Nation-States

Nation-States

&⊂ Consciousness and Competition ⊃&

NEIL DAVIDSON

Haymarket Books
Chicago, Illinois

Published in 2016 by
Haymarket Books
PO Box 180165
Chicago, IL 60618
773-583-7884
www.haymarketbooks.org
info@haymarketbooks.org

ISBN: 978-1-60846-568-2

Trade distribution:
In the US, Consortium Book Sales and Distribution, www.cbsd.com
In Canada, Publishers Group Canada, www.pgcbooks.ca
In the UK, Turnaround Publisher Services, www.turnaround-uk.com
All other countries, Publishers Group Worldwide, www.pgw.com

Cover design by Eric Kerl. Cover image of pro-independence march in
Edinburgh supporting a Scottish independence referendum to be held
on September 18, 2014.

This book was published with the generous support of
Lannan Foundation and the Wallace Action Fund.

Printed in Canada by union labor.

Library of Congress Cataloging-in-Publication data is available.

10 9 8 7 6 5 4 3 2 1

For Alan Rae

Contents

Preface

The term "nation-state" conjoins two others: "nation," a collective social identity; and "state," a structure of political power. Territorial states have existed since the emergence of class society around 3000 BCE, but nation-states are a much more recent phenomenon—so recent, in fact, that they are characteristic of only one type of class society, capitalism, whose origins lie a mere five hundred years ago, and which attained complete global dominance only in the late twentieth century.

Yet although the two aspects of nation-states are inseparable, the academic literature, including that written by Marxists, tends to discuss them in the context of separate disciplinary fields: adherence to national identity is a subject for social psychology, or perhaps the cultural studies branch of sociology; relationships between states are the province of the international relations wing of political science. Writers who do attempt to deal with both aspects of nation-states tend to either oscillate between collective identity and political structure or treat them in historical sequence. In Hagen Schulze's impressive survey of European states from the era of Charlemagne, for example, the first three parts of his book are respectively titled "States," "Nations," and "Nation-States"; but the subject matter of the third simply reverts to that of the first: it emphasizes states at the expense of their national form.[1] Most discussions, however, do not even make these distinctions and simply use "nation" as a synonym for "state" throughout.[2]

Any analysis of the nation-state form must therefore attempt to span the gulf between the individual citizen's "consciousness" of national identity and the geopolitical "competition" between capitalist states. I am only too aware that most of the pieces reprinted here fail to achieve this integration and are too one-sidedly focused on questions of identity, in part because I only recognized the existence of the problem relatively late in the period during which they were written. Chapter 7, at least, is a first approximation of what an attempt might look like.

◆

The bridge between social identity and state form in political life is of course national*ism*, the term encompassing both the ideology that all peoples should have their own nation-states and a series of specific movements to establish or defend those nation-states. In one of his foundational essays on the subject, "The Modern Janus," Tom Nairn argued that nationalism's historical role as the vehicle for overcoming uneven development meant it could be compared to the two-faced god of his title: one face pointing forward, toward "modernity"; the other face pointing backward, "desperately into the past, to gather strength wherever it can be found for the ordeal of 'development.'" And because this tension between past and future was inescapable, it was delusional to imagine that any nationalism could be either wholly positive or wholly negative: "In short, the substance of nationalism as such is always morally, politically, humanly ambiguous." It was of course both possible and necessary to draw up criteria by which nationalisms could be supported or opposed, but these criteria were in a sense separate from claims about the *nature* of nationalism.[3]

One can agree with this position without accepting, as Nairn has increasingly tended to do, that nationalism is both inevitable and, regardless of its inherent ambiguities, desirable.[4] It is, for example, difficult to conceive of *any* positive features in the far-right nationalisms currently contending for office or—in their Fascist variants—for control of the streets in Europe today. But even the contemporary nationalisms that are situated on the left of the political spectrum accept the economic order of capital—those associated with peoples who are clearly oppressed, like the Palestinians, as much as those associated with peoples who are clearly not, like the Scots. There are no limits to how reactionary nationalisms can be, but there are limits to their radicalism.

Nevertheless, the dominant Marxist position, from Marx and Engels's own writings during the revolutions of 1848–49 onward, has been that it was necessary to distinguish between different national movements as a basis for supporting some and opposing others.[5] The 1896 London Congress of the Second International passed a resolution declaring that it stood "for the complete right of all nations to self-determination."[6] As was quite often the case with the Second International, the adoption of a position did not mean that constituent parties or individual members regarded themselves as bound by it. It is clear from the debates at the 1907 Stuttgart Congress, for example, that many leading figures in the International did not support self-determination for the colonies and were prepared to express this view in unashamedly racist terms.[7] As was also quite often the case with the Second International, however, revolutionaries in that body tried both to uphold Congress policy and to clarify what it would mean in concrete terms if consistently applied.

Lenin was at the forefront of these attempts. Unfortunately, his desire to retain fidelity to the 1896 resolution led him into arguing that there were no difficulties with the notion of a "right" to self-determination, when clearly there were: who or what, for example, is supposed to confer such a right? One need not accept Luxemburg's belief in the ultimate pointlessness of national self-determination under capitalism to recognize the truth of her assessment: "A 'right of nations' which is valid for all countries and all times is nothing more than a metaphysical cliché of the type of 'rights of man' and 'rights of the citizen.'"[8] If we dispense with vacuous references to "rights," however, the essence of the policy is uncontentious. As Lenin wrote, "the proletariat confines itself, so to speak, to the negative demand for recognition of the *right* to self-determination, without giving guarantees to any nation."[9] In other words, socialists support the democratic demand of national groups ("peoples") to be able to make an unimpeded decision about their constitutional status ("self-determination") without necessarily supporting the particular decision that they make—indeed, they may argue against it.

Lenin's most important contribution to debates on the national question was to highlight the distinction between "oppressed" and "oppressor" nations, as a basis for deciding which national movements should be sup-

ported and which opposed by socialists. The former were those nationalities held against their collective will within the remaining absolutist or
tributary empires of the Habsburgs, Romanovs, and Ottomans; or the
colonies and semicolonies of the great powers in Africa, Asia, Latin America, and of course Ireland. These national movements had to be supported,
whatever the exact nature of their politics, which were in most cases un-
informed by socialist aspirations. On the other hand there were the "oppressor" nations (or, in the case of the absolutist and tributary empires,
states) that prevented the oppressed from achieving independent statehood.
The nationalisms of these oppressor states had to be opposed, above all by
the working class within them. It was in this context that Lenin drew his
famous analogy with the right to divorce: people should have the right to
divorce, but this does not mean that every couple should necessarily do
so. The assumption is that a situation of national oppression is analogous
to an unhappy or abusive marriage, in which the abused or oppressed can
be expected to exercise their "right" to divorce or secession:

> [The masses] will . . . resort to secession only when national oppression
> and national friction make joint life absolutely intolerable and hinder
> any and all economic intercourse. In that case, the interests of capitalist
> development and of the freedom of the class struggle will be best served
> by secession.[10]

The distinction between oppressor and oppressed was never an entirely adequate device for establishing the attitude of Marxists toward national movements. It had nothing to say about the attitude of socialists
to nations that may have had legitimate grounds for claiming that they
were oppressed—as Serbia did in 1914, for example—but were also part
of a wider inter-imperialist struggle in which one side manipulated their
situation. Nor did it provide guidance in a situation where a socialist revolution in a multinational empire—like Russia in 1917—might result
in some of the formerly oppressed nations seeking to secede *from* a workers' state, as for example Ukraine attempted to do during the early stages
of the Russian Revolution. My argument here is not that the positions
Lenin and the Bolsheviks adopted in these cases were necessarily
wrong—although in relation to Ukraine I think there is a strong argument that they were—but rather that they were based on a wider set of
political considerations than simply the oppressor/oppressed distinction.[11]

However, it could be legitimately argued that these were exceptional cases and that in general the categories of oppressor and oppressed allowed socialists to arrive at correct operational conclusions.

Whether the distinction is still as helpful today is less certain. Lenin tended to work with highly schematic revolutionary periodizations. For him, 1789–1871 was the era of the bourgeois revolution in Western Europe (which omits the Netherlands, England, and Scotland at one end, and the western parts of the Austro-Hungarian Empire at the other); 1905 marked the opening of the bourgeois revolution in Eastern Europe (and "the East" more generally). In the context of this discussion, however, the relevant issue is not the inflexibility of his periodizations, but rather the fact that Lenin saw the question of national self-determination as peculiar to the era of bourgeois revolution. In other words, it was not a question that would remain eternally valid until the global triumph of the socialist revolution. It was specifically relevant to a situation in which three remaining absolutist or tributary empires (Austria-Hungary, Russia, and Turkey) and eight capitalist powers (the UK, the Netherlands, Belgium, France, Germany, Spain, Portugal, the US, and Japan) had between them reduced the rest of the world outside Europe, North America, and Australasia to colonial or semicolonial status.

The world remains deeply uneven and unequal in terms of power and influence, but it *is* now divided into a system of nation-states. The historic formation of this system was accomplished during the sixty years between the opening of the First World War and the end of the postwar boom. Imperialism as an aspect of capitalism continues, of course, but while colonial regimes still exist—Chinese control over Tibet is one example—old-style colonialism is unlikely to be resurrected in any general way. Much to the chagrin of those who want the US to take up the White Man's Burden, it shows no sign of doing so in this sense.[12] If we leave aside the reunification of Ireland, the two main national questions still unresolved from the era of decolonization are those of the Palestinians and the Kurds, both exceptional in different respects: the former because the Palestinians no longer possess a territory in which to exercise self-determination, having been expelled from it by the Zionist colonial-settler regime; the Kurds because they are spread across the territories of five different nation-states and have different relations with each. The Kurdish example also illustrates the difficulty of simply attempting to apply the oppressor/oppressed distinction, given the quite different political trajectories taken by the Iraqi and Syrian Kurds in relation to US imperialism, the internal regimes in the territories they control, and much else besides.

However, the biggest problem for Marxists in deciding what attitude to take to national movements has not been these long-standing struggles for self-determination, but rather two relatively recent phenomena. One is where former nation-states have entered a process of complete disintegration, as in Yugoslavia during the 1990s and in several states in Central Africa and the Middle East more recently. What attitude should the left take in these cases, where different religious, tribal, or "ethnic" groups are struggling against each other to seize territory and resources?[13] It is completely futile for the left to play the game described by Alex Callinicos as "hunt the progressive nationality": one can and must oppose Western intervention on behalf of one side or the other without having any illusions that any side represents a more progressive option. The other is the emergence, or in some cases the reemergence, of "stateless nations" seeking autonomy or independence in the long-established capitalist states of the West. In some cases these had an earlier history of oppression, in others not; but by the 1980s differences between Catalonia and Quebec on the one hand and Scotland on the other were marginal. Today, the former are no more "oppressed" than the latter.[14] But simply rejecting on that basis their demands for self-determination is to embrace a stultifying formalism that takes no account of the exigencies of the class struggle or the dangers of inadvertently supporting the existing constitutional structures of the leading capitalist nation-states. Ironically, it was Lenin himself who indicated a superior approach in the very article in which he set out the oppressed/oppressor distinction:

> The demand for a "yes" or "no" reply to the question of secession in the case of every nation may seem a very "practical" one. In reality it is absurd; it is metaphysical in theory, while in practice it leads to subordinating the proletariat to the bourgeoisie's policy. The bourgeoisie always places its national demands in the forefront, and does so in categorical fashion. With the proletariat, however, these demands are subordinated to the interests of the class struggle. Theoretically, you cannot say in advance whether the bourgeois-democratic revolution will end in a given nation seceding from another nation, or in its equality with the latter; *in either case*, the important thing for the proletariat is to

ensure the development of its class.[15]

These considerations need not be confined to the era of what Lenin calls "the bourgeois–democratic revolution."[16] In our own time, I take "subordinated to the demands of the class struggle" to include the following, although this is not intended as an exhaustive list:

> For socialists . . . the question of support for particular national demands (not for particular nationalisms) is determined by their relationship to the struggle for socialism, regardless of whether the nation concerned is oppressed or not. Furthermore, it should openly be undertaken with the purpose of weakening the support of workers for that nationalism. In this context several questions have to be asked. Does support strengthen or weaken the capitalist or imperialist state? Does support strengthen or weaken the class consciousness and organization of the working class? Does support strengthen or weaken the tolerance of people of different nations or "races" for each other?[17]

These questions are answered in the affirmative for the Scottish independence movement, discussed in the final essay reproduced here, but that conclusion assumes an entire argument about the nature of the nation-state and its relationship to capital, which is set out in the preceding chapters. It is to them that we now turn.

◆

The pieces that follow are set out in chronological order of composition and publication. As in *Holding Fast to an Image of the Past* and *We Cannot Escape History*, I have reproduced them without alteration, except to introduce a greater consistency of style, for the correction of factual errors, and for the addition of material previously omitted for reasons of length. Chapter 5 on the Enlightenment contains the majority of these restorations. Although only chapters 4.1 and 9 deal directly with Scotland, the specific experiences of the country where I was born and in which I continue to live have obviously influenced my general approach to the national question. With the exception of chapter 9 the pieces reproduced here offer theoretical reflections on nation-states rather than analyses of particular national movements.

The devolution referendum of September 11, 1997, resulted in majorities for a Scottish Parliament (74.29 percent) with tax-varying powers (63.48 percent). This body was subsequently created by the Scotland Act 1998, which was passed by the UK Parliament on November 17, 1998. I wrote the first chapter of the current volume in the months that followed the opening of the Scottish Parliament on May 12, 1999. Like chapter 9, this one emerged out of my immersion in a particular campaign, although in this case the subject matter is slightly tangential to it. I will now briefly reconstruct the history of that campaign from a combination of my memories and those of other participants, and from documents still in my possession, as an example of the type of political context that creates the need for theoretical analysis.

NATO forces began bombing the Serbian capital, Belgrade, on March 24, 1999, ostensibly to protect the Albanian Kosovars from being ethnically cleansed by the local Serb population and their allies in Serbia itself. Opposition to the bombing centered on three arguments. First, NATO had other motivations for intervening than those stated. It clearly was not concerned with the general rights of refugees, since, for example, the Kurds in northwest Turkey were not considered suitable subjects for intervention, even though their suffering was quite equal to that of the Albanian Kosovars, and the state responsible for it was actually part of NATO. In fact, the intervention ("Operation Allied Force") was intended to assert the imperial authority of the US over potential enemies, but also over its European allies.[18] Second, it legitimated the idea that the US and its allies had the right to militarily intervene wherever and whenever they chose. Third—and for a majority of opponents the most important reason—the bombing would kill and injure innocent people and for this reason bring about, or at least exacerbate, the very situation it was supposed to prevent, since the Albanian Kosovars would be blamed for Serbian deaths. Indeed, the bombing provided the perfect excuse to intensify the expulsions, the majority of which took place after it started.[19] Variations on all of these arguments would of course have to be deployed soon afterward, in opposition to the invasions and occupations of Afghanistan and Iraq, for which the Kosovo crisis was in many respects a miniature dry run.

A small demonstration had been held on the Mound in Edinburgh the day after the bombing began. At the time I was a member of the Scottish Committee of the Socialist Workers Party (SWP). I wrote, at its behest, to comrades in that city on April 3, 1999, asking them to come ("and—more importantly—to bring as many people as possible with you") to a public antiwar meeting we had organized on a united front basis, for the following Wednesday at the Royal British Hotel on Princes Street. The meeting took place less than a month before the first election to the new Scottish Parliament, and so that evening an audience of around a hundred heard speeches from a platform of several candidates, including the SWP's Willie Black, Catriona Grant of the Scottish Socialist Party (SSP), and one from the Scottish National Party (SNP), although I can no longer recall who this was. They spoke alongside local Labour MP Tam Dalyell and "a representative from the Kurdish Workers Party (PKK) and a Serbian opponent of Milošević." Toward the end of the meeting, which had been advertised as "Edinburgh Against the Bombing," I stood up and—as is traditional at these events—announced a collection for the room, saying also that the organizers would be writing to everyone who had left their contact details to let them know about forthcoming campaign activities, although there was as yet no formal campaign in which to be active. Since I seemed to have acquired responsibility for coordinating the SWP's antiwar work in the city, I duly wrote on April 9 as "acting secretary" of the putative campaign, inviting attendees to an organizational meeting upstairs in the historic drinking establishment then favored by the Edinburgh left, the Café Royal on West Register Street.

Not for the first time in the history of the socialist movement—nor, I suspect, the last—the numbers who actually turned up for this meeting were fewer than we might have hoped. There were definitely four of us, although there may have been a few more. One of them was Jim Aitkin, schoolteacher, poet, former International Officer for the Scottish Campaign for Nuclear Disarmament, and member of the Communist Party of Great Britain (CPGB) prior to its dissolution in 1992. Jim would become chair of the campaign. Another was Alan Rae. Originally from Clydebank, Alan had joined the Fourth International's official British franchise, the International Marxist Group, in the late sixties after being involved in the Vietnam Solidarity Campaign. He worked at Linthouse, one of the shipbuilding firms that constituted the Upper Clyde Shipbuilders, but left the yard in December 1970, six months before the famous work-in against closure began, Both men now found themselves sitting in a room with a mere handful of other people and wondering if they were wasting their time.

They were not. In fact, the campaign, somewhat portentously rechristened the Edinburgh Campaign Against War in Europe (ECAWE), quickly became an effective local group, not least because of the work of the comrades mentioned in the preceding paragraph and the others who helped get it started, particularly Danny McGowan, Martin Walker, and Terry Wrigley. ECAWE met once a week at the Edinburgh Trades Council and, between meetings, did what campaigning groups do: leafleted, petitioned, posted flyers, called or joined demonstrations, picketed politicians who supported the bombing, spoke at trade union branches and sought their affiliation, wrote letters to the local press, and carried out joint work with other groups like the Campaign for Nuclear Disarmament. We rediscovered what we had previously found out during the Gulf War at the beginning of the decade: some religious groups, above all the Quakers, were committed and reliable, while some small Trotskyist sects were divisive and manipulative, treating the campaign mainly as a means of promoting their current fixation ("Independence for Kosovo!"). One of the demonstrations we supported, in Glasgow on June 5, was addressed by Nicola Sturgeon, then a newly elected SNP member of the Scottish Parliament, now leader of that party and Scottish first minister.

The Milošević regime surrendered on June 9, and the situation in Kosovo subsided into an uneasy cessation of hostilities—it would be too much to describe it as "peace," given the reverse ethnic cleansing that was now visited on the Serb population in retaliation for what had been done to the Albanian Kosovars. We kept a watching brief for several weeks, but once it was clear that the bombing had stopped, the group effectively dissolved itself in July. Did our activities make any difference? They did nothing to stop the bombing but were not entirely wasted for all that. The arguments of ECAWE and similar groups in cities across Scotland and the UK did not meet with instant acceptance from the people we were trying to convince, and—mercifully for its victims—the whole NATO intervention had taken less than six weeks, which is a very short period in which to build a campaign, compared with the subsequent run-up to the invasions of Afghanistan and Iraq. No public discussion is ever completely wasted, however, and in addition to bringing new people into political activity, the campaigns also helped begin the process of winning an anti-interventionist majority that emerged with the great antiwar movement three years later and the formation of the Stop the War Coalition.

Among ECAWE's activities was a conference at the University of Edinburgh on May 23, "Against NATO's War in the Balkans," attended by 170 people. The conference allowed us to discuss the implications of what was happening in a more reflective way than was possible in our weekly meetings. The initial timetable shows that *Observer* journalist Nick Cohen was originally scheduled to speak on the plight of refugees, although he later withdrew—I suspect because his growing support for Western intervention on "humanitarian" grounds prevented him from associating with an explicitly antiwar platform. The actual program produced some extraordinary conjunctions, particularly a session in which military historian John Erickson—a supporter of NATO throughout the Cold War—spoke alongside the late Chris Harman, a SWP Central Committee member, against the bombing. Chapter 1 was originally presented as a paper there and subsequently accepted for publication in *International Socialism* (ISJ) by then-editor John Rees. My article, however, was not a critique of imperialist intervention but rather of a key ideological assumption about the conflict, namely that it was essentially about "ethnicity."

I had been struck, during the original 1992 fragmentation of Yugoslavia and the Rwandan genocide three years later, by the way in which the term "ethnicity" was stretched by media commentators to the point where it could encompass both Muslims (a religion) and Tutsis and Hutus ("tribal" identities). If the term "race" was now quarantined with scare quotes because it referred to nonexistent biological distinctions between human groups, then it seemed to me that "ethnicity" should be regarded as dangerous for precisely the opposite reason: it imposed an identity on individuals based on some culturally acquired group characteristic (linguistic, religious, or occupational), which was then used to define them to the exclusion of all else. Ironically, although "ethnicity" was increasingly used as an *alternative* to "race" in postwar social science, in social life, however, it ended up as a *synonym* for it, above all in relation to Islam: members of this group behave in certain ways because of an all-determining characteristic—in this case their religious beliefs—that allows or perhaps compels "us" to discriminate against them. The problems associated with promiscuous use of the term "ethnicity" have since been demonstrated by attempts to use it as an explanatory master category for the entire twentieth century.[20] In the face of this I stand by my conclusion that it would be for the best if the term could either be abandoned completely or at least treated with the utmost skepticism.

Considerations on the usefulness of "ethnicity" as a concept overlapped with my main theoretical focus during this period, the historical emergence of Scottish national consciousness. While the ECAWE was attempting to mobilize antiwar sentiment in and around the Scottish capital, I was simultaneously negotiating with Pluto Press the publication of what would become my first book, *The Origins of Scottish Nationhood*, which appeared in 2000. My central argument was that a territorially inclusive (that is, including the Highlands) Scottish identity only emerged after the 1707 Treaty of Union, once the Scottish state had been dissolved. In order to defend this shocking exercise in revisionism I had, however, to begin both by defining what I meant by "nation" and related terms and by tracing the historical emergence of the institutions and identities that they describe. Since I argued that these were the product of a relatively recent process of development, I was consciously aligning myself with what is usually referred to as the "modernist" tendency in nation theory.[21] Chapters 2 and 3 are extracted from *Origins*, where these theoretical discussions precede a critique of the anachronistic notion that a Scottish "nation" existed as far back as the opening of the Wars of Independence in 1296. These chapters are not, however, specifically concerned with Scottish experience; indeed, my point was precisely that this experience had to be understood as the local manifestation of general historical laws.

The journal *Historical Materialism* (HM) invited John Foster, perhaps the leading historian associated with the post-1992 fragments of the CPGB, to review *Origins*, which he duly did in an article published in 2002.[22] Foster's objections to what I had written were partly based on my claims about the economic backwardness of Scotland before 1707, and partly based on my association of nationalism with capitalist development. Behind these objections lay Foster's adherence to Stalinist conceptions of "the Scottish people" and the supposed connection between their national identity, which apparently dates back to the tenth century, and radical politics. In making this critique Foster ignored the substantive content of the book—thus avoiding any engagement with the actual evidence I had assembled for the late development of Scottish national identity—and concentrated instead on the theoretical chapters and those giving a summary of developments down to 1707. My response, reproduced here as chapter 4.1, was met by a rejoinder from Foster that focused almost exclusively on methodological and theoretical issues and involved the accusation that I was effectively, if perhaps unconsciously, operating within Weberian categories. That's fighting talk where I come from, although I was unsure whether I should be more offended by his suggestion that I was unaware of my own theoretical assumptions or by the claim that they were supposedly derived from the doyen of bourgeois sociology. In any event, I wrote a further response, reproduced here as chapter 4.2, but never submitted it to HM as it was then over three years since *Origins* had appeared, and I was more interested in advancing the arguments about the Scottish bourgeois revolution contained in *Discovering the Scottish Revolution* (2003) than in revisiting my earlier work. In retrospect I should have submitted it, as Foster's challenge did make me engage with Weber in a way I had hitherto neglected. More importantly perhaps, it also forced me to take seriously the need to follow Marx and Engels's method rather than building a case on the selective quotation of particular judgments, since their reflections could on occasion be just as expressive of contemporary prejudices as those of lesser thinkers.[23]

◆

Chapters 5 and 6 deal with two supposedly antithetical attempts to provide universalist alternatives to the particularism of nation-states, the former focusing on the Enlightenment and the latter on the extent to which Islam has undergone a comparable experience.

Chapter 5 was commissioned in 2005 by Harman in his role as editor of the ISJ and published in that journal the following year, after extensive rewriting and cutting on his part. This was only partly for reasons of space. Harman wanted the article to be published quickly, but was unsure about my argument toward the end (particularly the section entitled "Reason, Power, and the Interests"). He therefore found it expedient to discard the entire section rather than engage in a prolonged debate over the nature of rationality. I wasn't particularly bothered by this—one of the duties of socialist authors is to produce hack work to order ("we need an article on . . .")—but the arguments in the published article were more basic than I had originally intended. The original version is published here in its entirety for the first time.

I would probably have offered Harman an article on the subject even if he had not invited me to write one, such was my revulsion at the way in which nominally left-wing supporters of the wars in Afghanistan and Iraq invoked Enlightenment traditions to justify what Richard Seymour calls "the liberal defense of murder."[24] Many people on the left who shared my revulsion at the posturing of B52 liberals and New Atheists essentially accepted their claims and concluded that if Richard Dawkins or the late Christopher Hitchens (a duo delightfully conflated by Terry Eagleton as "Ditchens") represented Enlightenment values, then the Enlightenment itself must be rejected.[25] The same conclusions have been drawn again more recently in the wake of the Charlie Hebdo murders. There were of course preexisting anti-Enlightenment positions associated with postmodernists who oppose it on relativist grounds and postcolonialists who do so on the basis of its supposed Eurocentrism; but this was different. For some on the left it was as if the Enlightenment was simply an ideological justification for the slave trade or the extermination of First Nation Americans; many seemed completely unaware that leading Enlightenment figures opposed these atrocities *on the basis of their Enlightenment beliefs*. It is true that the Enlightenment was a highly contradictory movement that cannot simply be "defended" in an uncritical way, but neither can we abandon it without disabling ourselves. Marxism seeks to complete, perhaps even transcend, Enlightenment thought, but it is part of the same project and would be unthinkable without it. In a sense we have two tasks. One is to understand that Enlightenment thought has at least three aspects: the arguments that were always apologetic or manipulative; those that contained partial insights important insofar as they advanced the cause of the bourgeoisie in its revolutionary phase; and those that were and are of genuinely universal validity. The second task is not to confuse any one of these aspects with any other.

Chapter 6 was originally conceived of as part of the preceding chapter but quickly acquired a life of its own. It ended up as a separate article published in the SWP magazine, *Socialist Review*, also in 2006. Although it was concerned with the same set of controversies, it approached them from the perspective of Islam, by then increasingly regarded as the antithesis of Enlightenment values. Against the claims of the New Atheists, I argued that Islam was not immune to rationality and actually had a much better record in this regard than Christianity. Insofar as Islam did begin to fall behind the West, it was not a function of religion but rather of the type of states in which Islam tended to be embedded—but these states were also characteristic of societies in which Hinduism and Confucianism were the dominant religions. The real argument was about the connection between capitalism and the Enlightenment, and the extent to which the tributary states of the East were able to prevent the former from developing beyond a certain point, which then left them vulnerable to Western pressure or conquest.[26] None of this had anything intrinsically to do with Islam (or Hinduism or Confucianism). The point was well made by Ernest Gellner, after the Iranian Revolution but several years before the current wave of Islamophobia began to gather momentum. He imagined an alternative future in which the Muslim army had defeated the Franks at the Battle of Tours in 732:

> No doubt we should all be admiring Ibn Weber's *The Kharejite Ethic and the Spirit of Capitalism* which would conclusively demonstrate how the modern rational spirit and its expression in business and bureaucratic organisation could only have arisen in consequence of neo-Kharejite puritanism in northern Europe. In particular, the work would demonstrate how [this] could never happen had Europe stayed Christian, given the inveterate proclivity of that faith to a baroque, manipulative, patronage-ridden, quasi-animistic and disorderly vision of the world.[27]

In other words, it is possible to imagine a world in which Islam had adapted to the emergent feudal structures of northwestern Europe with exactly the same outcome as what in fact took place, because religion was not the determining variable.

◆

In chapters 7 and 8, from the late 2000s and early 2010s, I have edited together several different pieces that had their origin in a single research inquiry but—for reasons wearily familiar to most people employed in higher education—ended up being published as separate chapters and articles. These are the most "academic" pieces to be reproduced here, not—I hope—in the sense of being irrelevant, but because they originally appeared in peer-reviewed journals and books from reputable publishers, rather than in the pages of the socialist press. They emerged from the intersection of three major debates in which I was (and to an extent remain) involved during these years: the nature of uneven and combined development, the relationship between nation-states and capital, and the role of the far right in contemporary capitalist societies. My writings dealing specifically with the first of these subjects have been republished elsewhere; the remaining two have a chapter each here.[28]

Chapter 7, on the relationship between nation-states and capital, argues that nation-states cannot be conceived as having a merely contingent relationship to capital, nor do they operate according to a "logic" that happens to intersect with that of capital at certain points. These positions seek to avoid the temptations of reductionism or functionalism, but instead court opposite dangers. Above all they risk abandoning the Marxist injunction to treat the social world as a totality, regarding it instead as a jumble of self-contained fragments, "levels" or "autonomous spheres" that have no necessary connection with each other. On the contrary, capital requires multiple nation-states, as no other state form, still less the absence of a state, could facilitate accumulation to anything like the same degree. This is what links the two aspects of nation-states highlighted at the very beginning of this preface: competition among rival states and national consciousness within the minds of citizens. The first unifies the capitals within the territorial area controlled by the state, and the latter divides the working class exploited within it.

The question of nationalist ideology is also a theme of chapter 8, although the focus here is on specifically right-wing versions which are by no means always a necessity for capital. I attempt to establish that right-wing social movements have existed in the past and continue to do so now: it is simply a comforting illusion to imagine that they are manufactured out of whole cloth by manipulative millionaires and have no wider base. Whatever else might be said about the Da'esh group, which emerged after the component parts of this chapter were written, it has its own internal dynamic and is not acting for invisible wire-pullers elsewhere in the wreckage of the Middle East, although it may inadvertently advance their goals. The activities of right-wing social movements are not always "in the interests of capital" in an uncomplicated way, or sometimes at all. They are always strongly nationalistic and do seek to divide workers on racial or ethnic grounds, but even the form this usually takes—halting or reversing migration—is scarcely a policy favored by large-scale capital. The implication for the left is that we cannot automatically take opposite positions to those supported by the far right, such as—to take one of the most contentious issues possible—the UK Independence Party (UKIP) demand for British withdrawal from the European Union (EU). Withdrawal would in fact provoke a crisis for the British nation-state, of a type that has been relatively rare in its history—which is one reason why the left should support it, whatever UKIP may say.

◆

Possible withdrawal from the EU is only one possible source of crisis for the British state. The other, far more likely to occur in the short term, is Scottish secession. Chapter 9 was written in the days immediately before and after the Scottish independence referendum of September 18, 2014, when 44.7 percent of those registered voted for independence, but 55.3 percent voted against. It is perhaps the most politically engaged of all the pieces collected here—unsurprisingly, since the campaign for a Yes vote was one of the most exciting and transformative moments in my lifetime as a political activist. Any discussion of the referendum written immediately after the result is bound to lack the perspective that chronological distance can bring; there are occasions, however, when analytical detachment needs to be balanced against the immediacy of what has happened. It is, after all, moments like the referendum that theoretical discussions about nations, nationalism, and nation-states are designed to inform. However, since this piece reads rather differently than previous chapters for reasons other than my personal involvement in the process it describes, an explanation for its stylistic distinctiveness is called for.

On September 10, at the beginning of the frenetic final week of the campaign, I received an email from Susan Watkins, editor of *New Left Review* (NLR). The editorial board had read and liked a piece I had written on the forthcoming referendum in *Radical Philosophy*.[29] Would I be able to write the postreferendum analysis for NLR? This came as something of a surprise, as I had expressed major disagreements with the journal's editorial stance on a number of occasions and criticized several of its leading contributors—not least Tom Nairn, its main commentator on matters Scottish. On the question of the referendum, however, we were in agreement that the left should support a Yes vote. There was a problem, though: the tone and to a certain extent the content of the piece would be determined by the outcome of the ballot on September 18, but it had to be submitted by October 3, leaving me little more than two weeks to write it. I made the deadline with only a few days' slippage and a couple of thousand words over the limit—practically a footnote by my usual excessive standards. I then found myself on the receiving end of a series of queries from the editorial board, asking for elaboration on a number of points. Could I give examples of media bias against the Yes campaign? How did the nature of the local economy in a No-supporting city like Aberdeen compare to a Yes-supporting one like Glasgow? What had been the trajectory of Labour and SNP votes since the establishment of the Scottish Parliament in 1999? Only after I sent no fewer than four supplementary texts—around 24,000 words in total, added to the original article—did the requests for further information cease. The one specific addition the NLR had wanted to make was a section referring to Nairn's original explanation for the emergence of Scottish nationalism, to which I was of course invited to add my own critique, which I duly did when I received the article for final review a few weeks later. I was perfectly happy with the content of the published piece, which came in at just under 9,000 words; but in literary terms it is a hybrid, with passages written by me interspersed with others written by Watkins on the basis of the material I sent her. In some respects therefore she should be credited, if not as coauthor, then certainly with far greater input than is usual for an editor.

◆

The mass mobilizations against a seemingly endless succession of Western interventions in Central Europe, the Middle East, and North Africa did at any rate unite all serious sections of the left in Britain; the 2014 Scottish independence referendum divided them. The majority of Labour Party members and the fragments of the Communist Party were opposed, and many individuals on the revolutionary and radical left more generally felt unable to support the breakup of the British state on what they saw as a nationalist basis. In effect, their arguments—and although I disagree with them, these are not by any means absurd or ignoble arguments—were that this would destroy the unity of the British working class and do so in a way that would also trap Scottish workers within nationalist ideology. I have set out my objections to these arguments in chapter 9 and elsewhere, and will not repeat them here.[30] The point is that despite disagreements over this issue, the different sections of the left will have to find ways of working together, not only in Scotland but in all those nation-states where subnational demands for independence are being raised.

On a more personal level, however, it is also true that individual relationships were put under strain where people took opposing positions on the referendum. I described above how I met Alan Rae in 1999 while setting up a campaign against the NATO bombing of Serbia, and I have known him as a friend and comrade ever since. Alan joined the SWP either during or shortly after the campaign, but as someone who combines a mercurial temperament with doggedness in defending what he regards as matters of principle, he subsequently had what might be described as a volatile relationship with the party. He (and I) left for good in 2013, more or less at the point when the referendum campaign was about to take off in earnest. We disagree about the attitude socialists should take to Scottish independence, but if the left is serious about being, in Robert Burns's words, "of independent mind," then these differences in perspective are only to be expected.[31] I am glad, therefore, to have the opportunity to dedicate this book to Alan, to whom Burns's description certainly applies.

Neil Davidson
West Calder
West Lothian
Scotland
UK
August 17, 2015

Chapter 1

The Trouble with "Ethnicity"*

INTRODUCTION

The concept of exploitation is central to the Marxist understanding of history and contemporary society. But not all social conflicts can be immediately reduced to the struggle between exploiters and exploited, and to explain these conflicts we require other concepts. The most important is that of "oppression." This refers to systematic discrimination by one social group against another on the grounds of characteristics either inherited (skin color, biological sex) or socially acquired (religious belief, language). The experience of oppression cuts across class lines, although that experience is more or less severe depending on where its victims are

---

* Based on a talk given at the conference "Against NATO's War in the Balkans," organized by the Edinburgh Campaign Against War in Europe and held at the University of Edinburgh on May 23, 1999. Originally published in *International Socialism* 2:84 (Autumn 1999).

placed within the class structure. Some forms, like the oppression of women, have persisted throughout the existence of class society, while others, like racism, are specific to capitalism. Sometimes the reasons, or pretexts, for the oppression of a group may change over time. During the feudal era, for example, Jewish people were persecuted for their religious beliefs, but as capitalism developed this persecution increasingly focused on their supposed race. Whatever the reason or pretext, however, ruling classes throughout history have instigated or endorsed the oppression of different groups in order to maintain or create divisions among those over whom they rule. Recently, groups have increasingly been subjected to oppression on the grounds of their ethnicity. The most extreme form of such oppression has become known as "ethnic cleansing."

The term "ethnic cleansing" is an English translation of the Serbo-Croatian phrase *etničko čišćenje*. It was first used in Yugoslavia, not in the conflicts that erupted after the end of the Cold War but by the Croatian Ustaše during the Second World War, to describe the policy of killing or expelling Serbs, Jews, Gypsies, and Muslims from the Fascist state the Ustaše briefly set up with Nazi support. The first use during the current events was by the Croatian Supreme Council of the Judiciary in 1991, after the Croatian declaration of independence from Yugoslavia, to describe the actions of Serb guerrillas who were attempting to drive Croatians out of areas where Serbs were in the majority: "the aim of this expulsion is obviously the ethnic cleansing of the critical areas ... [to] be annexed to Serbia."[1] The phrase only began to appear in the British press and thereafter in popular usage during the war that began in Bosnia-Herzegovina the following year, when Bosnian Serb forces, initially backed by the Milošević regime in Belgrade, started expelling Muslims and Croats from those parts of the state territory that the former considered to be Serbian. The first area to be "cleansed" in this way seems to have been the Croat village of Kijevo in the otherwise Serb-dominated province of Krajina, during August 1991.[2] Since then the term has been used to describe not just events in former Yugoslavia (where all sides became involved in the practice to some extent) but also similar—and in some cases even worse—occurrences distant in space and time. On the one hand, the term was being extended spatially to events such as the massacres in Rwanda during 1994, which took place in societies geographically distant from Yugoslavia and quite different in terms of their historical development. On the other hand, the term was also extended chronologically back to events such as the expulsion and killing of Armenians by Turks at the end of the First World War, which were historically distant and had not previously been discussed in these terms.[3]

"Ethnic cleansing" presupposes the existence of different ethnic groups. The majority of people who opposed the NATO bombing of Yugoslavia also opposed the "ethnic cleansing" of Kosovar Albanians that NATO used to justify it, arguing that bombing not only intensified the hatreds that made ethnic cleansing possible but also made it easier to carry out, by forcing the removal of the international monitors who had provided some check on the Serb paramilitaries. Nevertheless, opponents tended to share with supporters of the war—and indeed with the people carrying out the "ethnic cleansing"—the view that there were genuine ethnic differences between groups in former Yugoslavia. From this perspective, while ethnic differences such as those between the Serbs and the Kosovar Albanians should occasion mutual respect rather than oppression, the differences themselves cannot and should not be denied. This position is inadequate, and I want to argue instead that we need to go beyond opposition to "ethnic cleansing"—which of course means all "ethnic cleansing," not only that of the Kosovar Albanians—and question the validity of the term "ethnicity" itself.

Since the argument that follows may be liable to misrepresentation, I should perhaps make one central point clear from the start. Ethnicity is often equated with culture, most frequently with that of minority populations in Western Europe and North America, or with non-Western cultures more generally. (Older readers may remember a time in the late 1960s and early 1970s when Guatemalan pottery or Afghan textiles were regularly described as "ethnic" when being marketed in Britain, as if "ethnicity" were some special property they possessed.) I am not arguing against cultural diversity, still less suggesting that socialists should abandon their duty to defend people whose culture is under threat or who are suffering from any of the other forms of oppression outlined above. Lenin pointed out the necessity for socialists to be "tribunes of the people" nearly a hundred years ago, in words that still retain their relevance: "Working-class consciousness cannot be genuine political consciousness unless the workers are trained to respond to *all* cases of tyranny, oppression, violence, and abuse, no matter *what class* is affected—unless they are trained, moreover, to respond from a Social-Democratic [i.e., revolutionary socialist] point of view and no other."[4] For socialists, therefore, it makes no difference whether particular groups of people are oppressed because of their language, religion, nationhood, or ethnicity; in each case our duty is to defend the oppressed and show solidarity with them, particularly where socialists themselves belong to the dominant linguistic, religious, national, or—assuming for the moment that such a thing exists—ethnic group.

My point is rather that the way in which the notion of "ethnicity" is currently and increasingly being used contains a number of problems for the left. Two stand out in particular. On the one hand, those who approve of ethnicity as the affirmation of a cultural identity, insofar as they emphasize supposedly innate differences between human social groups, are in danger of lending credibility to the current form taken by racist ideology. On the other hand, those who disapprove of ethnicity as a manifestation of (real or imagined) exclusionist tribalism are in danger, insofar as they suggest that "ethnic" nationalisms are particularly prone to oppressive behavior, of obscuring those characteristics that *all* nationalisms have in common, whether they are oppressor or oppressed or fall into neither of these categories. Our first task is therefore to distinguish among the various ways in which the term "ethnicity" has been used and to assess their respective validity.

KINSHIP, OCCUPATION, AND IDENTITY

"Ethnicity" has been defined in three ways: first, where members of a group have a common line of descent and consequently a shared kinship; second, where they have a common position within the international division of labor and consequently a shared occupation; and third, where they have one or more cultural attributes in common and consequently a shared identity. The first and second reasons assume that ethnicity can be defined objectively, the third that it can be defined subjectively. As we shall see, it is the subjective definition that is currently dominant.

Kinship

Social groups who share a common line of descent, or groups whose members interbreed exclusively with each other, thus maintaining the same genetic inheritance, are usually referred to in anthropology as endogamous groups. Such groups would have been universal at the origins of human evolution but are, however, virtually impossible to find today. Indeed, recent archaeological and anthropological work suggests that mass human migration—often across entire continents—occurred much earlier in history than was previously believed, and resulted in the erosion of endogamy within the original tribal societies. One writer notes that, as a result of these factors, "the common ancestry of 'the people' was always partially fictive" within tribal society.[5] But once we move onto the terrain of recorded history, the multiple genetic inheritance of the global population is indisputable—a fact that also makes the existence of different "races" a fiction impossible to sustain. Susan Reynolds has rightly criticized the tendency of medieval historians to describe the barbarian invaders of the Roman Empire as biologically distinct "tribal" entities, based merely on the continued use of their original group names. "This must be wrong," she points out. "Once barbarians had been converted to orthodox Christianity and prohibitions on intermarriage had been lifted, it must have been hard to distinguish them from 'Romans' who were already mixed genetically and were increasingly barbarized culturally."[6]

The main constituent nations of Britain are a case in point. Early in the eighteenth century Daniel Defoe mocked the pretensions of his countrymen to ethnic purity in his satirical poem "The True-Born Englishman":

> In eager rapes, and furious lust begot,
> Between a painted Briton and a Scot.
> Whose gend'ring off-spring quickly learn'd to bow,
> And yoke their heifers to the Roman plough:
> From whence a mongrel half-bred race there came,
> With neither name nor nation, speech nor fame.
> In whose hot veins new mixtures quickly ran,
> Infus'd betwixt a Saxon and a Dane.
> While their rank daughters, to their parents just,
> Receiv'd all nations with promiscuous lust.
> This nauseous brood directly did contain
> The well-extracted blood of Englishmen.

As Linda Colley, who quotes this passage, comments: "Defoe's uncompromising insistence on the ethnic diversity of England, its early exposure to successive invasions from Continental Europe, and the constant intermingling of its people with the Welsh and Scots, was fully justified in historical terms."[7] Similar intermingling took place in Scotland during the "Dark Ages" between 400 and 1057. "The period has, with justice, been called 'an age of migrations,'" writes Michael Lynch, "when the different tribal peoples—Picts, Scots, Angles, Britons and Scandinavians—who inhabited the mainland of modern-day Scotland moved, fought, displaced and intermarried with each other."[8] And to these, of course, could be added the Norman English who were invited to settle in Scotland during the reign of David I (1124–53), and who were themselves descended from Viking settlers in part of what is now France.

In an extreme case like that of the native Australians it might be supposed that endogamy was maintained until the arrival of the European colonists, but in fact they too had interbred with Papuan and Polynesian immigrants many centuries before the Dutch or the British set foot on their continent.[9] As the late Eric Wolf wrote of the ethnic composition of the world in 1400: "If there were any isolated societies these were but temporary phenomena—a group pushed to the edge of a zone of interaction and left to itself for a brief moment in time."[10] In short, even before capitalism had penetrated all corners of the world in the search for markets and raw materials, the growth of trade, conquest, and migration had already made the existence of endogamous gene pools increasingly rare. Of course, this does not mean that various groups have not claimed, and in some cases perhaps even believed, that they were descended from the pure stock of some ancestral group, but it is important to understand that these claims and beliefs are based on a myth of kinship, not a reality.

Occupation

Like the modern notion of "race," the origins of the occupational definition of ethnicity lie in the colonial expansion of capitalism outside of its European heartlands. From the origins of systematic racial slavery in the sixteenth century, "race" has been a general term used to override differences among peoples by categorizing them on the basis of physical characteristics, of which skin color was the most important. (As we shall see below, the racisms directed against the Catholic Irish and, by extension, the Highland Scots were exceptions in that they were based on religion and language rather than physical appearance.)[11] There were massive differences in social development between the Shona-speaking peoples of southern Africa, who built and lived in the stone city of Great

Zimbabwe during the fifteenth and sixteenth centuries, and the hunter-gatherers who inhabited Australia at the same time. Yet to ideologists of "race" they were both indistinguishably "black." At first, during the process of primitive accumulation, racism was used to justify the assignment of specific roles within the system (for instance the role of slave), but later on it was used to consign members of "races" who had migrated to the metropolitan centers either to the reserve army of labor or to the group of workers with the worst pay and conditions in the labor force.

"Ethnicity," on the other hand, was a term designed to distinguish between groups within overall "racial" categories, in those sections of the labor market in which they had established themselves. The capitalist mode of production requires the subordination of labor to capital, but in the European colonies it also required that the labor force be internally divided. As Wolf notes, the allocation of workers to invented ethnic categories is doubly effective in this respect, first "by ordering the groups and categories of laborers hierarchically with respect to one another" and second "by continuously producing and re-creating symbolically marked 'cultural' distinctions among them." On the one hand, groups were allocated specific roles both within the production process and in social life more generally. On the other hand, they were encouraged to identify with these roles and to defend them against other groups. Wolf is therefore right to say that these ethnic identities are not "'primordial' social relationships," but "historical products of labor market segmentation under the capitalist mode [of production]."[12] Sometimes the identities built on the existing division of labor in precolonial society; sometimes they were wholly new and based on the division of labor within the new industries that the colonists established.

In Rwanda and Burundi before colonization there were three distinct groups—Hutus, Tutsis, and Twas, with the former two being numerically the most significant.[13] In each case group membership passed down through the male side of the family. Is this an example of the "kinship" ethnicity that I earlier consigned to prehistory? In fact, although group membership at birth was determined based on that of the male parent, it was possible to move from Tutsi to Hutu in the course of your own life. All three groups spoke the same language, and the distinctions between them were principally based on the fact that they performed different social roles: the Hutu farmed, the Tutsi reared cattle, and the Twa hunted. A

7

cattle owner was a Tutsi by definition, which meant that Hutus and Twas could "become" Tutsis if they were able to accumulate sufficient wealth to become cattle owners themselves, a transition that was marked ceremonially. Since longhorn cattle were the main form of disposable property, people who owned cattle were therefore a significant part of the ruling class, but there were also Tutsis who owned few cattle and whose social position was proportionally less important. The situation is further complicated by the fact that some Hutus were members of that section of the ruling class who owned large farms, without becoming Tutsi. As Charlie Kimber writes: "The Hutu-Tutsi distinction in pre-colonial Rwanda and Burundi was not a simple class distinction (because you could be a poor Tutsi or a rich Hutu), nor was it an ethnic distinction (because you could be born into one group and die as another)."[14] It did, however, *become* an ethnic distinction, with the arrival first of the German and then of the Belgian colonial administrations. Under these regimes, real occupational stratification that designated people as being Hutu, Tutsi, and Twa transformed into a set of imaginary ethnic distinctions among separate "tribal" groups, one of which (the Tutsi) was privileged over the others in the colonial hierarchy and in the immediately postcolonial state.

Rwanda shows how existing occupational roles in existing populations can become the basis of new ethnicities imposed by colonialism. More commonly, ethnicities have developed among migrant groups responding to dislocation and industrialization. The emergence of ethnicity in the Gezira region of the Sudan, after the beginning of cotton production in 1925, demonstrates this process. The British recruited workers from various West African groups, all of whom were Muslims and most of whom spoke Hausa. Unlike the local Sudanese, these immigrants were already accustomed to wage labor in their own homelands, which had been industrialized earlier, and they were consequently more likely to meet their quotas. The British tended to replace local workers with the immigrants. In response to their displacement, the Sudanese began to refer disparagingly to the West Africans as "Fellata," a term that has overtones of slavish obedience. The West Africans in turn began to distinguish themselves from the Sudanese precisely on the basis of their supposedly greater capacity for hard work, a distinction linked to the adoption of a fundamentalist Islam far stricter than that practiced by the Sudanese, which was enshrined in their self-description as "Takari": a respectful term for pilgrims to Mecca from West Africa. As Thomas Eriksen concludes from this episode: "Contemporary ethnicity or 'tribalism' is not, in other words, a relic of the past but a product of modernization processes leading up to the present."[15]

The sugar industry in the French colony of Mauritius provides an extreme example of how a wide range of characteristics can be fitted to occupational roles, becoming ethnicities as a result. Indians, members of a national group, were recruited as laborers in the cane fields. Brahmins from among these Indians, adherents of a religious sect, were made foremen; Creoles, who were descendants of slaves and consequently identifiable by their skin color, tended to be skilled workers; Chinese or "mulattos"—one a national group, the other defined by skin color—held the middle managerial positions; the estate managers were invariably French settlers, who were both a national group and identifiable by their white skin, but needless to say did not have an "ethnicity."[16]

We might say, therefore, that the term "ethnicity" is valid in this sense when it is used to describe either the way in which existing occupational patterns in precapitalist societies were used by European colonists to classify the population into supposedly endogamous groups, or when the migrations set in motion by colonialism led groups to define themselves as either endogamous or possessing some quality or characteristic that distinguished them from the native populations around them. What has confused the issue is that the word "ethnicity" was not in general use at the time these developments were taking place (roughly between 1875 and 1945), but this would not be the first time that something has existed in the world before the language has been developed to describe it.[17] The term could be usefully employed now in relation, for example, to the situation of Chinese traders in Indonesia or Korean traders in Los Angeles, but the term is generally not used with this degree of specificity. On the contrary, it is the third and final notion of "ethnicity," that of identity, which is currently sweeping all before it.

Identity

In answer to the central question of why groups come to identify themselves as having a particular "ethnicity," Anthony Smith has argued that an ethnic community—that is, a community whose members have not had their "ethnicity" imposed on them from outside, but distinguish themselves in this way—has six main attributes: "a collective proper name, a myth of common ancestry, shared historical memories, one or more differentiating elements of common culture, an association with a specific 'homeland,' and a sense of solidarity for significant sectors of the population."[18] This attempts to incorporate a belief in kinship relations as part of the definition. It is not clear why these are "ethnic" attributes rather than simply "national" ones. Indeed, the definition of a nation that Smith gives a few pages earlier in the book could be substituted without affecting his argument: "A nation can therefore be defined as *a named human population sharing an historic territory, common myths and historical territories, a mass, public culture, a common economy and common legal rights and duties for all members.*"[19] (The similarity is perhaps unsurprising, given that Smith is attempting to argue for the importance of ethnicity in the formation of national identity.) It is perfectly possible for a particular social group to identify themselves as having an "ethnic" identity without possessing all or any of the attributes listed by Smith, as the example of the Bosnian Muslims makes clear. Like all classificatory lists, its elements are somewhat arbitrary. Perhaps in realization of this, some writers have abandoned any attempts at precise definition.

In 1953 David Reisman became the first person to use the term "ethnicity" to mean identity, and he was quickly followed by other North American sociologists.[20] Their usage has clear affinities with the notion of a "status group," introduced by Max Weber to describe differentiation that happens at the social level (as opposed to occupational class, at the economic level, or party interest at the political)—although as we shall see, Weber was skeptical about the usefulness of "ethnicity" as a way of describing identity and tended to use the term more to describe the character of endogamous groups.[21] In the hands of his American followers the terms were used to describe those groups who did not belong to the white Anglo-Saxon Protestant population—that is to say, everyone who was not descended from the original English, Scottish, and "Scots" [i.e., Protestant] Irish settlers. Exceptionally, German immigrants were allowed to merge with the WASPs, at least where they too were Protestants.[22] Ethnicity was therefore reserved for "minorities" identified by attributes as diverse as skin color (blacks), religion (Jews), or country of origin (Italians). This lack of specificity brings to mind the famous conversation between Humpty Dumpty and Alice during her adventures through the looking glass:

"When I use a word," Humpty Dumpty said, in a rather scornful tone, "it means just what I choose it to mean—neither more nor less."

"The question is," said Alice, "whether you can make words mean so many different things."

"The question is," said Humpty Dumpty, "which is to be the master—that's all."[23]

Stuart Hall, here playing the role of Humpty Dumpty, has offered the following definition of "ethnicity": "By 'ethnicity' we mean the commitment to those points of attachment which give the individual some sense of 'place' and position in the world, whether these be in relation to particular communities, localities, territories, languages, religions or cultures."[24] If the term encompasses "communities, localities, territories, languages, religions or cultures," then it is difficult to see what could *not* be defined as "ethnic." An American sociologist, Abner Cohen, once proposed that City of London stockbrokers should be considered an "ethnic" group by virtue of their group identity.[25] He was not being entirely serious, but the proposal takes the mad logic of "ethnic identity" to its conclusion in Bedlam. More seriously, the census that British citizens will be required to complete in 2001 asks respondents to define their own "ethnicity" from a core list that consists of four nations (Bangladesh, China, India, and Pakistan), one continent (Asia), and two skin colors (Black and White)—although these latter two are subdivided, the first into "Black: African," "Black: Caribbean," and "Black: Other," and the second into "White: British" and "White: Other." In fact, most uses of the word "ethnic" are in place of some other word (like "communities, localities, territories, languages, religions or cultures"), the use of which would give far greater precision of meaning. The result of not doing so, as the South African Marxist Neville Alexander rightly says, is "to reduce the diverse reasons for the emergence of group solidarities to a single quality called 'ethnicity,' thereby obscuring precisely what has to be explained—the basis of such solidarity."[26] Weber made the same point, in more academic language, much earlier in the century:

All in all, the notion of "ethnically" determined social action subsumes phenomena that a rigorous sociological analysis . . . would have to distinguish carefully. . . . It is certain that in this process the collective term "ethnic" would be abandoned, for it is unsuitable for a really rigorous analysis.

In the next paragraph Weber describes how "the concept of the ethnic group ... dissolves if we define our terms exactly."[27] Ethnicity, in short, becomes a way of labeling people through the use of an ideological supercategory that includes virtually any characteristic they might conceivably possess.

There is a further problem. Hall assumes "ethnicity" can be divided into "bad" and "good" forms that more or less correspond to that of the majority populations of metropolitan imperialist states on the one hand and of their minority immigrant communities on the other. Of the former, Hall writes: "In the face of the proliferation of cultural differences, and the multi-ethnic character of the new Britain, and threatened on the other side by the encroaching trauma of an emerging European identity, we have seen over the past decade a particularly defensive, closed and exclusive definition of 'Englishness' being advanced as a way of warding off or refusing to live with difference—a retreat from modernity no exercise in managerial newspeak or the 'new entrepreneurialism' can disguise or deflect."[28] Of the latter, however, we learn that it is "not an ethnicity which is doomed to survive, as Englishness was, only by marginalizing, dispossessing, displacing and forgetting other ethnicities." On the contrary, these immigrant communities have a "politics of ethnicity predicated on difference and diversity."[29] It is difficult to see how Hall could explain conflict between youth of Afro-Caribbean and South Asian descent on this basis (or indeed, that between those of Afro-Caribbean and Korean descent in Los Angeles). And while a model of "ethnicity" derived from the British (or rather "English") experience can certainly be generalized to other Western European imperialist nations like France, in a region like the Balkans, where historically there has never been a dominant "ethnic" group, it has no explanatory power whatsoever.

THE INTERNATIONALIZATION OF CAPITAL, CRISIS, AND IDENTITY POLITICS

The editors of a recent reader on ethnicity begin by reflecting on the sudden upsurge of interest in their subject:

> For at least 150 years liberals and socialists confidently expected the demise of ethnic, racial, and national ties and the unification of the world through international trade and mass communications. These expecta-

tions have not been realized. Instead, we are witnessing a series of explosive ethnic revivals across the globe. In Europe and the Americas ethnic movements unexpectedly surfaced from the 1960s and 1970s, in Africa and Asia they have been gaining force since the 1950s, and the demise of the former Soviet Union has encouraged ethnic conflicts and national movements to flourish throughout its territory. Since 1990 twenty new states based largely upon dominant ethnic communities have been recognized. Clearly, ethnicity, far from fading away, has now become a central issue in the social and political life of every continent. The "end of history," it seems, turns out to have ushered in the era of ethnicity.[30]

Why has the upsurge of "ethnic" identification taken place now? For this sense of "ethnicity" to become established required two general conditions. The first condition is the need to *distinguish* one group from another. As Thomas Eriksen has stressed, "ethnicity is essentially an aspect of a relationship, not a property of a group." In other words, cultural distinctiveness in itself does not confer "ethnicity" on a group, but only when it is contrasted with the culture of another group: "For ethnicity to come about, the groups must have a minimum of contact with each other, and they must entertain ideas of each other as being culturally different from themselves."[31] But for this to happen the differences must themselves be considered important, and there are only certain circumstances in which this is the case. The most important of these circumstances, and the second condition, is rapid social change. As Malcolm Cross notes: "A man living in a world where change is largely absent does not need to be reminded of his culture in order to affirm his identity."[32] Where that change is destructive of established ways of life, and in some cases whole societies, and class politics does not offer an alternative, then distinguishing oneself as part of a specific group in order to struggle over the resources, or scavenge what you can from the rubble left by the onward march of international capital, may appear to be the only available option—even where group membership may previously have meant little or nothing to the people concerned.

Across the developing world in particular, the state is increasingly failing to deliver any form of social redistribution to the most disadvantaged. And some areas, most of which are in Africa, have seen not just increasing poverty but actual social collapse, brought on by economic crisis, which the state has been unable to prevent. In these circumstances an "ethnic" community, often constructed by colonial powers that have long since departed, can provide what the state cannot. David Brown writes: "If the state claiming to be the cultural nation cannot offer the necessary protection, then it is the cultural nation claiming to be the potential state which offers the next best bet."[33] As we have seen, Rwanda provides a particularly tragic example of what can result from the residue of Western-invented "ethnicities" in a situation of acute social crisis: the genocide of 1994, far from being the expression of age-old "ethnic" animosities, was prepared by the destructive impact of colonialism on Central Africa.

The left should be at the forefront of opposition to this, reasserting the realities of class against the myths of ethnicity, but all too often it is handicapped by its refusal to accept that "identity" can ever be irrelevant, or mystified, or simply a cover for sectional interests. As Adam Kuper writes: "So although the popular American notion of cultural identity has been stretched beyond ethnic groups to other kinds of minorities, it remains doubly essentialist: one has an essential identity, and this derives from the essential characteristic of the collectivity to which one belongs."[34] In most cases, however, there are no "essential" characteristics, or indeed, any need for these collectivities to have existed for any length of time: "In actuality, a sense of ethnic community can develop among individuals who neither share significant cultural attributes nor who are particularly distinctive from their neighbors; and it can refer to commonalities of circumstance which developed within living memory, and to attributes which clearly do not objectively derive from common ancestry."[35] The more developed world—in this case the Balkans—provides us with the best example of how, unlike in Central Africa, "ethnicities" can arise with virtually no prior basis.

Unlike their parents, or even their grandparents, many of the people who came to be described as "ethnic Muslims" in Bosnia-Herzegovina had never been inside a mosque in their lives—at least until they began to be identified in this way for the purposes of persecution. It was only then that religion took on the significance it now has for them. As this example suggests, the distinction between "imposed" and "chosen" ethnic identities is not one that can be sustained, since there are many cases where groups that have been identified as possessing a particular attribute and discriminated against on that basis have subsequently chosen militantly to assert that identity in response to their oppressors. It was not inevitable that such identities become dominant among groups where particular attributes exist. As Misha Glenny writes of the Bosnian Muslims: "Although largely secular, the explicit religious origins of the Muslims' identity (they have no specific ethnic or linguistic criteria to differentiate themselves from Serbs or Croats, neither do they have a Belgrade or Zagreb to turn to for material, political or spiritual aid) have made the process of defining their nationhood exceptionally difficult." It is interesting that Glenny, who is otherwise one of the most insightful of journalistic commentators on the Balkan situation, sees this as a problem, rather than a hopeful basis for overcoming the divisions within Bosnian society, noting that "many Muslims incline toward aspects of either Serbian or Croatian culture."[36] But before sides became fixed in the Bosnian war, it was by no means certain that residual religious belief would be inflated until it became an imaginary essence by which these people were defined: "Before the war . . . when the Serbs still hoped to keep Bosnia in Yugoslavia, the media frequently highlighted similarities with the Muslims, while Croats often stressed that Bosnia had been part of historical Croatia and that most Bosnian Muslims were originally of Croatian descent."[37] In other words, these Muslims could have been absorbed into either Serb or Croat "ethnicities," in which case the supposedly essential nature of their Islamic identity would never have arisen.

The developed world has not remained untouched by the rise of—or perhaps one should say the retreat to—"ethnicity." The crisis in Western Europe and North America is clearly not of the same order as that in the Balkans, still less Central Africa, but similar pressures are at work. Where reforms are increasingly hard to come by, as a result of the political parties that have traditionally represented the working class refusing to challenge the bourgeoisie to the minimal extent of taxing them at significantly higher rates than their employees, two collective solutions remain for improving conditions. One is the road of class struggle, of forcing redistribution, either directly from the bourgeoisie in the form of higher wages and better conditions, or indirectly by forcing the state to intervene through legislation or increased taxation. The other road, the road more frequently traveled, is not to struggle for redistribution from the capitalist class to the working class, but to struggle—or more precisely, to lobby—for resources to be redistributed from one section of the working class to another, or from one region to another, or . . . from one "ethnic" group to another. If groups can become politically organized and consequently put electoral pressure on local or national politicians, then they, or more usually their representatives, can lobby for "affirmative action" on their behalf. As Eric Hobsbawm has written:

> There are good reasons why ethnicity (whatever it is) should be politicized in modern multi-ethnic societies, which characteristically take the form of a diaspora of mainly urban ghettoes, combined with a sharp increase in the occasions for friction between ethnic groups. Electoral democracy produces a ready-made machine for minority groups to fight effectively for a share of the central resources, once they learn to act as a group and are sufficiently concentrated for electoral purposes. At the same time, for reasons both of politics and ideology, and also of changing economic organization, the mechanism for defusing interethnic tensions by assigning separate niches to different groups, atrophies. They compete not for comparable resources . . . but for the *same* resources in the same labor or housing or educational or other markets. And in this competition, at least for the disadvantaged, group pressures for special favors ("affirmative action") is the most powerful weapon available.[38]

The latter strategy has a long history in postwar Britain, stretching back to the 1960s. It has only been since the onset of economic crisis in the following decade that it came to full maturity. Ambalavaner Sivanandan notes acidly the "scramble for government favors and government grants . . . on the basis of specific ethnic needs and problems" by "minority" groups following the Brixton riots of 1981 and the recommendations of the Scarman report. What this did, writes Sivanandan, was

> on the one hand, to deepen ethnic differences and foster ethnic rivalry and, on the other, to widen the definition of ethnicity to include a variety of national and religious groups—Chinese, Cypriots, Greeks, Turks, Irish, Italians, Jews, Moslems, Sikhs—till the term itself became meaningless (except as a means of getting funds). This "vertical mosaic" of ethnic groups, so distanced from the horizontal of class politics, then became even more removed by the policies of "Left" Labour councils who, lacking the race/class perspective which would have allowed them to dismantle the institutional racism of their own structures, institutionalized ethnicity instead.[39]

The problem is not simply the compromises and downplaying of radical demands that are required to receive state funding, but the fact of competition between communities. Nor is it even the case that such funding as is available invariably goes to the working-class areas, since the middle class can play the lobbying game to far greater effect and will generally reap whatever benefits are to be had. It would be bad enough if accepting the existence of ethnicity merely meant condoning an endless splintering into rival groups to divide up the crumbs left by global capital, but there are even worse implications. The most serious of these is the relationship between ethnicity and racism.

"ETHNICITY" AND THE NEW RACISM

For many on the left (as well as academics and officials in government agencies) it is perfectly acceptable to talk about ethnicity (without quotation marks), where it is no longer acceptable to talk about "race." There are, in other words, no such things as "races," but there are such things as "ethnicities." As Steve Fenton writes:

> The term race is associated with mistaken science, it connotes physical difference and, frequently, color. It is typically seen as malign and racial ideologies have been associated with compulsion and regimes of oppression. By contrast, ethnic can be taken as an analytic term in social science, is often seen as the voluntary identification of peoples, and as (at least potentially) benign.[40]

The problem is that the notion of ethnicity is all too often used to invoke precisely the qualities that used to be invoked under the now discredited notion of "race." To understand why, it is necessary to trace the previous major shifts in racist ideology.

Marxist accounts of the origins and development of racist ideology tend to see three moments in the history of capitalism as decisive in determining its precise form. The first is slavery, and the need to justify enslaving millions of fellow human beings at the very moment when men were being declared equal and in possession of certain unalienable rights. The second is colonialism, and the need to justify the conquest and subsequent domination of foreign peoples. The third is immigration, and the need to justify discrimination against peoples who were usually encouraged to come to the metropolitan centers in the process of reconstruction after the Second World War. The respective justifications for treatment of nonwhite populations differed in each case, moving from their less than human nature (making it permissible to enslave them) to their backwardness (requiring the guidance of the more advanced white "races") to the competition they posed to the white populations for jobs and housing (requiring an end to immigration and—in extreme versions—the repatriation of existing immigrants).[41]

In an important book published in 1981, however, the Marxist philosopher Martin Barker argued that we were now seeing the rise of a "new racism," which "can refuse insults: it need never talk of 'niggers,' 'wogs' or 'coons.' It does not need to see Jews as morally degenerate, or blacks as 'jungle bunnies.' Nonetheless in subtle but effective ways it authorizes the very emotions of hostility that then get expressed in these terms."[42] The "newness" of this racism is not in its reliance on the pseudosciences of sociobiology and ethnology for justification—pseudoscience has been a feature of racism since the invention of phrenology in the mid-nineteenth century—but in the claim that they demonstrate the social incompatibility of groups with different cultures. There have been two historical precedents for this shift in meaning, in which entire peoples were defined by virtue of what had previously been seen as an acquired characteristic—religion in the first, culture more generally in the second—rather than biology.

The first was in Ireland. In his work on the origins of racism, Theodore Allen defines racial oppression as the reduction of "all members of an oppressed group to an undifferentiated social status, a status beneath that of any member of any social class within the colonizing population." Allen argues that racism originated not from innate propensities on the part of different groups to distinguish themselves from and discriminate against other groups (the "psycho-cultural" argument), but as a conscious ruling-class strategy to justify slavery as an economic system in the epoch where formal equality (for males) was increasingly the norm (the "socio-economic" argument). Although his argument is mainly concerned with the racial oppression in the Americas, Allen identifies a precursor of white colonial attitudes to the Native Americans and to African slaves: in the British (i.e., Lowland Scot and English) treatment of the Irish from the Anglo-Norman period onward. With the Reformation, however, the religious difference between the Protestantism of the British settlers and the Catholicism of the Irish natives provided an additional element to the racism of the former: "What had fed primarily on simple xenophobia now, as religio-racism, drank at eternal Springs of private feelings about 'man and God.'" There were also more material reasons. As Allen strongly argues, the construction of "religio-racism" against the entire Irish population was a conscious choice on the part of the English ruling class and their Scottish allies. Ireland was a crucial strategic territory in the struggle between Catholic and Protestant Europe, hence the impossibility of co-opting sections of the Catholic Irish ruling class for the purposes of social control: they could not be trusted to take the British side in the conflicts with Catholic Spain and France. The alternative, of course, was to attempt to convert the Catholic population to Protestantism, but this was unthinkable for most of the eighteenth century, for two reasons. First, the Ascendancy comprised a relatively small minority of the population whose wealth and power would have been threatened if a majority had been allowed to share its legal privileges. Second, the majority of Protestants below the ruling class proper were Dissenters, most of them Presbyterians, and consequently excluded from the privileges available to communicants with the Anglican Church of Ireland. Mass conversion of the Catholic population was likely to lead to the converts joining the Dissenting branch of Protestantism rather than that of the great landowners, raising the prospect of the majority of the population uniting against the Ascendancy. After this came near to happening anyway, in 1798, the British ruling class and their Irish extension responded by incorporating the Dissenting element through the Orange Order, but more importantly by shifting the nature of Catholic oppression from a racial to a national basis "*by the incorporation of the Irish bourgeoisie into the intermediate buffer social control system.*" In short, once Catholics were allowed to participate in ruling Ireland, the system of "religio-racial" oppression had to be abandoned.[43] There are problems with this analysis, not least in the functionalism of the explanatory framework, where changes are the result of intentional maneuvers by the ruling class. It is also the case that Irish people in Britain continue to experience racism as the dominant form of oppression. Nevertheless, Allen is clearly right to note that the use of religion—an attribute that we would now regard as "ethnic"—as the basis of racial identification was rare at the time. In a situation where the oppressed population is of the same skin color as the oppressors, this shift was probably inevitable.

The second precedent was in South Africa. One of the intellectual founders of apartheid (which means "separate development") in South

Africa was W. W. M. Eiselen. As Kuper points out, Eiselen rejected the notions of black inferiority dominant among his countrymen: "Not race but culture was the true basis of difference, the sign of destiny." But although different cultures should be valued in their own right, their individual integrity should also be preserved: "If the integrity of traditional cultures were undermined, social disintegration would follow." Segregation of the races was necessary, not to preserve unequal relations between white and black, but the cultural differences between them.[44] This was the theoretical basis on which apartheid was built.

What is disturbing, given these precedents, is that the notion of "ethnicity," particularly when it is used in its cultural sense, has increasingly become a substitute for "race," a coded way of reinventing racial categories without making skin color the key issue, in similar ways to those pioneered in Ireland and South Africa. And it is not simply racists who are responsible for this. The Race Relations Act 1976 defines a "racial group" "by reference to one or more of the following: color, race, nationality (including citizenship) or ethnic or national origins."[45] A Commission for Racial Equality publication setting out the Racial Equality Standard for local government in Scotland asks that: "The Standard should be adopted and used both by authorities that have relatively substantial ethnic minority populations in their areas and those whose ethnic populations are smaller and more scattered."[46] The assumption that ethnicity represented a minority deviation from a majority norm should in itself make us deeply suspicious, but it is only since the 1970s that the racist undercurrents of the term have become completely obvious. As Neville Alexander points out, quoting one of the American sociologists responsible for popularizing the term during the 1940s, "ethnicity" is useful "as a means of avoiding the word, yet retaining its meaning."[47]

Alex Callinicos rightly argues that the "new" racism has arisen as a result of the discredit into which the notion of biologically distinct races has fallen—partly as a result of advances in knowledge that have undermined any scientific basis for such beliefs, partly (and one suspects far more) as a result of the use to which such beliefs were put during the Holocaust. (Hence the modern convention, which I have followed here, of placing the word "race" in quotes, indicating that the concept is wholly ideological and has no referent in the world.) Callinicos also argues, however, that the "newness" of this racism is more apparent than real, since biological racism and, related to this, ideas of black inferiority are still very much alive, and in any case the "new" cultural racism often involves the same type of stereotyping as the "old" biological racism.[48] There is some force in these criticisms. Given, for example, the attempt by Charles Murray in *The Bell Curve* to explain black underachievement on the basis of genetic inheritance, it would be very foolish to predict the imminent disappearance of biological racism.[49] Nevertheless, there are reasons to believe that the *dominant* form of racist ideology is taking a new form in which questions of "ethnicity" are central.

First, the emphasis on culture is not related to biology in the sense of indicating that some human beings are genetically superior or inferior to others, but in the sense that human beings are naturally hostile to those with different cultures: "we may all share a common human nature, but part of that very shared nature is the natural tendency to form bounded social units and to differentiate ourselves from outsiders."[50] This has become part of the discourse of even the extreme right, in British politics at least. During the campaign that preceded the elections to the European Parliament on June 10, 1999, a British National Party (BNP) leaflet intended for distribution across Scotland called for opposition to the "uprooting of our culture and to mass immigration" and for support of "the preservation of our unique Scottish identity within a free Britain." Voters were invited to find out more about the Fascist election campaign to save sterling and "to preserve the cultural and ethnic identity of Scotland and the British people."[51] The object here is to bait the hook that catches the unwary with references to culture and ethnicity in a way that makes a point of *not* referring to racial stereotypes.

Second, and more importantly, we are seeing the naturalization of "ethnic" characteristics. Attributes or properties like religion or language that were once regarded as socially acquired and consequently amenable to change are increasingly being treated *as if* they were naturally occurring and permanent. Indeed, in the case of nationalism, Tom Nairn has argued that they *are* naturally occurring and permanent, leading him to claim that "differential cultural development (including language) may have had a function unsuspected by previous historians and theorists. . . . If internal species-diversity through cultural means has always been 'human nature,' presumably it will go on being so—in a way that has nothing to do with blood or race."[52] The idea—supported by NATO and large sections of the liberal press—that different "ethnic" groups in the Balkans "naturally" want to separate themselves from other groups, if necessary by terror and expulsion, is clearly one practical application of this theory. As long as ethnicity is assumed to have a real existence then the pressure is always there to accept the logic of these supposed differences, which is that all the states in the Balkans must have a single dominant "ethnic" group, no matter what the cost to the other groups who might have lived there for as long or longer.

The same thinking lies behind the Northern Ireland Peace Agreement. Increasingly, the language in which the conflict in the North is described is abandoning the notions of "religious sectarianism" in which it was conducted for so long, and adopting that of "ethnic division" instead. Mere religious belief may decline with secularization, as it has across most of the British Isles, but if religion has become part of your very nature, then all you can do is keep the two sides ("communities") hermetically sealed off from each other. In other words, Protestant and Catholic religious beliefs have become the basis of "ethnic identities" and these in turn are assumed to function in the same way as "racial characteristics" once did. In addition to passing over the role that the British state has had in creating and maintaining the conflict, this ideological transformation also has another advantage for the ruling class, in that it absolves it from finding any permanent solution other than "peaceful coexistence." The question of language illustrates both how the state pretends to "evenhandedness" while supporting the Unionist position, and the way in which the social divisions in the North are treated as "cultural."

Since 1968 there has been a revival of interest in Irish culture and of the Gaelic language in particular among Catholics in the North. Since this interest has rightly been associated with political republicanism, or at the very least with the desire to assert a political identity in the face of a state that denies or marginalizes it, the educational and cultural activities involved have tended to be organized and financed by the communities themselves, rather than by the state. In 1994, however, the government-sponsored Cultural Traditions Group expressed its concern that Gaelic was associated with republicanism and arranged to fund a trust to enable Protestants to learn the language in settings where they would not be troubled by these associations. As Bill Rolston points out, this is not "symmetry," but "an exercise in depoliticizing a cultural movement. It is multiculturalism as counterinsurgency." The same Cultural Traditions Group also provides funding for the "Ulster-Scots" language, whose supporters set up the Ulster Scots Society in, by a curious coincidence, 1994.[53] There is no such language. The only Scottish language is Gaelic, and even "Scottish-Scots" is a dialect—in fact several dialects—of English); but such claims help to establish the myth that there are two parallel communities, with equivalent traditions, not a divided society in which one community is oppressed.

The difficulty is that if we lack a word to describe the victims of racism, since we reject the concept of "race," then the concept of ethnicity seems to offer an alternative. If what I have argued here is correct, however, ethnicity is rapidly turning into the thing it was originally introduced to oppose. What Kuper has written of contemporary American anthropology seems applicable to much of the left: "it repudiate[s] the popular ideas that differences are natural, and that cultural identity must be grounded in a primordial, biological identity, but a rhetoric that places great emphasis on difference and identity is not best placed to counter these views. On the contrary, the insistence that radical difference can be observed between peoples best serves to sustain them."[54]

"ETHNIC" VERSUS "CIVIC" NATIONALISM

There is however, another danger with the use of "ethnicity." It is sometimes argued that "ethnic" nationalisms that supposedly lead to the purging of entire populations as in Yugoslavia can be combated by an alternative, "civic" nationalism based on politics, not tribe. James Kellas describes this as "inclusive" in the sense that anyone can adopt that culture and join the nation, even if that person is not considered to be part of the "ethnic nation."[55] "Civic" nationalism is frequently presented as the only true form of nationalism. Certain nationalisms—like that of Serbia—are said to be inherently oppressive precisely because they are based on an "ethnic" identity. The contrast is often made between this kind of nationalism and one described as "civic" or "social"—Scottish and Catalan nationalism, for example, are frequently described in this way, not least by Scottish and Catalan nationalists themselves.

George Kerevan, former Trotskyist and currently the SNP spokesperson for the environment, used his column in *The Scotsman* newspaper recently to distinguish the nationalism of his party from that of the Milošević regime:

There is nationalism in the sense it applies to Hitler or Milošević. Call it ethnic or tribal nationalism. In fact, don't call it nationalism at all, because it's not about building modern nations. This is a reactionary, tribal, exclusive ideology espoused in times of economic and political change by those social orders who are being usurped or threatened by the process of modernization.... But there is another, totally different meaning of the word nationalism—nation building. Building the common institutions of an inclusive civil society that alone mobilizes the talents, energies, and co-operation of the population to create a modern industrial society.[56]

Note that nationalisms of which Kerevan disapproves (not least because they threaten to discredit his own nationalism by association) are dismissed as mere "tribalism." Conversely, "civic" nationalism is with equal frequency presented as not "really" being a form of nationalism at all, and only the "tribalism" of Milošević, which, as Michael Ignatieff puts it, "legitimizes an appeal to blood loyalty," is designated as such. In either event, the desired effect is to protect "civic" nationalism from any suggestion that it appeals to blood and soil.[57] Now Marxists do distinguish between different forms of nationalism, in particular between those of oppressors and oppressed, but this is not what is being argued here.[58] What is interesting about the argument regarding "civic" nationalism is that it is precisely the one that has historically been used to defend multinational oppressor nationalisms like those of Britain and the US.

During the Scottish parliamentary elections of May 1999, the Scottish *Daily Record* issued a warning to its readers that the nationalism of the SNP could lead to the type of brutality exercised by the Serbs against the Kosovar Albanians. Here the British nationalism supported by both the *Daily Record* and its party of choice, the British Labor Party, simply disappears from view, despite the fact that it has been used to mobilize support for actual, as opposed to hypothetical, bloodletting for nearly three hundred years and is doing so again in the Balkans while I have been writing this article. The notion that British nationalism is not "really" nationalism at all is of course a venerable theme of ruling class ideologues. It was first systematically expressed by the historian Lord Acton in an article of 1862 where he argued that the multinational character of the British nation ensured that "freedom" (in the economic sense understood by mid-Victorian liberals) was secure: "The combination of different nations in one State is as necessary a condition of civilized life as the combination of men in society." One of the benefits conferred by this arrangement was that the "intellectually superior" would elevate "inferior races" hitherto corrupted by despotism or democracy. It takes little effort to insert the names of England in the first category and Scotland (or possibly "the Celts" more generally) in the second. How different this beneficent fusion was to the situation elsewhere in Europe! "Where political and national boundaries coincide, society ceases to advance, and nations relapse into a condition corresponding to that of men who renounce intercourse with their fellow-men."[59] It takes equally little effort to insert the name of France within this category.

This analysis, or second- or third-hand versions of it, clearly informs the attitude of contemporary supporters of the British state, such as Gordon Brown, who are happy to dilate on their abhorrence of (Scottish) nationalism while simultaneously offering their support for British bombers whose sides are decorated with the Union Jack. Social psychologist Michael Billig has characterized the everyday nationalism of the established imperial states as "banal nationalism": "'Our' nationalism is not presented as nationalism, which is dangerously irrational, surplus and alien." Other people have nationalism; at best, "we" have patriotism. Billig aims his comments specifically at the situation in the US, but they have a broader applicability: "The wars waged by US troops; the bombing in Vietnam and Iraq; the bombast of successive US presidents; and the endless display of the revered flag; all of these are removed from the problems of over-heated nationalism."[60]

As these comments suggest, there are significant difficulties for socialists in attempting to use "civic" nationalism as an alternative to "ethnic" nationalism. Two in particular stand out. The first is that the category of the "civic" avoids any engagement with the fact that there are certain activities that nation-*states* must undertake, regardless of how nonethnic they may be. As Billig complains, "[Ignatieff] does not describe how 'civic nationalists' create a nation-state with its own myths; how the civic nations recruit their citizenry in war-time; how they draw their boundaries; how they demarcate 'others' behind those boundaries; how they resist, violently if necessary, those movements which seek to rearrange the boundaries; and so on."[61] The second is that, as we have seen, ethnicities can either be invented to categorize groups by their enemies or as self-identification by those groups themselves, without any reference to real or imaginary kinship relations: culture can just as easily be made the basis of ethnicity as blood-and-soil tribalism. Precisely because ethnicity is a socially constructed category, however, ethnic categorizations can be produced anywhere with the same disastrous results that we have seen for the last ten years in the Balkans. Consequently there is no reason why "civic" nationalism cannot in turn be transformed into "ethnic" nationalism under certain determinate conditions, just as it was in Germany—a modern, developed, and highly cultured capitalist society—during the 1930s.[62] This is a conclusion that adherents of "civic" nationalism are, of course, most anxious to avoid.

The example of Scotland is worth considering in this context for two reasons: on the one hand, because the historical record demonstrates how even this most civil of societies first rose on a sea of ethnic blood; on the other, because the contemporary situation contains all the elements needed for an "ethnic" nationalism to arise—and in this Scotland is no different from most other Western European nations, although it tends to evade the scrutiny to which English nationalism is rightly subjected. The modern Scottish nation was created through two processes: the destruction of Highland society and the incorporation of its imagery into the national self-image; and the consolidation of that image through participation in the conquest and colonization of North America and India. Both processes included ferocious episodes of what we would now call "ethnic cleansing."

The Highlanders were considered to be no better than the Catholic Irish; indeed, their language and persons were often described in this way in both the Lowlands and England. One self-proclaimed "gentleman" of Derby, on whom Highlanders were quartered during the Jacobite occupation of that town in 1745, expressed every existing prejudice possible about the Highlanders in the space of one brief letter. First, their appearance: "Most of the men, after their entrance into my house, looked like so many fiends turned out of hell, to ravage the kingdom and cut throats; and under their plaids nothing but a various sort of butchering weapons were to be seen." Even though these fiends in human form proceeded to eat and drink this gentleman out of house and home (unaccountably failing to cut either his throat or those of his family), he could still find amusement in their religious observance: "What did afford me some matter for an unavoidable laughter, (though my family was in a miserable condition) was, to see these desperadoes, from officers to the common men, at their several meals, first pull of their bonnets, and then lift up their eyes in a most solemn manner, and mutter something to themselves, by way of saying grace—as if they had been so many primitive Christians." As if, indeed. His greatest abuse, however, is reserved for their language: "Their dialect (from the idea I had of it) seemed to me, as if a herd of hottentots, wild monkeys in a desert, or vagrant gypsies, had been jabbering, screaming, and howling together; and really this jargon of speech was very suited to such a set of banditti."[63] The conflation of "hottentot," "monkey," and "gypsy" is suggestive and horrifying, but no different from what was commonly said about the Irish. And this is how they were treated in the aftermath of the Battle of Culloden. Discussing the brutality shown to the defeated Scottish Highlanders by the British army, the historian Alan MacInnes has written that the actions of the victorious Hanoverian troops involved "systematic state terrorism, characterized by a genocidal intent that verged on 'ethnic cleansing.'"[64] At the forefront of these atrocities were the Lowland Scots.

As the warrior vanguard of British imperialism, however, the Highlanders behaved no better than the Lowlanders or the English. The Native Americans, to whom the Highlanders have been so frequently and inaccurately compared, might have expected different treatment at their hands than was generally dispensed by settlers from elsewhere in the British Isles. Alas, this was not the case. There were individual examples of intermarriage, or even of Highlanders adopting Native American lifestyles, but as James Hunter writes: "Most North American Indian native peoples . . . would have been hard pressed to distinguish between the behavior of Scottish Highlanders or any other of the various types of European with whom they came in contact." In some cases this behavior contained particularly bitter ironies: "Emigrants to Cape Breton Island, many of them refugees from clearances . . . showed not the slightest scruple about displacing the area's traditional inhabitants, the Micmac, from territories the latter had occupied for much longer than there had been Gaelic-speaking Scots in Scotland."[65] Scotland was of course *itself* an imperial power—or, as an integral part of the British state, at least a major component of one. We are fortunate to have an excellent description of imperial rule in Asia by James Callender, a Scottish radical active during the 1780s and 1790s:

In Bengal only, we destroyed or expelled within the short period of six years, no less than five millions of industrious and harmless people; and as we have been sovereigns in that country for about thirty-five years, it may be reasonably computed that we have strewn the plains of Indostan with fifteen or twenty millions of carcasses....The persons positively destroyed must, in whole, have exceeded twenty millions, or two thousand ... acts of homicide per annum. These victims have been sacrificed to the balance of power, and the balance of trade, the honor of the British flag.[66]

Nor is the type of racism associated with empire something of the distant past. As late as 1923 a Committee of the Church of Scotland, asked to consider the effects of Irish immigration to Scotland, produced a report to the General Assembly in which the Catholic Irish were described as "a people by themselves, segregated by reason of their race, their customs, their traditions, and, *above all*, by their loyalty to their Church." The Scottish and Irish "races" could never mix, nor even live together, because: "The Irish are the most obedient children of the Church of Rome; the Scots stubbornly adhere to the principles of the reformed faith [i.e., Protestantism]. The Irish have separate schools for their children; they have their own clubs for recreation and social intercourse; they tend to segregate in communities, and even to monopolize certain departments of labour to the exclusion of Scots."[67]

It should be obvious, therefore, that it is historically inaccurate to claim that the Scottish nation has had a purely "civic" national identity, and politically myopic to imagine that a full-blown "ethnic" nationalism could not reemerge here under certain conditions. The materials are there in the traditions of Protestant sectarianism, militarism, or even simply "whiteness." On the latter point it is worth noting that the Commission for Racial Equality reported in May 1999 that Scotland had 1,087 recorded racial incidents during 1997–98, compared to 441 in Wales and 13,437 in England. Although Scotland is home to only 2.1 percent of "ethnic minorities" in Britain, it recorded 7.3 percent of all racially motivated incidents. In Central Scotland, where the majority of incidents were reported, the percentage was fifteen times higher than in Central London. None of these remarks are intended to contribute to *Daily Record*–style hysteria about Scottish nationalism. The chances of an ethnic national movement arising in the near future strike me as unlikely, and the SNP is equally unlikely to be a vehicle for such a nationalism should it arise, but it is necessary to remind ourselves that there are no nations on earth, be their nationalisms ever so "civic," where "ethnic" divisions could not be invented and "cleansing" imposed if the material conditions were right.

CONCLUSION

It could be argued that I am displaying too great a concern with mere terminology, and, given the way in which the academic left is currently obsessed with language, this would be an understandable response. Nevertheless, the dire political consequences that have previously followed the widespread adoption of certain terms ("patriarchy," for example) tend to suggest that terminological shifts not only register changed ways of thinking but also encourage such changes. As the Russian Marxist Valentin Voloshinov wrote, "the word is the most sensitive *index of social changes*," and if, as Voloshinov also suggests, the word is "an arena of class struggle," then it is high time that we began to wage it over the word "ethnicity."[68]

In his recent book on culture, Kuper concludes with sentiments that are equally relevant to this discussion:

> Unless we separate out the various processes that are lumped together under the heading of culture, and look beyond the field of culture to other processes, then we will not get very far in understanding any of it. For the same sort of reason, cultural identity can never provide an adequate guide for living. We all have multiple identities, and even if I accept that I have a primary cultural identity, I may not want to conform to it. Besides, it may not be very practical. I operate in the market, live through my body, struggle in the grip of others. If I am to regard myself only as a cultural being, I allow myself very little room to maneuver, or to question the world in which I find myself.

Kuper notes that there is a final objection to defining ourselves in this way, which he describes as "moral," but which is actually political: "It tends to draw attention away from what we have in common instead of encouraging us to communicate across national, ethnic, and religious boundaries, and to venture between them."[69] Although rendered in liberal individualistic terms, this is well said. For socialists, the aim is to overcome the divisions that are increasingly described as "ethnic" by removing the oppressions that give them significance, not to perpetuate or add to them. This may mean supporting oppressed nations or peoples, but the notion of "ethnicity" is ultimately a means of dividing people up into ever more arbitrary classifications. At best, under the guise of celebrating "cultural difference," it only obscures what most working people, which is most people, have in common by emphasizing relatively superficial aspects of our social world. At worst, in a struggle for scarce resources such as that currently being played out in the Balkans, it can be used as a means of marking down certain people for persecution. As I have tried to suggest, there is no reason why we in Britain should feel complacent about the implications of "ethnic cleansing" for ourselves. The necessary elements of "ethnicity" can always be assembled from whatever historical relics are lying around, if economic crisis and social collapse are sufficiently severe. The anthropologist Marcus Banks wrote recently of ethnicity: "Unfortunately . . . it is too late to kill it off or pronounce ethnicity dead; the discourse on ethnicity has escaped from the academy and into the field."[70] This is too pessimistic. To dispense with the concept, we must first dispense with the social conditions that require the thing to which it refers; but it is possible to make a start. To paraphrase Alasdair MacIntyre in another context: understanding the uses to which "ethnicity" has been put leads comprehensively to the conclusion that it is a term no honest person should continue to use.[71]

◦ Chapter 2 ◦

What Is National Consciousness?*

INTRODUCTION

Readers should bear three points in mind during what follows. First, although the theoretical basis of this chapter is the classical Marxist tradition, I have also drawn from the general literature of nation theory where it is compatible with historical materialism, however unwelcome that affinity may be for the writers concerned. Second, although that literature is now extensive and continues to grow, I refer to their work only where it usefully illustrates positions that I want to accept or reject, rather than providing yet more commentary on the major contributors, or (worse still) commentary on their commentators. This chapter is a framework; it is not intended to be a comprehensive survey. Third, for the purposes of clarity many of these positions are posed in starkly antithetical terms

---

* Originally published as chapter 1 of *The Origins of Scottish Nationhood* (London: Pluto Press, 2000).

that will require subsequent qualification. The first concerns the definition of nationhood.

DEFINING A NATION

Definitions of nationhood tend to fall into one of two categories, which rely on either objective or subjective criteria. There is no agreed-upon Marxist position and little help to be gained from Marx or Engels themselves since, as Michael Löwy has noted, "a precise definition of the concept of 'a nation'" is absent from their writings on the national question.[1] Consequently, their successors have tended to take one of the existing sides in the debate.

On the objective side the most famous definition was given by Stalin in an article of 1913 called "Marxism and the National Question," which unfortunately has exerted an influence over the left far in excess of its theoretical merits, which are slight. Stalin writes: "A nation is a historically evolved, stable community of language, territory, economic life and psychological make-up manifested in a community of culture." Furthermore, we learn that "it is sufficient for a single one of these characteristics to be absent and the nation ceases to be a nation."[2] These positions have been accepted by many who would otherwise have nothing to do with Stalinist politics. In an article discussing the Scottish national question Bob Mulholland quotes part of the above passage, then writes of Stalin that "his succinct definition makes sense and undoubtedly applies to the national characteristics of the Scottish people."[3] In fact, his "succinct definition" is merely an extensive checklist of criteria, against which can be matched the attributes of those peoples seeking the status of "nation." Eric Hobsbawm has noted the "shifting and ambiguous" quality of all objective criteria, which "makes them unusually convenient for propagandist and programmatic, as distinct from descriptive purposes."[4] These characteristics are clearly present here, but perhaps the most obvious deficiency of these specific criteria is that many nations currently recognized as such would be denied the title, and contrary to what Mulholland says, one of these would be Scotland. Many nations which have successfully attained statehood would also have to admit that they had attained their position through false pretences. Take Switzerland as an example.

Switzerland fails the Stalinist criteria on at least two counts, those of language (there are five official languages: German, French, Italian, and two dialects of Romansh) and religion (there are two major religions: Roman Catholicism and Calvinist Protestantism). Yet the territory of Switzerland did not change from 1515 to 1803, and during those three centuries the vast majority spoke dialects of German, only at the later date incorporating Italian speakers. Only in 1815 did it acquire territories with significant French-speaking populations in Valais, Geneva, and Neuchâtel, courtesy of the Holy Alliance. The state itself was only established in 1815, and as late as 1848 it was still enforcing religious divisions within the cantons: Protestantism was unlawful in Catholic areas and Catholicism illegal in Protestant ones. After the revolutions of the latter year (which actually began in Switzerland), these restrictions were lifted and the territory of the state divided on a linguistic basis instead. Only in 1891, six hundred years after the event, did the state decide that the founding of the original Confederation of Schwyz, Obwalden, and Nidwalden in 1291 constituted the origin of the Swiss nation.[5]

It should be clear even from this brief account that the Swiss nation exists even in the absence of the elements that are supposed to constitute nationhood, not because of them. It might be protested that Switzerland is an exceptional case, but Scotland faced similar (and in some respects even more extreme) difficulties, yet also succeeded in becoming a nation. It is perhaps appropriate that Leon Trotsky, the man who did most to uphold the classical Marxist tradition against Stalin, also offered an alternative to his checklist procedure using precisely the example of Switzerland:

> The Swiss people, through their historical connections, feel themselves to be a nation despite different languages and religions. An abstract criterion is not decisive in this question, far more decisive is the historical consciousness of a group, their feelings, their impulses. But that too is not determined accidentally, but rather by the situation and all the attendant circumstances.[6]

The specific reasons why the Swiss, the Scots, or any other people originally came to feel themselves a nation have to be separately discovered in each case, but this subjective feeling of identification is the only attribute that all have in common. In the words of the Zionist Ahad Ha'am: "If I feel the spirit of Jewish nationality in my heart so that it stamps all my inward life with its seal, then the spirit of Jewish nationality exists in me; and its existence is not at an end even if all my Jewish contemporaries should cease to feel it in their hearts." Elie Kedourie, who quotes this passage, adds:"Here are no superfluous appeals to philology or biology, no laborious attempts to prove that because a group speaks the same language, or has the same religion, or lives in the same territory, it is therefore a nation."[7] As Hugh Seton-Watson writes,"a nation exists when a significant number of people in a community consider themselves to form a nation, or behave as if they form one."[8]

Do we need to make such a stark choice between objective and subjective definitions? Might not the notion of "ethnicity" provide a way of transcending their opposition? As we saw in the previous chapter, "ethnicity" can be defined in three ways: kinship, occupation, or identity. In the context of this discussion, the kinship or occupational definitions of ethnicity are irrelevant. There are no longer any endogamous kinship groups and have not been for centuries or possibly even millennia (although there are, of course, groups who believe that they share the same genetic inheritance). There are certainly occupational groups, but these are by no means all "national," and even those that are can never be the basis of nations, precisely because their definition as such is only possible in relation to a preexisting external national homeland: Chinese traders in Indonesia can only be defined as Chinese because "Chinese" is already a recognized national category. The third definition is the only relevant one, and it is entirely subjective.[9] If ethnicity does not provide a third way between objective and subjective definitions, what difficulties are commonly raised in relation to the latter that might prevent us adopting it? There are two.

The first tends to be raised on the left. Does granting national status to any group that claims it not involve recognizing the right to self-determination of Zionists like Ha'am, South African white supremacists, Ulster Loyalists, and other groups whose goals socialists oppose? This objection is based on a misunderstanding. Recognizing that the aforementioned groups consider themselves to be nations does not in any way imply *support* for them. Whether or not one supports a national group surely depends on an assessment of the role it plays in world politics, not the mere fact of its existence. The distinction between oppressor and oppressed nations, first drawn by Marx and later refined by Lenin, is obviously a helpful guide in making such an assessment, although it is clear that many nations in dispute—of which Scotland is one—fall into neither of these categories.[10] The point is perhaps made clearer if considered in relation to existing imperial powers: I am, generally speaking, opposed to the activities of the French state; I do not for that reason seek to deny the existence of the French nation.

The second is more concerned with the theoretical than the political implications of subjectivism. According to Hobsbawm, subjective definitions are "open to the objection that defining a nation by its members' consciousness of belonging to it is tautological and provides only an a posteriori guide to what a nation is."[11] Such definitions would, however, be tautological only if group members did not already know what a nation was. Since they do, a group that decides it is a nation is saying, in effect, "we are the same kind of group as these other groups that have declared themselves nations." The only group of which this could not have been true would have been the first to declare itself a nation, since it would have had nothing to measure itself against. Once a group decides it is a nation, it usually also discovers that it has always been one, or (in the Scottish case at least) that it has been one since 1296, or perhaps 1320.

In the discussion that follows the word "nation" will therefore be used to describe a human community that has acquired national consciousness. Benedict Anderson famously wrote of the nation that exists in this consciousness that: "It is *imagined* because the members of even the smallest nation will never know most of their fellow-members, meet them, or even hear of them, yet in the minds of each lives the image of their communion." According to Anderson all communities beyond the original tribal groupings (and perhaps even they) have faced this problem of numbers and consequently have had to "imagine" themselves as a collective, although in different ways depending on the nature of the community. Consequently, he argues, "imagining" in this sense is neutral and does not involve "falsity" or "fabrication."[12] Leave aside whatever value judgments we may wish to make for the moment; it is nevertheless clear that national consciousness is different from other forms of collective consciousness, but in what way? It is first necessary to identify what they all have in common. The Russian Marxist Valentin Voloshinov wrote that "the only possible objective definition of consciousness is a sociological one." By this Voloshinov means that consciousness is not an individual but a collective attribute. It is produced by people internalizing the meaning of the ideological signs that their social group has produced and used over time in the process of interaction. As a result: "Individual consciousness is not the architect of the ideological superstructure, but only a tenant lodging in the social edifice of ideological signs."[13] We distinguish between specific forms of collective consciousness not by the ways in which they come into being or the ways in which the resultant communities are "imagined," but by the relationships they bear to external social reality, which are different in each case. These distinctions can be seen most readily if we compare national consciousness to another form of consciousness: class.

NATIONAL CONSCIOUSNESS AND CLASS CONSCIOUSNESS

All the analytic concepts that we use to describe certain types of social relationship—class, nation, state—are abstractions. What is crucial is their underlying relationship to the reality from which they are abstracted. For Marxists, "class" is an objective condition independent of what a person perceives their condition to be. In the classic statement of this position, Geoffrey de Ste Croix writes: "A class (a particular class) is a group of persons in a community identified by their position in the whole system of social production, defined above all according to their relationship (primarily in terms of the degree of ownership or control) to the conditions of production (that is to say, the means and labor of production) and to the other classes."[14] For a class in a subordinate position within "the whole system of social production" to become an effective contender for power it must first become *conscious*, both of its own position and of the antagonistic relationship with the dominant class that this position entails. As Marx explains in relation to the working class: "Economic conditions had first transformed the mass of the people of the country into workers. The domination of capital had created for this mass a common situation, common interests. This mass is thus already a class against capital, but not yet for itself. In the struggle . . . the mass becomes united and constitutes itself as a class for itself."[15] It may be, as Georg Lukács once suggested, that in situations where the process has not taken place, it is nevertheless possible to imagine what type of consciousness the working class might have if its members were collectively aware of their position: "By relating consciousness to the whole of society it becomes possible to infer the thoughts and feelings which men would have in a particular situation if they were able to assess both it and the interests arising from it in their impact on immediate action and on the whole structure of society. That is to say, it would be possible to infer the thoughts and feelings appropriate to their objective situation. The number of such situations is not unlimited in any society."[16] Their position as workers does not, however, depend on their awareness of it, for it is certain that many (perhaps most) workers under capitalism have never achieved full awareness of their position; indeed, this is one of the necessary conditions of their remaining workers under capitalism.

There is, however, another position, also claiming to be Marxist, which argues against an objective definition of class. Edward Thompson has given it its clearest expression: "And class happens when some men, as a result of common experiences (inherited or shared), feel and articulate the identity of their interests as between themselves, and against other men whose interests are different from (and usually opposed to) theirs."[17] Some writers have used this definition of class to argue for the essential similarity between the processes by which classes and nations are formed.[18] In fact, Thompson's original definition does not relate to the formation of classes at all, but to the formation of class consciousness, the process of becoming a "class for itself."[19] Nevertheless, with the necessary adjustments it does indeed become an excellent definition of how nations "happen": "And nationhood happens when some people, as a result of common experience (inherited or shared), feel and articulate the identity of interests as between themselves, and against other nations whose interests are different from (and usually opposed to) theirs." The point here, and the reason why I have stressed the objective nature of social class, is that where nations are concerned, the situation is reversed. Contrary to what is written by Stalin and all other objectivist theorists of the nation, there is no underlying reality of nationhood that can be brought to the level of consciousness. Consequently, to revert to the Marxist distinction between a class "in itself" and a class "for itself," we can say that a national group becomes "a nation for itself" when members of the group learn to think of themselves and each other as members of the same nation, but there is no such thing as "a nation in itself."[20] As George Kerevan once pointed out, national consciousness "is materially determined by the external appearance of bourgeois society"; class consciousness is materially determined "by its essence."[21] Class consciousness arises through a process of recognizing real common interests, a recognition that is only possible as a result of social classes having a material reality prior to consciousness. National consciousness arises through a process of constructing imaginary common interests, a construction that can result in the establishment of a territorial nation–state, but only at that point will the nation have a material reality outside of consciousness. The resulting difference in aspiration may be summed up schematically by saying that a member of a social class may achieve class consciousness (bring their consciousness in line with reality), while a group with national consciousness may achieve statehood (bring reality in line with their consciousness).

NATIONAL CONSCIOUSNESS AND NATIONALISM

I have suggested that national consciousness does not always involve the objective of attaining statehood. In his attempt to specify what distinguishes the nation from other "imagined communities," Anderson stresses the existence of both territorial limits "beyond which lie other nations" and sovereignty embodied in a state.[22] In this Anderson stands in a long tradition within social science. Max Weber wrote that "a nation is a community [of sentiment] which normally tends to produce a state of its own."[23] Alfred Cobban concluded, still more decisively, that "a nation is a community which is, or wishes to be, a state."[24] For John Breuilly the active participation in realizing that wish is decisive: "The constant reiteration of the statement 'I am French' is empty unless linked to some notion of what being French means. In turn, that meaning can become politically effective only if shared by a number of people with effective organization. It is the shared meanings and their political organization that constitute a form of nationalism rather than the purely subjective choices of individual Frenchmen."[25] Other writers have gone still further. According to Anthony Smith: "A nation can . . . be defined as *a named human population sharing an historic territory, common myths and historical territories, a mass, public culture, a common economy and common legal rights and duties for all members.*"[26] The difficulty with this definition is that if nationhood is even partly dependent on economic and legal factors, then—contrary to what Smith says elsewhere in his writings—nationhood must involve not only the desire for statehood, not only participation in or support for the struggle to achieve it, but its actual attainment, for it is difficult to see how else "a common economy and legal rights and duties" could have any reality.

All the writers cited directly above fail to distinguish between what I have defined as national consciousness and nationalism, and treat the former merely as an aspect of the latter. Montserrat Guibernau, for example, writes that "the fragmentary nature of current approaches to nationalism originates from their inability to merge its two fundamental attributes: the political character of nationalism as an ideology defending the notion that state and nation should be congruent; and its capacity to be a provider of identity for individuals conscious of forming a group based upon a common culture, past, project for the future, and attachment to a concrete territory."[27] And, in the context of Scotland, Tom Nairn has written of the difference between what he calls Upper Case Nationalism and lower case nationalism. The first represents the specific political demand for a nation-state (but not necessarily membership in the Scottish National Party); the second represents a more general identification with the Scottish people, compatible with a variety of political positions; but both types can be accommodated under the heading of nationalism.[28] In fact, the sense of mutual recognition implied by the term "national consciousness" is different from nationalism. It is perfectly possible for a people to develop national consciousness without subsequently becoming nationalists—the majority of modern Scots are the living proof of this contention, at least as far as Scottish, as opposed to British, national consciousness is concerned—but it is *not* possible to build a nationalist movement without (at least a minority of) a people previously developing national consciousness. The two have also been known to develop simultaneously, but for the purposes of clarity I will treat national consciousness as a more or less passive expression of collective identification among a social group, and nationalism as a more or less active participation in the political mobilization of a social group for the construction *or* defense of a state.

Smith has argued against purely political definitions of nationalism on the grounds that "not all nationalisms have in practice opted for independent statehood," citing the Scottish and Catalan examples. He asserts that a consequence of defining nations politically is that they can only then be said to exist when embodied in a state, leading to a situation where "Scotland cannot become a 'nation' until the majority of Scottish voters agree with the Scottish National Party's platform and vote for an independent Scottish 'nation-state.'"[29] Here we see the consequences of failing to distinguish between national consciousness and nationalism.

The Scottish people already have national consciousness and would therefore constitute a nation even if there were no organizations committed to Scottish statehood—as indeed was the case prior to the 1920s. Similarly, Michael Biddiss asks rhetorically whether "a deep pride in Welshness only be accorded the status of nationalism proper when it is harnessed to the program of Plaid Cymru?"[30] The answer is: not necessarily, but it must be harnessed to *some* program for the establishment of a Welsh state, otherwise "deep pride" remains an expression of national consciousness, rather than nationalism.

WHAT NATIONAL CONSCIOUSNESS IS NOT

Nationalism is not the only concept to be confused with national consciousness. In the following section I want to distinguish between national consciousness and four related concepts—national identity, "banal nationalism," patriotism, and cultural nationalism—to which it bears a superficial resemblance and with which it is often used interchangeably.

National identity

The most widely used of these concepts is that of "national identity," which is unsurprising, given the totemic authority with which the concept of identity in general is currently endowed. The supposed transition from modernity to postmodernity, whose precise date is disputed but most commonly placed in the first half of the 1970s, is held to have produced a number of unprecedented social effects: "Post-modernism argues that late or post-modern societies are impelled by constant and rapid social change which makes a fixed and immutable sense of self redundant." According to this argument, there has not only been an increase in the *speed* with which identities can be exchanged, but also a change in the *type* of identities associated with modernity—principally those of class—to others, which are the basis of the "new social movements such as feminism, black struggles, nationalist and ecological movements."[31] Michael Billig quotes John Shotter as writing that "'identity' has become the watchword of the times," but then adds: "The watchword, however, should be watched, for frequently it explains less than it appears to."[32] There are a number of reasons why the current significance ascribed to identity requires that we mount a watchtower, but two are particularly relevant to this discussion.

The first is that the significance of identity is not new. One of the chief characteristics of modernity was precisely "constant and rapid social change" in which, as one moderately well-known text of 1848 has it, "all that is solid melts into air."[33] It is therefore curious that these characteristics are now being claimed for postmodernity. It may be therefore that people who lived during earlier stages of industrial capitalism had a wider and more fluid range of identities (religious, regional, artisanal) than is patronizingly assumed by modern social theorists. It was certainly during this period that national identity became available for the first time, at least for the majority of the populations of Europe and the Americas. Another corollary is that perhaps the supposedly fabulous range of identities available to those of us who live during the current late stage of capitalism comprises little more than the various consumer groups identified as targets for niche advertising. Stuart Hall has given the game away to a certain extent when he writes: "But the fact is that greater and greater numbers of people (men *and* women)—with however little money—play the game of using things to signify who they are."[34] As Ambalavaner Sivanandan has written of this passage: "Who are these people . . . unless it is those who use cardboard boxes under Waterloo Bridge to signify that they are the homeless?"[35]

The second is that, even if we accept that identities have some increased significance in contemporary social life, some are of greater significance than others and cannot be exchanged for others. As Billig has stressed:

> Not all identities should be considered as equivalent and interchangeable. Perhaps the postmodern consumer can purchase a bewildering range of identity-styles. Certainly, the commercial structures are in place for the economically comfortable to change styles in the Western world . . . national identity cannot be exchanged like last year's clothes. . . . One can eat Chinese tomorrow and Turkish the day after; one can even dress in Chinese or Turkish styles. But *being* Chinese or Turkish are not commercially available options.[36]

National identity is therefore of great significance, but is it the same as national consciousness? For some writers it is. Take, for example, the following—in most respects unexceptionable—passage by Guibernau: "In my view nationalism is a sentiment that has to do with attachments to a homeland, a common language, ideals, values and traditions, and also the identification of a group with symbols (a flag, a particular song, piece of music or design) which defines it as 'different' from others. The attachment to all these signs creates an identity; and the appeal to that identity has had in the past, and still has today, the power to mobilize people."[37]

My quarrel is not, at this point in the argument, with the concept of nationalism outlined here but with the concept of national identity. As Billig writes: "One should not presume that an identity is a hidden psychological state, as if there is a wordless, psychological or neurological state of 'having an identity.'"[38] The signs to which Guibernau refers do not *create* an identity, they *are* themselves an identity, or rather they are part of one. Identities are the *ensemble* of all the external signs through which people show both to themselves and to other people that they have chosen to be identified in that particular way. These signs can be as visible as particular types of clothing or as audible as particular ways of speaking, but most often they are simply the ways in which people respond to being addressed in a particular way. If, for example, I began to wear the kilt as my regular form of dress, where I had previously worn trousers, began to include Scottish words in my conversation, where I had previously spoken only English, and began to hail the abilities of the Scottish national football team, where I had previously expressed admiration for the Italian side, the observer might reasonably conclude that—questions of my sanity apart—I was asserting my Scottish national identity by displaying the signs that are generally recognized as carrying this message.

Ross Poole has noted the variety of ways in which the term "identity" has been used and the consequent ambiguity that has arisen over its meaning. As far as national identity is concerned, he discerns two dominant uses. The first corresponds to the way in which I understand national identity: "In one sense, identity refers to what is characteristic of and perhaps specific to a particular group or community: in this sense, national identity designates the particularities of tradition, politics, history, geography and culture insofar as these enter into a prevailing conception of a nation." The second corresponds to the way in which I understand national consciousness: "On the other hand, the term is often used to refer to a mode of individual existence—a way in which individuals conceive themselves and others. In this sense it is individuals who have identities (or sometimes search for them), and national identity is a certain kind of shared self-awareness."[39] As Billig notes: "National identities are forms of

social life, rather than internal psychological states; as such, they are ideological creations, caught up in the historical processes of nationhood....
A 'national identity' is not a thing; it is a short-hand description for ways
of talking about the self and community."[40] National consciousness, however, is precisely the "internal psychological state" that then seeks expression in the outward signs of identity. This does not mean that for every
form of consciousness there is a corresponding "identity" that one "has"
(recall Billig's strictures about identity not being a thing):Thompson wrote
of the "robustness" of "customary consciousness" in eighteenth-century
England, but the people of whom he writes did not have a "customary
identity." They rather took part in certain rituals, gave utterance to certain
types of speech, or had certain expectations of how much should be
charged for staple goods, all of which they recognized as "customary."[41]
Similarly, there is class consciousness, but there is no "class identity," at
least for the working class.The outward signs of class-belonging change
as the class itself is restructured and as new and different occupations—
with corresponding forms of dress and speech—arise to replace the old,
which are then invariably lamented as "traditional," even though they
may only have existed since the latter half of the nineteenth century.

"Banal nationalism"

If the concept of "national identity" is virtually omnipresent in the contemporary discourse of the nation, then that of "banal nationalism" is
unique to its creator, the social psychologist Billig, from whose work I
have already drawn. Billig uses the concept to stress both the ubiquity of
nationalism and its unexceptional quality:"The metonymic image of banal
nationalism is not the flag which is being consciously waved with fervent
passion; it is the flag hanging unnoticed on the public building."[42] Billig
appears to consider "banal nationalism" an example of what Voloshinov
calls a "behavioral psychology":"Behavioral psychology is that atmosphere
of unsystematized and unfixed inner and outer speech which endows our
every instance of behavior and action and our every 'conscious' state with
meaning."[43] I have found this to be a useful concept, particularly in de-
flating the assumption within long-established nation-states (which often
happen to be the most powerful states in the world system) that they are
immune from nationalism. Banal nationalism is not, however, the same as
national consciousness. No matter how everyday or undemonstrative the

former is, it is still an expression of loyalty to the nation as a state, as the image of the flag employed by Billig makes clear, whereas the latter is an expression of identification with the nation as a social group who may not have attained statehood and may not even aspire to do so.

Patriotism

"Patriotism" in the modern sense seems to have come into use in the late seventeenth century, but was first systematically formulated in England by Henry Saint John, Lord Bolingbroke, during the 1720s. He drew on three sources. The first was the tradition of Greek and Roman thought, reclaimed from antiquity by Machiavelli, where political "virtue" was ensured by balance between the different elements of the constitution, namely king, lords, and commons. "Corruption" was the consequence of any of these elements attaining ascendancy over the others, and patriotism was the expression of resistance to this imbalance. The second was the notion that the ancient constitution of the English itself was handed down from the unsullied period of the Anglo-Saxons, before the Norman Conquest. The third was the belief that, with the Reformation, England became an elect nation, not necessarily in a religious sense but one where England is seen as the home of Liberty.[44]

Bernard Crick writes of this period in British history that "patriotism could, indeed, positively adhere to the Dynasty, Parliament, the Protestant religion and the rule of law (or negatively to hating and fearing Papists and the French) in both England and Scotland, but patriotism does not always imply nationalism."[45] This is plausible if we are simply using the term "patriotism," as the late Ernest Gellner did, to refer to any of the different feelings of group loyalty possible before nationalism came into being.[46] In eighteenth-century England, however, the term did not denote any old loyalty, but exactly the same loyalty as is now denoted by the term "nationalism": it is how people spoke of nationalism before that term came into common use during the early nineteenth century. This is certainly how it was received in France, where, in 1750, the treatise by Bolingbroke was translated and published anonymously as *Lettres sur l'esprit de patriotisme et sur l'idée d'un roi patriote.* As Robert Palmer notes:

> Patriotism was invoked in 1789 because the course of eighteenth-century
> thought had prepared and developed it.... It was nationalism, if we take

the word in its larger sense to mean the idea that a man depends for his well being, his possession of rights, his hope for self-improvement, his duties and obligations, his faith in a cause for which he is willing to die, not on God, the king, humanity, class, or something vaguely called society, but on his nation or *patrie*. And this idea showed a remarkable growth in the forty years before the Revolution.[47]

This usage became general in Europe and North America following the French Revolution of 1789. In their address to the Scottish Society of the Friends of the People in 1792, for example, the United Irishmen quite naturally discussed the constitutional changes of the previous decade in these terms: "The patriots won reform, but the revolution itself was nominal and delusive."[48] It is therefore quite wrong to argue, as for example Peter Taylor does, that it was only the Anglo–British who claimed to be patriots rather than nationalists.[49] During the classic period of bourgeois revolution, from 1776 to 1848, it was the term used by both those who wished to reform the existing capitalist states (in the United Netherlands and Britain) and those seeking to create new capitalist states on their model (in the American colonies and France).[50]

What has confused the question of patriotism is that the meaning of the term underwent a change during "the long nineteenth century." Crick is, of course, the biographer of George Orwell, and he has praised the distinction that his subject drew between "patriotism" and "nationalism" as one of "extraordinary importance."[51] Yet if we turn to the essay from 1945 in which Orwell makes this distinction, we find the following definitions: "By 'patriotism' I mean devotion to a particular place and way of life, which one believes to be the best in the world but has no wish to force upon other people. Patriotism is of its nature defensive, both militarily and culturally. Nationalism, on the other hand, is inseparable from the desire for power."[52] As Orwell explains elsewhere in this essay, he is using "nationalism" in a highly idiosyncratic way, but it is also clear that he is using the term "patriotism" quite differently from a British patriot urging war on France in the 1740s or, for that matter, a French patriot urging war on Britain in the 1790s, neither of which could remotely be called "defensive."

In fact, the distinction drawn by Orwell between patriotism and nationalism had already been formalized by the Dutch historian Johan Huizinga in a lecture given under German occupation in 1940. According to Huizinga, the former corresponds to "the will to maintain and defend what is one's own and cherished," and the latter to "the powerful drive to dominate, the urge to have one's own nation, one's own state assert itself above, over and at the cost of others." Superficially, this distinction appears close to the one that I have drawn between national consciousness and nationalism, an impression strengthened by the existence of several Dutch terms for "national awareness," "sense of nationality," and "national consciousness," which Huizinga aligns with patriotism but not with nationalism: "The dividing line between patriotism and nationalism, however one may understand the latter, is in theory absolutely clear: the one is a subjective feeling, the other an objectively perceptible attitude." In practice, however, he concedes that the distinction is less clear.[53]

Both writers were displaying a common attitude, which crystallized in the face of Fascism, where members of the Allies in particular defined their own nationalism as inward-looking and pacific, or at any rate defensive, compared to the aggressive imperialism of the Axis powers. Indeed, so different was this feeling that it should not be classified as nationalism at all, but as patriotism. This may be understandable, but it is scarcely very plausible, given the way in which nationalist rhetoric was used to rally the defense of the Dutch and British empires, and would shortly be invoked again during the Cold War to justify massive levels of arms spending "in defense of British values"—something of which Orwell, in his more acute moments at least, was painfully aware.[54] The distinction between good "patriotism" and bad "nationalism" is now in general use, but is totally meaningless—except to indicate which nationalism the users themselves support, since they will refer to it as "patriotism."[55] During the eighteenth century the term "patriotism" was therefore a precursor to "nationalism," because the latter term was not yet available. During the twentieth century it was used as an alternative to "nationalism" because of the disgrace into which the latter had fallen (partly as a result of the hysteria that accompanied the First World War, even more so because the Axis powers used nationalism to justify their conquests and the horrors that ensued).[55] In both cases it is a thoroughly political concept.

Cultural nationalism

The distinction between cultural nationalism (emphasizing the "ethnic characteristics" of a people) and political nationalism (expressing the "col-

lective will" of a people) first emerged, respectively, in works by Johann
Herder and Jean-Jacques Rousseau during the third quarter of the eighteenth century.[56] The distinction between *Kulturnation* and *Staatsnation*
was systematized by Friedrich Meinecke in 1907: "We may distinguish
between an earlier period, in which nations on the whole had a more
plantlike and impersonal existence and growth, and a later period, in
which the conscious will of the nation wakens in that it feels itself to be
a great personality (even if only through the instrumentality of its leaders)
and claims the hallmark and right of the developed personality, namely,
self-determination."[57] These remarks suggest a distinction very close to
mine, between cultural identification and political mobilization, which
is reinforced by John Plamenatz:

> Nationalism is primarily a cultural phenomenon, though it can, and often
> does, take a political form. It is related to, but different from, both patri-
> otism and national consciousness. . . . And national consciousness is only
> a lively sense of, and perhaps also a pride in, what distinguishes one's own
> from other peoples. It is a sense of cultural identity. It was strong among
> the Greeks, the Romans and the Italians of the Renaissance as it had
> been anywhere in the last two centuries. But these three peoples were
> free of nationalism because they felt no need to preserve a threatened
> culture . . . Nationalism, as distinct from mere national consciousness,
> arises when people grow aware, not only of cultural diversity, but of cul-
> tural change, and share some idea of progress which moves them to com-
> pare their own achievements and capacities with those of others.[58]

There are two reasons for doubting the assimilation of national consciousness to cultural nationalism. The first is the assumption that culture
is by definition unpolitical. Smith has argued that to deny movements
intent on renegotiating their position within a multinational state the
title of nationalism is untenable because it "overlook[s] the centrality of
national culture and social regeneration in their movements, an ideal that
is common to so many other 'nationalisms.'"[59] Accordingly, culture may
in certain circumstances be as central to a nationalist movement as political activity. For example: "Where political nationalism fails or is ex-
hausted, we find cultural nationalists providing new models and tapping
different kinds of collective energies, thereby mobilizing larger numbers
of hitherto unaffected members of the community." Smith cites the Irish

Gaelic revival after the fall of Parnell in 1891 as an example of this.[60] These movements are nationalisms, but not because culture in itself has the same significance as politics. On the contrary, it is because cultural mobilization in these circumstances is simply politics carried on by other means, where normal means are no longer available; but this is still a political project. And it is possible to generalize the argument still further. Frederick Barnard has argued that the distinction between cultural and political nationalism is in every circumstance untenable, and was so even when Herder and Rousseau set out their respective positions. Both men "were equally anxious to advance a doctrine of nationhood which involved the transformation of both culture and politics":

> The significance of "cultural nationalism" is not in its being apolitical or non-political but in directing attention to a profound change in the source of political legitimization. Culture now emerges as something not only potentially relevant to politics but something indispensably *necessary*. A nation is no longer simply a community bound by spiritual ties and cultural traditions. Indeed . . . it is precisely the infusion of culture with political content, which characterizes modern nationalism. Nationalism, on this view, is unthinkable without the appeal to cultural values. But for this change to come about, for culture to be invoked in the making of political claims, culture must itself be viewed in its political contexts.[61]

The second reason is the period during which cultural nationalism is said to have existed. In the quote Meinecke is discussing the failure of—among other *Kulturnations*—the ancient Greeks to form a *Staatsnation*. As we have seen, Plamenatz discusses not only the Greeks but also the Romans and—with slightly more plausibility—the Italians of the Renaissance. Both writers imply, in other words, that nations have always existed, but have not always succeeded in forming states. As Moses Finley acidly observes: "Modern critics of Greek particularism should first decry their failure to have an industrial revolution." The ancient Greeks, in other words, did not have the structural capacity to form a nation-state: "If one asks, Of what nation, territory or country was Ptolemy king?, the answer is that he was not king 'of' anywhere, neither in his titulary nor on his coins nor in any official documents, whether edicts, letters or treaties. He was just 'King Ptolemy,' of wherever his writ ran at any moment. And the same was true of the other Hellenistic rulers, major or minor. That is what *dynasteia* signified."[62] As this suggests, certain forms of consciousness only become possible when the historical conditions are ready for their appearance. When were the conditions ready for the appearance of national consciousness? How did it then become transformed into nationalism?

✆ Chapter 3 ✆

From National Consciousness to Nation-States*

INTRODUCTION

"The surest sign that a society has entered into the secure possession of a new concept," writes Quentin Skinner, "is that a new vocabulary will be developed in terms of which the concept can then be publicly articulated and discussed." He takes the example of how the term "state" emerged during the Reformation to describe "a form of public power separate from both the ruler and the ruled, and constituting a supreme political authority within a certain defined territory."[1] Yet the state had existed for thousands of years before the concept was required. With "nation" the situation is reversed. The word "nation" had existed for hundreds if not

---

* Originally published as chapter 2 of *The Origins of Scottish Nationhood* (London: Pluto Press, 2000).

thousands of years before it acquired its current meaning, but as Valentin Voloshinov explains, "the word is the most sensitive index of social changes, and what is more, of changes still in the process of growth, still without definitive shape and as yet not accommodated into already regularized and fully defined ideological systems."[2] We can see the social changes to which the word "nation" provides an index by briefly surveying how the word was used in the medieval period.

The Vulgate Bible, for example, when first produced in the third century, rendered the original Greek "ethnos" as the Latin "natio," although in the New Testament the terms "gens" and "populus" are also used interchangeably—understandably, since these all refer to the original Middle Eastern tribal formations whose dismal fate the authors of the Book of Jeremiah take such delight in recounting. "Natio" was in turn translated as "nacioun" in the first English versions of the Bible produced in the fourteenth century, and this passed into the Authorized Version of 1611 as "nation."[3] What did "natio" mean in late medieval and early modern Europe? "A kingdom was never thought of merely as the territory which happened to be ruled by a king. It comprised and corresponded to a 'people' (*gens, natio, populus*), which was assumed to be a natural, inherited community of tradition, custom, law, and descent."[4] "Natio" was therefore one of a variety of terms, along with "gens" and "populus," used to designate a people. "Peoples" were in turn defined by two characteristics, which Susan Reynolds calls "common biological descent" and "common culture."

The origin myths that establish "common biological descent" had three main sources, all of which had been established by the sixth or seventh centuries. The first was developed in sixth-century Byzantium to classify the barbarian peoples by their supposed descent from the Germanic god Mannus. The second, which was first set down in a seventh-century Frankish chronicle, traced the Franks back to the arrival of exiled Trojans in the Rhineland following the fall of their city, a lineage that was quickly claimed by other peoples for themselves. The third, created in the seventh century by Isidore of Seville, claimed that the peoples of Europe were descended from Japheth, son of Noah. By the first millennium the three genealogies were increasingly being combined into one: "By the eleventh century, the *Historia Brittonum*, with its various additions, derived the British from the Trojan Brutus, taking in Alanus/Alaneus (i.e., the deutero-Mannus) by the way, then showing the descent of the Trojans from Noah, and adding Noah's descent from Adam and from God for good measure."[5]

The most significant aspects of the "common culture" were language and law. More precisely, if the feudal idea of nation was defined racially, then the feudal idea of race was itself defined linguistically: "Language makes race," wrote one medieval writer, Claudius Marius Victor.[6] It was in this basis of common language that the student fraternity in medieval universities was usually, if not exclusively, divided into "nations" from the thirteenth century onward. Indeed, the first recorded use of the term "nationalism" was in relation to the founding of Leipzig University in 1409, as the result of an academic dispute between the Bohemian "nation" and the three other "nations" at Prague University. As Anthony Smith reports, however: "The sense in which the term was used was restricted: a union to defend the common interest of one of the four 'nationes' among the Leipzig professors."[7] Nor was it only academic communities that were defined in this way. So too were the knightly orders: "The Hospitallers in the Levant were grouped into tongues according to their place of origin in Western Europe."[8] Identification of language with race is close to what we would now call "ethnic" as opposed to "national" identity. Robert Bartlett has noted the emergence of a "politicized linguistic consciousness" during the later Middle Ages in which the word for "language" also comes to mean "the people," leading to a situation where "ethnic and linguistic identity tended to blur into one another."[9] As late as the publication of the French *Dictionnaire de l'Académie* in 1694, the nation was still defined as those who spoke the French language and were subject to French laws.[10] In the words of John Hale: "'Nation' then meant, as it had in the organization of the General Councils of the church in the fifteenth century and still did in the social organization of universities, a group of individuals with a common place of origin." And as Hale makes clear, such "nationalism" as did exist was the cultural expression of xenophobia toward other "races."[11]

These racial distinctions did not necessarily imply any degree of solidarity between their members. The international ruling class and their clerical ideologues communicated with each other in Latin and would have had more in common with each other than did members of the peasant masses over which they ruled, even supposing—and this is a major supposition—that they shared the same vernacular in the first place. One basis for the myth of the Norman Yoke in English history—of a Saxon "race" oppressed by Normans—is the fact that the court did indeed speak in Norman French until the mid-fourteenth century. There were, of course, particular group loyalties in the premodern epoch, but these cannot be equated with nationalism. Reynolds has criticized the view that European medieval kingdoms were "predestined 'nation-states,'" which moved "through the attainment of 'national consciousness' to find [their] own rightful boundaries in the nation-state." Leaving aside the fact that not all succeeded in doing so, this perspective assumes that the "values and solidarities" of medieval Europeans were the same as our own: "Language like this casts a blanket of muddled anachronisms over medieval institutions and ideas." In their place, Reynolds uses the term "regnal" to describe the kind of solidarity felt by the inhabitants of a kingdom toward the monarch or—more important in the context of Scotland after 1286 or even 1603—the institution of monarchy.[12] As Brendan O'Leary has written: "Most of those who discuss 'nations' before 'nationalism' are in fact establishing the existence of cultural precedents, and ethnic and other materials subsequently shaped and re-shaped by nation-builders." Those who do so, and "assimilate the materials upon which nationalists will draw, to nationalism itself," are both falling victim and contributing to a "conceptual confusion."[13] In some cases regnal solidarity is one of the "other materials" out of which nationalism was constructed: it should not be confused with the finished product.

What other forms of consciousness were available during the medieval period? Everyone was a believer in the Christian faith and, as a necessary concomitant of this, a member of a Christian congregation. Everyone also belonged to one of the Three Estates, but—with the exception of the merchants—it is unlikely that many of the Third Estate regarded themselves in this way. Identification with your Estate was the preserve of members of the First (clergy) and the Second (nobility), not the Third (commons). Both religion and rank were universal sources of identity, unconnected with belonging to particular locations or populations. At the local level all territories and peoples were subjects of one royal dynasty or another, who often ruled over widely disparate languages and cultures without attempting to unify them into one. For the vast majority of the population who lived on the land, the apex of the feudal pyramid represented by the monarch would have been unimaginably distant. Unavoidably, their identities would have been suffocatingly local.

On the one hand, the sociological tradition derived in equal parts from Émile Durkheim and Max Weber emphasizes the need for societies to achieve cohesion during the process of industrialization, overcoming its disintegrative impact on agrarian society by imposing a common culture coincident with the territory of the state. The key figure here is neither Durkheim nor Weber but rather Ernest Gellner, for whom "the roots of nationalism in the distinctive structural requirements of industrial society are very deep indeed." At least three aspects of industrial society produce this requirement: "mobility," "communication," and "size due to refinement of specialization." These constitute a particular kind of culture: "The maintenance of this kind of inescapably high (because literate) culture requires protection by a state, a centralized order-enforcing agency or rather group of agencies, capable of garnering and deploying the resources which are needed both to sustain a high culture, and to ensure its diffusion through an entire population, an achievement inconceivable and not attempted in the pre-industrial world."[14] Nationalism here essentially subsumes the role religion played in what Weberians call traditional or agrarian societies. In effect they dismiss the idea that nations are permanent aspects of the human condition, only to reintroduce it as applicable after the process of industrialization has begun.

On the other hand, Marxists emphasize not industrialization as such but the dominance of the capitalist mode of production. So doing, they recognize that because the capitalist mode dominated some areas long before industrialization proper, national consciousness—and in some cases a fully formed nationalism—existed in those places before the second half of the eighteenth century. Given the frequency with which the existence of nationalism before 1789 is offered as a supposedly devastating critique of the Marxist position, it is perhaps necessary to elaborate on the latter point. As Michael Mann has noted, industrialization simply arrives too late to play the role Gellner assigns to it. To argue that nations only appeared at some stage in the later eighteenth century would be as absurd as arguing that capitalism only appeared at the same period.[15] (It should be noted, however, that toward the end of his life, Gellner tended to argue that "industrialization" also included the earlier "commercialization" of society, before large-scale production had been introduced—

a position closer to the Marxist one.)[16] In fact, national consciousness took as many centuries to become the dominant form of consciousness as the capitalist mode of production did to become the dominant mode of production, and it did so as a consequence of the latter.

National consciousness developed in three stages. In the first, which I call that of psychological formation (c. 1450–1688), it emerged unevenly across Europe (and its colonial extensions) among the most advanced economic groups, as a response to socioeconomic changes set in train by the transition to capitalism. In the second, which I call that of geographical extension (1688–1789), groups with an emergent national consciousness in the Netherlands and England succeeded in elevating this new psychological state into political movements, which led others (first in North America, Ireland, and France, then generally) to aspire to national status, even if their level of social development had not previously allowed national consciousness to arise. In the third, which I call that of social diffusion (1789–1848), national consciousness began to emerge in the social classes below the rulers of the new nation-states, partly as the result of deliberate indoctrination, but far more so as the by now inevitable pattern of life experience within societies shaped by the nation-state form.

PSYCHOLOGICAL FORMATION

Four main elements combined at the origin of national consciousness: all reflect to a greater or lesser extent the impact of capitalism on feudal society. The first element was the formation of externally demarcated and internally connected areas of economic activity. Europe had emerged from the first crisis of feudalism by the second half of the fifteenth century as a system of states that, the Swiss Confederation apart, was still dominated by the feudal mode of production. It was a system, however, increasingly adapted to elements of capitalism. In this context, the importance of capitalist development is less in the domain of production than of circulation, for it was in the creation of trade networks that merchant capital began to link up dispersed rural communities both with each other and with the urban centers to form an extensive home market.

Linked directly to this element was a second, the adoption of a common language by the communities that were being connected to each other at the economic level. During the mid-sixteenth century Charles de Roulles complained that, when traveling across France, he encountered eight different ways of saying "yes" and "no."[17] The need to communicate for the purposes of market exchange began to break down the distinctiveness of local dialects, forging a language common, or at least comprehensible, to all. Language in this way began to set the boundaries of the economic networks referred to above, boundaries that did not necessarily coincide with those of medieval kingdoms. Clearly such economic and linguistic unification was far easier in a small centralized kingdom like England than in a territory like the German Empire. As Hale writes: "In practice Germany was a congeries of independent units comprising some thirty principates . . . fifty ecclesiastical territories, about one hundred counties and sixty self-governing cities."[18] Indeed, establishment of state frontiers often determines what is considered a dialect of a particular language and what is considered a separate language. As J. Derrick McClure has pointed out, Flemish and Dutch are now considered separate languages, and both are as near (or as far) from German as the English spoken in London is from the English spoken in Cornwall. If the German state had evolved to include Flemish-speaking Belgium and the Netherlands, however, then Flemish and Dutch would be considered dialects of German.[19] Any standard form is, as McClure nicely puts it, usually "one out of a number of dialects which has, for fortuitous reasons, undergone a process of social climbing," usually because it happened to be the dialect spoken in the commercial and administrative center of the state.[20] Michael Billig has suggested that the concept of "a language" is an invention of the epoch of the nation-state, and "if this is the case, then language does not create nationalism, so much as nationalism creates language; or rather nationalism creates 'our' common-sense, unquestioned view that there are, 'naturally' and unproblematically, things called different 'languages,' which we speak." The same is true for dialect: "The notion of 'dialect' becomes crucial to maintain the idea of separate languages: it seems to account for the fact that not all speakers of a language speak in the same way."[21] The formation of standard forms of language was immeasurably aided by the invention of printing and the possibilities it presented for the codification of language in mass-produced works. Of the twenty million books published by 1500, 23 percent were already in the vernacular, rather than Latin.[22] These would not have been produced unless an audience of the literate already existed who understood their contents, but their effect was to extend the size of that audience, since printers could not produce works in *every* local dialect, only in the one that had emerged as the standard form, or in those that were in competition to do so. The first northern German translation of the Bible in 1479 had to be produced with double columns, one each for the Saxon and Frankish dialects of the language: an edition that extended to even the main dialects of southern Germany would have been impossible to produce in readable form.[23] The increasing standardization of language then fed back into its original economic formation, as the merchants whose trading networks had originally defined the territorial reach of linguistic comprehensibility increasingly identified themselves with that territory, to the exclusion of rivals who spoke a different language. The rise of the vernacular was accompanied by the decline of Latin as a lingua franca, a process virtually complete by the mid-sixteenth century and expressed in the new profession of interpreter, now necessary to make vernacular diplomatic exchanges mutually comprehensible.[24]

As this reference to international relations suggests, the third element was the character of the new absolutist states. Absolutism was the form taken by the feudal state during the economic transition from feudalism to capitalism. Yet the absolutist states did not arise automatically as the expression of some immanent tendency within this process. The replacement of the estates monarchy by this more centralized apparatus was rather the political response of the feudal ruling class to the socioeconomic pressures—different in degree and combination throughout Europe—set in train by the first crisis of the feudal system, and the greater significance of capitalist production in the economies that emerged afterward. The fourteenth-century crisis of the feudal system involved a generalized fall in rural productivity followed by demographic collapse, as the combined effects of famine and disease afflicted the inhabitants of town and country alike. In these circumstances the landowning nobility could only maintain—let alone increase—their level of income by systematically extending the area controlled by the state to which they owed allegiance (thus increasing the number of peasants under seigniorial control) and intensifying their exploitation of both long-standing and newly conquered peasant communities. The former brought conflict between states that encroached on each other's territories, a process exemplified by the Hundred Years' War between England and France (1337–1453).

The latter brought conflict within states, between the lords and the peasantry, who violently opposed increased exactions in a great series of risings that began in maritime Flanders in the 1320s and ended (in Western Europe at least) in Catalonia in the 1470s. Both the effective pursuit of external military aggression and the suppression of internal revolt required the agency of a centralized, coercive state power greater than the territorially dispersed structures typical of the first period of feudalism proper (c. 1000–1450). For our purposes two main characteristics of this emergent state form were of central importance.

One was the relative autonomy of the absolutist states from their class base—the nobility. The collective interests of the feudal ruling class did not necessarily correspond to the individual interests of its constituent feudal lords. Consequently the latter did not, in the main, directly control the state apparatus, either through inherited membership of their feudal estate or appointment to regal office. On the contrary, since they regularly went to war with each other and, less regularly, combined to make war on the monarch, it was essential that the apparatus be operated by a bureaucracy responsible to the crown and not to specific noble interests. Inseparable from this strengthening of central power was a weakening of the power of the lords in two areas. Collectively, the lords were the dominant estate within any parliament and could use this position to thwart the wishes of the monarch. The relative success of the absolutist monarchies therefore depended on (and could almost be measured by) the extent to which they managed to suppress their particular national assembly—the longevity of French absolutism compared to the English variant being very marked in this respect. Individually, the lords held jurisdictional authority within their own superiorities, which provided, on the one hand, a (theoretically) untrammeled supremacy over the peasants and, on the other, a territorial base for resistance to the monarch, particularly when combined with a system of military land tenure. Aspirant absolutists therefore sought to dominate the peasantry directly, without relying on local noble intermediaries. By 1688, wherever this displacement of power had been achieved successfully—as it had in France, Spain, Prussia, and Sweden—the responsibility for extracting the surplus from the peasantry had been assumed by the central state, and the mechanism of surplus extraction changed from rent to tax: the local autonomy of the nobles was thereby greatly reduced.

The other characteristic was the hegemony that the absolutist states exercised over the class that would eventually overthrow them—the bourgeoisie. For the bourgeoisie, the absolutist state was important as a means of controlling civil disorder within the towns and protecting the towns themselves from the demands of individual nobles; for the absolutist state, the bourgeoisie were important as a source of revenue, as personnel to fill the offices of state, and most importantly as a social force that the monarchy could muster in the face of collective noble opposition. Yet this dependent relationship left the bourgeoisie as an influence upon the state, not a codeterminer (with the nobility) of its class nature. Absolutism placed the bourgeoisie in a protected but subordinate place within the social order, which had the paradoxical effect of allowing socioeconomic advance while imposing political retardation.

In the context of this discussion, it is important that in several respects these innovations invested the territorial state with far greater political significance than had the estates monarchies that preceded them. The local jurisdictions that characterized the classic epoch of military feudalism began to give way to greater concentration of state power, notably through the introduction of standing armies and, partly in order to pay for them, regular centralized taxation. Death and taxes both involved bureaucracies that required a version of the local language, comprehensible across the state territory, with which to conduct their business, thus strengthening the second, "linguistic" element referred to above. They also had two unintended effects. On the one hand, the introduction of regular taxation and the adoption of mercantilist policies reinforced the economic unity that had begun to emerge spontaneously from the activities of merchant capitalists. On the other, the military rivalry that characterized the new system necessitated mobilizing the active support of the bourgeois minority as a source of financial backing and administrative expertise. Despite these innovations it is nevertheless important not to mistake the role of absolutism in the birth of nationhood, which was that of a midwife, not of a mother. The issue is often elided by reference to the influence of "the modern state" in the creation of nations, but this is to dissolve the difference between the absolutist state and its genuinely modern bourgeois successor.[25] The law is important in this respect. John Cairns writes of the rise of the legal works titled "institutes" or "institutions" in the seventeenth century: "This element of national unification in law, the creation of a common law within one nation state, is found in the French institutional writers, who, while France was a country with a multiplicity of differing laws and jurisdictions, felt able to produce institutions of the law of all France."[26] This process was not one of unifying the law, however, but of adding together all the different laws that pertained throughout the territory of the state. It would take the Revolution of 1789 to establish a unified French law. More generally, the arrival of nationhood coincided not with the establishment of the absolutist states but with their overthrow.

The fourth and final element is an example of what Eric Hobsbawm calls "proto-nationalism," or what I prefer to call "proto-national consciousness." Under this heading Hobsbawm describes several types of "collective belonging." The most relevant to this discussion are "supralocal forms of popular identification which go beyond those circumscribing the actual spaces in which people passed most of their lives," examples of which might be local manifestations of a global religious belief.[27] The ideology of absolutism involved stressing the deeds of religious figures such as saints who were associated with the territory of the realm, but it was the Reformation that made religion more than an ideologically pious enhancement to the image of the ruling dynasty. Wherever Protestantism became the dominant religion within a given territory after 1517, it contributed to the formation of national consciousness by allowing communities of belief to define themselves against the intraterritorial institutions of the Roman Catholic Church and the Holy Roman Empire. In part, this happened through the availability of the Bible in the vernacular, but this in turn was dependent on the existence of preexisting linguistic frameworks in which market transactions and state administration could be carried out. In short, Protestantism acted as a stimulus to national consciousness only to the extent that the development of capitalism had provided it with the framework to do so. Naturally, the process went furthest in England, but even there it was not until after the death of Elizabeth I in 1603 that Protestantism came to be separated from regnal solidarity with the monarch.[28] Eventually, Catholicism would play the same role, but as Josep Llobera writes: "Religion was not sufficient to define national identity, particularly in religiously homogeneous areas, where there was more than one nation competing for hegemony." Llobera uses the example of Catalonia in the nineteenth century to illustrate how "the local church, and particularly the rank and file clerics—who were closer to the people—might have helped to vehiculate a nationalist ideology which went against state nationalism," but it is important to note that because the Catalan church was the same as that of the central Spanish state, it could not act as a focus for Catalan nationalism until the epoch of nationalism had arrived in the eighteenth century, when the continued use of the language made it the main vehicle for preserving Catalonian national consciousness.[29]

GEOGRAPHICAL EXTENSION

What precipitated the formation of national consciousness out of these four different elements? It was the bourgeois revolutions that effected the final transformation of the term "nation" from one that signified "a people" as a race group to one that stood for "the people" as a community—although one of the most divisive issues within all bourgeois revolutionary movements was precisely how "the people" should be defined. As late as 1743, Jean-François Melon could define the French nation as "about a thousand men as against twenty million others."[30] In one respect, therefore, the great French Revolution was about extending—forcibly, in some cases—the definition of "the French nation" to include the twenty million others. Yet whatever limits were set on membership, the struggle against absolutism required the mobilization of at least a large minority of "the people" to achieve the expulsion or destruction of the royal dynasty. This could only be done by providing some form of identity that could embrace the often very different forms of opposition to the crown, regardless of whether the ruler in question was foreign (as in the case of Spanish Habsburg dynasty in the Netherlands) or native (as in the case of the Stuart dynasty in England).[31] Nationalism provided this identity.

Initially, it was an identity adopted principally by the bourgeoisie. Since the very term "bourgeoisie" is frequently subjected to ridicule, it is perhaps worth explaining what is meant by the term. Ellen Meiksins Wood has attacked the notion, allegedly held by more orthodox Marxists than her, of "the bourgeois as an agent of progress":

> We have got so used to the identification of bourgeois with capitalist that the presuppositions secreted in this conflation have become invisible to us. The burgher or bourgeois is, by definition, a town dweller.

Beyond that, specifically in its French form, the word used to mean nothing more than someone of non-noble status who, while he worked for a living, did not generally dirty his hands and used his mind more than his body for work. That old usage tells us nothing about capitalism, and is likely to refer to a professional, an office-holder, or an intellectual no less than to a merchant.

Wood calls attention to the flawed "logic" whereby "the ancient town-dweller gives way to the medieval burgher, who in turn develops seamlessly into the modern capitalist" and endorses "a famous historian" who regards this view of history as involving "the perennial rise of the middle classes."[32] It is true that the origins of capitalism had no necessary connection with the growth of the towns. (This is a position associated with the thinkers of the Scottish Enlightenment and with the Marx and Engels of *The German Ideology*, where that work displays the Scottish influence.) It seems to me, however, that dislodging the bourgeoisie from the position they have occupied in Marxist accounts of the rise of capitalism gives far too much ground to anti-Marxist historians who wish to expunge from the historical record not only the "rising bourgeoisie" but any notion that fundamental social change takes place through class struggle.[33] Some Marxists have responded to such attacks not by effectively conceding the argument, like Wood, but by avoiding the contested terminology, like Christopher Hill.[34] Neither of these options is satisfactory. The term "bourgeoisie," like a number of terms (one of which, as we have seen, is "nation"), changed in meaning over time. By the time Marx used the term in the 1840s, it stood, in relation to town-dwellers, both for something shallower than previously (because it excluded the new class of industrial laborers) and for something wider (because it included rural capitalists). In short it meant capitalists, both rural and urban, in the literal sense of those who owned or controlled capital, but also a larger social group over which capitalists as such were hegemonic. Hal Draper describes the bourgeoisie in this sense as "a social penumbra around the hard core of capitalists proper, shading out into the diverse social elements that function as servitors or hangers-on of capital without themselves owning capital."[35] These social elements tended to include lawyers and—in eighteenth-century Scotland at least—ministers of religion.

Recognizing the role of the bourgeoisie as the initial bearers of national identity can prevent historical misunderstandings. I wrote earlier of the need to distinguish between national consciousness and nationalism for analytic purposes.[36] Nevertheless, at the point of origin the two are inseparable. This is important, since (as we saw in the previous chapter when considering "cultural nationalism") some writers have argued that national consciousness existed long before nationalism. Breuilly—who is a modernist—uses two essays by Dante to argue that national consciousness could be found as early as the thirteenth century. In one, "On Vernacular Language," Dante claims to have discovered an Italian language, which he in turn identifies with the Italian nation and argues for its use by poets. In the other, "On the Monarchy," Dante argues for the establishment of a universal monarchy to establish harmony across Christendom as a whole, not only in the Italian Peninsula. Breuilly argues that the divergence between these two positions is proof of both "the existence of some kind of national consciousness and concern with national language and cultural identity in late thirteenth and early fourteenth-century Europe" and "the non-existence of nationalist consciousness."[37] The "illustrious vernacular" of which Dante spoke was in fact the Florentine dialect, adopted by intellectuals like himself who belonged to the bourgeoisie of the most advanced Italian city-state. As Gramsci asked: "Does not this mean that two conceptions of the world were in conflict: a bourgeois-popular one expressing itself in the vernacular and an aristocratic-feudal one expressing itself in Latin and harking back to Roman antiquity?" With the decline of the communes and the reimposition of feudalism, the attempt to establish a vernacular means of expression was destroyed along with its social basis: "After a brief interlude (the communal liberties) when there is a flourishing of intellectuals who come from the popular (bourgeois) classes, the intellectual function is reabsorbed into the traditional caste, where the individual elements come from the people but where the character of the caste prevails over their origins."[38]

In other words, the national consciousness expressed by Dante was linked to the very early development of capitalism in Italy, whose defeat meant that the possibility of national unification was taken off the historical agenda for another five hundred years. In these circumstances the aspiration for a universal monarchy was an *alternative* to a nationalism that had been blocked, and whose literary manifestations would soon themselves be abandoned. National consciousness could not flourish, or even take root, where the conditions for capitalist development were no longer present, and for it to be consolidated across Europe, even if only among the bourgeoisie, there had to be at least one case where it successfully made the transition to nationalism and then became embodied in a nation-state. Only when there were concrete examples of nationhood could different groups know what they were conscious of, regardless of whether they then went on to develop nationalisms of their own or not.

The capitalist nation-state became a permanent feature of the international state system only toward the end of the hundred years between the end of the English Revolution in 1688 and the beginning of the French Revolution in 1789. Thereafter, new nations could be manufactured regardless of whether the original elements were present or not—although an economic infrastructure and common language would, of necessity, have to be introduced at some point for a sense of national consciousness to be consolidated. As Billig writes of the construction of the French nation during the revolutionary years after 1789: "Because the project was being pursued in its own name (policies were to be justified in the name of 'the nation'), it had to assume its own reality before being effected in practice."[39] The ideological dominance of nationalism over the population depended, however, on *when* a particular revolution occurred in the overall cycle of bourgeois revolutions. In the two states where bourgeois revolutions were successfully completed before or during 1688—the Dutch and the English—the existence of national consciousness was directly proportional to the extent to which the postrevolutionary state developed a centralized apparatus, rather than a federal or confederal structure. In this respect English nationalism— "God's firstborn," as Liah Greenfield calls it[40]—was as far in advance of its Dutch predecessor as it was of its American successor, which similarly remained an alliance of semiautonomous states down to 1865.[41]

Three American academics have recently argued that the view of nineteenth-century Europe as the epoch of nationalism must be abandoned. During the French Revolution: "The nation is divided by class and regional strife, widely unsupported or even resisted by a disenchanted or uninterested population, and ruled by narrowly based governments dependent on terror, conscription and foreign wars." The Italian Risorgimento and German unification were similarly empty of national content: "Nationalism was limited and contradictory in both cases, sometimes exploited, usually disregarded;

not only the masses but also even the elites had little choice. The appeal of unification to these elites may in fact have been more economic than nationalist. The course of events was governed by traditional cabinet diplomacy in pursuit of great power interests, specifically the goals of Prussia and Piedmont as determined by Bismarck and Cavour. In their calculations, nationalism played no significant role."[42] The problem with this analysis is that the authors treat nationalism as an independent political variable, a "thing in itself," so to speak. If it transpires that other interests may have been involved, then nationalism must therefore be of no account. But nationalism can only ever be a vehicle by which "other" interests are advanced; to believe otherwise is to accept the myth of nationalism itself, which these authors evidently do. It is of course true that the majority of these elites were concerned to build states, rather than nations, but the latter was a necessary concomitant of the former, in conditions of industrialization. This is the meaning of the famous quip by the Piedmontese politician Massimo d'Azeglio, which they quote but evidently fail to understand: "We have made Italy, now let us make Italians."[43] As the great nationalist leader Giuseppe Mazzini wrote before Italy was "made": "The nation is the universality of Italians, united by agreement and living under a common law.... Without unity of belief and a social consensus, without unity in political, civil and penal legislation, without unity in education and representation, there is no nation."[44]

After 1848 all ruling classes intent on creating states on the British or French models were forced to embrace nationalism, not because they personally were capitalists, or even, more broadly, members of the bourgeoisie, but because all of them—Prussian Junkers, Japanese samurai, Italian monarchists, and eventually Stalinist bureaucrats—were engaged in building industrial societies dominated by the capitalist mode of production. The example of Italy, cited above, is typical of how ruling classes were faced with the need to diffuse consciousness of being a nation down from elite level into the mass of the population, a large and growing proportion of whom were not the bourgeoisie and petty bourgeoisie who had originally formed the nation, but workers. The difficulties involved should not be underestimated: as late as the 1860s, as many as a quarter of the inhabitants of the French state did not speak French: "French was a foreign language for a substantial number of Frenchmen, including almost half of the children who would reach adulthood in the last quarter of the century."[45] In many respects, however, the difficulties involved in developing such a consciousness among workers were less extreme than in the case of the peasantry.

SOCIAL DIFFUSION

Before discussing the nature of national consciousness among the working class, it will be necessary to return to the concept of class consciousness, or more precisely of *reformist* class consciousness, since this provides the context within which national consciousness and nationalism develop. Ralph Miliband has argued that class consciousness at the individual level operates as a series of four "distinct and ascending levels," rising from "perception of class membership," to a perception of the immediate interests of that class, to possessing "the *will* to advance the interests of the class," to a "perception of what [the advancement of class interests] requires, not simply in immediate terms, but in more general, global terms."[46] Miliband rightly says that the degree to which classes become conscious of their position varies according to what kind of class they are. Exploiting classes have always displayed a far greater awareness of their position than the majority of those whom they exploit—indeed, this is a precondition of their continuing to exploit them. Exploited classes, on the other hand, have shown far less awareness. He is wrong, however, to say in relation to the working class that any worker who is not committed to the revolutionary overthrow of capitalism is not class-conscious.[47] On the contrary, there is an intermediate form of class consciousness where one accepts the system as an unchanging feature of human society but rejects the way in which specific aspects of it negatively impact the lives of working-class people—that is, a state in between failing to recognize oneself as a member of the working class at all and fully recognizing the revolutionary role of the working class. For most workers, most of the time, this is the norm, not the exception. In this sense, Lenin was absolutely right to argue that "the history of all countries shows that the working class, exclusively by its own effort, is able to develop only trade union consciousness, i.e., the conviction that it is necessary to combine in unions, fight the employers, and strive to compel the government to pass necessary labor legislation, etc."[48] The notion of "trade union consciousness" is not, however, a particularly helpful one, since the type of reformist consciousness Lenin describes can and does exist outside of trade unions, whose members have always tended to be a minority of the world working class. The ascent to revolutionary class consciousness occurs when workers see that the negative aspects of their lives are not accidental but direct effects of how the system operates, and that it is possible to replace the system in its totality.

Reformist consciousness was originally a product of the social conditions produced by the transition to capitalism, or more precisely by the process of capitalist industrialization: first in Britain and subsequently wherever the process took place. It is sometimes said that the industrial working class (and this essentially means the British industrial working class) was revolutionary at the moment of its formation and subsequently became reformist through a combination of political defeat in 1848 and economic expansion thereafter. But while the working class was certainly insurrectionary in its formative years, this is not the same as being revolutionary. The restricted nature of politics in the late eighteenth and early nineteenth centuries meant that even reforms had to be fought for with arms in hand. The debates over moral versus physical force in both the Chartist and earlier Radical movements were not so much about reform versus revolution as about how best to achieve reform, through peaceful means or otherwise. In fact, reformist consciousness was established very early in the history of the British working class and will be reproduced as long as capitalism exists, but we are concerned here with its origins. Four developments lay behind it.

First, once the initial shock of industrialization passed, workers came to accept that capitalism was not a passing aberration but a new form of society that might have many years of vitality ahead of it. The apparent permanence of the system forced accommodation and adaptation, however grudgingly, from the new exploited class, whose horizons were anyway limited by the "dull compulsion" to work, raise families, and recover from the savage exertions that the factory system demanded.

Second, although these conditions provoked resistance, the fact that the new system generated its own defensive illusions made it less likely that a generalized revolutionary class consciousness would emerge out of such resistance. Under slavery, feudalism, or any other class society before capitalism, exploiters used physical force or the threat of it to make direct producers hand over the surplus they produced. Under early capitalism, they relied instead on a kind of economic discipline: workers feared the poverty that would result from being sacked. It could be argued that this tactic, or at least the hunger and deprivation that resulted from it, was also a form of violence, but the impact on consciousness was different, at least partly because workers appeared to engage in fair exchange with the capitalist: they contracted to work for a certain number of hours and were paid accordingly. The actual process of exploitation, the fact that the worker produced more than that for which she or he was rewarded, was hidden from view.[49] As a result, although workers were usually hostile to their own particular boss, this did not necessarily generalize into opposition to the system as a whole, since meanness or ill-treatment of the workforce could be put down to his personal qualities (or the lack of them), rather than to the necessities of exploitation.

Third, since workers would nevertheless not come to a conditional acceptance of capitalism based purely on the illusions thrown up by the economic operation of the system, both the capitalist state and individual capitalists made a conscious effort to persuade workers of the virtues of the system, a project rehearsed in church sermons and classroom lessons well before the advent of the mass media to whom such instruction is left today.

Fourth, although trade unions grew out of worker resistance, the goal of these new organizations, whatever rhetoric was employed about the (invariably distant) overturning of the system, was improving the condition of the working class within the system itself.

In Britain, where both industry and the working class developed first, reformism as a form of working-class consciousness was a fact by 1832, although it took another fifty years before it became embedded in political organizations. In other words it clearly predates the extension of representative democracy, the advent of imperialism, the creation of the welfare state, or any of the other mechanisms that are often cited as having secured the consent of the working class. The resulting form of consciousness was famously described by Gramsci as "dual" or "contradictory": on the one hand accepting the permanence of the system, on the other rejecting the effect of its operation.[50] The most basic expression of this contradiction is an acceptance by workers of the wages system, accompanied by a rejection of the particular level of wages that they are being offered, but it extends to all aspects of social life. The following incident, recorded by Wilhelm Reich after an encounter on an Austrian train during the 1930s, illustrates these contradictions in perhaps their most extreme form:

> A young worker, clearly a married man, was saying that all the laws were made for the rich and were rigged against the poor. I pricked up my ears to hear what else this class-conscious worker might have to say. He went on: "Take the marriage laws, for example. They say a man's entitled to beat his wife. Well I can tell you, only a rich man can beat his wife. If you're poor, you always get pulled up for it." Whether what he was saying is correct or not isn't the point. It is highly indicative of what goes on inside an average worker's head. As a poor man, he contrasts himself with a rich man and senses his inequality: so far as that goes, he has the beginnings of a class conscious mentality. But at the same time he would dearly love to be able to beat his wife *within the law*! And his class sense makes him feel at a disadvantage in this particular respect. Bourgeois sexual morality fights class consciousness in his mind.[51]

What then is the relationship of national consciousness to this reformist consciousness? As George Kerevan points out, workers are confronted by "two materially conditioned allegiances": on the one hand "*nationalism*, reflecting the social position of the individual caught in the allegiances of civil society and its exterior state"; on the other "*proletarian internationalism*, reflecting the class position of the worker and the kernel of the socialist mode of production developing within capitalism."[52] But precisely because nationalism reflects the position of the worker in civil society, it never manifests itself in a pure form. Alex Callinicos writes: "Dual consciousness within the Western working class is characterized by the acceptance of two identities—as worker and as citizen, as member of a class and as member of a nation-state. These identities imply an involvement in different kinds of social conflicts, the class struggle between capital and labor and the power struggle between nation states."[53] As the reference to dual consciousness here suggests, national consciousness does not compete with revolutionary class consciousness *directly* for the allegiance of workers, but as a key element in reformist class consciousness. Indeed, one might say that workers remain nationalist to the extent that they remain reformist. And from the point of view of the capitalist class in individual nations, it is absolutely necessary that they do so, or the danger is always that workers will identify not with the "national" interest of the state in which they happen to be situated but with that of the class to which they are condemned to belong, regardless of the accident of geographical location. Nationalism should not therefore be seen as something that only "happens" during separatist movements on the one hand, or during Fascist and imperialist manifestations on the other: the capitalist system generates nationalism as a necessary, everyday condition of its continued existence.

Benedict Anderson once argued that the origins of national consciousness lay in the collapse of "three fundamental cultural conceptions" during the rise of capitalism: the identification of "a particular script-language" (such as Latin in Christendom) with access to religious truth; the belief that society was organized in a natural hierarchy, at the summit of which were "monarchs who were persons apart from other human beings"; and a view of the inseparability of cosmology and history that rendered "the origins of the world and of men essentially identical." The interconnected decline of these three notions meant that human beings required "a new way of linking fraternity, power and time meaningfully together."[54] As Chris Harman has noted, however, this argument makes the connection of nationhood with capitalist development contingent rather than necessary, with the former simply allowing expression for an "existential yearning" and providing an outlet for "the satisfaction of innate psychological needs."[55] It is possible, however, to reformulate Anderson's position in a way that does not assume an eternal human condition but rather looks to how nationalism answers particular social needs that are produced by the atomized nature of capitalist society. In one respect Gellner is right to say that mass nationalism was a product of industrialization, but his insight was too focused on the functionality of nationalism for industrial societies. Industrialization, and the related process of urbanization, together produced the changes in human consciousness that made nationalism *possible* for the subordinate classes, and this is worth at least as much attention as the fact that they produced the more complex societies that made nationalism *necessary* for the dominant class. It is all too easy to ignore how unprecedented these experiences were (and still are) for the people undergoing them.

Take a relatively late but well-documented example of industrialization. During the early 1930s the Russian psychologist Alexander Luria undertook a number of behavioral studies in Uzbekistan and Kirghizia, both areas of what was then Soviet Central Asia. These were areas where the economy was largely precapitalist and the majority of the population was illiterate. The first five-year plan provided for more intensive industrialization of regions like Central Asia than in the USSR more generally. Accordingly: "Industrial production, and numbers of workers employed in industry, expanded more rapidly in Central Asia and Kazakhstan, and in the Urals and West Siberia, than in the rest of the USSR." Furthermore, this was from a lower level: "While 9.4 percent of the Soviet population lived in these republics, they contained only 1.5 percent of those employed in large-scale industry; and most industrial workers were Russians." By 1934 this had completely changed, with the number employed in large-scale industry nearly trebling from 53,000 to 158,000: "The increase in the working class in these areas took place against the background of the forcible transfer of a large part of Central Asian agriculture to the production of cotton, and the forcible settlement of the nomadic Kazakhs, many of whom died from starvation in the subsequent famine, or emigrated from Kazakhstan."[56]

Both regions were therefore experiencing what Luria later called "a radical restructuring of their socioeconomic system" as a result of Stalinist collectivization and the industrialization process, and these "radical changes in class structure were accompanied by new cultural shifts." These included the universalization of literacy and numeracy, as well as fundamental changes in agronomy. "As a result, people became acquainted not only with new fields of knowledge but also with *new motives for action.*" These developments produced new forms of consciousness in which "abstract" rather than "situational" thinking came to predominate, modeled on the new state-capitalist social relations rather than those of petty commodity production. As Luria notes:

> Sociohistorical shifts not only introduce new content into the mental world of human beings; they also create new forms of activity and new structures of cognitive functioning. They advance human consciousness to new levels. We now see the inaccuracy of the centuries-old notions in accordance with which the basic structures of perception, representation, reasoning, deduction, imagination, and self-awareness are fixed forms of spiritual life and remain unchanged under differing social conditions. The basic categories of human mental life can be understood

as products of social history—they are subject to change when the basic forms of social practice are altered and are thus social in nature.[57]

The second great influence on the forms of human mental life is the process of urbanization that in most cases accompanies industrialization. Here I simply want to quote from Georg Simmel, writing in Germany before the First World War, as he describes the influence of urbanism in an evocative passage from his great essay "The Metropolis and Mental Life":

> The psychological foundation, upon which the metropolitan individuality is erected, is the intensification of emotional life due to the swift and continuous shift of external and internal stimuli. Man is a creature whose existence is dependent on differences, i.e., his mind is stimulated by the difference between present impressions and those which have preceded. Lasting impressions, the slightness in their differences, the habituated regularity of their course and contrasts between them, consume, so to speak, less mental energy than the rapid telescoping of changing images, pronounced differences within what is grasped at a single glance, and the unexpectedness of violent stimuli. To the extent that the metropolis creates these psychological conditions—with every crossing of the street, with the tempo and multiplicity of economic, occupational and social life—it creates in the sensory foundations of mental life, and in the degree of awareness necessitated by our organization as creatures dependent on differences, a deep contrast with the slower, more habitual, more smoothly flowing rhythm of the sensory-mental phase of small town and rural existence.[58]

In short, industrialization and urbanization, particularly when combined into one process, develop new structural capacities, new modes of experience, and new psychological needs in the people who have to work in the factories and live in the cities. Tom Nairn has argued for the "functionality" of nationalism in meeting the new needs created by these two processes:

> Nationalism could only have worked, in this sense, because it actually did provide the masses with something real and important—something that class consciousness postulated in a narrowly intellectualist mode could never have furnished, a culture which however deplorable was larger, more accessible, and more relevant to mass realities than the

rationalism of our Enlightenment inheritance. If this is so then it cannot be true that nationalism is just false consciousness. It must have had a functionality in modern development, perhaps one more important than that of class consciousness and formation within the individual nation-states of this period.[59]

It is this need for some collective sense of belonging with which to overcome the effects of alienation, the need for psychic compensation for the injuries sustained at the hands of capitalist society, that nationalism fulfills, in the absence of revolutionary class consciousness but in conjunction with reformist class consciousness. One might say that the origins of national consciousness see the emergence of an identity-ensemble adequate to the historical conditions of generalized alienation. The initial experience of peasants and rural laborers plucked from their communities and dropped into the urban hells of Glasgow, Manchester, Berlin, Turin, or Petrograd is clearly relevant to the period under discussion here, but the needs produced by capitalist industrialization are permanent. As Kerevan writes, "if individuals only face one another in the market connected by money relations; then their social unity as individuals is reflected in only one all-embracing unit of civil society—the nation."[60]

There are obvious similarities between what Marx himself said about religion and what I am saying here about nationalism. The former has of course long been subjected to both careless and deliberate misrepresentation. The point of the passage containing the reference to "the opium of the people" is not that religion is a drug administered by a ruling class to dull the senses of the people, but that it is manufactured by the people themselves to fill the void created by what the later Marx would call their alienation: "*Religious* suffering is at one and the same time the expression of real suffering and a protest against real *suffering*."[61] In this sense nationalism is the modern form of religion, with the state (or forces seeking to establish a new state) occupying the organizational role once played by the church.

The ideological role played by the ruling class in reinforcing nationalism is therefore only possible because nationalism already provides one possible means of meeting the psychic needs created by capitalism. Nevertheless, many critics of Marxism find it hard to accept any suggestion that nationalism is ultimately linked to the ideological defense of capitalism. Gellner once claimed that in Marxist theory nationalism is simply "a conscious distraction of populations from the real underlying conflict between classes, the obfuscation perpetuated in the interests of ruling classes, having much to fear from class consciousness, and much to gain from the encouragement of a spurious national consciousness."[62] Breuilly certainly assumes that this is the Marxist position and has argued that nationalism is "too pervasive to be reduced to the ideology and politics of this or that class or set of classes" and "too complex and varied to be understood as a reaction to a particular type of economic relationship or disparity."[63] These writers, who are by no means the most unsympathetic to Marxism, protest too much.

Once a capitalist nation-state has been established, those who control the apparatus always seek to consolidate the hold of nationalism among the people who inhabit its territory. States need conscripts for their armies, citizens to pay taxes, workers who accept that they have more in common with those who exploit them at home than they do with their fellow-exploited abroad. The latter was particularly important in the early years of the nation-state, since there is some evidence to suggest that members of what Peter Linebaugh and Marcus Rediker call the "Atlantic working class" of the eighteenth century, prior to industrialization, were not primarily national in their consciousness: "At its most dynamic the eighteenth-century proletariat was often ahead of any fixed consciousness. The changes of geography, language, climate, and relations of family and production were so volatile and sudden that consciousness had to be characterized by a celerity of thought that may be difficult to comprehend to those whose experience has been steadier."[64] This made it imperative that loyalty to a state be secured, and the nation was the means. Since the eighteenth century, British workers have often been asked to accept rises in interest rates, cuts in wages and services, or participation in imperialist wars, but never for the benefit of British capitalism, always for the benefit of the British nation, for "the national interest." And it is not only the state that makes such appeals. The organizations of the working class themselves reinforce reformist class consciousness within a national context. At the most elementary level this is because such organizations are unwilling to challenge the nationalism within which political discourse is conducted, for fear of being labeled unpatriotic. More importantly, however, it is because they seek either to influence or to determine policy within the confines of the existing nation-state.

Typically, therefore, nationalism is invested with the contradictory character of the reformist worldview. As Voloshinov notes: "The ruling class strives to lend the ideological sign a supraclass, external character, to extinguish or exhaust the struggle of class relations that obtains within it, to make it the expression of only one, solid and immutable view."[65] It cannot do so:

> Existence in the sign is not merely reflected but refracted. How is this refraction of existence in the ideological sign determined? By an intersecting of differently orientated social interests within one and the same sign community, i.e. *by the class struggle*. Class does not coincide with the sign community, i.e., with the community which is the totality of users of the same set of signs for ideological communication. Thus various different classes will use one and the same language. As a result, differently orientated accents intersect in every ideological sign. Sign becomes an arena of the class struggle.[66]

Linda Colley provides us with a concrete example from our period in which the relevant sign or word is "Britons." She notes of one man rioting against increases to the cost of bread during the Jubilee of George III: "The 'Old Price' rioter at Covent Garden, who was seen on jubilee day 1809 carrying a placard 'Be Britons on the 25th but riot on the 26th' was admitting that his protest was a partial one as well as accepting that patriotism necessarily involved celebration of the monarchy."[67] "Be Britons, but riot" sums up with admirable brevity the contradictions and the limits of working-class nationalism as an element of reformist consciousness.

• Chapter 4 •

Marxism and Nationhood: Two Replies to John Foster*

• 4.1 Stalinism, "Nation Theory," and Scottish History* •

INTRODUCTION

The Origins of Scottish Nationhood was an attempt to resolve two problems, one of history and the other of contemporary politics. The historical problem was the apparent failure of the Scottish nation to conform to the modernist conception of nationhood, in which national consciousness first develops during the transition to either capitalism (in classical Marxism) or industrialization (in classical sociology). If Scotland was a

---

* Originally published in *Historical Materialism* 10, no. 3 (2002) as a reply to John Foster, "Review of *The Origins of Scottish Nationhood*," *Historical Materialism* 10, no. 1 (2002).

nation in 1057 or 1320, as is so often claimed, then either it must be an exceptional case or the designation must also be extended to England, France, or any other unified kingdom of the medieval period. Since general theories abhor exceptions, we must conclude either that modernism is wrong, or—my preferred alternative—that Scotland achieved nationhood not in the Dark Ages or the medieval period but after the Treaty of Union with England.[1]

One attraction of the latter, admittedly counterintuitive proposition is that it offers an explanation for the second problem: why Scottish nationalism has failed, for more than thirty years, to win more than minority support, even under the Thatcher and Major regime—indeed, the Scottish National Party has never subsequently repeated the percentage of the poll it achieved in the general election of October 1974. In other words, it explains why most Scots were able to display high levels of both Scottish national consciousness and British nationalism. If a Scottish nation only came into existence after the construction of the British state, and if the formation of this Scottish national consciousness was historically inseparable from the formation of British national consciousness, then for Scots, particularly working-class Scots, "Britishness" may have taken political priority because it was at the level of the British state that crucial class battles had always been fought out.

John Foster once argued that there were five main "theoretical problems posed by Scotland's history as a nation": the origins of Scottish nationality; the end of Scottish statehood; the survival of Scottish nationality; the duality of Scottish and English national allegiances; and the timing of demands for greater Scottish self-government.[2] As can be seen from the summary above, my book deals with the first four, and given that I disagree with the solutions that Foster has proposed to these problems, I turned to his review expecting to meet an unfavorable critical response. In this at least I was not disappointed. I *was* disappointed, however, to find that Foster had chosen not to engage with what I had actually written but to dismiss my argument a priori, on theoretical grounds. Foster ignores most of my material on Scotland, except for issues concerning Scottish economic history—issues that are important in their own right, but peripheral to this discussion.[3] Indeed, most of his review is a critique of the general positions set out in my first two chapters.[4] Foster tells us that Marxism is not wrong over the origin and class content of nationhood—I have simply failed to understand it properly. Marxism apparently posits no necessary connection between nationhood and capitalism, or indeed any mode of production.[5]

I do not intend to repeat my arguments about either nationhood in general or Scottish nationhood in particular, since they are set out at length in *Origins* and space is short. I want to focus instead on two issues. First, the arguments with which Foster seeks to challenge my understanding of Scottish history. Second, the theoretical assumptions that Foster himself brings to this debate, since these raise issues that are of concern not only to socialists based in Scotland, like Foster and myself, but to the left more generally.

Some peculiarities of Scottish development

Foster has consistently argued that Scottish nationhood is a product of feudal, not capitalist, development.[6] He nevertheless claims (perhaps as a fallback position) that I underestimate the extent of agrarian capitalist development in Scotland before 1707.[7] His substantive critique begins with a simple mistake: "One of Davidson's proofs for the non-capitalist character of Lowland Scottish society prior to 1707 is the incorporation of feudal land payments into the Act of Union. He does not examine the origin of these payments. When did they begin? The fifteenth century. At this point they represented a historically extremely early attempt to monetarize land-holding and bring it legally into line with the property requirements of Roman-based law." "Why on earth should this be happening in barbaric Scotland?" he asks, apparently confusing my argument with that of Hugh Trevor-Roper.[8] I do not in fact refer, anywhere in the book, to the incorporation of feudal land payments, but leaving that aside for the moment, what was feuing, and why does Foster think it so important?

Feuing took place as follows. The feudal superior would grant a charter conferring perpetual heritable possession to the feuar (frequently a tenant) in return for a large initial down payment and payment thereafter of a fixed annual sum. Even after land had been feued out, however, the legal rights of the superior over his domains (his heritable jurisdiction) remained in place, so that even those peasants who were no longer tenants could not completely escape his authority. It is the incorporation of the heritable jurisdictions, which were specifically retained under section 20 of the Treaty of Union, that I refer to in the book.[9] The powers these jurisdictions conveyed extended, in some cases, to the death penalty, and I know of one case where this was carried out (by drowning) as late as 1679.[10] Nor were they simply a superstructural phenomenon: the baronial and regnal courts through which power was exercised also served as the means by which the lords oversaw the process of agricultural production. In 1707 jurisdictions of this kind existed nowhere else in Western Europe, because they had either been destroyed by bourgeois revolution (as in the United Netherlands and England) or been subsumed into those of the absolutist state (as in France or Spain). In short, they represented the legal embodiment of feudal social relations in the Scottish countryside. Their preservation was one of the inducements through which the capitalist English ruling class gained the acquiescence of their feudal Scottish counterparts in the Treaty of Union, by reassuring them there was no intention of initiating bourgeois revolution from above as the Cromwellian regime had done in the 1650s.

Given that these social relations prevailed in Scotland at and beyond the point of Union, it is difficult to take seriously the claim that "rural social structures" were "transformed" during the fifteenth century by "Scotland's position as a supplier of wool to the proto-capitalist textile industries of Flanders and Italy," a process that supposedly resulted in "agricultural defeudalisation."[11] Mere growth in the *extent* of a feudal economy does not necessarily translate into a change in its *nature*. Scottish sales of wool to areas of capitalist production in Flanders and northern Italy during the fifteenth century did not make the Scottish economy capitalist, any more than Prussian sales of grain to areas of capitalist production in Holland during the sixteenth century made the Prussian economy capitalist. The issue is surely the nature of productive relations in Scotland and Prussia, not in the areas to which they sold their commodities. Foster in any case exaggerates the importance of Scottish wool exports. It is true that these were originally equal to those of England, but as Isabel Guy has shown, the performance of the industry was not sustained after 1460. Decline occurred in four stages: "1460–1475, a period of unsteady prosperity; 1476–1533, a gradual decline; 1534–1542, an apparent upsurge; but from 1543 until the end of the century, a dramatic and irreversible slump." The last stage ultimately heralded a period of "long-term contraction," which might have mattered less if the trade in woven cloth—a manufactured good rather than a raw material—had kept pace with that of England. But whereas Scottish wool exports were generally around 20 percent of the English, cloth exports were only around 2 percent.[12]

More important than the fortunes of the wool industry, however, is the fact that it was not in any case the key to the feuing movement. The timing is all wrong. As Foster himself notes, feuing as a method for disposing of land had been taking place on the lands of that greatest of medieval landowners, the Catholic Church, since the fourteenth century. The process was encouraged more widely, however, by an act of the Scottish Parliament of 1458, the very point at which the decline of the wool industry began. Out of the 3,061 feu charters of church lands granted by the 1580s, only 106 were granted before 1500, and even excluding all cases where the date is uncertain, a minimum of 1,562, or over half, were granted after the Reformation of 1560, which suggests where the real impetus behind the movement lay.[13]

The feudal lords needed to increase their immediate disposable income but were restricted by the physical limits of what could be appropriated from their tenants; many were therefore tempted into changing the nature of occupancy on their lands. It occurred to at least some of the nobility, however, that they need not stop at feuing their own lands but could progress to church lands, the annual revenue of which was nearly £400,000 in 1560—ten times what those of the crown made, divided up among a mere three thousand clergy (out of a population of eight hundred thousand).[14] The church began to appear not merely as a contributor to their financial difficulties but as a potential solution. Yet there was urgency to such considerations. The example of the Reformation in England, where clerical abuses had been one of the justifications for the assault on the church, led to pressure for self-regulation in Scotland. Three councils—in 1549, 1552, and 1559—passed statutes seeking to curb the activities of the unregenerate clergy. The greater lords feared that an internally reformed church might provide them with less excuse to seize its assets while simultaneously challenging their existing exploitation of church offices. The lesser lords had always resented paying tiends (i.e., tithes) they could not afford to a church they did not control, and some of them at least were prepared to follow the magnates, if only to remove these financial burdens.

Here is at least one motivation (although scarcely the only one) behind the Scottish Reformation. Walter Makey is surely correct to write of the outcome that "these changes made significant adjustments in the structure of feudal Scotland without undermining its foundations; blood was drained out of the first estate and transfused into the second."[15] The only area where feuing left any permanent residue of independent yeoman farmers was in the southwest, the base for the Covenanting revolt against the absolutist Stuart monarchy between 1660 and 1688. The heroism of the later Covenanters is unquestionable, but their regional isolation tells its own story about the failure of a rural capitalist class to develop across Scotland as a whole before the eighteenth century.

Foster overestimates the extent of Scottish development before 1746 only to underestimate it afterward: "Davidson attributes what he claims was the sudden transformation of a backward post-feudal Scotland to its access to the most advanced technology from England."[16] My purpose in chapter 10, to which Foster alludes, was not primarily to discuss the economic transformation of Scotland, although my "claim" as to its "suddenness" is supported elsewhere in the book by figures showing the sharp upward trajectory, from the mid-eighteenth century, of output in coal, linen, and tobacco, and of income from rent in land.[17] It was rather to show the material conditions that permitted new forms of national and class consciousness to arise, and it is in this context that the theory of combined and uneven development is of crucial significance. To reduce it, as Foster does, to the mere acquisition of advanced technology—a commonplace of orthodox "developmental" economics in the vein of Gerschenkron—reveals his continuing inability to come to terms with Trotsky's contribution to Marxism. Trotsky's point, developed in relation to tsarist Russia but also relevant to Scotland after 1746, was that economically backward countries do not have to plod through the successive "stages" of development beloved of both the Second International and Stalinism, but can leap over entire transitional stages. What is transformed is not simply the technology employed by workers but the social relations within which that technology operates, with all that implies for ideology, culture, and politics.

By playing down the formidable development of capitalism in Scotland after 1746, Foster leaves himself with no explanation for the greater industrial militancy of Scottish over English workers in the Scottish General Strike of 1820. This event, which involved over sixty thousand workers, was absolutely decisive in shaping the Scottish working-class movement of the nineteenth century, yet it has been largely ignored by Scottish labor historians.[18] Foster ignores it too; I will suggest some reasons why this may be the case below.

Imagined continuities

Foster begins his critique by objecting to my methodology: "Immediately, however, it is important to stress that [Davidson's approach] is *not* the only Marxist approach to the national question. Marx's own position was decisively different. The hallmark of this alternative tradition is precisely its dialectical approach to the historical process, one that does not abstract class or nation in a mechanical, or sociological, way."[19] He opposes my attempt to identify nations with particular characteristics and specific historical times: "[Davidson] uses sociological rather than dialectical definitions of class and nation, and unilaterally links national identity to capitalism."[20] I have no idea what "sociological" means here, except that it is something Foster dislikes. (He also finds me guilty of "prioritizing sociologically-derived definitions.")[21] In fact, my work is only sociological in the sense that I am dealing with a particular form of consciousness, and as Valentin Voloshinov once noted: "The only possible objective definition of consciousness is a sociological one."[22] It is true, however, that I unilaterally link national identity to capitalism.

Definition and periodization are the basis of any scientific inquiry. In *Origins* I invited those historians of Scotland who reject my definition of nation (and related terms) to present their alternatives, on the grounds that they must presumably have some prior conception of what a nation is in order to be able to say that Scotland was one in, say, 1320.[23] No one has yet replied, but Foster effectively absolves them (and himself) from so doing by the simple expedient of saying that the nation is in a constant process of change over time, and that any attempt to define it is a sociological imposition on the dialectical fluidity of the historical process. Since both Foster and I consider ourselves to be working within broadly Leninist categories, it might be useful to see what this most unjustly maligned of revolutionaries has to say on the subject.

In his discussion of imperialism, Lenin noted "the conditional and relative value of all definitions in general, which can never embrace all the concatenations of a phenomenon in its full development"—before going on to list what he regarded as the five main features of the phenomenon in question.[24] He made similar remarks in relation to periodization: "Here, of course, as everywhere in nature and society, the lines of division are conventional and variable, relative, not absolute. We take the most outstanding and striking historical events only approximately as milestones in important historical movements."[25] Appropriately enough, Lenin is discussing the period between 1789 and 1871, during which nationalism played a generally progressive political role as part of the bourgeois revolutions.

In order to clarify this point, let us take an analogy from political economy. If we define capitalism simply as the exchange of commodities on the market, or as a factor of production, then we could argue with the Austrian marginalists that it has existed since the beginning of class society.[26] In this connection, Marx commented that "the bourgeois economy thus supplies the key to the ancient, etc. But not at all in the manner of those economists who smudge over all historical differences and see bourgeois relations in all forms of society. One can understand tribute, tithe, etc., if one is acquainted with ground rent. But one must not identify them."[27] If we define capitalism on the basis of competitive accumulation based on generalized wage labor, however, then a different picture emerges. Capital, as a set of social relations subordinate to those of feudalism, can be detected in Flanders or the Italian city-states of the thirteenth century. Capitalism can be seen as the dominant mode of production across specific state territories with the emergence of the Dutch and English nation-states in the sixteenth and seventeenth centuries. The capitalist system only emerges on a global scale after 1848. This is not to impose some schematic series of stages on historical development; it simply acknowledges that at a particular point in world history something changed, and in order to identify the nature of that change we need to draw distinctions between the periods before and after. To do otherwise not only makes it extremely difficult even to say what we are talking about (which I suspect is partly the point) but reduces Marxist theory to a confidence trick, and the theoretician to a shyster who can produce suitably "dialectical" definitions in conformity with the tactical requirements of the moment—an abiding characteristic of the Stalinism that still forms the basis of Foster's theoretical assumptions.

It is even unclear whether Foster is claiming (in a manner analogous to "those economists who smudge over all historical differences and see bourgeois relations in all forms of society") that nationhood *is* associated with every mode of production, or just that that it *can be* associated with any mode of production. Foster claims to have traced the genealogy of this purportedly "dialectical" approach, in which nations appear everywhere and anywhere in history, back to Marx and Engels themselves in "their correspondence from the 1860s and 70s, in *Grundrisse* and in Marx's *Ethnological Notebooks* of 1881–2 which formed the basis for Engels's *Origin of the Family, Private Property and the State*. It was this perspective that was taken forward by Lenin in his critiques of Bauer, Luxemburg and Stalin and further developed by the Soviet ethnographers of the 1960s, most notably by Yuri Bromley. Unfortunately none of this literature is referred to by Davidson."[28] There is, however, a good reason why this literature is not referred to by Davidson: the works by Marx, Engels, and Lenin do not take the positions Foster claims for them, and the ideological content of those by Bromley and his colleagues makes their scientific value considerably less than Foster claims.

Marx certainly believed that there were some aspects of our nature, our species being, that were unchanging, including the need to cooperate with other human beings in the production and reproduction of social life.[29] There is no evidence that he thought a propensity to form nation-states was among them. Foster informs us that Marx never saw fit "to draw an indelible line between nationality in the modern era of capitalism and what went before."[30] At one level this seems to be correct. As Paul James writes:"We should recall that Marx and Engels used the word 'nation' to apply to polities, from the Phoenician tribes to the still-to-be-unified land of imperially connected principalities, margraviates, and bishoprics called 'Germany.'"[31] But these usages reflect a lack of rigor in applying the term "nation," not a worked-out theoretical position.[32]

Foster writes that, in the *Grundrisse*, Marx is primarily concerned with "the fundamental importance of social entities larger than the family for human development":"On them depended the creation of a socially dynamic division of labor. Like instrumental language, such social entities, bonded by specific cultural identities, provided 'the first precondition for the appropriation of the objective conditions of life.'"[33] The section from which Foster quotes ("The Chapter on Capital") in fact traces the alternative routes through which precapitalist property relations—"Asiatic, Slavonic, ancient classical, Germanic"—emerged from the original clan communities. The basis for all of them is the settling of migratory clans on specific sites where the community is subsequently modified by biology and environment: "This naturally arisen clan community, or, if one will, pastoral society, is the first presupposition—the communality of blood, language, customs—for the *appropriation of the objective conditions of their life*, and of their life's reproducing and objectifying activity." What on earth has this to do with nationhood? Foster's language becomes noticeably cloudy at this point in the argument—as well it might. Is he *really* saying that the "social groups larger than the family" that arose during the tribal stage of development are related to contemporary nations? Human groups have always developed collective forms of identity, but labeling them all as "national" is an anachronistic procedure made possible by Foster's refusal to define what a nation is. Marx himself points out the problem with such claims for continuity only pages later in the *Grundrisse*:

> The survival of the commune as such in the old mode requires the reproduction of its members in the presupposed objective conditions. Production itself, the advance of population (this too belongs with production), necessarily suspends these conditions little by little; destroys them instead of reproducing them, etc., and with that, the communal system declines and falls, together with the property relations on which it was based. . . . *Not only do the objective conditions change in the act of reproduction, e.g. the village becomes a town, the wilderness a cleared field, etc., but the producers change, too, in that they bring out new qualities in themselves, develop themselves in production, transform themselves, develop new powers and ideas, new modes of intercourse, new needs and new language.* The older and more traditional the mode of production itself—and this lasts a long time in agriculture; even more in the oriental supplementation of agriculture with manufactures—i.e., the longer the real process of appropriation remains constant, the more constant will be the old forms of property and hence the community generally.[34]

In other words, Marx sees the initial—for want of a better word—"ethnic" formations dissolve as the division of labor becomes more complex, and nothing in the *Ethnological Notebooks* contradicts this view.[35]

A position that sees nationhood arising under any form of class society and not only under capitalism does not, however, necessarily involve arguing that nationhood will continue under socialism. It could be claimed that the nation is an institution (like the family) that is a product of the transition *to* class society, rather than any specific form *of* class society, and will dissolve with the last form of class society, which happens to be capitalism. Foster opts for primordialism, claiming support from, of all places, the "Manifesto of the Communist Party." Apparently, "the workers have no country" really means that the workers should have a country, that they would have one had they not been excluded from ownership by the bourgeoisie, and that they will have a country if they can lead the other social classes against the rulers: "Marx and Engels are not claiming that nations will themselves disappear when the proletariat is victorious. What is set to disappear is the hostility between them."[36] Let us concede that this is one possible interpretation of what Marx and Engels believed at this stage in their development. But their development did not stop at this stage. In particular, their views on the state did not remain as they were in 1848.

In 1848, Marx and Engels argued for the proletariat to seize control of the existing state and "wrest, by degrees, all capital from the bourgeoisie . . . centralize all production in the hands of the state, i.e., of the proletariat organized as a ruling class." Only in the future ("in the course of development"), after having "swept away the conditions for the existence of class antagonisms and of classes generally," will we have "an association, in which the free development of each is the condition of the free development of all."[37] The change in attitude to the state indicated by the Paris Commune—"the political form at last discovered under which to work out the economical emancipation of labor"—is decisive here.[38] The shift from conquering to destroying the state also has implications for the "nation" prefix, as can be seen from the *Critique of the Gotha Program*, which has, I believe, more significance for us than the jottings from other writers recorded or summarized in the *Ethnographic Notebooks*. Marx attacks the collapse of the German Workers' Party into "the narrowest national viewpoint" associated with Lassalle:

> It is perfectly self-evident that in order to be at all capable of struggle the working class must organize itself *as a class* at home and that the domestic sphere must be the immediate arena for its struggle. To this extent its class struggle is national, not in content, but as the Communist manifesto says, "in form." . . . And to what is the internationalism of the German Workers' Party reduced? To the consciousness that the result of their efforts "will be *the international brotherhood of peoples*"—a phrase borrowed from the bourgeois League of Peace and Freedom and which

is intended to pass as an equivalent for the international struggle against the ruling class and their governments. Not a word, therefore, of the international role of the working class![39]

Lenin inherited these positions and therefore does not provide support for Foster's genealogy either.[40] He saw the duty of socialists to defend the equality of nations, by opposing oppressor nationalisms (like the Great Russian in Poland or the Great British in Ireland) and supporting the rights of the oppressed. This remains the case today, although not every nation can be neatly identified as oppressed or oppressor—Scotland being a case in point.[41] Beyond this duty, however, he saw the demand for equality not as an end in itself but as a means of overcoming the divisions between nations and, ultimately, their existence: "And at the same time, it is their [i.e., the Russian proletariat's] task, in the interests of a successful struggle against all and every kind of nationalism among all nations, to preserve the unity of the proletarian struggle and the proletarian organizations, amalgamating these organizations into a close-knit international association, despite bourgeois strivings for national exclusiveness."[42]

In this context Foster completely misrepresents "Critical Remarks on the National Question," as indeed does Bromley.[43] Lenin does not refer to the nation as such when he states that each nation contains a proletarian culture in addition to a bourgeois and a clerical culture: "We take *from each* national culture *only* its democratic and socialist elements; we take them *only* and *absolutely* in opposition to the bourgeois culture and bourgeois nationalism of *each* nation." What Lenin is saying is that object of the socialist movement is not to preserve the "proletarian" aspects of that culture but to create an international culture drawn from all these cases: "The slogan of working-class democracy is not 'national culture' but the international culture of democracy and the world-wide working class movement."[44] Take one more example, although others could be cited. In "The Discussion on Self-Determination Summed Up," he describes the purpose of overcoming the inequality between nations as not the perpetuation of their existence but "the *practical* elimination of even the slightest national friction and the least national mistrust for the accelerated drawing together and fusion of nations that will be completed when the state *withers away*."[45] Later in the same article he writes of "the common goal" being "the closest association and eventual *amalgamation of all* nations."[46] In short there is nothing in the classical Marxist tradition that can be enlisted to support the notion of theoretical continuity between Marx and Bromley.

In fact, it is the latter who is the real source of Foster's position. According to Bromley, "ethnos (in the narrow sense of the term) can be defined as a firm aggregate of people, historically established on a given territory, possessing in common relatively stable particularities of language and culture, and also recognizing their unity and difference from other formations (self-awareness) and expressing this in a self-appointed name."[47] Two implications flow from this definition. The first is that ethnos defines human difference: "And when we speak, for example, about the French ethnos–people, it always implies that it has definite features distinguishing it from all other peoples and that this difference is consolidated through everyday ethnic consciousness."[48] The second is that ethnos transcends historical time: "The Ukrainian ethnos, for instance, existed under feudalism and capitalism, and continues to exist under socialism."[49] But neither of these implications should cause concern: "The fact that today the peoples of the USSR have a socialist culture that is common to all of them in content does not lead to the disappearance of the national forms of culture. On the contrary, this culture harmoniously combines with national cultures, with progressive national traditions that have further developed under the conditions of soviet reality and are gradually becoming the attitudes of all the soviet people."[50] Presumably no one reading the above passage will imagine that Bromley in any way represented a dissident trend among the Soviet academy. His views reflected the dominant ideology of the Russian ruling class.[51] In fact, as Banks notes, his work "was an attempt to tackle an obvious problem within the Soviet Union head on." That problem was the continued existence of national consciousness among the non-Russian population of the USSR and of Russian nationalism at the level of the state. As Banks explains: "Ethnos theory provides a bridging mechanism, by positing a stable core which runs through all the historical stages any society will undergo."[52]

But Bromley's work was also intended to solve another problem. As Banks puts it: "Under Stalin, the claims of any constituent parts of the Soviet Union to political independence were ruthlessly suppressed." Even those that had expressed no open nationalist ambitions were treated as potential threats to the unity of the state. Consequently, the ruling class employed varying methods of control, ranging from mass deportations (as in the case of the Crimean Tartars) to the dilution of "ethnic" administrative areas with "ethnic" Russians (as in the case of the Buryats in 1937).[53] These were the perfect conditions for transforming national consciousness into nationalism. Naked oppression tended to be replaced after 1953 with what Suny calls "a deeply contradictory policy" that "on the one hand, nourished the cultural uniqueness of distinct peoples and thereby increased ethnic solidarity and national consciousness in the non-Russian republics, and on the other, by requiring conformity to an imposed political order frustrated full articulation of a national agenda." Economic modernization "produced the possibility of communication and interaction, repression and reproduction of cultural practices, that made nationality more articulate and nationalism the most potent expression of denied ambitions."[54] Given the fantasies propagated by Bromley (and repeated by Foster), there is a certain grim satisfaction in the fact that the death blow to the USSR was delivered by the revolt of the very oppressed nationalities who were supposed to have found their freedom in socialist "ethnos."[55] The continued existence of nationalism in the USSR (and under the other Stalinist regimes) was not a proof that nationhood has no necessary connection with specific modes of production but an index of how far from socialism and, indeed, identical with capitalism these societies were.

Even if we accept that nations will not continue to exist under socialism, however, is it not possible that nationalism may play some role in the *struggle* for socialism? Foster thinks so, and invokes Voloshinov: "Voloshinov argued for an analysis of language in a way that actively and materially reflected the balance of class forces at a particular moment. Language represented a constant dialectic between inherited meanings and their polemical redefinition in terms of the real, concrete unfolding of the contradictions of class society. In the long term there could never be, for Voloshinov, any unilateral, static enforcement of one interpretation. Unfortunately, Davidson himself does not adopt Voloshinov's approach."[56] There are, however, two theoretical problems with the use Foster makes of Voloshinov's work. The first is indicated in a statement by Foster's colleague Charles Woolfson, in his pioneering study of Voloshinov and his school. Summarizing his conclusion on the multi-accentuality of the sign, Woolfson writes: "Each word, therefore, can have a multiplicity of meanings."[57] This is true—but each word does not therefore have an *infinite* multiplicity of meanings. As Alex Callinicos writes: "The term 'nation' preserves in all its usages the same sense, referring to a community bound to a unified state and transcending class antagonisms."[58] And this leads us to the second problem. Voloshinov refers to words, not things, but the nation is not just a word whose meaning can be disputed. It is the typical form of consciousness that arises from the material reality of the nation-state form. As Slavoj Žižek has pointed out: "Consciousness (ideological appearance) is also an 'objective' social fact with an activity of its own . . . bourgeois 'fetishistic' consciousness is not simply an 'illusion' masking social processes, but a mode of organization of the very social being, crucial to the actual process of social (re)production."[59]

This, I think, brings us to the heart of the problem with Foster's (non)definition of a nation. On the one hand, a nation-state is a territorially bounded political entity; on the other, national consciousness is a form of collective group self-identification, which may or may not correspond to an existing nation-state, but which would be unthinkable without the existence of nation-states. "The nation," however, is a metaphysical concept, and Foster uses it in the same mystified way as the bourgeois revolutionaries who first raised it as a political slogan. "Transformation or submergence [of a nation] will depend on how far, within the pre-existing nationally-bounded political economy, a revolutionary class emerges that is capable of leading this process and defining new, more progressive universal values."[60] This statement describes some of the early bourgeois revolutions (a small minority: were "progressive universal values" really hegemonic in the Italian Risorgimento, German unification, or the Meiji Restoration?), but it simply ignores the differences between them and proletarian revolutions. The bourgeoisie has to win allies because, as a minority class, it has never been in a position to take power on its own behalf. It cannot achieve hegemony over these allies simply with abstract doctrines of equality, nor can it openly proclaim that the overthrow of the ancien régime will in fact result in new forms of economic inequality: the nation is the ideological means by which the different class interests opposed to feudal absolutism were temporarily reconciled. The working class does not need to conceal its real aims in this way. What has confused the issue, once again, is the politics of Stalinism.

As with his use of Marx and Lenin to bolster Bromley, Foster is using Voloshinov to give some theoretical substance to the real source of his position, the Bulgarian Stalinist Georgi Dimitrov. In this case what all the talk about dialectical subtlety amounts to is a defense of the Popular Front, launched by Dimitrov in his keynote speech as General Secretary of the Communist International to the Seventh World Congress in August 1935.[61] In this speech we learn of the need to recapture national revolutionary traditions from the right and take seriously the patriotic feelings of the working class: "*National forms* of the proletarian class struggle and of the labor movement in the individual countries are in no contradiction to proletarian internationalism; on the contrary, it is precisely in these forms that the international interests of the proletariat can be successfully defended."[62] It is important to understand that, although the Popular Front is often treated as a return to sanity after the madness of the Third Period, in many respects it simply represented an equally disastrous mirror image of the earlier strategy. If the Third Period involved an isolationist sectarianism toward other parties of the left, the Popular Front involved a promiscuous embrace of bourgeois parties for essentially electoral purposes. The latter strategy remained central to the Communist parties, at least in the West, from the 1930s until their demise after 1989—to disastrous effect, as the outcomes in France and Spain in the 1930s and Chile in the 1970s confirm. Scotland was no exception, although here it led to factory closures rather than torture chambers.[63] Yet Foster wants to carry on with the same failed strategy. "Faced with the challenges posed by such entities as the European Union, Davidson's approach threatens to abandon anything that is progressive and democratic to chauvinist and nationalist misuse."[64] The proper response to this type of claim has been well made by David Harvey:

> Too frequently the response [of the left] is an overly simplistic argument that runs along the following lines: "because NAFTA and Maastricht are pro-capitalist we fight them by defending the nation state against supra-national governance." . . . The left must learn to fight capital at both spatial scales simultaneously. But, in so doing, it must also learn to coordinate potentially contradictory politics within itself at the different spatial scales, for it is often the case in hierarchical spatial systems (and ecological problems frequently pose this dilemma) that what makes good political sense at one scale does not make good politics at another

(the realization of, say, automobile production in Europe may mean plant closures in Oxford or Turin). Withdrawing to the nation state as the exclusive strategic site of class organization and struggle is to court failure (as well as to flirt with nationalism and all that that entails).[65]

Foster claims that "the *Origins of Scottish Nationhood* is unlikely to convince many of those who support an independent Scotland, and this is because it does not engage with those moments in history which many Scots see as defining what is progressive, democratic and collective in their culture."[66] What are these moments? For most nations the individual bourgeois revolutions are central to radical traditions. For Scottish socialists, however, the Scottish bourgeois revolution cannot occupy the same place that comparable events do for socialists in England and France—or even in Italy and the US. On the one hand, unlike 1642 in England or 1792 in France, there is no point in the Scottish revolution where popular interventions were *decisive* in shaping the outcome. The key turning points do not involve the revolutionary crowd storming Edinburgh Castle or a *levée en masse* overwhelming royalist armies against all odds, but deals struck in snuff-filled rooms off Edinburgh High Street and royal troops hunting down defeated peasants across Culloden Moor. On the other hand, unlike what transpired in 1870 in Italy or 1871 in Germany, the end result was not the establishment of a modern nation-state but the dismantling of its foundations and their absorption into a new state dominated by a historic enemy. Whichever way the matter is approached, both "the people" and "the nation" are absent.

As a result, the moments of Scottish radicalism are few and far between. The War of Independence is one: when the Scottish contingents of the Communist Party of Great Britain marched on May Day in 1938, they carried pictures of William Wallace and Robert the Bruce, not to mention Calgacus.[67] Unlike the English Peasants' Revolt of 1381, however, the War of Independence incorporated plebeian discontent into the service of the native ruling class and defused the revolt from below. It comes as no surprise, therefore, that the general strike of 1820 does not feature heavily in such a heavily nationalist tradition of revolt. Even though it reflects well on the Scottish working class (where was the English general strike?), it was too much part of an all-British movement of radical reform to be assimilated. Scottish radicals at the time did not rely solely on imagery of

William Wallace, but of the Magna Carta and the Bill of Rights—the English tradition of radicalism that offered them, as it had their bourgeoisie beforehand, a substitute for their own absent history of radicalism.

Interestingly, Foster and Woolfson once understood that the working class in Scotland had to operate on a British political level:

> [The United Kingdom state] established a common labor market. At the same time it sought to use pre-existing national identities to split the new proletariat. Consequently, those who wished to end or limit exploitation had to make it their first endeavor to bridge this national diversity, and to create a single "labor" identity. In doing so they drew both upon the experience of the immediate struggles and the pre-existing progressive and radical elements within each national culture. It was not, therefore, spontaneously but only as the result of sharp struggle that the national unity of a "British" trade union movement was achieved.[68]

Two comments are necessary here. First, the constant reiteration of "pre-existing national identities" (such as "the Scottish people") within the working-class movement remains as great a threat to the unity of the British working class as it was at the moment of its formation. Second, the formation of the "British" working class traded a loss in internationalist perspective for a gain in organizational coherence. If this is true of "Britishness," it is doubly so of "Scottishness." In their great (if flawed) work *The Many-Headed Hydra*, Peter Linebaugh and Marcus Rediker have noted that "the years 1790–1792 were a revolutionary moment. Egalitarian, multi-ethnic conceptions of humanity had not evolved in isolation, but rather through solidarity and connection, within and among social movements and individuals." They cite one example: "The friendship of Olaudah Equiano and Thomas and Lydia Hardy proved that Atlantic combinations—African and Scot, Englishwoman and African American man—were powerful and of historic significance." With the triumph of the counterrevolution across the Atlantic—a movement in which the authors rightly identify the dissemination of racism as central—these bonds began to dissolve: "Organizations such as the L[ondon] C[orresponding] S[ociety] would eventually make their peace with the nation, as the working class became national, *English*. With the rise of pan-Africanism, the people in exile became a noble *race* in exile. The three friends became unthinkable within ethnic and nationalistic historiography. . . . What began as repression thus evolved into mutually exclusive narratives that have hidden our history."[69]

Something of the internationalism that was lost with the formation of national labor movements is currently being rebuilt in double-sided rejection of the market order. On the one hand, international trade-union solidarity is being reforged. Early in 2001 there have been strikes in Belgium and Spain, and mass rallies in Portugal and Germany against the General Motors decision to shut down car production at Luton. On the other, the wave of demonstrations against the institutions of global capital in Seattle, Washington, Melbourne, Millau, Prague, Davos, Quebec, and Genoa shows the rebirth of a movement that sees international capitalism as the enemy and organizes on an international basis to oppose it. At a historical moment like this, the response of socialists must surely be better than trying to confine these new activists within the box (or, as I would have it, the prison) of their own nations? We have far more to learn from the activities of contemporary French workers and students than we have from a largely mythical Scottish past.

CONCLUSION

Toward the end of his review, Foster makes the following criticism of my work: "Davidson's own approach lacks the subtlety needed to capture the structured unevenness that has marked the development of Scotland's industrial economy. It is this that provides much of the superficial plausibility for the nationalist case."[70] Leaving aside the important-sounding but meaningless notion of "structured unevenness" (what national economy has ever industrialized evenly?), what I think this means is: "Scottish workers think that the industrial decline of their nation is the result of subordination to England. They are wrong, but because they are congenitally incapable of sustaining an internationalist viewpoint, all we can do is wearily unfurl our 'progressive' national banners once again over the usual gaggle of dissident Tories, Kirk ministers, and STUC officials, and appeal to New Labor to have mercy." A more patronizing and potentially disastrous strategy would be hard to imagine in the current climate. For nationalists to advocate nationalism is one thing, but for socialists to accommodate to it because they believe that the working class can only be won by pandering to an aspect of their existing reformist consciousness is quite another. It is the latter attitude, actually more dangerous than outright nationalism, that I criticize in the afterword.[71] Foster presumably thinks that I am referring to somebody else. I am not. *De te fabula narratur.*

꧁ 4.2 The Public Memoirs and Confessions of an Unconscious Weberian [†] ꧂

INTRODUCTION

For nearly twenty-five years, since the publication of *Scottish Capitalism*, John Foster's version of how the Scottish nation was formed has been virtually unchallenged on the left.[72] There are several reasons for this absence of debate, but the main one is that the majority of Scottish socialists agree with him, at least in broad outline. This broad acceptance of his position is not restricted to the left, either. To demonstrate this, readers will have to forgive me for returning to another review of the book that initiated this exchange.

While completing the final draft of *The Origins of Scottish Nationhood*, I came across an article by the Scottish historian Richard Finlay, in which he argued that Marxist theories of Scottish national identity that claim it did not arise until the period of the French Revolution are (and here I paraphrase slightly) crude, reductive, simplistic, and not worth the attention of serious historians.[73] What provoked this outburst, in an article about the enduring influence of the Covenanters, remains a mystery to which Finlay's footnotes provide no solution. In my view this is what Marxist historians *should* have been arguing about Scotland (with the caveat that no national identity simply "emerges" in the space of a year or a decade, but only after a long process of prior development); but I knew of hardly anyone who had explicitly taken this position in print except myself, and my own book had yet to appear.[74] I was therefore able to point out in an endnote that the only authors to whom Finlay explicitly referred (Nairn, Dickson) did not hold the positions he ascribed to them—indeed, they and the majority of Scottish Marxists held a position close or identical to his own: namely, that Scottish nationhood dated back to the Wars of Independence or even earlier. In the same note

[†] Previously unpublished rejoinder to John Foster, "Marxists, Weberians and Nationality: A Response to Neil Davidson," *Historical Materialism* 12, no. 1 (2004). Written in 2004.

I identified one of the leading Marxist exponents of this position and cited him later in the book: John Foster.[75]

Imagine my delight then, when, as if to confirm their affinity, both Finlay and Foster reviewed my book and criticized it in broadly similar terms. In response to my evidence about the changed nature of consciousness after 1746, Finlay wrote: "What this shows is that national identity is reinvented in response to particular national circumstances, but then so what? It has always been reinvented and was doing so before this period, and what is more was reinvented after this period."[76] But my argument is precisely that national identity (or, as I prefer, national consciousness) could not have been "reinvented" before the mid-eighteenth century, because it had to be "invented" first. Finlay partly conceded this, but went on to claim that it was of no significance: "Admittedly, Scotland is not a nation [before 1707] in the way that Davidson defines a nation, at this time there is only one, England. Yet, this stands in contradistinction to the ideas of most historians inside and outside of Scotland who would argue that the Scots had most of the necessary features to qualify as a nation state in the period before 1603 or certainly before 1707."[77] So, by my definition Scotland was not a nation before 1707, but by the definition of "most historians" it was. Foster, of course, does have a specific founding period in mind, between the eleventh and thirteenth centuries. He also claims (rightly) that "most historians" would agree this period saw the birth of the Scottish nation.[78] And what definitions did these historians use in arriving at this conclusion? Silence. Whenever one believes the Scottish nation to have come into being, one would have to employ some definition of nationhood ('the necessary features") in order to recognize the moment at which it occurs; but apparently this is undialectical.

A book that appeared after mine, Neal Ascherson's *Stone Voices*, also took issue with a host of—as usual—nameless modernists intent on denying the national content of the Declaration of Arbroath (1320): "The 'primordialists' may overstate their case about the antiquity of nationalism, but it is difficult to deny that recognizable ideas about a relationship between national and individual liberty were around in medieval Scotland. . . . There is something wrong with academic studies of nationalism. They define it too tightly and force it into Procrustean categories." The reader may find some of these comments familiar from Foster's latest piece, even down to the presence of Procrustes. According to Ascherson, although modernists may be right in some cases, we are wrong in those of oppressed small nations like Scotland. As a consequence, no general theory is possible: "The fact is that the emergence of a concept of the nation was an untidy development, ill-suited to cramming into exclusive 'stages.' [The Declaration of] Arbroath shows that quite 'un-modern' communities could invent an abstract terminology of nationhood when they needed to do so, and that the identification of personal and national independence could happen in very different times and places."[79] Again, these comments may sound familiar. My purpose in quoting from Finlay and Ascherson is not, of course, anything so crass as to imply that they are "unconscious" Stalinists because they share positions with Foster, nor that Foster "unconsciously" shares whatever theoretical positions—if any—Finlay or Ascherson adheres to. It is simply to point out that, after all his laborious expositions of the dialectic, after all his quotations from Marx and Lenin, Foster leaves us with a view of Scottish history that is acceptable to every mainstream academic, editor, and politician in Scotland and probably the world: nations have existed for a very long time—and they will exist from now on! In his review Finlay wrote that that to reject, as I do, the view that Scottish nationhood existed before the eighteenth century, "is to fly in the face of, for want of a better expression, common sense." This is praise indeed, for as Gramsci once pointed out, "common sense is an ambiguous, contradictory and multiform concept, and . . . to refer to common sense as a confirmation of a truth is a nonsense."[80]

Far from boldly upholding some iconoclastic Marxist position, then, Foster is simply reproducing the dominant ideology, "common sense," insofar as it concerns nationhood— which, incidentally, is not to be confused with the views of a handful of non-Marxist sociologists, political scientists, and historians who have taken a modernist position on the emergence of nations. It is worth insisting on this, since modernism has never been the dominant theory of nationhood. Elie Kedourie's book *Nationalism* (1960) and Ernest Gellner's essay "Nationalism" (1964) probably represent the initial modernist texts, but the real concentration occurs for a relatively brief period, from the late 1970s to the early 1990s. Gellner's final work, *Nationalism* (1997), is an epilogue to this entire canon. What does a modernist position involve? According to one representative survey of the field: "For modernists, national consciousness in the modern age has to be seen as qualitatively different from that in

Scotland of the Declaration of Arbroath or England of Shakespeare or Elizabeth or Cromwell. They argue that instead there has been a radical shift in what we now understand as nationalism, that it only comes with modernity that a sense of national identity comes to pervade all classes, or emerges as the overriding identity."[81] Despite the absurd objections that are sometimes lodged against the modernist arguments, no modernist denies that human groups possessed identities before the emergence of capitalism; what they deny is that these identities were national in character. As Gellner wrote:

> It is no part of my purpose to deny that mankind has at all times lived in groups. On the contrary, men have always lived in groups. Usually these groups persisted over time. One important factor in their persistence was the loyalty men felt for these groups, and the fact that they identified with them. This element in human life did not need to wait for some distinctive kind of economy. . . . If one calls this factor, generically, "patriotism," then it is no part of my intention to deny that some measure of such patriotism is indeed a perennial part of human life. . . . What is being claimed here is that nationalism is a very distinctive species of patriotism, and one which only becomes pervasive and dominant under certain social conditions, which in fact prevail in the modern world and nowhere else.[82]

However, modernism never held unchallenged sway. Overlapping with the publication of the key modernist works were others that expressed skepticism of their claims. An early forerunner was Anthony D. Smith's *The Ethnic Origins of Nations* (1971), but during the 1990s Liah Greenfield's *Nationalism* (1992), John Hutchinson's *Modern Nationalism* (1994), and Adrian Hastings's *The Construction of Nationhood* (1997) signaled the turning tide, although the final collapse into essentialism came with Emmanuel Todd's *La Diversité du monde* (1999).[83] The key thesis of this last work has been approvingly summarized by Tom Nairn:

> His idea was that such variations [into nations] must explain most of what has happened in modern times: the diversity of Homo Sapiens derives from a remote ancestry of kinship patterns, nuclear, communitarian or stem-family, sibling egalitarianism or its contrary, cousinate or non-cousinate marriage, and so on. Such trends underlie the contemporary checkerboard of national states, and can be used to account for phenomena such

as Nazism and Communism. . . . Just as the practical utility of the unconscious was to assist patients toward conscious readjustments in living, so
recognition of contemporary society's primordial side should help us re-
gain political control, to use and transcend the inheritance.[84]

A more typical version of anti–modernism has been given by Hastings, a member of the Anglo-Saxon school of "perennialist" thinkers on
nations and nationalism:

> Nationalism owes much to religion, to Christianity in particular. Na-
> tions developed . . . out of a typical medieval and early modern expe-
> rience of the multiplication of vernacular literatures and of state systems
> around them, a multiplication largely dependent on the church, its
> scriptures and its clergy. Nation-formation and nationalism have in
> themselves almost nothing to do with modernity. Only when modern-
> ization was itself already in the air did they almost accidentally become
> part of it, particularly from the eighteenth century when the political
> and economic success of England made it a model to imitate.[85]

Terminology apart, Foster's criticisms are identical to those of my non-
Marxist critics and the broader intellectual tradition of which they are
part. Now, if I were a Marxist, rather than an unconscious Weberian, I
would be worried about this convergence.[86] Did the Marxist revolution
in thought really take place in order that we could reach exactly the same
conclusions as those enshrined in bourgeois ideology?

My intention in writing *The Origins of Scottish Nationhood* was not
to engage particularly with Foster, but with these much more widespread
beliefs. His review and subsequent response to my reply, however, provide
a useful opportunity to demonstrate the falsity of Foster's claims to represent Marxist thinking on this subject. Foster is a skillful, if dishonest,
debater who employs two main tactics. One, which I will discuss here,
can be called "misrepresentation by omission"; the other I will return to
at the end of this chapter. Misrepresentation by omission involves ignor-
ing most of my substantive material and focusing instead on two preliminary theoretical chapters and a third whose function was to provide
a summary historical background. Thus, at one stroke, Foster both relieves
himself of the necessity of actually confronting the evidence with which
I support my central thesis, and gives to unwary readers the impression

that *The Origins of Scottish Nationhood* concerns the period leading up to the Treaty of Union in 1707. In fact it deals with the period from 1746 to 1820. My entire discussion of pre-Union Scotland is contained in the mere twenty-eight pages of the third chapter, of which two—to which Foster devotes almost all his attention—deal with the Treaty of Union.[87] The attention that Foster gives to my supposed methodology is, I think, designed to divert attention from my actual argument.

It would take an inordinate amount of space to correct all of the—I think quite conscious—distortions to which these methods give rise. I will therefore concentrate on replying to the two key charges that Foster levels at *The Origins of Scottish Nationhood*. First, that in terms of social theory I employ a Weberian, rather than Marxist, methodology to define nations. Second, that in terms of political strategy I deny both the national context of the class struggle and the national traditions of resistance upon which the working class and the oppressed must draw. Anything I might say here in response to the objections that Foster raises about the empirical accuracy of my account of Scottish history has been rendered redundant by the publication of *Discovering the Scottish Revolution* (2003), which contains my actual views on the Treaty of Union and several other matters besides.[88] Nevertheless, there is one historical point that I cannot forbear to raise, since it provides me with the title of this reply.

At one point in his critique, Foster notes that I make reference to the similar views of Sir Walter Scott and his protégé James Hogg on the question of Britishness. He then adds: "But [Davidson] makes no mention at all of Hogg's greatest work, *Confessions of a Justified Sinner*. This was written specifically to challenge Scott's artful and destructive caricature of the Covenanting and Cameronian tradition in *Old Mortality*."[89] Everything in these two sentences is wrong. Hogg did not write *The Private Memoirs and Confessions of a Justified Sinner* (1824) to refute Scott. He had, six years previously, nearly completed a novel about the later (post-1660) Covenanters called *The Brownie of Bodsbeck*, when Scott published his book on the same period, *Old Mortality*. Hogg publicized *The Brownie of Bodsbeck* as a reply to Scott, with whose treatment of the Covenanters he was in strong disagreement; but since most of it was written before *Old Mortality* appeared, it was not so much a reply as a different perspective on the same events. But Hogg was no uncomplicated admirer of the Covenanters either, as such a position would scarcely have been compatible with his Tory politics and nostalgic Jacobitism, both of which positions he shared with Scott.[90] In any case, *The Private Memoirs and Confessions of a Justified Sinner* is not concerned with the Covenanters or the Cameronians as social movements; it is above all a satire on the impact of extreme forms of doctrinal Calvinism on the individual psyche and the catastrophic intellectual and moral consequences to which this can lead:

> [Lady Dalcastle] had imbibed her ideas from the doctrines of one flaming predestinarian divine alone; and those were so rigid, that they became a stumbling-block to many of his brethren, and a mighty handle for the enemies of his party to turn the machine of state against them.... Wringhim had held in his doctrines that there were eight different kinds of FAITH, all perfectly distinct in their operation and effects. But the lady, in her secluded state, had discovered another five,—making twelve in all; the adjusting of the existence or fallacy of these five faiths served for a most enlightened discussion of nearly seventeen hours; in the course of which the two got warm in their arguments, always in proportion as they receded from nature, utility, and common sense.[91]

Ironically, if there is a character more sympathetic than any of the others it is George Cowlan, the Laird of Dalcastle and the protagonist's father, who "had not intentionally wronged or offended either of the parties": "During all the dreadful times that has overpast, though the laird had been a moderate man, he had still leaned to the side of the kingly prerogative, and had escaped confiscation and fines, without ever taking any active hand in suppressing the Covenanters."[92] If anything, this makes Cowlan precisely the type of character representative of the "middle way," which Scott's own heroes typically represent.[93] No, Hogg was no more a Covenanter than I am a Weberian, as I shall now demonstrate.

WHY I AM NOT A WEBERIAN

In his original review Foster suggested that there might be different Marxist approaches to the question; his second contribution makes clear that he believes there is in fact only one—his own. I say "his own" approach because although Foster positions himself as the guardian of a Marxist orthodoxy that he claims dates back to Marx himself, I still regard it as wholly imaginary. However, since I stated my objections to these claims in my first reply, I will not repeat them here. After demonstrating to his own satisfaction that Marx was in agreement with him, Foster then surveys a range of later Marxist writers—Kautsky, Bauer, Trotsky, Lenin—in search of my theoretical antecedents. He draws the perfectly correct conclusion that since none of them equated the origins of the nation with capitalism, my views on nationhood cannot have been influenced by any of them. Consequently, since my position does not derive from any identifiable Marxist source, I must instead have derived it (albeit "unconsciously") from Weber and his followers, whom he claims did hold this position.[94]

Foster also thinks he has found further evidence for my supposed Weberianism because I "make frequent use of definitions drawn from writers in the Weberian school and it is largely from this source that Davidson takes his key assumption: that the nation is a capitalist phenomenon."[95] In fact, I draw from only two sociologists who could seriously be described as Weberians (Gellner and Mann), one historian from the same Communist Party tradition as Foster himself (Hobsbawm), and a number of political scientists who do not fit easily into either camp.[96] And in any case: so what? I do not draw from their methodology or their definitions so much as from their substantive conclusions, and Marxists have always had this relationship to non-Marxist thought. I will reveal the secret of my actual theoretical inspiration in due course, but for the moment it is enough to note that there are three, fairly fundamental problems with claims concerning my Weberianism. First, I do not employ a Weberian methodology. Second, Weberians, including Weber himself, do not claim that nations are the product of capitalism—or at any rate, they do not necessarily do so. Third, many of the claims that Weber did make about nations are in fact completely compatible with those made by Marx, Engels, and other Marxists of the classical tradition.

Weberian and Marxist methodologies

Take the question of Weberian methodology first. Here is the central passage from the same work by Weber from which Foster quotes:

> An ideal type is formed by the one-sided *accentuation* of one or more points of view and by the synthesis of a great many diffuse, discrete, more or less present and occasionally absent *concrete individual* phenomena, which are arranged according to those one-sidedly emphasized viewpoints into a unified analytical construct. In its mental purity, this

mental construct cannot be found empirically anywhere in reality. It is a *utopia*. Historical research faces the task of determining in each individual case, the extent to which this ideal construct approximates to or diverges from reality.[97]

Weber puts this methodology to work in, for example, his famous discussion of types of authority—charismatic, patriarchal, bureaucratic, and so on. This is not how I proceed. Foster endlessly counterposes his supposedly Marxist dialectical definition of the nation to my supposedly Weberian sociological one, but I barely discuss "the nation" at all, for the simple reason that I regard "the nation" (like that other notion so beloved of Stalinism, "the people") as a piece of metaphysical claptrap that is almost always used in the way that Foster uses it: with conscious intent to mystify. The only definition I offer of the nation is the following sentence: "In the discussion that follows the word 'nation' will therefore be used to describe a human community that has acquired national consciousness." National consciousness in turn is "a more or less passive expression of collective identification among a social group, and nationalism [is] a more or less active participation in the political mobilization of a social group for the construction *or* defense of a state."[98] Now, if Foster really thinks that this is an example of an "ideal type," then it can only be because he has read Weber's work with as little care as he has evidently read mine. Far from being "formalistic," "dogmatic," etc., this about as minimalist a definition as you can possibly get. Its subjectivist basis was, however, a conscious rejection of a *real* "formalistic," "dogmatic," and objectivist position, associated not with Max Weber, who wrote very little on this subject, but with Joseph Vissarionovich Stalin, who also wrote very little on this subject, although it has regrettably been all too influential. Focusing on national consciousness has the very great advantage of forcing the discussion of "the nation" onto the terrain of what human beings have actually thought, believed, and felt rather than on some abstract quality—"nationhood"—that supposedly exists in history above and outside them. However, if the definition is not to remain tautological then it is also necessary to explain how national consciousness first arose in history: "Only when there were concrete examples of nationhood could different groups know what they were conscious *of*, whether or not they then went on to develop nationalisms of their own."[99] To this end I attempt to trace how four interrelated elements of capitalist development—economic (an internal market), linguistic (a common language), political (the absolutist state), and religious (Protestantism)—combined over several centuries to produce national consciousness within particular territories.[100]

In other words, this was an attempt to identify the historical *process* that led to the emergence of what we now know as national consciousness, drawing examples from several different countries, not an attempt to erect a static model of "the nation." For although national consciousness cannot be seen, smelt, or dropped on your foot, it can at least be discussed with some certainty as to what it is we are discussing. Note that, for all the importance Foster apparently ascribes to a dialectical definition of the nation, he never once tells us what that definition is! This certainly allows him a degree of flexibility denied the rest of us. We are only told that it (whatever "it" is), this endlessly changing, infinitely flexible thing, the nation, preexisted capitalism and will continue under socialism, its character changing along with the balance of class forces dominant within society at any time. The reader will have to forgive my exasperation, but debating with Foster is like wrestling with jelly. For him, nations appear to have no distinct qualities at all. Simply add the magic wonder ingredient, dialectics, and, like Humpty Dumpty in *Through the Looking Glass*, you too can make words mean anything that you want them to mean.

There is, there has to be, some procedural ground in common between all forms of social science. Every methodology that aspires to science has to employ the method of abstraction, of identifying the common features of a phenomenon from various instances until one has a workable definition. What distinguishes the dialectical method from others is the extent to which it is based on an engagement with the historical evidence. This is true of any concept that Marxists may wish to make, bourgeois revolution, absolutism, representative democracy, or whatever. "Dialectical method is about liberating our understanding of a constantly changing world from the imposed rigidity of *a priori* concepts."[101] But why does Foster assume that concepts or definitions have to be *a priori*? Let us take, not for the first or last time, the example of Lenin.

By the time Lenin came to write *Imperialism*, he had rediscovered Hegel's writings, notably *The Science of Logic*, and was excitedly commenting on them in what would become the *Philosophical Notebooks*. There can therefore be no suggestion that his work during this period represents some predialectical position on his part. Yet Lenin does not avoid definition. He does comment on the problems associated with definitions, but not on the grounds that they are contrary to the dialectical method: "Very brief definitions, although convenient, for they sum up the main points, are nevertheless inadequate, since we have to deduce from them some specially important features of the phenomenon that has to be defined. And so, without forgetting the conditional and relative value of all definitions in general, which can never embrace all the concatenations of a phenomenon in its full development, we must give a definition of imperialism that will include the following five of its basic features." After which he goes on to summarize his famous characteristics of imperialism discussed earlier in the pamphlet, ranging from the concentration of capital to the formation of international monopolies and the territorial division of the world by the great powers.[102] The definition is necessary, both to distinguish imperialism as a stage of capitalism from earlier forms of imperialism dating back to the origins of human society—there are clear parallels here with nationhood, incidentally—and also to distinguish it from Kautsky's notion of imperialism as a mere policy that capitalists could avoid if they wished and that might even be against their interests. Since Foster has been quoting from Lenin for over three decades, he is undoubtedly as familiar with these passages as I am. So why is it permissible to define imperialism "rigorously," but not any other phenomenon? Or—since I note that Foster has not stopped using such concepts as "state-monopoly capitalism" or "labor aristocracy"—is it only "nation" that is to be exempt?

Weber, nationalism, and capitalism

However, even if I did use Weberian methodology, it would in no way lead me to the conclusion that nations emerged only with capitalism. Foster quotes only from Weber's methodological writings, rather than his substantive works, so his assertions about Weber's views on the history of nations are—dare I say it—logical deductions about what Weber should believe on the basis of his methodology, rather than what he actually did believe. That is in itself quite a Weberian way of proceeding, although it would be cruel to press the point.[103] I do understand, however, why Foster chose not to consult those writings in which Weber discusses nationhood, since, brief though they are, they do not support his thesis. In his famous inaugural lecture of 1895, Weber refers to the conflict between Polish and German peasants in East Prussia as one involving "two nationalities" that "have competed for centuries on the same soil." Later in the same speech, Weber gave his concept of nationality a racial component: "We do not have peace and human happiness to hand down to our descendants, but rather the *eternal struggle* to preserve and raise the quality of our national species." For Weber the nation, which he identifies with a people, predates the formation of the capitalist state: "For us the nation-state is not something vague which, as some believe, is elevated ever higher, the more its nature is shrouded in mystical obscurity. Rather, it is the worldly organization of the nation's power."[104] The racial component tended to reduce in his later writings, but the assumption that "nation" precedes the modern state is constant. In an article written during the First World War, for example, he writes: "Any numerically 'large' nation organized as a *Machtstaat* [i.e., a state competing for power on the international arena] finds that, thanks to these very characteristics, it is confronted by tasks of a quite different order from those devolving on other nations such as the Swiss, the Danes, the Dutch, or the Norwegians."[105] In his more theoretical considerations on the subject Weber noted the "ambiguity" of the term "nation," but nevertheless defined it as "a community of sentiment which would adequately manifest itself in a state of its own." As for the conditions of national emergence, these have nothing specifically to do with capitalism: "The consular, and at the same time nationalist, reaction against the universalism of the papacy in the waning Middle Ages had its origin, to a great extent, in the interests of the intellectuals who wished to see the prebends of their own country reserved for themselves and not occupied by strangers via Rome.... At that time, however, the linkage to the national language *per se* was lacking; this linkage ... is specifically modern." Why? "Today quite considerable pecuniary and capitalist interests are anchored in the maintenance and cultivation of the popular language."[106]

Given that Weber followed Nietzsche in regarding phenomena as irreducibly different from each other, we should not be surprised to find that he makes no claims concerning the relationship of nationhood to capitalism. Nor does he even claim that there are elective affinities between the two phenomena, which would have been open to him on the basis of his methodology. Foster's assertion that Weber believed nations only appeared with capitalism is therefore untenable. Foster partly protects himself by referring to Weberians rather than to Weber himself, but the claim is no truer of them than it is of their master. Contrary to what Foster claims, "the Weberian School" do not view "the nation and nationalism as the exclusive product of capitalism" any more than their founder did.[107] As I pointed out in *The Origins of Scottish Nationhood*, one of my disagreements with Gellner—the Weberian whose discussion of these issues I have otherwise found most helpful—occurred precisely because he saw industrialization as the basis of these phenomena, rather than capitalism.[108]

Smith, Marx, Engels, Weber

Weber's views are, however, quite similar to those of Marx and—especially—Engels. Foster argues that Marx and Engels did not equate nationhood with capitalist development: "There is no suggestion that the nation is the exclusive creation of the bourgeoisie or capitalism."[109] As proof, he quotes two paragraphs from *The German Ideology*, which begins and ends with the following passages: "The relations of the different nations among themselves depend on the extent to which each has developed its productive forces, the division of labor and internal intercourse. . . . These same relations are to be seen (given a more developed intercourse) in the relations of different nations to one another."[110] On the basis of this quote Foster claims that "[Marx and Engels] associate the structure of a nation with the development of its productive forces and its internal division of labor, but, although treating the nation generally as a unit of politico-economic organization, they make no specific link with capitalism as such."[111] But what are Marx and Engels actually talking about here? In the passage quoted by Foster we find the following sentence: "How far the productive forces of a nation are developed is shown most manifestly by the degree to which the division of labor has been carried." How can a "nation"—in the sense of a collective identity—possess productive forces? The problem here is that much of the language in which *The German Ideology* is written is taken directly from Enlightenment writers, particularly those of the Scottish Historical School. As Hobsbawm writes, "the least satisfactory use of the 'nation'" is precisely "the sense in which Adam Smith uses the word in the title of his great work." Why is this usage unsatisfactory? "For in this context it plainly means no more than a territorial state, or, in the words of John Rae, a sharp Scottish mind wandering through early nine-teenth-century North America criticizing Smith, 'every separate commu-nity, society, nation, state or people (terms which as far as our subject is concerned, may be considered synonymous).'"[112] Michael Mann makes a similar point: "True, Adam Smith's famous tract, *The Wealth of Nations*, in-scribed 'nations' in the title. But his nations were mere geographic exam-ples, playing no role in his theory. He used 'Scotland' and 'England' (national regions) interchangeably with 'Great Britain' (a national state) to illustrate his points . . . 'Nations' were absent from the theories of classical economists."[113] In other words, when Marx and Engels talk about "the re-lations of different nations to each other," they clearly mean "the relations of *territorial states*—or peoples who aspire to have their own territorial states—to each other." What else could they possibly mean? Note also this later passage: "Generally speaking, large-scale industry created everywhere the same relations between the classes of society, and thus destroyed the peculiar features of the various nationalities. And finally, while the bour-geoisie of each nation still retained separate national interests, large-scale industry created a class which in all nations has the same interest and for which nationality is already dead; a class which is really rid of all the old world and at the same time stands pitted against it."[114] We can see here the functional utility to Foster of refusing to define his terms, dialectically or otherwise: it enables him to press into the service of his argument any use of the word, even when the historical context makes it clear that this is quite different from modern use.

It is relatively easy to show that Marx and Engels used the word "nation" in several different ways. The passages that follow are taken from three articles written by Engels in 1884. All refer to his own nation of Germany and are all conveniently located in the same volume (26) of the *Collected Works*. (I am assuming here that Foster shares my view that, although Marx and Engels obviously had different areas of specialist knowledge and interest, their views can be taken as one.)[115] The first comes from his notes on the tribal period of the Germanic peoples. Here, Engels refers to the Roman invaders as one of the "conquering nations" and to the tribal victory over Rome in 9 AD that established the independence of their territory as "a great gain," "even if in fact all the subsequent history of the Germans had been nothing but a long se-ries of national disasters."[116] Nations therefore stretch back to antiquity.

The second comes from a discussion of (to use the title given by his editors) "the decline of feudalism and the rise of nation-states": "Out of the confusion of peoples that characterized the earliest Middle Ages, there gradually emerged new nationalities, a process whereby, it will be recalled, in most of the former Roman provinces the vanquished assimilated the victor, the peasant and townsman assimilated the Germanic lord. Modern nationalities are thus also the product of the oppressed classes." "Modern nationalities," which Engels argues are products of the early absolutist period, are therefore distinct from the ancient tribal or imperial "nations"—indeed, they are not yet nations at all: "Once the boundaries had been fixed (disregarding subsequent wars of conquest and annihilation, such as those against the Slavs of the Elbe) it was natural for the linguistic groups to serve as the existent basis for the formation of states; for the nationalities to start developing into nations." Engels distinguishes here between states and nations, but elsewhere in the same article appears to blur the line again, in the same manner as in *The German Ideology*: "In the whole of Europe there were only two countries in which the monarchy, and the national unity that was then impossible without it, either did not exist at all or existed only on paper: Italy and Germany."[117] But "national unity" in this context also means "state formation," which respectively took place during the Italian Risorgimento and German unification. The third example makes this explicit: "the interests of the proletariat forbade the Prussianisation of Germany just as much as the perpetuation of its division into petty states. These interests called for the unification of Germany at last into a *nation*, which alone could provide the battlefield, cleared of all traditional petty obstacles, on which proletariat and bourgeoisie were to measure their strength."[118] I invite readers to compare these various comments with those from Weber cited earlier and consider whether there is any substantial difference between them in relation to the use to which their authors put the term "nation." In other words, I am perfectly aware that Marx and Engels believed nations existed before capitalism. The point is rather that their views in this respect are incompatible with historical materialism.

What is the problem here? Foster writes: "It is a commonplace of Weberian sociology to claim that Marx failed to provide any satisfactory conceptual definition of class."[119] The implication is that I am essentially taking the same position in relation to their theory of the nation. The Weberians are, of course, wrong about Marx and class. The manuscript of *Capital* volume 3 famously breaks off during the discussion of this subject, but this does not mean that a coherent, systematic approach to class cannot be extracted from their various writings, as the exemplary discussion by Geoffrey de Ste Croix has demonstrated beyond doubt.[120] As I argue in *Origins*, the two concepts are not comparable.[121] However, even if they were, it is not possible to extract a similar synthesis on nationhood from their writings (or rather, their occasional references and passing mentions), for the simple reason that they never gave nationhood the same kind of consideration they gave to class, and neither did their followers. In the preface to the first edition of *The Question of Nationalities and Social Democracy* (1907), Bauer begins by identifying "one of the most intractable problems of domestic policy" and arguing that "Social Democracy is finding itself unable to evade the discussion of the relationship between the national community and the state," which suggests that he thought it had previously been able to evade such a discussion. He recognizes that this involves both "the application of Marx's method of social research to a new field of investigation" and "the risk of venturing beyond the limits set by disciplinary boundaries."[122] In *The Origins of Scottish Nationhood* I wrote, in a passage that Foster finds particularly objectionable, that "there is no agreed Marxist position and little help to be gained from Marx and Engels themselves since, as Michael Löwy noted, 'a precise definition of the concept of "a nation"' is absent from their writings on the national question. Consequently their successors have tended to take one of the existing sides of the debate."[123] It might have been more accurate to have said that there was very little systematic thought on the subject during the epoch of classical Marxism and what little there was—principally by the Austro-Marxists—essentially echoed conventional non-Marxist thinking on the subject. This is precisely why it was necessary for anyone working in the field of nationalism to look to the emergent school of modernist thinking on the subject.

A MARXIST APPROACH TO NATION THEORY

Does this mean that Marx and Engels have nothing to teach us in relation to "nation theory"? Of course not, but it is important to be clear about where these teachings are to be found. Instead of asking what Marxism has to say about the historical conditions for the emergence of certain forms of consciousness, which could then be applied in the case of national consciousness, Foster simply looks for references to "nation" in order to justify his own position. Yet it seems inescapable—to me, at any rate—that this aspect of their thought remained "pre-Marxist" and in many ways incompatible with historical materialism. In fact, as I have tried to demonstrate above, Marx and Engels used "nation" in the same ways as virtually everyone else until well into the twentieth century: either (following Smith) as a synonym for "territorial state" or (following Herder) as a synonym for "a people," often vacillating between the two and sometimes merging them. Since Foster's religious piety toward Marx and Engels prevents him from admitting that they might have ever been wrong, or their thought ever less than fully formed, or their positions ever simply inconsistent, he has to invest their every use of the term "nation" with an inner coherence that these uses do not in fact possess. It is not that there is this (undefined) thing called "a nation" that keeps changing down the centuries with different modes of production, but that Engels is clearly using the term "German nation" to mean several different things. In most cases he means no more than "the people who now live or who historically have lived in the territory currently occupied by the nation-state that is now called Germany."

As the preceding argument suggests, there is no mystery over the lineage of my theoretical position on nationhood. It is derived directly from Marx and Engels and expresses what I take to be the general Marxist position on the relationship between social being and consciousness: "The mode of production of material life conditions the general process of social, political, and intellectual life. It is not the consciousness of men that determines their existence, but their social existence that determines their consciousness."[124] These famous words, and not some untheorized remarks about German tribes, seem to me to be the right starting point for any discussion about national consciousness. One of their implications is that certain forms of consciousness are only possible under particular conditions. The point was further developed by Lukács: "The crudeness and conceptual nullity of [vulgar Marxist] thought lies primarily in the fact that it obscures the historical, transitory nature of capitalist society. Its determinants take on the appearance of timeless, eternal categories valid for all social formations. This could be seen at its crassest in the vulgar bourgeois economists, but the vulgar Marxists soon followed in their footsteps."[125] As Lukács points out, vulgar Marxism has "wholly neglected" the distinction between capitalist and precapitalist social formations: "Its application of historical materialism has succumbed to the same error that Marx castigated in the case of vulgar economics: it mistook purely historical categories, moreover categories relevant only to capitalist society, for eternally valid ones."[126]

The "nation" is one of these historical categories that are only relevant to capitalist society. In making this particular error, vulgar Marxists simply follow bourgeois "normal science." An example can be found in Hastings. Hastings has argued that "'nation'—the word and the idea"— existed in England at least since the sixteenth, and probably since the fourteenth, century.

> This does not, of course, prove of itself that the English were themselves at that time a nation, as we understand the term, though their frequent use of the term shows clearly enough that they thought they were. However, it is one thing to discuss whether the Chinese, say, under the Ming dynasty were a "nation" when one is taking a word entirely foreign to their society and seeing whether it can suitably be applied to them, and quite another to maintain that a word which we have inherited from our ancestors in continual verbal continuity is not relevant in a way they thought it was, but is one which in terms of historical understanding it is pointless to apply to them. Can the historian validly so redefine people against their own self-understanding?[127]

But was it their understanding? In a brilliant passage early in his book *A Short History of Ethics*, Alasdair MacIntyre makes the point that certain concepts used in the Hellenistic world at the time of Homer are almost impossible to translate into modern English. The gap between the two "marks a difference between two forms of social life": "To understand a concept, to grasp the meaning of the words which express it, is always at least to learn what the rules are which govern the use of such words and so to grasp the role of the concept in language and social life. This in itself would suggest strongly that different forms of social life will provide different roles for concepts to play." He continues the discussion with specific regard to types of moral conduct, but the argument is of broader application: "This whole family of concepts, then, presupposed a certain sort of social order, characterized by a recognized hierarchy of functions."[128] In other words, just because people used the term "nation" in, say, the fourteenth century, it does not follow that they meant by it what we mean by it—indeed, if we take Marxism seriously, then it is extremely unlikely that they could have done so. I have pointed out the historical fluctuations in meaning of the word "nation," as have several earlier writers, using different examples.[129]

It is not simply a matter of words, but of the forms of consciousness that the words express. Take, for example, the question of atheism as a historical phenomenon. One of the central concerns of Lucien Febvre's classic work from the 1940s was the historical moment at which it became possible for people to abandon their belief in God:

> Not to believe. Would you say the problem was simple? Was it so easy for a man, as nonconformist as he could conceivably be in other respects, to break with the habits, the customs, even the laws of the social groups of which he was a part, at a time when these habits, customs, and laws were still in full force; when, on the other hand, the number of freethinkers who were trying to shake off the yoke was infinitesimal; when there was no material in his knowledge and the knowledge of the men of his time either for forming valid doubts or for supporting those doubts with proofs that, on the basis of experimentation, could have the force of real, verifiable conviction?

Recognizing the force of these circumstances, Febvre concludes: "It is absurd and puerile, therefore, to think that the unbelief of men in the sixteenth century, insofar as it was a reality, was in any way comparable to our own. It is absurd. And it is anachronistic." And his view of those who insisted on claiming the opposite? "Wanting to make the sixteenth century a skeptical century, a free-thinking and rationalist one, and glorify it as such is the worst of errors and delusions."[130] There are problems with his analysis.[131] Nevertheless, the overall method is sound and considerably more materialist than that of Foster. The latter writes of Scottish identity during the period that followed the Viking invasions:

> If a transformation of cultural identities occurred during that period it would appear to be because such struggle defended social gains, experienced on a mass scale by the peasant population, which the new feudal mode of production embodied. To this extent the resulting Scots national identity, as with national consciousness in general, might be expected to contain and carry forward the progressive elements involved in that initial alliance of peasant and warrior lord and to have done so to a degree which feudal institutions themselves, as instruments of class rule and exploitation, could not.[132]

Here Foster is engaging in the venerable Scottish Enlightenment tradition of speculative history, since there is no evidence for the Popular Front against Marauding Nomads between "peasants and warrior lords" that he imagines existing at this time. Leaving that aside, however, the central point is this: could peasants (or warriors for that matter) in the tenth century have experienced comparable states of consciousness to those of modern Scots? I trust that not even Foster is claiming as much. But if we are talking about a different form of consciousness, then what is the point of referring to it as "national," when it bears no relation to what we currently mean by that term?

I noted earlier that Foster deployed two debating tactics. To "misrepresentation by omission" he adds the well-known "amalgam" or "lumping" technique. This involves, for example, marshaling statements by representatives of the classical Marxist tradition on different aspects of the national question—the historical conditions for the emergence of nations, the attitude that revolutionaries should take to specific national movements and demands, the possibilities of nations continuing to exist after the end of class society—and presenting them as if they were all part of a single argument that has to be accepted or rejected as a whole. In other words, Foster fails to draw any distinction between the views of Marx, Engels, and Lenin on the historical development of nationhood and their views on how socialists should relate to specific national demands, although there is no necessary connection between them. Yet all three men recognized the existence of particular national groups that they refused to support, either because doing so would have aided absolutist reaction and hence held back the development of capitalism and the working class (the Slavs in 1848), or because it would have involved taking sides in an inter-imperialist conflict in which these nations or peoples were simply subordinate pawns (the Serbs in 1914). It is perfectly possible to agree that Engels was right to oppose pan-Slavism in 1848 without doing so on the basis that the Czechs were a "non-historic nation," just as it is quite possible to agree that Lenin was right to support the Easter Rising whatever one believes about the antiquity or otherwise of the Irish nation.

Foster does remind his readers that Marx supported the Irish and Polish movements for national liberation, insinuating that I might not, despite the fact that in my first response I actually cited these as examples of national movements that socialists have always had to support. Finally, we are further reminded more generally that "Marx was thoroughly contemptuous of those who dismissed the relevance of national issues on the basis of a bogus internationalism—whether under the banner of Proudhon or Bakunin," a statement that not only implies that I also dismiss the national question, but that I do so on a petty-bourgeois anarchist basis—the ground for this accusation having been prepared on the previous page where Foster suggests that my views on the state might also be comparable to those of Bakunin.[133] Foster further insinuates that I adhere to an "abstract internationalism" that is unconcerned with the fate of my own or presumably any other specific nation. And he has a quote from Lenin to support his position:

> To take the first proposition (the working men have no country) and forget its connection with the second (the workers are constituted as a class nationally, though not in the same sense as the bourgeoisie) will be exceptionally incorrect. Where, then, does the connection lie? In my opinion precisely in the fact that the democratic movement (at such a moment, in such concrete circumstances) [sic] the proletariat cannot refuse to support it (and consequent [sic] support defense of the fatherland in a national war). Marx and Engels said in the *Communist Manifesto* that working men have no country. But the same Marx called for a national war more than once.[134]

Here I think we can agree with Lenin that Marx and Engels were not "muddlers who said one thing today and another tomorrow"; but what is the context for this hastily written and uncorrected letter to Inessa Armand? As the date reveals, it was written six months after the Easter Rising in Ireland and during the debates within the revolutionary wing of the Second International about national self-determination. Lenin was arguing against the position of those in his own party (like Bukharin) and on the revolutionary left more generally (like Luxemburg) who thought that socialists should not support national movements under any circumstances. In effect, the letter is a summary of the position Lenin had argued during the summer of the same year in "The Discussion on Self-Determination Summed Up." There is no doubt in my mind that on this occasion Lenin was right and Bukharin and Luxemburg were wrong; but what has this got to do with the formation of national consciousness or its transition into nationalism? It is perfectly possible—indeed, for Marxists, it is positively essential—to able to support national movements or national demands without making any concessions to nationalist ideology, especially those aspects that treat nations as a timeless aspect of the human condition. Lenin set out his vision of the demise of the nation-state under socialism with perfect clarity at exactly the same time as he was declaring his support for movements of national liberation:

> The aim of socialism is not only to end the division of mankind into tiny states and the isolation of nations in any form, it is not only to bring the nations closer together but to integrate them. And it is precisely in order to achieve this aim that we must, on the one hand, explain to the masses the reactionary nature of Renner and Otto Bauer's idea of so-called "cultural and national autonomy" and, on the other, demand the liberation of oppressed nations in a clearly and precisely political program that takes special account of the hypocrisy and cowardice of socialists in the oppressor nations, and not in general nebulous phrases, not in empty declarations and not by "relegating" the question until socialism has been achieved. In the same way as mankind can arrive at the abolition of classes only through a transition period of the dictatorship of the oppressed classes, it can arrive at the inevitable integration of nations only through a transition period of the complete emancipation of all oppressed nations, i.e., their freedom to secede.[135]

For Lenin, then, national secession was not an end in itself but a moment in the process of overcoming the existence of nation-states altogether.

Finally, why is Foster so anxious to recruit national identity into the service of socialism? At one point in his most recent intervention he writes: "For [Davidson], 'working-class consciousness' and 'national consciousness' are totally conceptually separate and opposed." Apparently I claim that "national consciousness denies class consciousness."[136] In fact, I do not refer to "working-class consciousness" as such, for the simple reason that you cannot seriously use the term without specifying what content it has at any given time. Only a small minority of workers will ever completely identify with the ideology of the ruling class. For most of the time most workers possess varying degrees of reformist working-class consciousness. Under non-revolutionary conditions, there is only another and still smaller minority who will possess revolutionary working-class consciousness: a consciousness that corresponds to the reality of their situation, in other words. Far from regarding national consciousness as a denial of working-class consciousness in general, I regard it as absolutely essential to the maintenance of reformist working-class consciousness and consequently an obstacle to the formation of revolutionary working-class consciousness. If, however, you reject the necessity for socialist revolution, or even the possibility of socialist revolution, then national consciousness does not represent a problem so much as an opportunity for harnessing workers to a reformist project. I have already explained in my initial response to Foster why this strategy has been politically and industrially disastrous, but I believe that it will also be increasingly unsustainable, precisely because of the dual nature of Scottish national consciousness.

CONCLUSION

The radical left in Scotland has increasingly come to support independence—"secession" in Leninist terms—from Britain. Unfortunately, most have done so on the basis of precisely the type of myths and fantasies about Scottish nationhood that Foster also invites us to embrace. The difference is that the new nationalist left have taken this to its logical conclusion by essentially becoming Scottish nationalists, while Foster and those who remain tied to the traditions of Stalinism continue to support the British nation-state. It is possible, of course, to support Scottish independence from a position that makes no concessions to nationalism of any sort but focuses instead on, for example, the difficulties it would pose for the British imperialist state and its nuclear arsenal. Should the issue of Scottish independence ever be seriously posed, then I suspect that we will hear far less from Foster about the need to engage with Scottish radical traditions, and far more about the need to maintain the unity of the British labor movement, which in this context will mean the unity of the Labour Party and individual trade-union bureaucracies. But working-class unity is not achieved by internally reproducing the territorial divisions of the capitalist nation-state system; it depends on the willingness of workers to take solidarity action in support of each other—if necessary, across borders, however recently they may have been established.

∞ Chapter 5 ∞

Enlightenment and Anti-Capitalism[*]

INTRODUCTION

What was the Enlightenment? The term has three overlapping meanings. The first refers to an intellectual and social movement that, like the Renaissance and the Reformation before it, characterized a specific historical period, in this case extending from the middle decades of the seventeenth century to—at the latest—the first decades of the nineteenth. The second refers to the traces left by that movement, theoretical works like Adam Smith's *The Wealth of Nations* or constitutional documents like the American Declaration of Independence (both dating from 1776). The third refers to certain methods of intellectual inquiry and principles of social organization that both animated the movement and informed its literary productions. It is because of the continued debate over the value of these methods and principles that the Enlightenment

---

* Originally published in *International Socialism* 2:110 (Spring 2006).

remains a contemporary issue and not merely a historical one, in a way that, for example, Renaissance assessments of classical humanism and Reformation debates over predestination do not.

The Enlightenment heritage is now under attack on two fronts. On the one side it is confronted by a partial reversion to pre-Enlightenment ideas. Defying all predictions of imminent secularization, religious belief is resurgent on a global scale, encompassing Christianity and Hinduism as much as Islam. On the other side, sections of the left have embraced ideas that claim to go beyond the Enlightenment, with a series of relativist and irrationalist positions that are usually lumped together under the name of "postmodernism," an academic fashion that is rapidly ceasing to be fashionable but has left a legacy of confusion for new generations of activists. Who then defends the Enlightenment? Right on cue, members of the liberal left have reinvented themselves as partisans for capitalist globalization, Western imperialism, and institutional racism, in the guise of upholders of Reason, Democracy, and Freedom of Speech. The obscene spectacle of highly paid journalists attacking the beliefs of Muslims, one of the most oppressed groups in British society, while draping themselves in the banner of Jefferson and Voltaire can only help persuade radicals—Muslim and non-Muslim alike—that the Enlightenment is indeed a Eurocentric conspiracy to defend the existing global order.

If we cannot simply "reject" the Enlightenment without depriving ourselves of some of the most important intellectual tools necessary for human liberation, neither can we uncritically "defend" it, as if it had no limitations, or as if there had been no positive intellectual developments since the early nineteenth century. In an article written during the last years of his life, the late Michel Foucault argued for resistance to what he called "intellectual blackmail" over the Enlightenment:

> One has to refuse everything that might present itself in the form of a simplistic and authoritarian alternative: you can either accept the Enlightenment and remain within the terms of its rationalism (this is considered a positive term by some and used by others, on the contrary, as a reproach); or else you criticize the Enlightenment and then try to escape the principles of rationality (which may be seen, once again, as good or bad). And we do not break free from this blackmail by introducing "dialectical" nuances while seeking to determine what good or bad elements there may have been in the Enlightenment.[1]

We do require dialectics, I think, but the essential point is right and can act as a useful starting point: we have to understand the Enlightenment as a totality, and not by cherry picking "good or bad elements" that happen to suit us. We can only do so by approaching the Enlightenment historically.

WHAT WAS THE ENLIGHTENMENT? COMPONENTS, CONTRADICTIONS, CAPITALISM

"The metaphor of truth as light is deeply rooted in Western thought," writes Alex Callinicos.[2] In fact, the metaphor has been more widespread than he suggests, since it occurs in the sacred books of all the major monotheist world religions.[3] Nevertheless, it was in the West that the metaphor of light (and that of its antipode, darkness) became secularized. The religious connotations of enlightenment were not abandoned immediately. Their continued coexistence is nicely captured in the epitaph that Alexander Pope wrote for Isaac Newton in 1730:

> Nature, and Nature's Laws lay hid in Night
> God said, Let Newton be! And All was Light.[4]

But by the end of the century God had been effectively replaced by Nature. In his *Cantata on the Death of Joseph II* (1790), Beethoven used a poem by Eulogius Schneider that begins: "Mankind rose up to the light." He was to reuse the same melody in *Fidelio* (1814), where, as Anthony Arblaster writes: "The words to which the melody is set . . . similarly employ the Enlightenment image of light dispersing darkness and fanaticism."[5] And *Fidelio* was not the first opera to employ this imagery. At the climax of Mozart's opera *The Magic Flute* (1791), Sarastro sings:

> The sun's golden glory has vanquished the night;
> The false world of darkness now yields to the light.

To which the chorus responds: "Hail, you new enlightened ones!"[6] Still in the German-speaking world, one splendid polemic that appeared in the August 1793 edition of the journal *Oberdeutsche Allgemeine Literaturzeitung* reflected on the period leading up to the French Revolution of 1789 in these terms: "The empire of ignorance and superstition was moving closer and closer towards its collapse, the light of *Aufklärung* [the age of Enlightenment] made more and more progress, and the convulsive gestures with which the creatures of the night howled at the dawning day showed clearly enough that they themselves despaired of victory, and were only summoning up their reserves for one final demented counter-attack."[7] Even enemies of the Enlightenment had to use the same terms. The Scottish reactionary John Robison, author of *Proofs of a Conspiracy against All the Religions and Governments of Europe*, asserted: "Illumination turns out to be worse than darkness."[8]

Components

At the heart of Enlightenment thought were three central claims. The first was that the natural and social worlds can be explained, and consequently acted upon, through the application of reason, without recourse to religion or other mystical beliefs. This represented a radical break with most sixteenth- and early seventeenth-century thought, which gave a privileged place to religious interpretations of reality. If there is one man who embodies the most radical elements of the Enlightenment it is "the supreme philosophical bogeyman" Baruch Spinoza.[9] And it is in his work that the metaphor of light is first turned against organized religion. In 1670 he attacked the "dogma" of organized religion:

> But what dogma!—degrading rational man to a beast, completely in-hibiting man's free judgment and his capacity to distinguish true from false, and apparently devised with the set purpose of utterly extinguish-ing the light of reason. Piety and reason—O Everlasting God!—take the form of ridiculous mysteries, and men who utterly despise reason, who reject and turn away from the intellect as naturally corrupt—these are the men (and this is of all things the most iniquitous) who are be-lieved to possess the divine light![10]

Spinoza was not in fact an atheist, but it was perfectly obvious in which di-rection his thought was leading. Early in the eighteenth century one English critic, Richard Blackmore, wrote of Spinoza in his poem *The Creation*:

> *For Heaven his ensigns treacherous displays;*
> *Declares for God, while he that God betrays;*
> *For whom he's pleased such evidence to bring;*
> *That saves the name, while it subverts the thing.*[11]

Three points are worth noting here. First, Spinoza and those who followed him in the next century were not primarily attacking Islam, Buddhism, or other religions mainly practiced outside Europe, but rather the dominant Christian church within their own societies. Second, free speech was not invoked in order to attack the weak and powerless, but the mighty combination of Church and State, which could bring to bear the Holy Inquisition, censorship, jail, mutilation, and even death. Third, and consequently, proclaiming their views involved an element of risk, which was not confined to the Catholic states. Spinoza wrote in the postrevolutionary United Netherlands, probably the most tolerant society in Europe, but still came under sustained attack for his views. Thomas Aikenhead was hanged for blasphemy in Calvinist Edinburgh in 1697.[12] In France before the Revolution of 1789, declaring your belief in Reason over Revelation was virtually to invite investigation. The police report on Denis Diderot, editor of the *Encyclopédie*, states: "He is a very clever boy but extremely dangerous." And he was dangerous, among other reasons, because "he speaks of the holy mysteries with scorn."[13] Reason, however, was desirable for more than the strength it provided to opponents of organized religion. It was seen as providing a means for people to act to change the circumstances in which they found themselves. As Immanuel Kant wrote in 1783, in one of the first self-conscious attempts to define the meaning of the Enlightenment project: "Once . . . man's inclination and vocation to *think freely* has developed . . . it generally reacts upon the mentality of the people, who thus become increasingly able to *act freely*."[14]

The second claim was that human history moves in a particular direction, characterized by progression rather than, as had previously been believed, by regression, stagnation, or recurrence. Reversals had been known to occur, of course, but the resumption of development had in each case brought humanity closer to the point where the rule of reason could be achieved. No human accomplishment was ever completely lost, thought Edward Gibbon, contemplating one of the most important of these reversals in *The Decline and Fall of the Roman Empire*: "We may therefore acquiesce in the pleasing conclusion, that every age of the world has increased, and still increases, the real wealth, the happiness, the knowledge, and perhaps the virtue, of the human race."[15] But the Enlightenment also saw progress as occurring in a much more specific sense, through successive stages of development characterized by what French and then Scottish thinkers called "modes of subsistence." As Adam Smith explained to his students in 1762, these were "first, the Age of Hunters; secondly, the Age of Shepherds; thirdly, the Age of Agriculture; and fourthly, the Age of Commerce."[16] And, as Smith's colleague Lord Kames observed in 1758, "these progressive changes . . . may be traced in all societies."[17] Therefore, although not all societies progressed at the same speed, all could potentially reach the same level of development. In other words, as Walter Bagehot later remarked, it was possible for everyone to rise "from being a savage . . . to be[ing] a Scotchman,"[18] or perhaps even an Englishman. In 1701 Daniel Defoe cautioned his English readers against the contempt they felt toward foreigners. Given time, he told his audience, these people, and the nations to which they belong, will reach our level: "From Hence I only infer, That an *English* Man, of all Men, ought not to despise Foreigners, *as such*, and I think the Inference is just, *since what they are to-day, we were yesterday, and tomorrow they will be like us*."[19] Patronizing as this now appears, it is essentially an optimistic and universal doctrine. It was obvious, however, that all societies were not undergoing these changes within the same historical timescale. In France, Anne-Robert-Jacques Turgot noted that all the different stages of social development were simultaneously being played out: "Thus, the present state of the world, marked as it is by these infinite variations in inequality, spreads out before us at one and the same time all the gradations from barbarism to refinement, thereby revealing at a single glance, as it were, the records and remains of all the steps taken by the human mind, a reflection of all the stages through which it has passed, and the history of the ages." But these stages were all points on the road to the same ultimate destination: "Thus the human race, considered over the period since its origin, appears to the eye of a philosopher as one vast whole, which itself, like each individual, has its infancy and its advancement. . . . Finally, commercial and political ties unite all parts of the globe, and the whole human race, through alternate periods of weal and woe, goes on advancing, although at a slow pace, towards greater perfection."[20]

The third claim was that human beings are possessed of universal rights, which are theirs simply by virtue of their being human, and not because they are members of a particular social estate or religious denomination. If the first two claims encompass *how* we know about the

world (through reason) and *what* we know about the society (it pro-
gresses), the third at the very least implies that society is currently insufficiently rational and that progress may not take place automatically. If,
as Smith and Kames suggest, all societies advance through certain stages
of development, then the human beings who make up those societies
must all share the same faculties, reason above all. Hegel wrote in his *En-
cyclopedia of the Philosophical Sciences* (1816): "Human beings are implicitly
rational; therein lies the possibility of equal rights for all people and the
nullification of any rigid distinction between members of the human
species who possess rights and those who do not."[21] The fact that Hegel
can only talk of "possibility" here acknowledges the fact that rights are
still an aspiration rather than a reality.

All three claims are combined in a report of 1818 by Thomas Jefferson to the legislature of Virginia on the subject of what should be taught
at the state university: "And it cannot be but that each generation suc-
ceeding to the knowledge acquired by all those who preceded it, adding
to it their own acquisitions and discoveries, and handing the mass down
for successive and constant accumulation, must advance the knowledge
and well-being of mankind, not *infinitely*, as some have said, but *indefinitely*,
and to a term that no-one can fix or foresee." The proof that these were
not "vain dreams" could be found in America itself, where "we have before our eyes real and living examples." Jefferson was convinced he knew
what had elevated the colonists over the original inhabitants: "What, but
education, has advanced us beyond the conditions of our indigenous
neighbors? And what chains them to their present state of barbarism and
wretchedness, but a bigoted veneration for the supposed superlative wisdom of their fathers, and the preposterous idea that they are to look
backward for better things, and not forward, longing, as it should seem,
to return to the days of eating acorns and roots, rather than indulge in
the degeneracies of civilization."

Note, however, that Jefferson does not think the Native Americans
are incapable of development, just unwilling to undertake what is necessary to attain it. Note also that the main object of his criticism is the
existing order in Europe. He writes that the doctrine that holds nothing
can ever be improved "is the genuine fruit of the alliance between
Church and State; the tenants of which, finding themselves but too well
in their present condition, oppose all advances that might unmask their

usurpations, and monopolies of honors, wealth and power, and fear every change, as endangering the comforts they now hold."[22] But there were limits to reason, progress, and universality.

Contradictions

The Enlightenment inherited from religious thought the notion that certain areas were not subject to rational explanation. In the 1650s Blaise Pascal wrote, in one of the most beautiful of the aphorisms that make up his *Pensées*: "The heart has its reasons of which reason knows nothing."[23] Shortly afterward Spinoza argued that "the way prescribed by reason is very difficult, so that those who believe that a people, or men divided over public business, can be induced to live by reason's dictate alone, are dreaming of the poet's golden age or a fairy tale."[24] The point was finally theorized in Scotland nearly a hundred years later by David Hume. Hume was no friend of what he called "superstition" but nevertheless made a fundamental distinction between "reason" and "the passions," a term that is best understood as meaning "needs" or "desires": "Reason is, and ought only to be the slave of the passions, and can never pretend to any other office then to serve and obey them."[25] In other words, we can act rationally in response to our passions, but the passions themselves are not susceptible to rational analysis.

If the trouble with reason was the limited extent of its applicability, the trouble with progress was the exceptions to which it appeared to give rise. The most important of these was concerned with the significance of biological distinctions between different human groups, or "races." Enlightenment thinkers were deeply divided on this issue. One tendency challenged the racist ideology that was being developed to justify the conquest of Native Americans and enslavement of Africans. Johann Gottfried von Herder, for example, was opposed to notions of European superiority and the "intolerable pride" it produced: "What is a measure of all peoples *by the measure of us Europeans* supposed to be at all? Where is the means of comparison?"[26] This trend in the Enlightenment inspired *Les amis des noirs*, whose ideas led Robespierre to abolish slavery in 1793, at the height of the revolutions in France and Haiti.[27] As Sankar Muthu writes: "Among the more remarkable features of such writings—an aspect that should give pause to those who theorize an intractable conceptual divide between universalism and relativism in moral and political thought—is that an increasingly acute awareness of the ir-reducible plurality and partial incommensurability of social forms, moral values and political institutions engendered a historically uncommon, in-clusive moral universalism."[28] Another trend, however, doubted whether people with black skin could even be regarded as fully human. In 1748 Montesquieu declared: "It is impossible for us to suppose these creatures to be men."[29] In his *Lectures on the Philosophy of History* from the early 1830s, Hegel noted that Africa was "the land of Childhood" and that this required the historian to "disregard the category of universality." Hegel assumes that Africans and their descendants are—exceptionally among the peoples—incapable of attaining personhood and therefore eligibility for human rights: "This condition [i.e., lack of self-control] is capable of no development or culture, and as we see them at this day, such have they always been."[30]

There is a contradiction between Hegel's earlier argument about the possibility of universal human rights and his rejection of "the category of the universal" for Africans, which is not explained simply by the pas-sage of time and the increasingly reactionary cast of his later political thought: there were limits to precisely how universal universality was going to be. Universality implied equal legal rights, but—even leaving aside issues of racial exclusivity—these rights were usually restricted along class lines. Michael Hardt and Antonio Negri have argued that we need to return to Enlightenment conceptions of democracy ("Back to the Eighteenth Century!") on the grounds that in this period the concept was still uncorrupted: "The eighteenth-century revolutionaries did not call democracy either the rule of a vanguard party or the rule of elected officials who are occasionally and in limited ways accountable to the multitude."[31] True, but neither did eighteenth-century revolutionaries or their predecessors believe that democracy "requires the rule of everyone by everyone." Take, for example, Hardt and Negri's hero, Spinoza. He certainly wrote several passages extolling democracy as the most effective method of government: "This system of government is undoubtedly the best and its disadvantages are fewer because it is in closest accord with human nature. For . . . in a democracy (which comes closest to the natural state) all the citizens undertake to act, but not to reason or judge, by di-visions made in common. That is to say, since all men cannot think alike, they agree that a proposal supported by a majority of voters shall have the force of a decree, meanwhile retaining the authority to repeal the same when they see a better alternative."[32] He did not, however, believe that everyone was capable of democracy. He wrote in the same work:

> I know how deeply rooted in the mind are the prejudices embraced under the guise of piety. I know too, that the masses can no more be freed from their superstition than from their fears. Finally, I know that they are unchanging in their obstinacy, that they are not guided by reason, that their praise and blame is at the mercy of impulse. Therefore I do not invite the common people to read this work, nor all those who are victims of the same emotional attitudes. Indeed, I would prefer that they disregard this book completely rather than they make themselves a nuisance by misrepresenting it after their wont.[33]

Similarly, Voltaire wrote in a letter of 1768: "We have never intended to enlighten shoemakers and servants—this is up to apostles."[34] As Paul Siegel astutely remarks, Voltaire's attitude toward the dissemination of Enlightenment ideas to the masses lies behind one of his best-known slogans: "If God did not exist, it would be necessary to invent him."[35] Religion was "necessary" for the common people, who might otherwise seek to apply reason to areas quite as uncomfortable to denizens of the coffee shops of Paris as habitués of the Palace of Versailles. Voltaire was a brilliant and courageous man, but there is no need to deceive ourselves, as the righteous Islamophobes who invoke his name constantly do, that he saw Enlightenment extending much beyond his own class—even if his attitude was partly motivated by fear of reactionary forces being able to mobilize popular feeling against religious or agrarian reforms.[36]

But the complexities of the doctrine of universality are perhaps best expressed in the American Declaration of Independence. Along with the French Declaration of the Rights of Man and of the Citizen, this is one of the most famous political expressions of Enlightenment thought. In the immortal words of the second paragraph: "We hold these truths to be self-evident, that all men are created equal, that they are endowed by their Creator with certain unalienable Rights, that among these are Life, Liberty and the pursuit of Happiness."[37] Anyone wanting to raise a laugh at the supposedly fraudulent claims of Enlightenment universalism need only quote the opening passage and then point out everyone it excludes: all women, Native Americans, slaves, and so on. But as Howard Zinn—not a writer noted for his subservience to received versions of American history—sensibly notes: "To say that the Declaration of Independence, even by its own standards, was limited to life, liberty and happiness for white males is not to denounce the makers and signers of the Declaration for holding the ideas expected of privileged males of the eighteenth century." To do so would be "to lay impossible moral burdens on that time."[38] However, the main issue with the Declaration is not the extent to which the Founding Fathers acted in part from self-interested motives, but the extent to which the existence of these motives means that their self-proclaimed universal values were—perhaps unconsciously—a cover for their particular interests. Michael Bérubé points out that "poststructuralism tends to argue that the emancipatory narratives of the Enlightenment are in fact predicated on—and compromised by—their historical and social origins in eighteenth-century racism and sexism," and "the social violence of the last two centuries of American society is not something to be corrected by a return to the Enlightenment rhetoric of rights but is, rather, a fulfillment of the symbolic violence constitutive of the Enlightenment itself."[39] Is it true that universality is "tainted" in this way? In fact, as Terry Eagleton remarks, it is "one of the greatest emancipatory ideas in world history . . . not least because middle-class society could now be challenged by those it suppressed, *according to its own logic*, caught out in a performative contradiction between what it said and what it did."[40]

Capitalism

The source of these tensions within the Enlightenment lies in its relationship to capitalism as a historical system. Critics of the Enlightenment have of course no doubts that there is a relationship, although they are less certain what it is. For Michel Foucault the regime of truth "was not merely ideological or superstructural; it was a condition of the formation and development of capitalism."[41] If Foucault credits the Enlightenment with giving rise to capitalism, the Indian "postcolonial" intellectual Partha Chatterjee sees the Enlightenment as dependent upon it: "For ever since the Age of Enlightenment, Reason, in its universalizing mission, has been parasitic upon a much less lofty, much more mundane, palpably material and singularly invidious force, namely the universalist urge of capital."[42]

Faced with reductive arguments of this sort, it is tempting to deny that any connection exists. This is the strategy pursued by Ellen Meiksins

Wood, who writes of such criticisms: "We are being invited to jettison
all that is best in the Enlightenment project—especially its commitment
to a universal human emancipation—and to blame these values for destructive effects we should be ascribing to capitalism."[43] I agree with
Wood that we need to indict capitalism for the threats with which humanity is currently faced, but this should not involve pretending that the
Enlightenment has nothing to do with capitalist development—a position that seems to fear the former will be tainted by association with the
latter. But we must surely take a different attitude to historical capitalism
in the epoch of its ascendancy over feudalism than we do to capitalism
today: then, the system was relatively progressive; now, it is absolutely reactionary. The question surely is: which elements of the Enlightenment
were particular to the economic and social conditions from which it initially emerged, and which are genuinely universal and consequently capable of being turned to different purposes?

Wood argues the case for separating the Enlightenment and capitalism in several moves. First, she identifies Enlightenment thought with
that of France. Second, she argues that many aspects of the French Enlightenment "belong to a social form that is not just a transitional point
on the way to capitalism but an alternative route out of feudalism." The
absolutist form of the French state was a distinct mode of production, in
other words. Third, Enlightenment demands were consequently neither
connected with capitalism nor directed against feudalism, but had to do
with the particular exclusions exercised by the aristocracy: "Their quarrel
with the aristocracy had little to do with liberating capitalism from the
fetters of feudalism." The universalism of the French bourgeoisie was directed against "aristocratic particularism." Fourth, this was capable of being
generalized into a much wider attack on tradition, from any quarter: "The
point is that in this particular historical conjuncture, in distinctly non-
capitalist conditions, even bourgeois class ideology took the form of a
larger vision of general human emancipation, not just emancipation for
the bourgeoisie." Fifth, she contrasts France with England, which she sees
as the geographical home of precisely the type of capitalist rationality for
which French Enlightenment thought is unjustly blamed, and effectively
denies that English thought in this period belongs to the Enlightenment
tradition at all: "The characteristic ideology that set England apart from
other European cultures was above all the ideology of 'improvement': not

the Enlightenment idea of the improvement of *humanity* but the improvement of *property*."[44] Wood effectively endorses the self-image of the bourgeoisie in its revolutionary phase, forgetting that its advocacy of universal social and political rights ignored precisely the economic inequalities that limited their effectiveness. Absolutism was not a separate, noncapitalist mode of production but simply the most developed form of the feudal state—a fact of which the French bourgeoisie were keenly aware.

The fixation on France is conventional. Robert Darnton, for example, writes: "[The Enlightenment] was a concrete historical phenomenon, which can be located in time and pinned down in space: Paris in the early eighteenth century."[45] Yet the English Enlightenment (which cannot in any event be reduced to an ideology of agricultural improvement) preceded the French and was the major influence on the very French thinkers whom Wood regards as completely distinct.[46] The difficulties with equating the Enlightenment with France or even Paris can be seen most clearly, however, if we examine one of the British nations Wood unaccountably fails to mention, no doubt because it sits uncomfortably with her thesis. Franco Venturi contrasts England with Scotland, to the advantage of the latter: "It is tempting to observe that the Enlightenment was born and organized in those places where the contrast between a backward world and a modern one was chronologically more abrupt, and geographically closer."[47] More specifically, as Alasdair MacIntyre notes: "The French themselves often avowedly looked to English models, but England in turn was overshadowed by the achievements of the Scottish Enlightenment. The greatest figures of all were certainly German: Kant and Mozart. But for intellectual variety as well as intellectual range not even the Germans can outmatch David Hume, Adam Smith, Adam Ferguson, John Millar, Lord Kames and Lord Monboddo."[48] Scotland surely has as much claim to be the center of the European Enlightenment as France, Edinburgh to be recognized as its capital as much as Paris. Yet the Scottish bourgeoisie were not faced with an absolutist state. On the contrary, they were faced with what was probably the most classically military-feudal society in Western Europe. Their Enlightenment was an attempt both to understand the socioeconomic changes that were taking place as a result of the transition to capitalism, and to consciously apply that understanding in order to hasten the process to a conclusion. It is no accident that the collective high point of Enlightenment thought emerged there after 1746, as the ideology of an intellectual vanguard intent on imposing a revolution from above against the remains of feudalism. *The Wealth of Nations* barely mentions the nation in which it was written, yet the entire work is concerned with the problem of how nations like Scotland could progress out of backwardness and attain the level of development already achieved by England.[49]

As this suggests, the Enlightenment was both a product of capitalist development and a contributor to its further expansion. Mikulas Teich describes it as following the Renaissance and the Reformation as third in a series of "historically demarcated sequences" encompassed by "the long-drawn-out transition from feudalism to capitalism." The transition displayed marked geographical and temporal unevenness between initiation and completion across or even within the nations, but each of these cultural and ideological sequences tended to manifest themselves simultaneously, or after only brief delays, on the international scene. As a result, their class content and social meaning differed depending on whether the nation in question was nearer to the beginning or the end of the process: "The promoters of the Enlightenment were socially a heterogeneous group, and from that point of view, the Enlightenment was a mixed 'aristocratic-bourgeois' movement. Insofar as it is possible to ascribe to it a common program it was reformist. Insofar as it was undermining the reigning feudal order it was revolutionary."[50]

Albert Hirschman has demonstrated that many of the arguments used in favor of capitalism by Enlightenment thinkers in Scotland and France were based not on admiration of capitalism itself but on the political and social benefits that economic development would supposedly bring. David Hume wrote, in his 1752 essay "Of Interest," that "it is an infallible consequence of all industrious professions, to beget frugality, and make the love of gain prevail over the love of pleasure."[51] Hirschman cites this passage as the "culmination" of early Enlightenment thought in this respect, because "capitalism is here hailed by a leading philosopher of the age because it would activate some benign human proclivities at the expense of some malignant ones—because of the expectation that, in this way, it would repress and perhaps atrophy the more destructive and disastrous components of human nature." And what were these aspects of human nature? "Ever since the end of the Middle Ages, and particularly as a result of the increasing frequency of war and civil war in the seventeenth and eighteenth centuries, the search was on . . . for new rules of conduct and devices that would impose much needed discipline and constraints on both rulers and ruled, and the expansion of commerce and industry was thought to hold much promise in this regard."

Drawing on the work of Montesquieu in France and Sir James Steuart in Scotland, Hirschman shows that "the diffusion of capitalist forms" was not, as Max Weber had claimed, the consequence of the desperate Calvinist *"search for individual salvation"* but of "the equally desperate search for a way of avoiding society's ruin, permanently threatening at the time because of precarious arrangements for internal and external order." The effects of capitalism were anything but peaceful and conducive to order, however, and the arguments raised at the time have been "not only forgotten but actively repressed." For Hirschman, this is necessary for the legitimacy of the capitalist order, since the "social order" "was adopted with the firm expectation that it would solve certain problems and that it clearly and abysmally fails to do so."[52]

Jürgen Habermas once argued that the "incompleteness" of the Enlightenment was part of the broader incompleteness of modernity as a whole.[53] The historian Louis Dupré has similarly written: "The Enlightenment remained a project; it never became a full achievement."[54] But this raises the question of what "completion" would involve. From the middle decades of the nineteenth century, those who claim to support the Enlightenment project have held two opposing positions in relation to its social goals. One is that, to the extent that it is possible for them to be accomplished at all, this has been done in the heartlands of capitalism and now needs to be extended to those parts of the world still languishing in premodernity. The other is that capitalism is only one of two possible forms of modernity, that Enlightenment social goals will only ever be partially attained under capitalist society, and that it will require the other, socialism, for them to be realized in full.[55]

The triumphant system had to suppress the radicalism of the Enlightenment, or at least transfer it from the social to the natural world. The reaction was sharpest in the places where capitalism was most fully established. In England, for example, the Royal Society was established in 1660—that is, in the year of the Restoration and the beginning of the conservative reaction to English Revolution—under the patronage of Charles II. According to Christopher Hill: "Monarchy was restored to preside over the rule of gentlemen and merchant oligarchies, the Royal

Society was established to check the advance of mechanic atheism." Accordingly, "the universe of correspondences and analogies" was replaced by "the abstract, empty, unfriendly mathematical universe of the Newtonians." Nor was it completely rational: "Fellows of the Royal Society came to the rescue of the irrational . . . in defending the existence of spirits and witches they were defending the existence of God."[56] Margaret Jacob describes how this version of rationality eventually encouraged suspicion of Enlightenment itself:

> Once we perceive the social and political meaning of Newtonian science and natural religion, a meaning rooted in the experience of the first of the great modern revolutions and in the rejection of republican and democratic forms of government, we can see why European radicals from the English Commonwealthmen of the 1690s through their Continental followers down to, in an attenuated sense, Blake and Coleridge, rejected the Newtonian understanding of nature. . . . In historical and ideological terms, Blake had understandable reasons for seeing Newton as one powerful symbol of a social and cosmic order from which he was alienated, a system "with cogs tyrannic." For Blake, with his unique vision, Newtonians were the true "materialists" in that they subjected people to the rule of an impersonal and mechanized nature divorced from the human order.

Jacob describes Newtonianism as "a vast holding operation against a far more dangerous rendering of Enlightenment ideals."[57]

Daniel Gordon is therefore correct to write that there was a general tension within "much Enlightenment thought" and it "was designed not merely to convince people to regard commercial society as the best regime, but also to dramatize the personal qualities of courage, patriotism, and refinement that one should cultivate in opposition to the very same regime." In this "double-edged mentality . . . we should see the dialectic as a process internal to the Enlightenment—a process in which a certain degree of historical optimism immediately produced doubts about the completeness of the society desired."[58] It was nevertheless in England that the tensions within the Enlightenment continued to be played out most closely. Toward the end of the eighteenth century Thomas Malthus attempted to place the argument against radicalism on a naturalistic footing, rather than the voluntaristic one to which earlier reactionaries like

Burke had adhered. Malthus argued that while human population growth took place geometrically, the food supply grew only arithmetically, a condition that would inevitably lead to the detriment of the poor. Defense of this doctrine led him to attack Smith, who had argued that accumulation led to an increase in wage goods and hence to a rise in the living standards of laborers. According to Malthus, however, only agriculture expanded the food supply, and accumulation that drew laborers away from the land to work in manufacturing would only exacerbate the problem. His conclusion was ultimately that the little protection afforded the poor by the poor laws should be abolished, so as to let the market work and prevent—or at least make them suffer the consequences of—thoughtless breeding.[59] Porter notes that this is the "most striking instance of the retreat into reaction" at the end of the eighteenth century. According to Malthus: "The program of boundless progress was intrinsically self-defeating—knowledge would produce growth, growth would increase wealth, wealth would then fuel a population explosion . . . The real obstacle was not the vices of the politicians but the nature of things." As Porter also notes, however, two of the first people to attempt to refute Malthus were doctors who "did so on the basis of enlightened reasoning." Both were Dissenters. One was Charles Hall, who wrote in an anti-Malthusian appendix to his The Effects of Civilization on the Peoples of the European States (1805) that the problem was not in nature but in a society based on "an exploitative economic order": "Politics played the major part: rulers created the problem and then blamed Nature." The other was Thomas Jarrold, whose reply to Malthus, Dissertations on Man, Philosophical, Physiological and Political (1806), claimed that "because 'man is not a mere animal,' fertility [is] not a biological constant but a social variable." Porter comments:

> Hall and Jarrold equally refuted Malthus, but from diametrically opposite directions. For Hall, hunger and poverty were the progeny not of Nature but of capitalism; for Jarrold, much as for Erasmus Darwin, modern capitalist society offered the escape from those Malthusian dilemmas. Hall believed, like [William] Godwin, that political action would eradicate poverty; Jarrold, that any overpopulation threat would wither away with growing prosperity. Both accused Malthus of a fatalism that followed from fathering on Nature arrangements which were essentially manmade, historical and political. Against Malthus's degrading vision—

man as a slave to sexual appetites—both Hall and Jarrold defended divine design and human dignity. And both looked forward to better things—"the period is hastening when the condition of mankind will be far better than it now is," Jarrold concluded; "already I fancy I have seen the first dawning of this wished-for morning." Both thus reaffirmed enlightened optimism.[60]

In the "Manifesto of the Communist Party" Marx and Engels summarized the role of the Enlightenment in the bourgeois revolution: "When Christian ideas succumbed in the eighteenth century to rationalist ideas, feudal society fought its death battle with the then revolutionary bourgeoisie." Capitalism needed to free the power of rational thought, but reason is not the possession of a single class, and once it became apparent that human beings had the power to transform their world along capitalist lines, the question inevitably arose of a further transformation. "The weapons with which the bourgeoisie felled feudalism to the ground are now turned against the bourgeoisie itself."[61] Realizing this, the bourgeoisie were concerned to limit the application of Enlightenment doctrines, particularly by claiming that it was simply a mistake, a dangerous illusion, to imagine that there could be anything beyond capital. "It was henceforth no longer a question whether this or that theorem was true, but whether it was useful to capital or harmful, expedient or inexpedient, in accordance with police regulations or contrary to them."[62] The working class and the oppressed would therefore have to maintain the traditions that the bourgeoisie had abandoned; but if they inherited a material interest in transforming the world that the bourgeoisie no longer had, they also inherited from the Enlightenment the power of reason as a means of effecting that transformation. "One of the most moving narratives in modern history," writes Eagleton, "is the story of how men and women languishing under various forms of oppression came to acquire, often at great personal cost, the sort of technical knowledge necessary for them to understand their condition more deeply, and so acquire some of the theoretical armory essential to change it." And, as he suggests, we retrospectively insult the memory of these people if we dismiss their struggle for knowledge as collusion with their own oppression.[63]

In Britain, the Enlightenment began to sink popular roots at the moment at which the small producers, artisans, day laborers, and minor state officials who had formed the democratic movement were beginning to be transformed into a working class. Edward Thompson has given us an evocative picture of the radical culture during the first decades of the nineteenth century, when the Enlightenment was beginning to become part of history: "A shoemaker, who had been taught his letters in the Old Testament, would labour through [Tom Paine's] *Age of Reason*; a schoolmaster, whose education had taken him little further than worthy religious homilies, would attempt Voltaire, Gibbon, Ricardo; here and there local Radical leaders, weavers, booksellers, tailors, would amass shelves of Radical periodicals and learn how to use parliamentary Blue Books; illiterate laborers would, nevertheless, go each week to a pub where Cobbett's editorial letter was read aloud and discussed."[64] Paine was a central figure in the literature of the popular Enlightenment. Between 1791 and 1793, the various editions of his earlier work, *Rights of Man*, may have sold as many as two hundred thousand copies in England, Wales, and Scotland: "Paine's book was found in Cornish tin-mines, in Mendip villages, in the Scottish Highlands, and, a little later, in most parts of Ireland."[65] Paine himself estimated, with his usual lack of modesty, that within ten years of the publication of part 1 in 1790, as many as five hundred thousand copies had been sold. Assuming that this is near the truth, and that four million British citizens were literate, nearly one reader in ten must have bought the book, and this does not account for the others who read it in pirated or serialized editions, or the illiterate who had it read aloud to them. As his most recent biographer notes, these figures made *The Rights of Man* "the most widely read book of all time in any language," selling proportionally more copies than the publishing sensation of the next generation, Sir Walter Scott.[66] As Thompson points out, Paine conducts his attack on the Bible "in language which the collier or country girl could understand": "When we consider the barbaric and evil superstitions which the churches and Sunday schools were inculcating at this time, we can see the profoundly liberating effect which Paine's writing had on many minds. It helped men to struggle free from a pall of religious deference which reinforced the deference due to magistrate and employer, and it launched many nineteenth-century artisans upon a course of sturdy intellectual self-reliance and inquiry."

But as Thompson also notes, "the limitations of Paine's 'reason' must also be remembered: there was a glibness and lack of imagination about it that remind one of Blake's strictures on the 'single vision.'"[67] We will return to this point in the next part of this chapter, since it points toward one reason for the more widespread left-wing suspicion of Enlightenment reason that was to emerge during the twentieth century. But in the early nineteenth century these suspicions were only held by relatively marginal figures like Blake. In Robert Burns's "A Man's a Man for a'That" (1795), it is "the man o' independent mind" who "looks and laughs" at the pretensions of the aristocracy.[68] In his poem "To Toussaint L'Ouverture" (1803), William Wordsworth wrote of the leader of the slave revolution in San Domingo that among his "great allies" was "man's unconquerable mind."[69] And these views were carried over into the working-class movement proper. The words of "L'Internationale" (1870) by the French socialist Eugène Pottier invoke "reason in revolt" and enjoin the "servile masses" to dispense "with all your superstitions." From his Fascist prison in the early 1930s, Antonio Gramsci recalled how in his youth he had been united with one of his non-Marxist lecturers, Umberto Cosmo, to promote the antireligious program of Benedetto Croce: "This point still seems to me today to be the major contribution to world culture of the modern Italian intellectuals, and it seems to me, furthermore, a conquest in the social political sphere which must not be lost."[70]

Socialists remained interested in the writings of the philosophes. During the 1870s Engels advised German socialists to "organize the mass distribution among the workers of the splendid French materialist literature of the last century," of which he said that "even today [it] stands exceedingly high as regards style, and still unparalleled as regards content."[71] Thirty years later Lenin thought this advice was still applicable in Russia as part of the struggle against the influence of religion over the working class.[72] Engels wrote: "The German working-class movement is the heir of German classical philosophy."[73] More generally, Lenin described Marxism as "the legitimate successor to the best that man produced in the nineteenth century, as represented by German philosophy, English [sic] political economy and French socialism."[74] Shortly after the Russian Revolution, Trotsky summarized the view of three generations of Marxists: "[Marxist] theory was formed entirely on the basis of bourgeois culture, both scientific and political, though it declared a fight to the finish upon that culture. Under the pressure of capitalist contradictions, the universalizing thought of the bourgeois democracy, of its boldest, most honest, and most far-sighted representatives, rises to the heights of a marvelous renunciation, armed with all the critical weapons of bourgeois science."[75]

Stuart Macintyre notes of the British socialist autodidacts of the period before the First World War that "they brooked no shortcuts in the search for knowledge" but often followed the great Enlightenment thinkers to Marxism: "Thus an original interest in the doctrine of creation could lead from the *Freethinker* to Darwin or Huxley, and thence to Haeckel's *Riddle of the Universe*, Morgan's *Ancient Society* and sometimes Engels's *Origin of the Family, Private Property and the State*; or an interest in history might commence with Gibbon, Macaulay, Lecky or Buckle and subsequently assume an increasingly sharp focus on the basis of the current social order, thus leading to Marx's historical writings."[76] T. A. Jackson, who eventually became one of the leaders of the Communist Party of Great Britain, recounted in his autobiography how he had been introduced to the Enlightenment philosophical tradition by coming across George Henry Lewes's *Biographical History of Philosophy*: "Lewes . . . led me to really study Bacon, Hobbes, and Locke, and better still, the mighty 'god-intoxicated' 'Master Atheist' Spinoza, and thereafter, Old Man Hegel and ultimately, and in consequence, Marx."[77] Duncan Hallas, a member of the second generation of British Trotskyists, concluded a selection of his favorite books with Voltaire's *Candide*, "the best pre-Marxian critique of society that I have ever read or re-read."[78]

The connection between scientific rationality and Marxism was perhaps best expressed by Engels's famous funeral oration at Marx's graveside, where he compared his friend's discoveries in relation to "human history" to those of Darwin in relation to "organic nature." The theme was picked up in an extraordinary speech by the German socialist leader Wilhelm Liebknecht:

> Science is the liberator of humanity. The *natural* sciences free us from *God*. But God in heaven still lives on although science has killed him. The science of *society* that Marx revealed to the people kills capitalism, and with it the idols and masters of the *earth* who will not let God die as long as they live. Science is not *German*. It knows no barriers, and least of all the barriers of nationality. It was therefore natural that the creator of *Capital* should also become the creator of the *International Working Men's Association*. The basis of science, which we owe to Marx, puts us in a position to resist all attacks of the enemy and to continue with ever-increasing strength the fight which we have undertaken.[79]

The importance of Darwin was immense, not only in Britain but even more so in Continental Europe, where the Catholic Church still dominated intellectual life.[80]

We should not exaggerate the extent of interest in Enlightenment thought. One survey, by an intelligent conservative, contrasts the nineteenth-century thirst for knowledge with today: "They wanted to read the best that had been thought and written. By the time the Great Reform Bill was passed in 1832, the mechanics' institutes, the working men's schools and the mutual improvement societies were to be found in almost every district. In Carlisle, at least 24 reading rooms were founded between 1836 and 1854 with a total of almost 1,400 members and 4,000 volumes."[81] Nevertheless, workers were as interested in popular entertainment between the world wars as they are today. Even in the Welsh valleys, legendary as the home of miners' libraries, "the intellectual climate could vary dramatically from mineshaft to mineshaft: as one collier explained, 'The conveyor face down the Number 2 Pit was a university,' where Darwin, Marx, Paine and modernist theology were debated, while 'the surface of Number 1 Pit was a den of grossness.'"[82] Similar contrasts could be found in Central Europe. As Norman Stone reports, "of books taken out of the Favoriten district headquarters of Vienna socialism, eighty-three per cent came under the heading *Belletristik*—i.e., 'penny dreadfuls'—and ... the pages of the heavier academic works were usually uncut after the first few," even those by leading theoreticians like Kautsky. "Did this mean that the working class were not as class-conscious as their leaders expected them to be," asks Stone, "or did it mean only that Kautsky was a crashing bore?"[83]

These traditions of popular Enlightenment thought are still alive. The American journalist Barbara Ehrenreich has recently recalled her parents in these terms:

> My family was originally blue-collar poor, but intensely committed to rationality, in a very positivistic and what I see now as a limited way. But they were militant about these things. And I came to respect this rationality as part of what gave them some dignity as against the bosses. . . . I always thought about rationality not that it was something the oppressor had and my people didn't have but that it was something you were more likely to encounter among the oppressed than among those who were busily trying to justify their position in society, regardless of truth.[84]

There are still attempts by liberals and Social Democrats to restore the sundered whole of the original Enlightenment. Gareth Stedman Jones, for example, has argued:"Contemporary social democracy should . . . revisit its original birthplace and resume the ambition of the late and democratic Enlightenment to combine the benefits of individual freedom and commercial society with the republican ideal of greater equality, inclusive citizenship and the public good."[85] This is literally utopian: we cannot return to the world of 1776 or 1789. For Marx, political emancipation was progress:"It may not be the last form of general human emancipation, but it is the last form of general human emancipation *within* the prevailing scheme of things."[86] But it was not the same as human emancipation."We know today that this idealized realm of reason was nothing more than the idealized realm of the bourgeoisie," wrote Engels in 1880:"The great thinkers of the eighteenth century could, no more than their predecessors, go beyond the limits imposed upon them by their epoch."[87] To be of their epoch was both their tragedy and the source of their greatness.

THE CONTEMPORARY DEBATE

The current debate over the Enlightenment is not concerned, however, with tragedy or contradiction, but is polarized between condemnation and appropriation. Let us return to the three positions that currently dominate discussion.

The religious revival

I wrote earlier that the issue of predestination was no longer at the heart of our contemporary concerns, but there are certainly people in the Anglo-Saxon world—currently sponsoring city academies in England and running school boards in the US—who would like to see it restored to that position. How seriously should we take this threat? Let us take one recent assessment from an impeccably establishment source, Lord May of Oxford, who has at various times been a professor of zoology at Imperial College, the Chief Scientific Adviser to the UK government, and the head of the Office of Science and Technology; he is currently a member of the House of Lords. He is not, in other words, someone who can be easily suspected of secretly plotting the downfall of Western civilization.

In an address to mark the end of his presidency of the Royal Society, May illustrated the danger of what he called "the darkness of fundamentalist unreason" by highlighting three "global" problems: "climate change, the loss of biological diversity, [and] new and re-emerging diseases." Scientists were attempting to find solutions to these, May said, but in each case were facing impediments from "campaigns waged by those whose belief systems or commercial interests impel them to deny, or even misrepresent, the scientific facts." Attempts to stop the spread of HIV/AIDS in Africa, for example, were being undermined by opposition to strategies based on condom use coming from the Catholic Church on the one hand, and by the US government, under pressure from fundamentalist Protestantism, on the other. May concluded: "The Enlightenment's core values . . . free, open, unprejudiced, uninhibited questioning and enquiry; individual liberty; separation of church and state . . . are under serious threat from resurgent fundamentalism, West and East."[88]

In the West, it is in the United States that the threat has assumed the most menacing proportions. Given the attention paid to the supposed irrationality of Islam, it is worth emphasizing the extent to which the US is also increasingly home to pre-Enlightenment views, with millions of Americans cleaving to precisely the type of religiosity that the Enlightenment sought to challenge. One survey found that 80 percent of Americans believe in an afterlife of some sort; 76 percent believe in heaven (and 64 percent that they will go there); 71 percent believe in hell, and while very few believe that *they* will go there, 32 percent believe that it is "an actual place of torment and suffering"; 18 percent believe in reincarnation, including 10 percent of born-again Christians, which suggests an uncertain grasp of their own belief system.[89] The challenge posed to the theory of evolution by creationism is often taken as emblematic of the fundamentalist challenge to the Enlightenment as a whole. For example, among the exhibits at the recently opened Museum of Earth History in Eureka Springs, Arkansas, is one showing Adam and Eve together with *Tyrannosaurus rex* and other dinosaurs in the Garden of Eden. Since, according to the Book of Genesis, God created all creatures that currently live or have ever lived on earth at the same time, dinosaurs must therefore have coexisted with humans. Given the premise, the logic is irrefutable. Nor are these views restricted to inhabitants of the Ozark Mountains; George W. Bush himself has declared: "The jury is still out on evolution."[90] As John Gray has pointed out, "nowhere else are there movements to expel Darwinism from public schools. In truth, the US is a less secular regime than Turkey."[91]

Marx and Engels both identified a central paradox of American culture as being that it was simultaneously the most purely bourgeois and the most in thrall to religiosity. Mike Davis once argued that the explanation lay in the absence of feudalism and the accompanying state church, which meant that the advent of liberal capitalism did not require an anticlerical "cultural revolution" of the sort that characterized the French experience.[92] This may explain the origins of American religiosity, but surely not its continued existence. Studies of religious belief conducted in the early 1990s suggested that 96 percent of Americans believed in God (although only 59 percent attended church services at least once a month). In the industrialized world, only Poland, with 97 percent (85 percent attendance), and Ireland, with 98 percent (88 percent attendance), registered higher.[93]

The explanation for this may lie in the way in which America has always had the most unrestrained form of capitalism, and the American people have been the least protected by collective provision. The relatively brief period of welfare capitalism (roughly between the 1930s and the 1970s) was followed by a ferocious reversion to a situation where families and communities were ripped apart by exposure to naked market relations. The psychic wounds caused to individuals by such devastation invite the healing touch of faith. As Ehrenreich writes of the middle-class job seekers she studied firsthand, certain kinds of religion not only cure alienated souls, they complement the individualist philosophy that wounded them in the first place. "If you can achieve anything through your own mental efforts—just by praying or concentrating hard enough—there is no need to confront the social and economic forces shaping your life."[94] Theodor Adorno once put the point in more theoretical terms, referring specifically to beliefs in astrology: "People even of supposedly 'normal' mind are prepared to accept systems of delusions for the simple reason that it is too difficult to distinguish such systems from the equally inexorable and equally opaque one under which they actually have to live their lives.[95]

The neoliberal onslaught experienced by the Americans is now the form of capitalism that is being exported everywhere. A recent survey of the rise of religious fundamentalism noted that modernity, "the very force that was once expected to render religion obsolete," was "in fact causing it to mutate and gather strength." The University of Helsinki estimates that two million Chinese every year are converting to evangelical Christianity, and that the number of new converts may reach three hundred million—a fifth of the current population.[96] However, it is not "modernity" as such that has produced these effects, but the specific form taken by *capitalist* modernity in its current multinational incarnation. "The combination of . . . two dimensions—socioeconomic anomie together with political and ideological anomie—has inevitably led people to fall back on other factors of social solidarity such as religion, family, and fatherland."[97] There is, however, an important difference between resurgent religion in the US and religion in the developing world. The fundamentalism of, for example, Iranian president Mahmoud Ahmadinejad contributes to the oppression of Iranians; the fundamentalism of US president George W. Bush contributes to the oppression not only of Americans but of peoples across the world. They may be equal in the irrationality of their views, but not in the extent of their powers.

In any case, is the religious revival the real source of threat to the Enlightenment? Attempts by the school board of Dover in Pennsylvania to introduce the teaching of intelligent design on an equal footing with Darwinism were opposed by parents, and the judge who heard the case declared the attempt to be unconstitutional.[98] May is surely right to identify the use of religious doctrine by the Catholic Church and the US State Department to exercise control of sexual and reproductive behavior as a greater threat to human well-being than personal belief in these doctrines. But as he also notes, this is not the only use to which fundamentalism is put:

> In the US, the aim of a growing network of fundamentalist foundations and lobby groups reaches well beyond "equal time" for creationism, or its disguised variant "intelligent design," in the science classroom. Rather, the ultimate aim is the overthrow of "scientific materialism," in all its manifestations. One major planning document from that movement's Discovery Institute tells us that "Design theory promises to reverse the stifling dominance of the materialist world view, and to replace it with a science consonant with Christian and theistic convictions." George Gilder, a senior fellow at the Discovery Institute, has indicated that this

new faith-based science will rid us of the "chimeras of popular science," which turn out to be ideas such as global warming, pollution problems, and ozone depletion.[99]

The Gilder to whom May refers is a free-market fanatic and one-time dot-com investment tipster who wrote: "It is the entrepreneurs who know the rules of the world and the laws of God."[100] The rejection of scientific materialism is a means of waging ideological war on any suggestion that there might be physical constraints on the unlimited expansion of capital. Indeed, many of the more conventionally religious believers show greater concern with the environmental crisis than the likes of Gilder. As *The Economist* reports: "A noisy movement among evangelical Christians, led by Billy Graham, argues that God has given man 'stewardship' of the earth; and thus it is man's responsibility to act on climate change."[101]

There are therefore two issues. One is the manipulation of religious beliefs on the behalf of factions within the ruling class. The other is the existence of these beliefs in the first place. The second is the more fundamental problem, but how to deal with it? One typical approach is that of Richard Dawkins, in a television series in which he attacked all religions for, among other things, their irrationality, refusal of scientific evidence, and encouragement of intolerance, and for conducting what he termed "child abuse" by deliberately subjecting young minds to beliefs that darken their world view at an impressionable age.[102] But Dawkins shows no understanding of (or interest in) why people might be predisposed to believe such things in the first place. Enlightenment thought on organized religion, which Dawkins essentially reproduces, assumes that it continues to exist because the majority of people are incapable of resisting indoctrination by their priests, presbyters, rabbis, or imams. Repeating Voltaire's splendid antireligious slogan from the eighteenth century, *écrasez l'infâme!* ("crush the infamy!"), may be invigorating, but it is also inadequate.

Some of the New Defenders of the Enlightenment come close to recognizing the problem, like Francis Wheen:

> The new irrationalism is an expression of despair by people who feel impotent to improve their lives and suspect that they are at the mercy of secretive, impersonal forces, whether these be the Pentagon or invaders from Mars. Political leaders accept it as a safe outlet for dissent, fulfilling much the same function that Marx attributed to religion—

the heart of a heartless world, the opium of the people. Far better for the powerless to seek solace in crystals, ley-lines and the myth of Abraham than in actually challenging the rulers, or the social and economic system over which they preside.[103]

Readers of Wheen's book *How Mumbo-Jumbo Conquered the World* will know that greater insight into the problem does not seem to have produced any greater awareness of the solution. Adherents of any religion are, however, unlikely to respond positively to a critique that casts doubt on their intelligence and ridicules their beliefs. Post-Enlightenment thinkers, notably Marx and Freud, who saw themselves as building on what the Enlightenment had achieved, sought to explain the social and psychological needs that make people require religion, and therefore they suggest alternative courses of action rather than simply denouncing believers for their irrationality. Thus, Marx famously wrote: "The criticism of religion is therefore in *embryo the criticism of that vale of tears* of which religion is the *halo*."[104] The implications were later independently drawn by Freud: "It is certainly senseless to begin by trying to do away with religion by force and at a single blow. . . . The believer will not let his belief be torn from him, either by arguments or prohibitions. And even if this did succeed with some it would be cruelty. A man who has been taking sleeping drafts for tens of years is naturally unable to sleep if his sleeping draft is taken away from him."[105]

Dawkins himself inadvertently provides an example of the very approach Freud is criticizing: "Michael Shermer, editor of *Skeptic* magazine, tells a salutary story of an occasion when he publicly debunked a famous television spiritualist. The man was doing ordinary conjuring tricks and duping people into thinking he was communicating with dead spirits. But instead of being hostile to the now-unmasked charlatan, the audience turned on the debunker and supported a woman who accused him of 'inappropriate' behavior because he destroyed people's illusions." Dawkins, for whom the human race has always been something of a disappointment, complains: "You'd think she'd have been grateful for having the wool pulled *off* her eyes, but apparently she preferred it firmly over them."[106] Dawkins's approach is simply unable to convince anyone not already predisposed to believe what he is saying.[107] Reading such endless bombast about "irrationality" brings to mind the extremely sensible advice given by Lenin to the Bolsheviks during the Russian Revolution of 1905, at a time when many Russian workers were under the influence of religion:

> Under no circumstances ought we to fall into the error of posing the religious question in an abstract, idealistic fashion, as an "intellectual" question unconnected with the class struggle, as is not infrequently done by the radical-democrats from among the bourgeoisie. It would be stupid to think that, in a society based on the endless oppression and coarsening of the worker masses, religious prejudices could be dispelled by purely propaganda methods. It would be bourgeois narrow-mindedness to forget that the yoke of religion that weighs upon mankind is merely a product and reflection of the economic yoke within society. No number of pamphlets and no amount of preaching can enlighten the proletariat, if it is not enlightened by its own struggle against the dark forces of capitalism. Unity in this really revolutionary struggle of the oppressed class for the creation of a paradise on earth is more important to us than unity of proletarian opinion on paradise in heaven.[108]

However, rather than leave the argument with a quote, excellent though it is, here is an example of the process of "enlightenment by struggle" to which Lenin refers, recounted by the Chilean writer Ariel Dorfman.

As a young student in the late 1960s trying to help the poor and migrant workers, Dorfman was involved in a "crusade against the industrial products of fiction" such as "comics, soap opera, westerns, radio and TV sitcoms, love songs, films of violence." One woman, a consumer of romantic fictions, approached him while he was digging a ditch in a local shantytown and asked him "if it was true that [he] thought people shouldn't read photo novels." He answered that he "thought that photo novels were a hazard to her health and her future." "Don't do that to us, *compañerito*," she said in a familiar, almost tender way. "Don't take my dreams away from me." Several years later, Dorfman met the same woman again, at the time of the radicalization associated with Salvador Allende's government: "She came up to me, just like that, and announced that I was right, that she didn't read 'trash' anymore. Then she added a phrase which still haunts me. 'Now, *compañero*, we are dreaming reality.' . . . She had outdistanced her old self, and was no longer entertained by those images which had been her own true love."[109] That woman's aspirations for liberation came to an end in the "first September 11th" of the Chilean coup. But the lesson remains for those people who imagine that the way to convince others of the need to "dream reality" is to insult, bully, and hector them from a position of assumed superiority.

The new atheism

And it is to these people that I now want to turn. The task of holding aloft the banner of the Enlightenment has been appropriated by a rightward-moving section of the liberal left, typically based in the media rather than the academy. This campaign is not, of course, one waged only by a handful of newspaper columnists. The law to ban the wearing of the hijab in French schools and colleges was supported by many French teachers, much of the left, and even the Trotskyist organization Lutte Ouvrière. Nevertheless, it is among media commentators that arguments about the need to protect the secular heritage of the Enlightenment have gained the greatest currency. The most striking thing about these arguments is their lopsidedness. The main target is not, for example, the campaign to introduce creationism into the science curriculum of American schools, or the refusal by the US government to take global warming seriously. Rather, it is the supposed threat to Western civilization from Islamic fundamentalism. Especially since 9/11 the slogan of "defending the Enlightenment" has been raised to justify support for what Robert Fisk calls "the great war for civilization" abroad and the repression of the Muslim population at home.[110]

Christopher Hitchens, one of the most vociferous media supporters of the War on Terror, gave a series of interviews explaining why someone long associated with the left had now aligned himself so decisively with the neoconservative agenda for the Middle East. Hitchens told *Scotland on Sunday* that since 9/11, he had been possessed by a mission "to defend the Enlightenment, to defend and extend the benefits of rationalism. By all and any means necessary."[111] Hitchens argued in the immediate aftermath of the attacks on the US: "The bombers of Manhattan represent fascism with an Islamic face, and there's no point in any euphemism about it. What they abominate about 'the West,' to put it in a phrase, is not what Western liberals don't like and can't defend about their own system, but what they *do* like about it and must defend: its emancipated women, its scientific inquiry, its separation of religion from the state."[112] Iraq was not, of course, involved in 9/11. Nor, the occasional opportunistic genuflection in the direction of Mecca aside, had the Ba'athist regime been anything other than a secular modernizing dictatorship. No matter, it too was an abomination to Enlightenment values and could be included under the general heading of "fascism," a term that has no scientific value in this context but is extremely useful for dragooning the liberal left behind the imperial war effort—for who could possibly argue against what Hitchens called "the forces of reaction"?[113]

For former left supporters of the War on Terror, the threat to the Enlightenment is not only from Islamic or Arabic "fascism" but from a left that has supposedly capitulated to it. According to Nick Cohen, one of the British-based B52 liberals: "For the first time since the Enlightenment, a section of the left is allied with religious fanaticism, and for the first time since the Hitler-Stalin pact, a section of the left has gone soft on fascism."[114] Why has the left behaved in this way? Because "when confronted with a movement of contemporary imperialism—Islamism wants an empire from the Philippines to Gibraltar—and which is tyrannical, homophobic, misogynist, racist and homicidal to boot, they feel it is valid because it is against Western culture."[115] The Ottoman Caliphate was, in fact, considerably more tolerant than many contemporary Christian kingdoms or empires.[116] A more important point, however, is the sheer sense of unreality that surrounds these claims. An empire is certainly being constructed "from the Philippines to Gibraltar," not by Muslims but by the very American state whose military apparatus Cohen is constantly exhorting to invade still more countries. Against this reality, one is tempted to quote a great passage from one of the founders of modern conservatism, Edmund Burke: "You are terrifying yourself with ghosts and apparitions, whilst your house is the haunt of robbers."[117]

And it is not only Islam abroad that is the subject of such hysteria. During the crisis caused by the publication of cartoons portraying the prophet Mohammed in the Danish newspaper *Jyllands-Posten*, several liberal commentators claimed the Muslim response showed that the difference between the West and the Islamic world was, in the words of Joan Smith, "between pre- and post-Enlightenment notions about the place of religion."[118] For some writers, the problem has been that the West has been insufficiently assertive of Enlightenment values in response to Islamic protests. Thus, Andrew Anthony has criticized the British media for failing to reproduce these "dramatically newsworthy cartoons" and thus supposedly failing to maintain the tradition of Paine, Shelley, and Hazlitt: "More than 200 years ago, in the age of reason, British writers offered up to the world the flame of liberty. Over the past two weeks, in the age of emotion, we appear to have found it too hot to handle."[119]

A more serious analysis was made by Fred Halliday, a former Marxist and an expert on international relations, who is worth quoting since he also supported the Great War for Civilization. Halliday made the obvious but sensible point that the majority of Muslims are not Islamists (his preferred term for Islamic fundamentalists). Internally: "The problem of 'Islam' in Western Europe is above all a problem of their Christian fellow citizens and of governments, not of any Muslim threat to the larger society: there are around 6 million Muslims in a Western Europe of over 250 millions." Externally: "'Islam' is not, in any serious sense, a threat to the West, militarily or economically: Islamic states have not been a military threat since the seventeenth century, and if there is an economic challenge today it comes from the Far, not the Middle East."[120]

Some supporters of the New Enlightenment realize that it is highly implausible to attack only Islamic fundamentalism without also attacking the Western variants. In one of the more readable and intelligent examples of the genre, Wheen begins by noting the coincidence of the return of Ayatollah Khomeini to Iran and the election of Margaret Thatcher as prime minister of Great Britain in the first half of 1979, both linked by their adherence to "two powerful messianic creeds": Islamic fundamentalism and neoliberalism. However, despite this apparent evenhandedness, Wheen comes down on the side of the US, as the Enlightenment's "most flourishing offshoot, the country damned by Islamists as the great Satan but exalted by Tom Paine as 'the cause of all mankind.'"[121] He does not even consider whether America's role in the world might have changed since the days of Lexington and Concord. And so it goes. Nick Cohen describes George W. Bush as "a Bible-bashing know-nothing whose strings were pulled by Big Pharma, Big Oil and the Big Guy in the Sky."[122] Might this have anything to do with his plans for US dominance of the Middle East? The issue simply vanishes from the diatribes against the left that follow. To Muslims no mercy; to the established order, endless indulgence. Hitchens correctly wrote in 1991 that "the real bridle on our tongues is imposed by everyday lying and jargon, sanctioned and promulgated at the highest levels of media and politics, and not by the awkward handful who imagine themselves revolutionaries."[123] This soon changed. In his entertaining demolition of some of the absurdities of political correctness, Robert Hughes was careful to balance his critique with attacks on what he calls "patriotic correctness"—indeed, one of his criticisms of PC is that it legitimates precisely the claims that conservatives make.[124] By 1994 even this was too much for Hitchens: "The fact is we need no instruction in the crimes of old-style nativist and prohibitionist censors. The pressing matter is the defense of free thinking from its false friends, not its traditional enemies."[125]

The philosopher Onora O'Neill has written that "contemporary liberal readings of the right to free speech often assume that we can safely accord the same freedoms of expression to the powerless and the powerful," and this is certainly the case for the writers quoted here.[126] Starting from an abstract, decontextualized idea of rationality, they claim to be attacking irrationality without fear or favor wherever they find it. It just so happens that the irrationality of the powerful tends to receive rather less attention than that of the powerless. The charge of irrationalism is so convenient, however, that the New Defenders have extended it from Muslims to other foes, notably in the environmental movement. Dick Taverne has come to the defense of genetically modified foods. After the usual chest beating (Taverne declares himself "a militant rationalist" and "a great admirer of the Enlightenment as a glorious period in human history"), we learn that alternative medicines and organic farming—and it is quite a cunning move to link the latter with the former, incidentally—represent "a deeply disturbing anti-Enlightenment reaction." Taverne claims that "there is a semi-religious streak in the green fundamentalists. When they say 'I don't give a damn about the evidence because I know I am trying to save the world,' then they are not a million miles from the creationists who say 'I don't give a damn about the evidence because it is written in the Bible.'"[127] Or again: "With its anti-science dogma, Greenpeace is in some ways our equivalent of the religious right in the US."[128] Taverne's pro-GM lobby group, the Association of Sense about Science, has received funding from, among others, Amersham Biosciences, GlaxoSmithKline, AstraZeneca, Pfizer, Oxford GlycoSciences, and the Association of the British Pharmaceutical Industry: one therefore suspects that something other than the dictates of pure reason may be at work here. As one of his supporters says: "Neither pressure groups nor companies are accountable or democratic, but at least companies face the discipline of the market."[129] Ah yes, the discipline of the market. Here we approach the issue that is really at stake—the notion that only the operation of the market can be truly described as rational. I will return to this issue in the third and final part of this chapter.

Why have so many one-time Marxists collapsed back into this highly selective version of the Enlightenment? Martin Kettle, for whom "the failure of socialism" is apparently the great lesson of the twentieth century, claims: "Too many haters of capitalism and the United States still cram everything into the frame of untruth and self-deception that says my enemy's enemy is still my friend because, even if he blows up my family on the tube, murders my colleagues on the bus or threatens to behead me for publishing a drawing, he is still at war with Bush, Blair and Berlusconi."[130] This is crude innuendo. Does Kettle actually know *anyone* who takes this position? It is a classic example of Stalinist tactics retained by repentant Stalinists. Behind it lies the heavy stench of defeat, of thwarted hopes and the rescaling of political ambitions to more modest proportions, of a world not transformed but at least made safe for *Guardian* columnists. To invoke the Enlightenment, with its great Promethean insistence that human beings can transform their world, in defense of this retreat is pitiable, and in some cases tragic. The talk is of rationality, but underneath lies the suggestion that human beings are prone to commit evil and therefore have to be controlled. But once you accept the notion of evil, there are certain consequences: "All the paraphernalia of the rule of law—of secure, enforceable individual rights, democratically based legislation, checks on power, independent judicial processes, the means of redressing injustice, the means of defending the polity and the community against attack, and so on—follow."[131] And antiterror laws, identity cards, Camp X-Ray, and the rest.

Postmodern relativism

There is one aspect of the argument of New Enlightenment liberals that carries some plausibility, and this is the attack on the absurdities of postmodernism. Halliday, one of the B52 liberals, is able to score points off the postmodernist left when he argues:

> If you are languishing in the jails of the Islamic guards in Iran, forced to wear medieval clothes on the streets of Tehran, being shot for your commitment to secularism in Egypt or Algeria, being driven from your home and possibly killed in Bombay or having your land stolen by people who claim it was given them by god, then it is little comfort as you protest in

the name of universal values to be told you are ethnocentric or not post-modernistically playful enough or that, sorry, after all, we cannot be sure that the rights you ask to be defended are properly founded.[132]

There can be few people on the left who do not oppose such things. But there is nevertheless sometimes a reluctance to come to the defense of the Enlightenment legacy, and in the words of a text with which Christian fundamentalists at any rate will be familiar: "If the trumpet give an uncertain sound, who shall prepare himself to the battle?"[133]

Until the middle decades of the twentieth century, virtually the only source of hostility to the Enlightenment, and to rationality more generally, was from the counterrevolutionary right; but there were some exceptions. Jonathan Swift was not a radical in any conventional left-wing sense.[134] Nevertheless, in his great satire *Gulliver's Travels*, some of the most lifeless and tedious creatures encountered by the hero are slaves to Reason:

> As these noble Houyhnhnms are endowed by Nature with a general disposition to all virtues, and have no conceptions or ideas of what is evil in a rational creature, their grand maxim is, to cultivate *Reason*, and to be wholly governed by it. . . . They have no fondness for their colts or foals, but the care they take in educating them proceedeth entirely from the dictates of *Reason*. . . . They will have it that Nature teaches them to love the whole species, and it is *Reason* only that maketh a distinction of persons, where there is a superior degree of virtue.[135]

Yet, as I noted in the previous section, there was a minority of radicals for whom reason itself was an oppressive power. As Roy Porter notes: "The Monochrome materialism of enlightened philosophy mirrored the sordid realties of capitalist oppression: industrialism, poverty, slavery, prostitution, war." The radical William Blake raged against Urizen ("your reason") in the figures of Bacon, Locke, and Newton, asking God to keep us "From Single vision and Newton's sleep."[136] On the socialist left, anarchists tended to be deeply suspicious of educated and technical experts, but not of the sciences and reason itself, something that is true even of Mikhail Bakunin or Jan Machajski, who was not an anarchist but developed very similar theories from within the Polish Marxist movement.[137] There were exceptions, but these tended to be on the intellectual margins. One was Georges Sorel, the French theorist of revolutionary syndicalism. According to Irving

Horowitz, Sorel was distinguished by his unwillingness "to grant the Enlightenment concept of progress its advanced function of restoring to human control the historical events which scholasticism attributed to providential edict." Indeed, he "remained convinced that Western European socialism retained the Enlightenment position on historical change because it was more concerned with reform than revolution."[138] Accordingly, he differed from most Marxists in two ways. First, he thought that the working class had to be inoculated against any aspect of bourgeois culture: "The proletariat must be preserved from the experience of the Germans who conquered the Roman Empire; the latter were ashamed of being barbarians and put themselves to school with the rhetoricians of the Latin decadence; they had no reason to congratulate themselves for having wished to be civilized." He saw his role as being to "help to ruin the prestige of middle-class culture," the acceptance of which had acted to retard the "class war." Second, he thought that what would mobilize the working class to revolutionary action was not "reason in revolt" but the particular myth of the general strike, "the *myth* in which Socialism is wholly comprised, i.e., a body of images capable of evoking instinctively all the sentiments which correspond to the different manifestations of the war undertaken by Socialism against modern society."[139] Yet as Irving Horowitz notes: "It is interesting that opponents of 'Jacobin' dictatorship *within* Orthodox Marxism, such as Rosa Luxemburg in Germany and Leon Trotsky in Russia, based their conclusions precisely on that tradition which Sorel saw as the leading culprit, the Enlightenment."[140]

Given the enemies the Enlightenment legacy gathered in the first half of the twentieth century, this was always a minority position. "The year 1789 is hereby erased from history," remarked Joseph Goebbels, the newly appointed Nazi Minister for Popular Enlightenment and Propaganda, in a radio broadcast of April 1, 1933.[141] By "1789," he meant not only the French Revolution but the entire tradition of Enlightenment thought that had contributed to it. During the 1930s, shortly after the Nazi seizure of power in Germany, Trotsky wrote of the petty-bourgeois supporter of Fascism: "To evolution, materialist thought, and rationalism—of the twentieth, nineteenth, and eighteenth century—is counterposed in his mind national idealism as the source of heroic inspiration." But one aspect of Fascism was precisely its ability to mobilize the most irrational impulses that continued to exist in bourgeois society:

Today, not only in peasant homes but also in city skyscrapers, there lives alongside of the twentieth century the tenth or the thirteenth. A hundred million people use electricity and still believe in the magic power of signs and exorcisms. The Pope of Rome broadcasts over the radio about the miraculous transformation of water into wine. Movie stars go to mediums. Aviators who pilot miraculous mechanisms created by man's genius wear amulets on their sweaters. What inexhaustible reserves they possess of darkness, ignorance and savagery![142]

In the face of this, Trotsky affirmed the Enlightenment tradition in the same way as Marx and Engels themselves, in *The History of the Russian Revolution*: "The historical assent of humanity taken as a whole, may be summarized as a succession of victories of consciousness over blind forces—in nature, in society, in man himself."[143] The optimism expressed here—in conditions of extraordinary difficulty between Stalin's consolidation of power in Russia and Hitler's accession to power in Germany— reflects the belief that Marxism inherited from the Enlightenment, that human beings have the capacity to remake the world. The subsequent history of the twentieth century undermined such optimism in four stages.

The first was the impact of the Second World War and the Holocaust. Although the First World War had shaken the bourgeoisie's own faith in progress and reason, it was the sequel that generated more widespread doubts. It is a common belief that "Auschwitz decisively closed the Enlightenment era of faith in the coordinated growth of reason, moral betterment, and happiness."[144] In fact, as Peter Novick has shown, the Holocaust did not attain its current universal significance until many years after the end of the Second World War.[145] What it did do was produce the first serious intellectual critique of the Enlightenment from the left. Theodor Adorno and Max Horkheimer wrote: "For the Enlightenment, whatever does not conform to the rule of computation and utility is suspect." Or more simply: "Enlightenment is totalitarian." Why?

Its untruth does not consist in what its romantic enemies have always reproached it for: analytic method, return to elements, dissolution through reflective thought; but instead that for enlightenment the process is always decided from the start. . . . With the extension of the bourgeois commodity economy, the dark horizon of myth is illumed by the sun of calculating reason, beneath whose cold rays the seed of the new barbarism grows to function. . . . By elevating necessity to the status of the basis for all time to come, and by idealistically degrading the spirit forever to the very apex, socialism held on too surely to the legacy of bourgeois philosophy. . . . As the organ of this kind of adaptation, as a mere construction of means, the Enlightenment is as destructive as its romantic enemies accuse it of being. It comes into its own only when it surrenders the last remaining concordance with the latter and dares to transcend the false absolute, the principle of blind domination. . . . The difficulties in the concept of reason caused by the fact that its subjects, the possessors of that very reason, contradict one another, are concealed by the apparent clarity of the judgments of the Western Enlightenment.

However, in a chapter written after the war and its full horror had become apparent ("Elements of Anti-Semitism"), they could still write: "Enlightenment which is in possession of itself and coming to power can break the bounds of enlightenment."[146] There is, in other words, still a tension within the Enlightenment that could be resolved in different ways. A similar sense of the contradictions is caught in a prize-winning essay of 1947 by the US liberal philosopher and politician Charles Frankel: "The general disrepute into which the dogma of necessary progress has fallen has cast a cloud not only over those elements in the beliefs of the *philosophes*, which may be defensible, but over the liberal philosophy in which the belief in human betterment through the use of intelligence is a ventral part." Nevertheless, he too thought it necessary to defend the philosophes: "But where they failed, it was essentially a failure of imagination . . . not due to their attachment to science, but to a metaphysical theory which exalted categories of physics into the exclusive properties of nature."[147]

The second stage was an effect of the postwar boom and the Cold War balance of terror. Enzo Traverso writes: "The defeat of Nazism, the Red Army's advance into Central Europe and the impressive growth of Communist parties in countries where they had played a leading role in the Resistance all encouraged a return in the postwar period to a philosophy of progress."[148] Callinicos has rightly criticized this passage insofar as it attempts to explain the absence of a Marxist response to the Holocaust.[149] It does, however, partly explain the maintenance of Enlightenment optimism, especially if taken together with effective full employment and the construction of the welfare state.

It was not the horror of the Holocaust that drove a relatively small minority to question rationality in this period, but the meaninglessness of postwar affluence and the threat of thermonuclear annihilation. In the 1950s, with the Cold War, the H-bomb, and the persistence of alienation even amid the "affluent" capitalism of the United States, there developed the subculture of the Beats that counterposed imagination to reason—a mood that found a much wider audience in the 1960s. In John Clellon Holmes's novel of the Beat Generation, *Go*, published in 1952 but set in the immediate aftermath of the Second World War, one of the main characters, Paul Hobbes, reflects on two of his friends from this circle: "They made none of the moral or political judgments he thought essential; they did not seem compelled to fit everything into the pigeon holes of a system. . . . They never read the papers, they did not follow with diligent and self-conscious attention the happenings in the political and cultural arena; they seemed to have an almost cultivated contempt for logical argument."[150] This attitude was transmitted more or less exactly into that of the 1960s counterculture. Leslie Fiedler wrote of its early adherents, using a term that would only come into widespread use twenty years later: "The post-modernists are surely in some sense 'mystics,' religious at least in a way they do not ordinarily know how to confess, but they are not Christians. Indeed, they regard Christianity quite as the Black Muslims (with whom they have certain affinities) do, as a white ideology: merely one more method—along with Humanism, technology, Marxism—of imposing 'White' or Western values on the rest of the world." If they had religion, it was "derived from Tibet or Japan or the ceremonies of the Plains Indians": "It is all part of the attempt of the generation under twenty-five, not exclusively in its most sensitive members but especially in them, to become Negro, even as they attempt to become poor or pre-rational."[151] Similarly, in the conclusion to the second edition of Norman Cohn's *The Pursuit of the Millennium* (1970), the author identifies both the revolutionary movements of the Third World and the drugged experimentation of the young in the West as modern forms of "medieval mysticism."[152] The rejection of conventional notions of reason is present in at least some of Bob Dylan's great songs of the 1960s. He expresses admiration for one woman because "she knows too much to argue or to judge."[153] In the case of another, it is her "useless and pointless knowledge" that is precisely the problem.[154] One pamphlet produced in San Francisco during the Summer of Love in 1967 advised its readers to "start unlearning everything they taught you, period," including "everything that prevents you seeing the world in dumb wonder again like a child."[155]

A link between the Marxist and countercultural critiques of Enlightenment was made in the work of Herbert Marcuse, a member of the Frankfurt School in exile from Nazi Germany, who relocated permanently to the US after the Second World War. "Auschwitz continues to haunt, not the memory but the accomplishments of man—the space flights; the rockets and missiles; the 'labyrinthine basement under the Snack Bar'; the pretty electronic plants, clean, hygienic and with flower beds; the poison gas which is not really harmful to people; the secrecy in which we all participate." His portrayal of a totally administered society that "appears to be the very embodiment of Reason" yet "is irrational as a whole" and has incorporated all traditional forms of opposition (i.e., the working class) had a certain appeal to student activists in particular. Like Hardt and Negri today, it is difficult to believe that Marcuse could have been easily comprehensible to anyone without training in German idealist philosophy; it is his overall message that made his reputation—that and the fact that he flattered his student bohemian readership by identifying them as part of the "substratum of the outcasts and outsiders, the exploited and persecuted of other races and other colors, the unemployed and the unemployable."[156]

The third and by far the most significant stage in the retreat from Enlightenment, however, was the aftermath of the movements for human liberation that we associate with the year 1968. The counterculture was a minor aspect of these movements, and most of its celebrated achievements, in relation to sexuality in particular, only became available to the Western working class a decade or more after it had faded, and even then only after years of struggle. The theories that informed it preexisted the upsurge itself and belong more properly to the period of economic boom. As two French writers recall: "For most of the students of our generation—the one that began its course of studies in the 1960s—the ideals of the Enlightenment could not but be a bad joke; a somber mystification. That, anyhow, was what was taught to us. The master thinkers in those days were called Foucault, Deleuze, Derrida, Althusser, Lacan."[157] But it took the defeat of the broader movement to bring to the surface the incipient irrationalism that the counterculture incubated. "What could be more reassuring," writes Callinicos, "for a generation, drawn first towards and then away from Marxism by the political ups and downs of the past two decades, than to be told—in a style decked out with the apparent profundity and genuine obscurity of the sub-Modernist rhetoric cultivated by '68 thought—that there is nothing they can do to change the world?"[158] Alan Sokal and Jean Bricmont also identify "political discouragement" with the rise of the new social movements. They point out that when the real sources of power and wealth are apparently unreachable, "science" can be attacked as a convenient substitute.[159] Two liberal critics of what they call the "higher superstition" of the academic left in the US have traced a third source: "[The] ... 'special competence' of the oppressed was deeply ingrained and has become unchallengeable within leftist circles." Not only do privileged groups "have no right to define reality for others," but also "the very state of being oppressed is somehow supposed to confer a greater clarity of vision, a more authentic view of the world, than the bourgeois trappings of economic, racial and sexual hegemony."[160]

In the postmodern mélange, and the broader currents of irrationality that circle round it, the problem with Enlightenment goals is apparently not that they remain incomplete but on the contrary that they have been all too perfectly realized. "The 'Enlightenment,' which discovered the liberties," wrote Michel Foucault in 1975, "also invented the disciplines."[161] And this judgment was more balanced than most. Take the three aspects of the Enlightenment that I discussed earlier in this chapter.

Reason was now the source of oppression. Goya, artistic conscience of the tragedy of the Spanish Enlightenment, called one of his etchings "The Sleep of Reason Produces Monsters." Not so, claimed Gilles Deleuze and Félix Guattari in 1977: "It is not the slumber of reason that engenders monsters, but vigilant and insomniac rationality."[162]

Progress was dangerous because it implied that human history might have a point. Jean-François Lyotard argued as follows, in what has retrospectively become the founding manifesto of postmodernism:

> I will use the term *modern* to designate any science that legitimates itself with reference to a metadiscourse ... making an explicit appeal to some grand narrative, such as the dialectics of Spirit, the hermeneutics of meaning, the emancipation of the rational or working subject, or the creation of wealth. For example, the rule of consensus between the sender and addressee of a statement with truth-value is deemed acceptable if it is cast in terms of a possible unanimity between rational minds:

this is the Enlightenment narrative, in which the hero of knowledge works towards a good ethico-political end—universal peace. . . . I define *postmodern* as incredulity towards metanarratives.[163]

Essentially the same viewpoint is expressed in the plain-speaking, accessible tones of the American philosopher Richard Rorty: "I hope we have reached a time when we can finally get rid of the conviction that there just must be large theoretical ways of finding out how to end injustice. I hope we can learn to get along without the conviction that there is something—such as the human soul, or human nature, or the will of God, or the shape of history—which provides a subject matter for grand, politically useful theory." Above all, Rorty concludes, we must avoid attempting to find a "successor to Marxism."[164]

Universality simply disguises the particular interests of the group invoking this slogan. Andrew Ross writes of the continuities between the liberal and Marxist traditions: "If those . . . are rooted in the Enlightenment project of social, cultural and political rationality, they are also tied to propositions about the universality of that project—as a social logic through which the world ought to transform itself in the image of Western men."[165] One feels a certain amount of disappointment that Ross did not add the words "able-bodied, white, and heterosexual" in front of the phrase "Western men," but the general drift is clear enough. Sandra Harding expresses her skepticism that "there is one world, one 'truth' about it and one and only one science that can, in principle, accurately represent that 'truth.'" Such claims imply an "ideal knower" who is "presumably the 'rational man' of Enlightenment Liberal political philosophy." The claims for science are made in bad faith, for "unexpected or destructive effects of modern sciences are attributed to politics, culture, or something else said to be outside science proper." It is time, Harding believes, that we faced up to the truth about science: "Maldevelopment and dedevelopment for the majority of the world's peoples have tended to be the now-obvious effects of the introduction of scientifically rational agriculture, manufacturing, health care, and so forth into the already economically and politically disadvantaged societies of the Third World."[166] *Health care and so forth?* A concomitant of these rejections of the Enlightenment is the celebration of "non-Western" knowledge. "The knowledge possessed by non-Western civilizations and by so-called primitive tribes is truly astounding. It aids its practitioners in their own social and geographical conditions and contains elements that exceed what the corresponding elements of Western civilization do for us. . . . Needless to say our rationalists are not at all pleased: they mumble darkly of 'relativism' and 'irrationalism,' new inarticulate substitutes for the old and never abandoned curse: *anathema sit!*"[167] In the case of Paul Feyerabend, his rejection of reason seems to stem from suspicion of the scientists and technicians that he identifies either as the servants of power or as a new ruling class.[168]

One measure of the extent to which these arguments had gone was revealed in a hoax contribution to the journal *Social Text* by Alan Sokal. In it, he described how "natural scientists, and especially physicists" still insisted on retaining "the dogma imposed by the long post-Enlightenment hegemony over the Western intellectual outlook, which can be summarized briefly as follows: that there exists an external world, whose properties are independent of any individual human being and indeed of humanity as a whole; that these properties are encoded in 'eternal' physical laws; and that human beings can obtain reliable, albeit imperfect and tentative, knowledge of these laws by hewing to the 'objective' procedures and epistemological strictures prescribed by the (so-called) scientific method." Note that we are being asked to reject these propositions and accept instead "that physical 'reality,' no less than social 'reality,' is at bottom a social linguistic construct."[169]

The arguments for local particularity and traditional belief against universalism and rationality, advanced for example by Edmund Burke in *Reflections on the Revolution in France* and Joseph de Maistre in *Study on Sovereignty*, are repeated today by some on the left in apparent ignorance of their origin in these founding texts of modern conservative political theory. "Man's cradle must be surrounded by dogma and when his reason awakens, he must find all his opinions ready made, at least those concerning his social behavior," wrote Maistre: "Nothing is more important for man than prejudice."[170] As two liberal critics note: "Maistre, in his counterrevolutionary ferocity, is the true spiritual ancestor of the 'postmodern' skepticism so dear to the hearts of the academic left."[171] Others are perfectly aware of where their ideas originate. Chantal Mouffe, for example, acknowledges: "One of the chief emphases of conservative thought does indeed lie in its critique of the Enlightenment's rationalism and universalism, a critique it shares with postmodern thought." Both are "predicated upon human finitude, imperfection and limits." She then goes on to praise the British conservative philosopher Michael Oakeshott.[172]

The fourth and final stage in the retreat from the Enlightenment followed the collapse of Stalinism in Eastern Europe, but by this point most of the intellectual damage had been done; 1989 simply confirmed the now-conventional wisdom. "Marxism, the last shoot stemming from both the Enlightenment and Christianity, seems to have lost all of its critical power," wrote Lyotard.[173] One imagines that it did not take the events of 1989 for Lyotard to reach this conclusion. For Václav Havel, "the fall of Communism can be regarded as a sign that modern thought—based on the premise that the world is objectively knowable, and that the knowledge so obtained can be absolutely generalised—has come to a final crisis."[174] As John Sanbonmatsu recounts:

> Like a virus travelling through the body of critical thought, postmodernism has succeeded by commanding the disciplinary apparatus nearest to account—stamping out genetic replicas of itself for export to other fields, other sub-disciplines, other geographies. Once secured in its discursive host, the virus takes hold again, blooms, sends off new messengers. Incubated in the elite universities of the capitalist metropolis, the institutional centers dominating the global trade routes of intellectual production and exchange, the virus has exported itself to the periphery. In the early years of the 21st century, postmodernism calved a new generation of postcolonial theorists on the Indian subcontinent, provided solace to dispirited activists in Latin America, attracted academic activists disenchanted with Marxism, and struck the fancy of Islamic fundamentalists in Iran. If it is true, as Mark Twain wrote, that a lie will travel halfway around the world while the truth is still putting on its shoes, then let us begin by noting that no theory of recent vintage has travelled as fast, or as far, as postmodernism has.[175]

But it is important to understand that the rejection of the Enlightenment extended to people who had not been influenced by postmodernism in any way.[176] According to Jonathan Glover, "Pol Pot had certainly never heard of the Enlightenment. But he was directly influenced by it, if only though the reading of the Communist newspaper *L'Humanité* in his student days in Paris. The 'philosophers,' Stalin and Mao, were also probably barely aware of the Enlightenment and would have had little patience with its thinkers. . . . But Stalin and his heirs were in thrall to the Enlightenment. They accepted the Marxist version: the revolution would bring about the reconstruction of society along 'scientific lines,' which would in the end give people better lives."[177]

Several generations of radicals or would-be radicals have now been educated in the conventional pieties of poststructuralism and postmodernism. Many of them view the Enlightenment with intense suspicion, as an instrument for the domination of the oppressed and the subjugation of nature, and as little else. Consequently, they are either unwilling or unable to defend it. Roger Burbach, an active supporter of the antiglobalization movement, describes "virtually all political parties . . . including those on the left" as "heirs of the Enlightenment project."[178] This is not intended as a compliment: "What I find particularly useful in postmodernism at this ideological juncture is its view that there are no absolute laws of history, as well as its contention that modernism and the faith in progress that began in the age of the Enlightenment are at the root of the disasters that have wracked humanity throughout this century."[179] Similar themes are present in the introduction to a widely read anthology of the movement: "For the time of single ideologies and grand narratives was over. People were sick of sacrificing themselves for the sake of gigantic game plans which didn't take account of their individual needs, their humanity, their culture, their creativity."[180]

These postures constitute for the left an intellectual version of what the CIA calls "blowback," or the unintended negative consequences for the US of its foreign policy.[181] Campaigns go on, but as Larry Laudan points out, "to the extent—and it is considerable—that the new left subscribes to strong forms of relativism, it has lost all theoretical rationale for such activity."[182] And as Elizabeth Wilson writes, since "we are given no reasons why we should believe in one thing rather than another; we might as well go in for Erhardt Seminar training as radical politics; Buddhism is as good as Bolshevism (or better); therapy replaces collective action; astrology is the name of the game."[183]

REASON, POWER, AND THE INTERESTS

Until now I have used the term "reason," and quoted other writers using it, as if we all mean the same thing and the meaning requires no explanation. But this is precisely the problem: we cannot uncritically accept bourgeois definitions of reason. James Holstun rightly comments of certain writings by Adorno and Horkheimer, although the point is more widely applicable, that "this near-postmodernist critique casts its net too wide and not wide enough, for it denounces all science, all rationality (including, presumably, itself) while letting slip the historically specific capitalist form of rationality."[184] What then is the "specific capitalist form of rationality"? In fact, bourgeois thinkers have provided at least three ways of thinking about rationality.

Instrumental rationality and value rationality

Max Weber distinguished between two types of rationality, instrumental rationality and value rationality. As Callinicos has noted, the difference is that "value-rationality is concerned with the ends of action, instrumental rationality with the means."[185] For Weber values (ends) are fundamental beliefs, which may themselves be irrational (the "warring gods" between whom he believed we all have to choose), but to which adherence can be given by rational means. In some ways this is a reformulation of Hume's distinction between "reason" (instrumental rationality) and "the passions" (value-rationality). Weber thinks that capitalist accumulation is a rational end, although one that may be chosen for irrational reasons, such as his famous "Protestant ethic." But once accumulation is engaged upon it is not a choice, rational or otherwise, because there are no alternatives. Unless capitalists choose to cease being capitalists they are subject to a compulsion—to continue in competitive accumulation—that is more terrible and severe than any imposed by a mere value system, however deeply held.

Although the means/ends distinction is helpful up to a point, it has severe limitations. In his last book, appropriately called *Farewell to Reason*, the anarchist philosopher Paul Feyerabend refers to Reginius (Magherita von Brenato), a Holy Inquisitor for the Catholic Church. Reginius had heretics tortured but did so in order to save them from what was in his eyes the infinitely worse fate of eternal damnation: "Within the framework of his thought Reginius acted as a responsible and rational human being and he should be praised, at least by rationalists. If we are repelled by his views and unable to give him his due then we must realize that there are absolutely no 'objective' arguments to support our repulsion."[186] Feyerabend wants to argue that there is no difference between Reginius and, say, Galileo, because both were exercising rationality within their own belief systems. In other words, for Feyerabend, there is only instrumental rationality; he regards the values themselves as beyond discussion. But unless we are prepared to collapse into absolute relativism, we need some way of distinguishing between different ends.

Constructivist rationality and evolutionary rationality

The second way of thinking about rationality makes another distinction, in this case between constructivist rationality and evolutionary rationality. It is provided by Friedrich von Hayek, a thinker influenced by Weber, but whose fanatical insistence on the necessity of the market lacks any of the ambiguities of his predecessor. Hayek described himself as an "antirationalist," by which he did not mean that he considered himself irrational. On the contrary, Hayek believed that there were two types of rationalism. Adherents of the first, "constructivist rationalism," "believe that human societies can be mastered by human beings and remodeled according to rational criteria. Human societies can be organized so as to abolish social evils such as poverty and violence." Adherents of the second, "evolutionary rationalism," among whom he numbered himself, show "a distrust of the powers of human reason, a recognition of the extent of human ignorance about the social and natural worlds, and therefore a stress upon the unexpected, unintended consequences of social action." According to Hayek, Bacon, Hobbes, Rousseau, Condorcet, Godwin, Paine, Priestley, Price, and Jefferson are constructivists; Mandeville, Constant, Hume, Smith, Ferguson, and Burke are evolutionists. Leaving aside the question of whether this classification is accurate with respect to these thinkers (it is not—all the Scottish thinkers mentioned here are arch-constructivists), Hayek has identified a real distinction. It is clear that Marxism, and socialist thought more generally, belong to the constructivist camp. Hayek rejects constructivism on the grounds that it is not really rational at all, since any attempt to assert human control over the market will result not simply in failure but in social regression to a state of premodernity, in which an economically unfree population is ruled by a dictatorship. Hayek was of course considerably less concerned with political and social freedom.[187]

Hayek is articulating a position we have already encountered, that only the rationality of market-based economic activity—capitalism—is really rational. But he finds evolutionary rationality quite compatible with religious mystification: "Mythical beliefs of some sort may be needed to bring [the construction and spread of traditions] about, especially where rules of conduct conflicting with instinct are concerned." The traditions to which Hayek refers are those of the market order: "We owe it partly to mystical and religious beliefs, and, I believe, particularly to the main monotheistic ones, that beneficial traditions have been preserved and transmitted long enough to enable those groups following them to grow, and to have the opportunity to spread by natural or cultural selection."[188] He is not alone. The veteran conservative sociologist Robert Nisbet has claimed that continued progress, conceived in capitalist terms, is linked to the continued influence of the Judeo-Christian tradition. Nisbet is therefore only in favor of certain kinds of irrationalism, arguing that "the present age of the revolt against reason, of crusading irrationalism, of the almost exponential development and diffusion of the occult, and the constant spread of narcissism and solipsism make evident enough how fallible were and are the secular foundations of modern thought."[189] The cynicism of these attitudes should be quite evident.

Rationality as power

The third and final way of understanding rationality arose first chronologically but has only become widely influential more recently. Here, rationality is simply a means to power, or perhaps the exercise of power itself. The thought of Friedrich Nietzsche, which ultimately lay behind postmodernism and gave it the little intellectual credibility it possessed, is inescapable in this context.[190] The conservative critic Allan Bloom noted that "the abandonment, encouraged by Nietzsche, of the distinction between true and false in political and moral matters" was for ideology to lose its pejorative connotations and become identified with values as such. "Marxists," he wrote, "still vaguely hope for a world where there are values without domination." And if we take "Marxists" to mean the American academic left against which his book is directed, then Bloom is right to conclude: "This is all that remains of their Marxism, and they can and do fellow-travel with the Nietzscheans a goodly *bout de chemin.*"[191]

Nietzsche opposed any attempt to systematically understand the world. "I mistrust all systematizers and avoid them," he wrote. "The will to a system is a lack of integrity."[192] It was useless to seek after the facts; "facts are precisely what there are not, only interpretation." Nor is there any objective knowledge: "Insofar as the word 'knowledge' has any meaning, the world is knowable; but it is *interpretable* otherwise, it has no meaning behind it but countless meanings—'Perspectivism.' It is our needs that interpret the world; our drives and their For and Against. Every drive is a kind of lust to rule; each one has its perspectives that it would like to compel all the other drives to accept as a norm."[193]

The first step we need to take here is indicated in a comment by Alain Boyer: "We have to stop interpreting Nietzsche and take him at his word."[194] Nietzsche does in fact talk in class terms, although the class he admires, a spiritual "aristocracy" (this is the term he uses) superior to the mass of "slaves," does not resemble any actually existing ruling class. For despite the supposed universality of the "will to power," Nietzsche does not see this as operating *within* the collective "body" of a "healthy aristocracy," only between that body and other, inferior bodies. The former must, "if it is a living and not a decaying body, itself do all that to other bodies which the individuals within it refrain from doing to one another: it will have to be the will to power incarnate, it will want to grow, expand, draw to itself, gain ascendancy—not out of any morality or immorality, but because it *lives*, and because life *is* will to power."[195] Ishay Landa writes: "Summing up the socio-political meaning of power in Nietzsche's thought, one finds that it should ultimately serve and protect 'the strong,' the noble, the aristocratic, but should *not* be exploited when it may damage their position and turn against them; in no case should it benefit 'the weak,' the lower classes, the rabble, the slaves." The source of Nietzsche's hostility to the Enlightenment is therefore not—or not only—his refusal of systematization: "He proposes agnostic vagueness and epistemological uncertainty as a social weapon in a social struggle. He wills causality no more; he wills no more truths that are universal, because these tend to translate themselves into universal claims, such as the claim to the 'dignity of man and labour.' If Nietzsche is the spiritual father of postmodernism, its most significant forerunner, then we have before us a telling piece of evidence regarding the reactionary impulse that initially triggered postmodernism, the very driving force that set it in motion."[196]

One can see therefore the problem for the postmodern appropriators of Nietzsche's thought. In Larry Laudan's imaginary dialogue between a Realist and a Relativist (the Nietzschean in this context), he has the following to say to the latter: "You tell us that the real precipitatory cause for a scientist to accept or reject a theory or paradigm is his calculation as to whether it will serve his professional and extraprofessional interests. By your own lights, therefore, if you want to explain why *you* hold the beliefs you do, I have to inquire about how those beliefs further your position and ambitions, the standing of your profession, the interests of the groups of which you are a part."[197] The Relativist's answer has generally been to argue that some perspectives have more value than others. True knowledge emerges from the experience of the oppressed. Harding, for example, writes: "Women—and men—cannot understand or explain the world we live in or the real choices we have as long as the sciences describe and explain the world primarily from the perspectives of the lives of the dominant groups. If we must learn about this society and its nature only from its 'natives'—that is, within conceptual frameworks and agendas restricted by the needs and desires of the peoples indigenous to the ruling class, race and gender—we cannot gain objective explanations of natures, of either our lives or theirs."[198]

At one level this is incontestable, and indeed—the term is not intended pejoratively in this case—common sense: the victims of oppression are in a better position to know the truth of their condition than their oppressors.[199] But the issue is not quite so simple. Different groups of oppressed people may have conflicting perspectives on the same situation; even more to the point, so can members of the *same* group. Which is the true knowledge? As Meera Nanda points out, "given that neither 'women,' the 'non-West,' nor 'non-Western women' make up uniform categories, situated knowledges end up privileging the most hackneyed stereotypes of feminine ways of knowing and the 'wisdom' of non-Western traditions over scientific methods of inquiry."[200] The greatest problem, however, is the one we have already discussed in relation to religion: in the words of Hume, "Men often act against their interest; for which reason the view of the greater possible good does not always influence them."[201] Feyerabend writes: "A mature citizen is not a man who has been *instructed* in a special ideology and who now carries this ideology with him like a mental tumor, a mature citizen is a person who has then *decided* in favor of what he thinks suits him best." And if that is that God created the universe in six days and rested on the seventh, what complaint could we possibly have. Indeed, Feyerabend anticipates precisely this and goes on to say: "It is the vote of everyone concerned that decides fundamental issues such as the teaching methods used, or the truth of basic beliefs such as the theory of evolution, or the quantum theory, and not the authority of bigshots hiding behind a non-existent methodology."[202] An appropriate answer to this obscurantism has been given by Andrew Collier:

> Which is better, that [cognitive practices] produce true information, or that they produce politically useful information, that is, information in which widespread belief would produce politically desirable results? The whole scientific socialist tradition has answered, bluntly and correctly: it is the oppressors who have something to hide—the oppressed have a class interest in the objective truth. So that, so far as the politics of liberation are concerned, the cognitive virtues of objectivity, clarity, logical rigor are also political virtues—even though they may indeed conflict with some short-term political advantage.[203]

What might a Nietzschean society look like? In fact, there is an extraordinary literary portrait of precisely this in a most unexpected place: Orwell's *Nineteen Eighty-Four*. This emerges most clearly near the end of the book, in a dialogue between O'Brien and Winston Smith in the torture chambers of the Ministry of Love. "We are not interested in the good of others; we are interested only in power." And power, as O'Brien explains, "is power over human beings":

> Over the body—but, above all, over the mind. Power over matter—external reality, as you would call it—is not important. Already our control over matter is absolute. . . .
> "But how can you control matter?" [Winston] burst out. "You don't even control the climate or the law of gravity. And there are disease, pain, death—"
> O'Brien silenced him by a movement of his hand. "We control matter because we control the mind. Reality is inside the skull. . . . You must get rid of these nineteenth-century ideas about the laws of Nature. We make the laws of Nature."

O'Brien's relativism even extends—in a particularly contemporary note—to disputing the existence of evolution:

> "The earth is as old as we are, no older. How could it be older? Nothing exists except through human consciousness."
> "But the rocks are full of the bones of extinct animals—mammoths and mastodons and enormous reptiles which lived here long before man was heard of."

"Have you ever seen those bones, Winston? Of course not. Nineteenth-century biologists invented them. Before man there was nothing. After man, if he could come to an end, there would be nothing. Outside man there is nothing."

"But the whole universe is outside us. Look at the stars! Some of them are a million light years away. They are out of our reach forever."

"What are the stars?" said O'Brien indifferently. "They are bits of fire a few kilometers away. We could reach them if we wanted to. Or we could blot them out. The earth is the centre of the universe. The sun and the stars go round it."

But O'Brien also concedes that it is possible for instrumental reason to be applied in certain limited circumstances: "For certain purposes, of course, that is not true. When we navigate the ocean, or when we predict an eclipse, we often find it convenient to assume that the earth goes round the sun and that the stars are millions upon millions of kilometers away. But what of it? Do you suppose it is beyond us to produce a dual system of astronomy? The stars can be near or far, according as we need them. Do you suppose our mathematicians are unequal to that?" Finally, he concludes: "But always—do not forget this Winston—always there will be the intoxication of power, constantly increasing and constantly growing subtler. Always, at every moment, there will be the thrill of victory, the sensation of trampling on an enemy who is helpless. If you want a picture of the future, imagine a boot stamping on a human face forever."[204]

John Newsinger has argued that *Nineteen Eighty-Four* is a fictional representation of those theories of the USSR that regarded it as a form of bureaucratic—or, in Orwell's own terminology, oligarchic—collectivism.[205] It may be, however, that Orwell's greatest insight was not in relation to the Stalinist societies of his own time but constituted a genuine prophecy about the unreason that has proved to be the necessary ideological counterpoint to the neoliberal capitalism of our epoch.

Conclusion

What attitude should socialists then take to the heritage of the Enlightenment, in the face of its genuine enemies and false friends? Let us return, for the last time, to the three areas I earlier defined as the central ideas of the Enlightenment, but this time in reverse order: universalism, progress, and reason.

As the postmodernists discourse endlessly on the wonders of difference and particularity, Fascist and other extreme right-wing politicians are perfectly aware of how useful antiuniversalism is for their ends. As Richard Wolin reports of developments in France during the 1990s: "Representatives of the European New Right such as Alain de Benoist began employing the claims of 'differential racism' to justify cultural separatism—as epitomized by Le Pen's cynical claim, 'I love North Africans but their place is in Maghreb'—and discriminatory legislation. At this point the vacuity of 'difference' as an ethical paradigm became painfully apparent."[206] Sometimes, however, the racism takes very traditional forms. Take, for example, a recent message from peace campaigner Cindy Sheehan to her supporters, which has been reproduced on several websites. In it, Sheehan recollects the following episode: "I got a hate email from a 'patriotic American' once who told me that when we see the mothers and fathers of Iraq screaming because their babies have been killed, that they 'are just acting for the cameras. They are animals who don't care about their children because they know they can produce another.'" Sheehan rightly points out: "This wicked rhetoric . . . dehumanizes us all."[207] And that seems to me to be the right response, the enlightened response, so to speak. One reason (among many others) for trying to stop our governments killing Iraqi children and subjecting their parents to the pain of loss is precisely because "they" are the same as "us," with the same relationships and the same emotions. In the face of the racism displayed by Sheehan's correspondent, invoking the "irreducibility of difference" or the other shibboleths of cultural relativism is actually worse than useless, because it goes halfway toward accepting the racist argument. If the Iraqis, the Chinese, the !Kung San, or whoever are all fundamentally different in some way, then the logic of this position, should one wish to follow it, is that it is permissible to treat them differently.

If socialists need to reassert the claims of universalism, they need to subject the second key idea, that of progress, to question. Let us define progress simply in terms of society's increasing ability to keep the world's population alive and capable of living a fully human life. Capitalism gave us, over a hundred years ago, the technology, skills, techniques, and productive levels with which socialism could have been established. It was not; but since then these capacities have continued to grow, notwithstanding the terrible crises with which the system is regularly afflicted. In the absence of socialism millions have suffered and died needlessly; but at the same time, if and when we do achieve it, we will do so on the basis of developments that earlier generations of Marxists could only have imagined.

Supporters of the system like Julian Simon claim that we can overcome scarcity on the basis of the existing economic order: "We now possess knowledge about resource locations and materials processing that allows us to satisfy our physical needs and desires for food, drink, heat, light, clothing, longevity, transportation, and the recording and transmission of information and entertainment. We can perform these tasks sufficiently well that the additional knowledge on these subjects will not revolutionize humanity. It still remains to us to reorganize our institutions, economies, and societies in such fashion that the benefits of this knowledge are available to the vast majority rather than a minority of all people." But there are threats to this imminent nirvana and, Dear Reader, we are responsible: "On the other hand, with greater progress comes greater freedom from pressing survival needs, which in turn enables people to indulge themselves in foolish, irrational and counter-productive thinking, and can lead to mass movements that impede progress."[208] Capitalism made possible improvements to living conditions, provided people were prepared to struggle for them; but what capitalism gives, or least allows, it can also take away. As Thomas Pogge notes: "The consequences of such extreme poverty are foreseeable and extensively documented: 14 per cent of the world's population (826 million) are undernourished, 16 per cent (968 million) lack access to safe drinking water, 40 per cent (2,400 million) lack access to basic sanitation, and 854 million adults are illiterate. Of all human beings 15 per cent (more than 880 million) lack access to health services, 17 per cent (approximately 1,000 million) have no adequate shelter, and 33 per cent (2,000 million) no electricity." And as Pogge carefully explains, even these grim figures may give an overly positive impression: "By focusing on human beings *alive at any given time*, all these statistics give less weight to those whose lives are short." These things are avoidable:

> One third of all human deaths are due to poverty-related causes, such as starvation, diarrhea, pneumonia, tuberculosis, malaria, measles and prenatal conditions, all of which could be prevented or cured cheaply through food, safe drinking water, vaccinations, rehydration packs, or medicines. . . . Not mentioned in the retrospectives and not shown on the evening news are the ordinary deaths from starvation and preventable

diseases—some 250 million people, mostly children, in the 14 years since the end of the Cold War. The names of these people, if listed in the style of the Vietnam War Memorial, would cover a wall 350 miles long.[209]

Pogge could be living on a different planet from Simon, although it is one inhabited by rather more people. How can progress and regress occur at the same time? As Esther Leslie points out in her outstanding study of Walter Benjamin: "As the bourgeois class secures economic and political power, progress, a cardinal strand in Enlightenment political rhetoric and social theory, unfolds in actuality its class inflections as economic and social progress for one class, presented ideologically as the universally significant progression of humanity itself." Technological improvements themselves are not necessarily progressive: "The easy identification of technological development with progress overrides questions of social form or production relations." The problem, however, is not the technological aspect of the forces of production as such, but, as Leslie suggests, the relations of production within which they occur. Although both develop, the tendency is always for the latter to retard the former: "Every inch of progress on a technological level under these relations of production, the oppressed suffer regression on a social level: like Marx's understanding of machinery as potential liberator that in *this* moment under *this* organisation of relations of production only intensifies our exploitation and, often, our discomfort."[210] Every discussion of progress must therefore start with the question: progress for whom?

This brings me to the final idea, that of reason itself. Of this we must ask, as we did of progress: rational for whom? The central difficulty was once identified by Max Horkheimer: "The difficulties of rationalist philosophy originate from the fact that the universality of reason cannot be anything else than the accord among the interests of all groups alike, whereas in reality society has been split up into groups with competing interests."[211] Capitalists have to pursue courses of action that, however rational they may be for individual members of their class, can be terrifyingly irrational for everybody else. The tobacco companies who are currently opening up huge new markets in southeast Asia for their drugs will, in due course, be responsible for a cancer epidemic in southeast Asia, which will in turn put intolerable pressures on the fragile health services of those countries, the costs of which will be borne by the working class and peasantry, leading to further internal instability and thus the threat of war—but none of this enters the calculations of the legal drug barons. A similar logic applies to the nuclear fuel and oil companies supporting George W. Bush in resisting even the most limited attempts to reduce gas emissions. The waters rise in Bangladesh and Mozambique, condemning thousands to death, but not until the shores of the US are underwater will this be factored into their calculations—and if the recent experience of New Orleans is anything to go by, perhaps not even then. Once accumulation is engaged upon it is not a choice, rational or otherwise, because there are no alternatives: they are subject to a compulsion terrible, severe, and inescapable.

We therefore cannot simply reject the Enlightenment without depriving ourselves of some of the most important intellectual tools necessary for human liberation. But neither can we pretend that it had no limitations, or that there have been no positive intellectual developments since the early nineteenth century. The task for socialists is to identify elements of the Enlightenment that were particular to the capitalist economic and social conditions from which it initially emerged but are genuinely universal and consequently capable of being turned to different purposes. Time has surely passed judgment on claims that capitalism continues to uphold Enlightenment: war, environmental catastrophe, increased impoverishment—these are the fruits of capitalist reason, capitalist progress, and the rejection of universality. Enlightenment social goals will only ever be partially attained under capitalist society, and even these limited gains are constantly under threat. In these circumstances, only socialism is capable of "defending the Enlightenment," but also—more importantly—of completing it.

◖◖ Chapter 6 ◗◗

Islam and the Enlightenment[*]

INTRODUCTION

In the current Western controversy over Islam one theme recurs with increasing predictability. Many writers are prepared to acknowledge Muslim cultural and scientific achievements, but always with the caveat that Islamic civilization never experienced an equivalent to the Enlightenment. "Islam never had to go through a prolonged period of critically examining the validity of its spiritual vision, as the West did during the eighteenth century," writes Louis Dupré. "Islamic culture has, of course, known its own crisis . . . yet it was never forced to question its traditional worldview."[1]

Muslims have responded in different ways to the claim that their religion has never produced an Enlightenment. Ziauddin Sardar has criticized

---

[*] Originally published in *Socialist Review* 2:304 (March 2006). I have restored footnotes omitted in the original publication and removed a quotation I wrongly attributed to Salman Rushdie.

it in the *New Statesman* on two grounds. On the one hand: "It assumes that 'Islam' and 'Enlightenment' have nothing to do with each other—as if the European Enlightenment emerged out of nothing, without appropriating Islamic thought and learning." On the other: "It betrays an ignorance of postmodern critique that has exposed Enlightenment thought as Eurocentric hot air."[2] So: Islamic thought was responsible for the Enlightenment, but the Enlightenment was intellectually worthless. This is not, perhaps, the most effective way of highlighting the positive qualities of Islamic thought. Sardar's incoherence is possibly the result of his own critical attitude toward Islamism. More mainstream Muslim thinkers generally take one of two more positions.

The first is that Islam, unlike Christianity, did not require Enlightenment because its tenets do not involve the same conflict between religion and science. As the Egyptian scholar Abdulaziz Altwaijri has written: "Western enlightenment was completely opposed to religion and it still adopts the same attitude. Islamic enlightenment, on the contrary, combines belief and science, religion and reason, in a reasonable equilibrium between these components."[3] Islam is certainly less dependent than Christianity on miracles or what Tom Paine called "things naturally incredible"—a point actually made by several Enlightenment thinkers—but ultimately, because Enlightenment thought counterposes reason to revelation, it casts doubt on all religions, Christianity, Islam, Judaism, Hinduism, and Buddhism alike.[4]

The second position is that although the Enlightenment represented progress for the West, it was a means of oppressing the Muslim world. A. Hussain asks: "Given that our people have been victims of these developments, then why should we appreciate them?"[5] It is also true that both the Islamic world and Muslims in the West have suffered and continue to suffer from imperialism and racism, but this is not the fault of the Enlightenment as such. Rather, it is an outcome of the failure of Enlightenment ideas to find their realization in socialism, and of the way they have been harnessed instead to the needs of capitalist expansion. In the hands of a resurgent movement of the working class and the oppressed these ideas can be turned against the warmongers and Islamophobes who falsely claim them as their own. The history of the Islamic world shows that it raised many of the themes that later became associated with the Enlightenment and did so earlier in time. The issue is therefore why the

Enlightenment became *dominant* in the West and not in the Islamic world—or, indeed, in those other parts of the world, like China, that had previously been materially more advanced than the West.

The comparative basis for the critique of Islam is the Enlightenment that occurred in Europe and North America between the mid-seventeenth and early nineteenth centuries, but notice how the terms of the argument are changed in relation to Islam. No one refers to a "Christian Enlightenment." If the Enlightenment is given any specificity at all, it is in relation to individual nations. Why is territoriality the basis for discussion of the Enlightenment for the West, but religion for the East?

A CHRISTIAN ENLIGHTENMENT?

The assumption is that the Enlightenment, like the Renaissance and Reformation before it, emerged out of what is usually called the "Judeo-Christian tradition." In other words, Christianity was intellectually open and tolerant enough ("Western values," etc.) to allow critical thought to emerge, with the result that religion could gradually be superseded and the separation of church and state brought about. The implication, of course, is that Islam has been incapable of allowing the same process to take place. The fate of Giordano Bruno (who was burned at the stake by the Holy Inquisition) or Galileo (who was threatened with the same fate) for daring to question the doctrines of the Catholic Church might, however, cast some doubt on the claim that Christianity is intrinsically open to scientific rationality.

At this point the argument usually shifts from Christianity in general to the role of Protestantism in particular, or more narrowly still that of Calvinism, but this is no more convincing. Writers as politically different as Antonio Gramsci and Hugh Trevor-Roper have explained that Protestant thought was in many respects a retreat from the intellectual sophistication of late medieval Catholic thought, as characterized by, for example, Erasmus.[6] Sixteenth-century Geneva and seventeenth-century Edinburgh were not places in which rational speculation was encouraged. The intellectually progressive role of Protestantism lies in the way in which some versions of the faith encouraged congregations to seek the truth in their individual reading of the Bible, rather than from received authority—an approach that could be carried over into other areas of life. The teachings themselves did not point in this direction. Justification by faith is an enormously powerful doctrine, but not a rational one, since it rests on the claim that the ways of God are unknowable to man, not least in His arbitrary division of humanity into the Elect (the saved) and the Reprobate (the damned). Edinburgh later became the center of perhaps the greatest of all national Enlightenments, but as James Buchan puts it in *Capital of the Mind*, his outstanding study of the city during the eighteenth century, in order to become the vanguard of European intellectual life Edinburgh had first to abandon the "theocratic fantasies" of the Church of Scotland.[7] And this was true across Europe and in North America. Whatever the specific religious beliefs of individual Enlightenment thinkers, however coded some of their arguments, the movement as a whole was at war with the Judeo-Christian tradition: it represents not the continuity of Western culture but a profound break within it. Far from being the apotheosis of Western values, the Enlightenment rejected the values that had previously been dominant.

Enlightenment thinkers therefore took a far more complex attitude to Islam than their present-day admirers would have us believe. As Jonathan Israel recounts in his important history *Radical Enlightenment*: "On the one hand, Islam is viewed positively, even enthusiastically, as a purified form of revealed religion, stripped of the many imperfections of Judaism and Christianity and hence reassuringly akin to deism. On the other, Islam is more often regarded with hostility and contempt as a primitive, grossly superstitious religion like Judaism and Christianity and one no less, or still more adapted to promoting despotism."[8] Edward Gibbon wrote in a remarkably balanced way about Muhammad and the foundation of Islam in *The Decline and Fall of the Roman Empire*, particularly given his generally critical attitude to Christianity.[9] But perhaps most startling of all was Mozart's decision to make the character of the Turkish ruler Pasha Selim the one most representative of reason and humanity in his opera *The Abduction from the Seraglio*, particularly given that, in his home city of Vienna, Turkey was regarded as the greatest threat to the Austrian Empire.[10] In general, then, the Enlightenment did not regard Islam as being any better or any worse than Christianity.

Perhaps we should therefore consider the possibility that the decisive factor in both the emergence of Enlightenment in the West and its failure to emerge in the East was not religion as such but the kind of societies in which religions took root. We will in any case have to qualify the claim

that Islam knew no form of scientific rationality. It was Muslim scholars
who translated and preserved the philosophy and science of Greece and
Persia, which would otherwise have been lost. It was they who transmitted it to their equivalents in Europe, who came to be educated at
Muslim hands in Spain and Sicily. But Muslim achievements in scientific
thought were not simply archival. The thirteenth-century Syrian scholar
and physician Ibn al-Nafis was first to discover the pulmonary circulation
of the blood. In doing so he had to reject the views of one of his predecessors, Avicenna—himself an important medical thinker, who among
other things identified that disease could be spread by drinking water.
Ibn al-Nafis died in his bed at an advanced age (he is thought to have
been around 80). Compare his fate to that of the second person to pro-
pose the theory of circulation, the Spaniard Michael Servetus, which was
less happy. In 1553, the same year as Servetus published his treatise, he
was arrested by the Protestant authorities of Geneva on charges of blasphemy, and—a splendid example of Western values, this—he was burned
for heresy at the insistence of Calvin, after refusing to recant.

The Islamic world not only produced scientific theory but considered
the social role of religion. Another philosopher and physician, Rhazes,
held the view "that religion was the cause of wars and was hostile to philosophy and science. He believed in the progress of science and he considered Plato, Aristotle, Hippocrates much greater than the holy books."[11]
No comparable figure in, say, tenth-century Normandy could have
openly expounded these views and expected to live. In some Muslim
states comparable positions were held at the highest level of the state. In
India the Mughul Emperor Akbar (1556–1605) emphasized "the path of
reason" (rahi aql) rather than "reliance on tradition" and devoted much
consideration to the basis of religious identity and non-denominational
rule in India. His conclusions were published in Agra in 1591–92, shortly
before Bruno was burned at the stake in Rome.[12] Akbar's minister and
spokesman Abu'l Fazl included several exasperated passages in his book
A'in-i Akbari, bemoaning the constraints imposed on scientific endeavor
by religious obscurantism: "From time immemorial, the exercise of inquiry has been restricted, and questioning and investigation have been
regarded as precursors of infidelity. Whatever has been received from father, kindred and teacher is considered as a deposit under Divine sanction
and a malcontent is reproached with impiety or irreligion. Although a

few among the intelligent of their generation admit the imbecility of this procedure in others, yet they will not stir one step in this direction them-selves."[13] Clearly, then, there is nothing intrinsic to Islamic society that prevented Muslims from engaging in rational or scientific thought. Yet these intimations of Enlightenment, which occurred at an earlier historical stage than in the West, never emerged into a similar full-blown movement capable of contributing to the transformation of society. Ibn al-Nafis was untroubled by authority, but his ideas had no influence on medicine in the Islamic world; in the West, where similar ideas were initially punished by death, they were also rediscovered and within a hundred and fifty years became part of mainstream medical thought. Ideas, however brilliant, are by themselves incapable of changing the world; they must first find em-bodiment in some social force. Why was this missing?

THE NATURE OF ISLAMIC SOCIETY

There were great transformations in Islam between, say, the death of the Prophet in 632 and the fall of Constantinople in 1453, but some under-lying characteristics remained throughout. The Islamic world rested on a series of wealthy cities ranging from Baghdad in modern Iraq to Cairo in modern Egypt to Cordoba in modern Spain. Connecting these urban centers was a system of highly developed desert and sea trade routes, along which caravans and ships brought luxury goods like spices and manufactured goods like pottery. The richness and opulence of this civ-ilization stood in stark contrast to impoverished, backward Europe.

But what was the basis of the underlying economy—the "mode of production"? Feudalism, the mode that dominated in Western Europe and Japan, was of minor importance in the states of the Muslim world, with the major exception of Persia (modern-day Iran) and parts of India. Instead, the dominant mode was what some Marxists, including the pres-ent writer, call the tributary mode.[14] The point here is not to enter into esoteric debates about classification but to note the consequences for the possibility of capitalist development. In Europe the feudal estates monar-chies presided over weak, decentralized states; power was devolved to local lords based in the countryside, and it was here, in their local juris-dictions, that exploitation was carried out through the extraction of rent and labor services. But precisely because of this fragmented structure, it was possible for capitalist production to begin in (as Marx put it) "the interstices" between different areas of parcelized sovereignty. The towns varied in size and power, and the claim that they alone were sites of capitalist development is simply untenable—for one thing, some acted as collective feudal lords in their own right—but some at least were free from lordly or monarchical domination and provided spaces where new approaches to production could develop. Attempts have been made to present the Enlightenment as a pure expression of scientific rationality, which coincidentally appeared in the epoch of the transition from feudalism and the bourgeois revolutions. But it must rather be understood as the theorization of these economic and political processes, though in many complex and mediated ways. (Although in some cases, Scotland above all, the connection is clear and direct—what else is *The Wealth of Nations* about?)

The conditions that allowed capitalist development, and hence the Enlightenment, did not exist to the same extent in the Muslim world. In the Ottoman Empire, which lay at its heart, there was no private property in land, no local lordship, and therefore little space for new approaches to production and exploitation to arise. The state was the main exploiter, and its officials consciously sought to confine potential alternative sources of power, hence their bias toward small-scale commerce and hostility toward large mercantile capital. Consequently, merchants tended to be from external "nations"—Jews, Greeks, or Armenians—not from the native Arab or Turkish populations. There is therefore nothing inherently stagnant about Islamic societies, but they stand as the best example of how ruling classes are consciously able to use state power, "the superstructure," to prevent new and threatening classes from forming, with all that implies about the thwarting of intellectual developments. "Asking why the Scientific Revolution did not occur in Islam," writes Pervez Hoodbhoy, exaggerating only slightly, "is practically equivalent to asking why Islam did not produce a powerful bourgeois class."[15]

Take the example of the Tunisian writer Ibn Khaldun (1332–1402), author of the *Kitab Al-Ilbar* or *Book of Examples* (usually referred to in English as *The Muqaddimah* or *Introduction to History*). His sociological insights identified the continuing struggle between civilizations as based, on the one hand, on towns and traders (*hadarah*), and on the other on tribes and holy men (*badawah*), the two endlessly alternating as the dominant forces within the Muslim world. Adam Smith and his colleagues in the Historical School of the Scottish Enlightenment could develop a theory that saw societies develop and progress upward from one "mode of subsistence" to another because they had seen this movement in England and wished to see it reproduced in Scotland. Ibn Khaldun saw only cyclical repetition in the history of Islamic society and could not envisage any way to break the cycle. His work could not transcend the society it sought to theorize.[16]

In the face of this, the doctrines and organization of Islam are difficult to separate out into independent factors. In Christian Europe, church and state were allied in defense of the existing order; in the Islamic world they were fused. There was no separate church organization. There were of course differences between branches of Islam: Shiites favored rule by charismatic imams, Sunnis a consensus among believers. But in neither was there an overarching church organization comparable to that of Christianity. Instead a federal structure arose that adapted to the individual states. It is difficult, therefore, to dissociate reasons of state from reasons of religion: a belief in predestination implied that it was impious or even impossible to attempt to predict future events, while a belief in utilitarianism focused intellectual investigation or borrowing only on what was immediately useful. Finally, as the boundaries of the Islamic world began to run up against the expanding European powers from the sixteenth century on, the idea of drawing on European methods and discoveries became all the more painful to contemplate for ruling elites accustomed to their own sense of superiority. As the Western threat grew, the control over what was taught became even more extreme.

PARTIAL REFORM

Chinese history tends to support the view that the key issue is not religion but the nature of the economy and "the corresponding form of the state." Like Islam, China encompassed a great civilization with important scientific and technical accomplishments, surpassing those of Europe. But here too was a bureaucratic tributary state acting to suppress emergent class forces and their dangerous ideas. Reading the work of one leading intellectual in seventeenth-century China, Wang Fuzhi (1619–92), it is difficult not to see him as a predecessor to Adam Smith in Scotland or the Abbe Sieyès in France, but his thoughts led to no immediate results.[17] In China, as in the House of Islam, the state acted to control the spread of dangerous thoughts. During the eighteenth century in particular, critical writings were censored or destroyed. The high point of this "literary inquisition," as it was known, ran between 1779 and 1789—the events of the latter year showing the distance that had opened up between China and Europe.[18] But China was not an Islamic country: the similarities lie not in religion but in economy and state, and it was these that led them to a common fate.

The temporary conquest of the Ottoman province of Egypt by French revolutionary armies in 1798 not only revealed military weakness but also heralded the violent intrusion of Enlightenment ideas into the sealed world of Islam. This led to an attempt, first in Egypt and Turkey, to adapt at least some of the technical, scientific, and military aspects of Enlightenment thought. Many of the aspects of Islam that are ignorantly supposed to be "medieval" traditions are actually products of this period of partial reform. As one historian notes: "Often wrongly regarded in today's West as a mark of medieval obscurantism, the *burkah* was actually a modern dress that allowed women to come out of the seclusion of their homes and participate to a limited degree in public and commercial affairs."[19] Another points out: "The office of ayatollah is a creation of the nineteenth century; the rule of Khomeini and of his successor as 'supreme Jurist,' an innovation of the twentieth."[20] The imperial division and occupation of the Middle East after the First World War froze and in some cases even reversed the process. It should not be forgotten, in the endless babble about Western superiority, that feudal social relationships—against which the Enlightenment had raged—were actually *introduced* into Iraq by the British occupiers after 1920, to provide a social basis for the regime.[21]

The subsequent history has been told in remorseless detail by Robert Fisk in *The Great War for Civilization* and cannot even be attempted here. The question is: after over a hundred years of imperialist intervention, does the Islamic world today have to reproduce the experience of the West, from Renaissance to Reformation to Enlightenment? In 1959 one Afghan intellectual, Najim oud-Din Bammat, wrote: "Islam today has to go through a number of revolutions at once; a religious revolution like the Reformation; an intellectual and moral revolution like the eighteenth-century Enlightenment; an economic and social revolution like the European Industrial Revolution of the nineteenth century."[22] History, however, does not do repeats. Trotsky's theory of uneven and combined development leads us to expect that these revolutions do not have to follow each other but can interlock and be compressed in time.[23] Christian Europe, after all, was incomparably less developed than Arab or Persian civilization in the tenth or eleventh centuries. But its very backwardness allowed it to incubate a far higher form of class society—capitalism—and hence to "catch up and overtake" its former superiors, and in the process to fragment, occupy, and destroy them.

When the Enlightenment came to the masses of the Islamic world, it came not as a recapitulation of the European experience of the seventeenth and eighteenth centuries, but in the form of Marxism, the inheritor in radicalized form of that experience. Unfortunately, the theoretical and organizational forms in which Marxism made its impact were Stalinist ones and consequently carried within them the seeds of disaster—most spectacularly in Iraq during the 1950s and in Iran during the 1970s, but more insidiously almost everywhere else. It is because of the catastrophic record of Stalinism and, more broadly, of secular nationalism that people who would once have been drawn to socialism see Islamism as an alternative path to liberation today.

What future then for Islam and the Enlightenment? We should remember the experience of the West. Our Enlightenment occurred when Christianity was older than Islam is now, and it did not occur all at once. People did not simply become "rational" and abandon their previous views because they heard the wise words of Spinoza, Voltaire, or their popularizers. It happened over time and because the experience of social change and struggle made people more open to new ideas, ideas that began to explain the world in a way that religion no longer did. Socialists in the West have to begin, as Lenin always insisted, with *politics*, with the actual context of institutional racism and military intervention that faces Muslims every day. The absolute obligation on socialists is first to defend Muslims, both in the West and in the developing world, and to develop the historic alliance at the heart of the antiwar movement. To say that they, or people of any faith, must abandon their beliefs before we will deign to speak to them is not only arrogant but displays all the *worst* aspects of the Enlightenment: "Here is the Truth, on your knees before it!"[24] Why should Muslims listen to people whose self-importance is so great that they make agreement with them a precondition of even having a conversation? As Ambalavaner Sivanandan has written: "When our rulers ask us old colonials, new refugees, desperate asylum seekers—the *sub-homines*—to live up to British values, they are not referring to the values that they themselves exhibit, but those of the Enlightenment, which they have betrayed. We, the *sub-homines*, in our struggle for basic human rights, not only uphold basic human values, but challenge Britain to return to them."[25]

Enlightenment cannot be imposed by legal fiat or at the point of a gun. The real precondition of debate is unity in action, where discussion can take place secure in the knowledge that participants with different beliefs nevertheless share common goals. It is, I suspect, more than a coincidence that those who are most insistent on the need for Islamic Enlightenment are the voices crying loudest for war. The original Enlightenment will never recur, but we may be seeing the first signs of a New Enlightenment, not in these voices but in the actions of those—Muslim and non-Muslim alike—who have taken to the streets to oppose them.

≈ Chapter 7 ≈

The Necessity of Multiple Nation-States for Capital*

INTRODUCTION

Imagine that at some point in the future a single global polity has come into being and taken ownership and control of the entire world economy. Society under these conditions could be organized in one of two different ways. One way would be without classes, where the state has been replaced by a "protogovernmental" or "protopolitical administration."[1] The other way would leave class divisions intact, but with state managers

---

* Originally published in *Rethinking Marxism* 24, no. 1 (January 2012). This version also incorporates passages from "Putting the Nation Back into 'The International,'" *Cambridge Review of International Affairs* 22, no. 1 (March 2009) and the whole of "Many Capitals, Many States: Contingency, Logic or Mediation?," in *Marxism and Global Politics: Challenging Global Capitalism*, edited by Alexander Anievas (London: Routledge, 2010).

now directly occupying the position of the ruling class. The first would be world socialism. The second would be entirely new in human history, although comparable futures have been imagined in science fiction since H. G. Wells's *A Modern Utopia* (1905), and many attempts to classify the USSR as either "totalitarian" or a new form of class society envisaged a dictatorial world state as the outcome of Russian victory in the Cold War.[2] From a Marxist perspective, such a monolithic economic entity would have one thing in common with socialism: it would have ceased to be capitalist, for the nature of capitalism is determined by competition, and competition requires "many capitals." A "universal" capital, as Marx put it, is a "non-thing," an impossibility.[3] But how feasible is this hitherto unknown form of class society?

Marx thought the "entire social capital" of an individual society could be united under a single capitalist or company.[4] Subsequent Marxist theorists of imperialism projected this theoretical possibility onto a global scale, with capital continuing to become ever more concentrated and centralized until it formed one body, which they variously described as a "general cartel," a "universal capitalist trust," or a "single world trust."[5] For the thinkers of the Second and Third Internationals, however, this new and universal Leviathan was highly unlikely ever to be realized. It is sometimes claimed that this was because they expected working-class revolution to cut short developments in this direction.[6] But there was another reason. Any consummation of trends toward centralization and concentration would also be prevented by political-military conflicts, both among the imperialist powers and between them and emerging capitalist states. The development of a global state is even less likely now, since the aspect of the period that made them most plausible—the interpenetration of state and capital toward an integral "state capitalism"—is no longer the dominant tendency within contemporary economies.

Leave aside then this object of literary fantasy, political paranoia, and Marxist speculation, and envisage instead the completely opposite configuration: no state, but many capitals. Those who have come closest to advocating this outcome have been adherents of what might be called anarcho-capitalist thought, from Max Stirner and John Calhoun in the mid-nineteenth century to Murray Rothbard and Ayn Rand in more recent times.[7] Yet the career path as a state manager followed by one of Rand's leading devotees, Alan Greenspan, suggests that their hostility is more to certain state functions—above all those concerned with welfare provision—than to the institution itself. As Greenspan inquires in his autobiography: "If taxation was wrong, how could you reliably finance the essential functions of government, including the protection of individuals' rights through police power?"[8] Marxists have not considered the possibility of capitalism dispensing with the state to be a very likely one either, although some have wondered why class rule takes this particularly "public" form rather than using private means of coercion.[9] The question has arisen in a different form more recently, in the context of debates over globalization. Fred Halliday, for example, has charged Marxists with failing to explain "why, if there is a world economy in which class interests operate transnationally, there is a need for states at all."[10] I will address why this need exists below, but for the moment, let us assume that capitalism always consists of many capitals and capitals always require a state. Does it follow that many capitals necessarily require many states?

If neither the bureaucratic collectivist nightmare nor the anarcho-capitalist dream is feasible, we are left with one alternative to the existing situation, which draws elements from them both: a single global polity under which economic life is still carried on by many competing capitals. The notion briefly surfaced in classical sociology, for example in Ferdinand Tönnies's *Gemeinschaft und Gesellschaft* (1887), which speculated on whether it would be possible to "abolish the multiplicity of states and substitute for it a single world republic, coextensive with the world market."[11] Most Marxist writers, however, believe that theoretically desirable as this outcome may be from the point of view of capital, it is unlikely to be achieved in practice.[12] Even those who are often grouped together as identifying the emergence of a "single state" are usually arguing something quite different. Michael Hardt and Antonio Negri, for example, claim that nation-states and imperialism as traditionally understood are no longer central to the capitalist world order; they have been superseded by a new and metaphysical "logic of rule," which they conceptualize as "empire." But while they argue that some states, notably the US, may be better adapted to these new conditions, they do not argue that states are ceasing to exist: "empire" has superseded states without replacing them.[13] At the other end of the spectrum, Leo Panitch and Sam Gindin claim that the US is now a global imperial power without precedent or peer, and has successfully incorporated all potential economic competitors into a single imperial protectorate, within which geopolitical rivalries are no longer conceivable. But here again there is no suggestion that all other nation-states are to be literally absorbed into the US. Indeed, the consolidation of US hegemony implies the continued existence of other states over which hegemony can be exercised.[14]

I do not find either of these arguments convincing, but the point is that neither suggests that a world state is imminent, or even possible. Malcolm Bull's claim that the European empires, the Soviet Union, and the current American hegemony were successive aspects of "a global state in all but name" is simply playing with words.[15] There are non-Marxist writers of a social-constructivist bent who claim that a global state will "inevitably" emerge, not as a function of capitalist development but because the dangers posed by the anarchy of the states system will drive actors into seeking unity.[16] Among Marxists, though, William Robinson is virtually alone in claiming that a global capitalist state is in the process of coming into being through existing transnational state apparatuses, and the problems with his position have already been convincingly demonstrated.[17] The debate is therefore less to do with whether a global state will emerge in the future than with precisely *why* one will not, and what the implications of this are for relationships between capitalist states. We can quickly dispense with two possible reasons.

Alex Callincos has argued that uneven and combined development offers an explanation, a position that some of his critics have also accepted.[18] Leaving the substantive issue aside for the moment, it is not clear to me that Callinicos is referring to *combined* development at all.[19] He invokes it at the beginning of his discussion, but almost immediately shifts attention onto the earlier and less comprehensive theory of *uneven* development. In particular, he draws from Lenin's *Imperialism: The Highest Stage of Capitalism* to show how "uneven development that both raises productivity and is economically destabilizing, is inherent in capitalism" and "constantly subverts the efforts to integrate 'many capitals' into a single entity."[20] But uneven development does not in itself provide an explanation for the continued existence of the states system. Individual states have coexisted with massive internal unevenness, in some cases carried over in different forms from the feudal to the capitalist period, without it necessarily leading to fragmentation. The long-standing status of the north/south divide in Italy and the later emergence of another distinct geographical area in the postwar "Third Italy" have not seriously threatened the integrity of the state.[21] Similarly, the Scottish Highland/Lowland divide shows how ongoing levels of unevenness, unparalleled in Western Europe, have existed at a substate, regional level within Britain since 1707.[22] Why could similar extremes of unevenness not be contained within a single global state? As we shall see, there are reasons why a single world state is unlikely, but the territorial unevenness of capitalism is not one of them.

A more plausible argument for the continued existence of many states can, of course, be made from sheer practicality, or what Ellen Meiksins Wood calls "the insurmountable difficulty of sustaining on a large geographical scale the close regulation and predictability capital needs."[23] Neil Smith agrees that "a nation-state that is too large finds it difficult to maintain political control over its entire territory" and further argues that states can also be too small to be effective for capital: "The geographical extent of the nation-state is constrained on the low end by the need to control a sufficiently large market (for labor and commodities) to fuel accumulation."[24] But even size is not decisive. As Vivek Chibber notes, "one could certainly imagine a federated system, in which administrative and regulative authority is localized, but sovereignty is not."[25] Something more fundamental is involved here.

In the *Grundrisse*, Marx comments that some determinations exist throughout history, while others exist only at certain times in history.[26] To which category do states belong? States have certainly existed in different forms since the origins of class society, but as Alasdair MacIntyre once noted, "the difference between one form of society and another is not just a difference in basis, and a corresponding difference in superstructure, but a difference also in the way basis is related to superstructure."[27] The issue is therefore whether or not we treat these different forms of state as also being different types of determination. Are there simply "states" that relate in particular ways to different social formations, or are there "feudal states" and "capitalist states," the character of which is determined by the dominant mode of production? What is capitalist about a capitalist state?

Any state has to play two roles: one of representation, to "promote and defend the ruling class and its mode of exploitation or supremacy"; the other, mediation of "the exploitation or domination of the ruling class over other classes and strata."[28] In neither case is every action necessarily in the direct collective interest of the ruling class. It is rather that "all other interests are regularly *subordinated* to the interests of the ruling class."[29] There are, however, particular functions that capitalist states must perform, of which three are particularly important. The first is the imposition of a dual social order: horizontally over competing capitals so that market relations do not collapse into "the war of all against all"; and vertically over the conflict between capital and labor so that it continues to be resolved in the interest of the former. The second is the establishment of "general conditions of production" that individual competing capitals would be unwilling or unable to provide, including some basic level of technical infrastructure and welfare provision.[30] The necessity of the state to perform these functions for capital was well made in appropriately homespun images by Barack Obama in a speech during his 2012 presidential reelection campaign:

> If you were successful, somebody along the line gave you some help. There was a great teacher somewhere in your life. Somebody helped to create this unbelievable American system that we have that allowed you to thrive. Somebody invested in roads and bridges. If you've got a business—you didn't build that. Somebody else made that happen. The Internet didn't get invented on its own. Government research created the Internet so that all the companies could make money off the Internet. The point is, is that when we succeed, we succeed because of our individual initiative, but also because we do things together. There are some things, just like fighting fires, we don't do on our own. I mean, imagine if everybody had their own fire service. That would be a hard way to organize fighting fires. So we say to ourselves, ever since the founding of this country, you know what, there are some things we do better together. That's how we funded the GI Bill. That's how we created the middle class. That's how we built the Golden Gate Bridge or the Hoover Dam. That's how we invented the Internet. That's how we sent a man to the moon.[31]

These first two functions are both mainly "internal" to the territory of the state. The third function of the capitalist state, on the other hand, is to represent the collective interests of the "internal" capitalist class "externally" in relation to other capitalist states and classes. But capitalist states also engage in other external activities—variously described as "international relations" or "geopolitics"—that sometimes appear to play no role in supporting national capitals and may even be detrimental to their interests. Does this mean that, in some respects at least, the states system is (absolutely or relatively) autonomous from capitalism? If so, it would mean treating the state as a "capitalist state" for the purposes of internal class relations, including relations within the capitalist class, but as a "state under capitalism" for the purposes of external relations.

I think this is a position that it is impossible for Marxists to adopt, but any alternative has to transcend the two most coherent Marxist explanations for the continued coexistence of many capitals and many states. Both deny that there is any intrinsic connection between capital accumulation on the one hand and the inter-state system on the other. One is the argument from historical contingency associated with Robert Brenner, Hannes Lacher, Benno Teschke, and Ellen Meiksins Wood. The other is the argument from overlapping autonomous logics associated with Giovanni Arrighi, Alex Callinicos, and David Harvey. Contingency suggests an accident of history, whereas logic implies a coincidence of interests, but neither allows for any deeper underlying relationship; the connection is simply fortuitous, for reasons of either timing or motivation.

Both these explanations should be regarded as clusters of related argumentation rather than straightforwardly shared positions. Each member of the former group starts from the same assumptions about social property relations but individually reaches different conclusions. Each member of the latter group proceeds from a different perspective on territorial and economic logics only to arrive at very similar conclusions. I should also make clear that I do not regard these clusters as equivalents. Whatever the merits of the former group in other areas—and these are not negligible—as far the question of geopolitical rivalry is concerned, the latter seems to me to have both a more realistic perspective and one that is consequently a better guide to political practice: my disagreements with them are concerned more with the arguments by which they reach their conclusions than with the conclusions themselves.

STATES OF CONTINGENCY

In recent years the autonomy of the capitalist state has become a key ideological component of neoliberal thought. Nigel Harris, for example, rejects the use of the phrase "capitalist state" as "a term of abuse," on the grounds that "any state operating in the modern world must reach some

working accommodation with businessmen, domestic or foreign, to secure long-term survival, but to call it capitalist when there are no non-
capitalists . . . is to use a distinction which is either redundant or contrasted
with only a hypothetical alternative (so it becomes not a description but
an affirmation of political commitment)."[32] One response to these claims
would be that the notion of a "capitalist state" is neither redundant nor
affirmative, but primarily historical, as in the past there have been slave
states, tributary states, varieties of feudal state (estates monarchy and absolutist), and even short-lived workers' states, above all in Russia between
1917 and 1928. But Harris—whose recent works exude all the genuine
if misguided sincerity of the convert—implies that "the state" is essentially
the same under all modes of production and merely interacts with them
in different ways. The recent history of capitalism suggests the problem
with this claim, given the way in which the neoliberal project was nur-
tured and advanced by state activity, under the initial vanguard regimes
of Pinochet, Thatcher, and Reagan.[33] The generally hypocritical and self-
serving nature of this kind of argument should be obvious.

A less tendentious and generally more plausible argument for the
autonomy of the state has been given by Michael Mann: "The nation-
state system of our own era was not a product of capitalism (nor, indeed,
of feudalism) considered as pure modes of production. It is in that sense
'autonomous.' But it resulted from the way expansive, emergent, capitalist
relations were given regulative boundaries by pre-existing states."[34] Political Marxists effectively take the same position.[35] According to Teschke:
"If capitalism had developed within the framework of a universal Empire,
it is hard to see why it would have caused its break-up into multiple territorial units. In other words, there is no constitutive or genetic link between capitalism and a geopolitical universe."[36] In a contribution written
with Lacher, the point is made more explicit: "Counterfactually, it is perfectly possible to imagine that had capitalism emerged within an imperial
formation—let us say the Roman Empire—it would not have required
the political break-up into multiple territorial units."[37] Let us leave speculation about alternative pasts aside.[38] Does this view of the relationship
between capitalism and the states system imply the possibility of their
separation in the future?

Not necessarily. "It may be," writes Lacher, "that territorial statehood,
while not originating within capitalism, has become so entrenched that

it is all but impossible to move toward a form of state that corresponds to capitalism's globalizing dynamic."[39] In effect, this position simultaneously denies that capitalism has an intrinsic need for the states system and affirms that the states system is likely to continue in existence at least as long as capitalism does. Lacher and Teschke argue that they came to be linked because capitalism grew up within an existing states system with its own established dynamics of competition: "Capitalism did not develop out of itself the system of territorial states which fragments capitalist world society. Inversely: capitalism is structured by an international system because it was born in the world of a pre-existing system of territorial states."[40] Justin Rosenberg has expressed similar views, adding that "one cannot, it is true, derive any logical necessity of political fragmentation from Marx's general theory of capital. But why would one wish to?" Rosenberg argues that we need to consider instead the nature of capitalism, for, "perhaps uniquely, it has no intrinsic need to overcome [political fragmentation] in order to expand its own reach or further its development."[41] The suggestion seems to be that since territorial fragmentation is not a problem for capitalism, it should not be one for Marxist analysis of capitalism either. But even at the empirical level, problems do nevertheless remain.

The preexisting world of territorial states included forms as different as "city states, empires, federations, republics, centralized kingdoms, loosely knit elective monarchies and many variants on them."[42] If the capitalist states system can be said to have inherited this framework, it is only in the banal sense that both the earlier and later systems involve a multiplicity of states, since neither the forms taken by precapitalist territorial states nor their systemic relationships bear any resemblance to those of capitalism. Let us assume, therefore, that we are talking about the dominant feudal-absolutist states and their relationships, rather than the precapitalist states system as a whole. Narrowed down in this way, the capitalist states system can indeed be said to have emerged from the preexisting states system, but only in the same way as the capitalist mode of production emerged from within the feudal mode of production. Each individual capitalist state was erected on the ruins of its feudal or absolutist predecessor. In some cases more of the rubble was recycled in the construction of the new building than in others, usually in the form of external ornamentation; but in none did the structure inherit or reproduce what had gone before. It could not, for the social contents were different and required different shelters—or prisons. In some cases these states bore the same names and continued to have the same rivals. As Louis Althusser writes, the formation of nation-states is the result of a struggle "whose objective is not the conquest of an already existing form, but the reality of the form that does not yet exist."[43]

Conventional histories trace the wars between England/Britain and France between 1688 and 1815 as if they were all essentially part of the same conflict, but this periodization masks the break of 1789. The wars for the hundred years before 1789 were fought to decide whether the mode of production embodied in the feudal-absolutist French state or in its capitalist-constitutional British rival would dominate Europe and its colonies. By the 1760s it was clear from victories in Scotland (1745–46) and Canada (1756–63) that the British had won this contest. The wars for the twenty-five years after 1789 were fought to decide which type of capitalist state, the conservative British or the radical French, would provide the model for the emergent bourgeois world. By the 1870s it was clear from the trajectory of state formation in Italy, Germany, and Japan that, in the short term at any rate, the British had also emerged victorious in this respect. It is true that between 1870 and 1914 these states all consciously emphasized the archaic, imperial role of their monarchies, and for the inattentive this may look like the assertion of "feudal" elements within the state, indicating an incomplete transition, as Tom Nairn claims is the case for Britain.[44] But this is to confuse form and content. An analogy can be drawn here with Marx's distinction between the formal subsumption of labor under capital in the period of manufacture, in which capital takes over existing labor processes as it finds them, and the real subsumption of labor under capital in the period of machinofacture, where capital creates the labor process anew in factories specially designed for this purpose.[45] In a similar way, state managers took over the outer forms of the existing absolutist states but internally transformed them into apparatuses capable of building an autonomous center of capital accumulation. The point was well made by Bukharin, writing of the ideology of the imperialist powers in the First World War: "These sentiments are not 'remnants of feudalism,' as some observers suppose, these are not debris of the old that have survived in our times. This is an entirely new socio-political formation caused by the birth of finance capital. If the old feudal 'policy of blood and iron' was able to serve here, externally, as a model, this was possible only because the moving springs of modern economic life drive capital along the road of aggressive politics and the militarization of all social life."[46] The preexisting symbolism of the crown was imbued with a sense of national unity against two main challenges: external imperial rivalry and internal class divisions.[47]

Brenner accepts that capitalism "transformed the component states of that system [of multiple feudal states] into capitalist states but failed to alter the multi-state character of the resulting international system."[48] But why was the feudal-absolutist dynamic overcome in all other respects, as its components were transformed by bourgeois revolutions from above or below, *except* that of the state system? His own historical work shows how the regimes in England and the United Netherlands did not carry through the "intrinsical union" that was considered by both during the common-wealth period. Instead, the consolidation of capitalism in both states led to renewed rivalry, including several wars.[49] More recent attempts to unite states at similar levels of development, such as those involving Egypt and Syria in the United Arab Republic between 1958 and 1961, have also failed. But capitalism did not simply fail to overcome preexisting territorial divisions: it added to them. With the important exceptions of German and Italian unification, it was, if anything, the emergence and consolidation of the feudal-absolutist state within Europe that acted to reduce the number of what Charles Tilly calls "state-like units" from a thousand during the fourteenth century to thirty on the eve of the First World War.[50] Conse-quently, it was the collapse of the Austro-Hungarian, Russian, and Ot-toman Empires at the end of that war that signaled the real beginning of the European states system as it is currently constituted. Nor did this process only take place in Europe: colonial territories that were originally created and sustained for centuries by absolutist regimes as unified admin-istrative areas, such as the Spanish-American Empire, disintegrated once capitalist development proceeded beyond a certain level, in that case into eighteen separate states.[51]

And the expansion continues to this day. According to the US De-partment of State list of "independent states" (not an entirely reliable categorization, since it includes Kosovo) the number is at an all-time his-torical high of 194 and continues to grow. The recent expansion needs to be kept in perspective, of course. With some major exceptions like

East Timor, Eritrea, and South Sudan, the majority of new states emerged
from the collapse of Stalinism in Europe, the consequent disintegration
of the USSR and Yugoslavia, and the sundering of Czechoslovakia. They
owe their existence to a historical event for which there is no equivalent
in modern history, other than perhaps the fall of the absolutist monarchies
at the end of the First World War. In the future, Iraq may share the fate
of Yugoslavia and Belgium that of Czechoslovakia, but no empire comparable to the Russian currently exists from which multiple states could
emerge as they did after 1989. Nevertheless, political fragmentation seems
to be as much a part of neoliberal globalization as economic integration.

Countervailing tendencies toward incorporation have been far less
strong, not least because in most cases they would have to involve military
conquest of one state by another, with all the risks that involves.[52] Consequently, for every success like the Chinese reclamation of Hong Kong,
there is a failure like the Iraqi invasion of Kuwait. In short, something
other than mere contingency seems to be involved here. The ubiquity
of the nation-state form and of neoliberal regimes does not of course
mean that nation-states have attained anything like equality. As Jean and
John Comaroff report:

> It is difficult to establish any terms in which, say, Germany and Guinea,
> Bhutan and Belgium, Uganda and the United States, England and Eritrea
> may be held to belong to anything but the most polythetic of categories.
> Nor are the substantive differences among them—differences that are
> *growing* as a result of their engagement with global capitalism—satisfac-
> torily captured by resort to vapid oppositions, to conventional contrasts
> like rich versus poor, North versus South, successful versus unsuccessful
> countries. In some places, as we all know, the state can hardly be said to
> perdure at all, or to perdure purely as a private resource, a family business,
> a convenient fiction; in others, the nation, as imagined community, is little
> more than a rhetorical figure of speech, the color of a football stripe, an
> airline without aircraft, a university barely open. . . . On the other hand,
> despite this variability in their political sociology, nation-states appear, at
> least in their exterior forms, to be more similar than ever before, con-
> verging on the same rule of law, enacting similar constitutions, speaking
> more and more English, borrowing from the same stock of signs and
> symbols, worshipping together at the altar of Adam Smith.[53]

LOGIC OF STATE AND LOGIC OF CAPITAL

An alternative way of understanding the relationship between the states system and capitalism is that it involves two overlapping but autonomous logics. The great merit of this approach is that it recognizes the continuing reality of imperialism as an aspect of capitalist development—indeed, it was initially developed to provide a defensible explanation of the "new imperialism" rather than of the relationship between states and capitals more generally. In presenting his version of the argument, Callinicos somewhat tentatively claimed that Marxist analysis of international relations necessarily involves a "Realist moment."[54] Given the criticism to which he has been subjected in response, I should begin by making clear that I do not think this is where the difficulty with his position lies.

I understand why Marxist practitioners in the discipline of international relations, who have to critically engage with the dominant Realist school on an ongoing basis, might feel undermined by what appears to be a concession, by a leading Marxist thinker, to their opponents.[55] We should however see the issue in less discipline-specific terms. Non-Marxist theories can be compatible with Marxism and have on occasion influenced it. A particularly relevant example here would be Lenin's acknowledgement of the superiority of Hobson over Kautsky and Hilferding on the question of imperialism.[56] Ernest Gellner's theory of nationalism is a more recent example. He refused to distinguish at any fundamental level between capitalist and "socialist" states and expected nationalism to be equally characteristic of them both.[57] In the case of the latter type of state, this is not to be explained by the persistence of bourgeois ideology or the similar idealist conceptions once invoked to explain why society under the Stalinist regimes resembled that of their Western capitalist opponents.[58] Rather, it was because both were examples of industrial societies that required nationalism for the purposes of cultural and ultimately political cohesion. I differ from Gellner in seeing the similarity between the US and the USSR as due to the fact that both are forms of capitalist rather than industrial society, but I endorse his insistence that the same socioeconomic logic will essentially produce the same cultural and ideological effects. One of the many advantages of this position is that it removes the need for any special explanation for inter-"socialist" wars, which so bemused that other great theoretician of nationalism, Benedict Anderson, and led him to seek the origins of nationalism in essentially—here comes that word again—contingent factors.[59]

Similar parallels can be found in Realism. Liberalism assumes that democracies tend to resolve issues through negotiation rather than violence, that they possess institutional barriers to breaking with this tendency, and that they are responsive to their populations, who are assumed to be opposed to war with other democracies.[60] At best, this overgeneralizes from the internal cohesion of the West during the Cold War. At worst, it ignores the structural limitations on liberal democracy, even in those states that are closest to the formal models of equality, participation, and representation. These limitations are currently being strengthened as political choice is minimized under neoliberal hegemony. Nor is there any logic in assuming that the populations of democratic states would support war against dictatorships but not other democracies. In theory, the populations of democracies have chosen their political rulers and consequently are responsible for their decisions; in actuality, the populations of dictatorships have not. Why then should the latter be subjected to the disasters of war for the sins of their leaders? The extent of popular opposition to the war in Iraq suggests that this was the reasoning followed by millions of people—people whose views were of course ignored, to a greater or lesser extent, by the "democratic" governments of the West.

By contrast, take a typical statement by leading Realist John Mearsheimer: "The structure of the international state system forces states which seek only to be secure nonetheless to act aggressively toward each other." This can be criticized not because he predicts that states—or at least states of a certain size—will behave aggressively but because he treats this type of behavior as a result of the mere fact of statehood, rather than of the states' class nature. Nevertheless, I agree with his claim that China will inevitably seek to transform "its economic might into military might and make a run at dominating Northeast Asia," regardless of whether it establishes bourgeois democracy or not, "because democracies care about security as much as non-democracies do, and hegemony is the best way for any state to guarantee its own defense."[61] In this debate it is not Callinicos but contributors who claim that capitalist states act for noncapitalist reasons who display Realist tendencies. Nevertheless, rather than describe Marxism as displaying a Realist moment, it might be better to say that Marxism intersects at different points with other theoretical traditions, of which Realism is one, to the extent they are capable of a partially scientific analysis of reality. There is, however, a genuinely "non-Marxist" moment in Callinicos's formulations, which he shares with a writer rather closer to the traditions of historical materialism than Mearsheimer, namely Harvey, although the positions in question were independently arrived at.

Unlike the argument from contingency, the argument from "two autonomous logics" has already undergone important shifts in meaning at the hands of its adherents. In Arrighi's original formulation, it referred to two different forms of state power, conceptualized as "territorialist" and "capitalist," whose logics intersect.[62] In Harvey's reformulation, the distinction is between the logics of territorial states and of capitalist economies, for which "the motivations and interests of agents differ." Harvey claims that although the logics are "distinct," they also "intertwine in complex and often contradictory ways": "The difficulty for concrete analysis of actual situations is to keep the two sides of this dialectic simultaneously in motion and not to lapse into either a solely political or a predominantly economic mode of argumentation."[63] The unsatisfactory nature of this reformulation—for Marxists at any rate—is that the so-called dialectic of territorial states and capitalist economies still requires you to show how the former has interests distinct from those of the latter without lapsing into explanatory pluralism. For Harvey this does not necessarily involve a major theoretical problem. One of his major achievements has been to reconstruct Marx's critique of political economy, but, as he describes, this was accomplished solely with reference to Marx's own texts, "without too much help from elsewhere."[64] More specifically, as Callinicos notes, "there has in general been very little sense of Marxism as a tradition (or indeed a cluster of partly overlapping, partly conflicting traditions) in his writing: the obverse of his intense involvement with Marx's economic texts is a relative inattention to the work of subsequent Marxists and certainly to the Marxisms of the Second and Third Internationals."[65]

Harvey is aware of this tradition, but although his work in *The New Imperialism* may reoccupy "the terrain of the classics," unlike his earlier work it does not engage with them. Harvey is prepared to adopt particular concepts from classical Marxism, such as Luxemburg's notion of "overaccumulation," but nowhere have these writings been integrated into his understanding of capitalism in the same way as *Capital* itself has.[66] Marx's own theory can be used, in Harvey's formulation, to "rub up against" several quite different forms of thought.[67] This can indeed be productive, but it is also possible to rub someone up the wrong way. Hannah Arendt's metaphysics of power, upon which Harvey draws, is suggestive and had been unfairly ignored, but as a scientific alternative to the work of Kautsky, Hilferding, Lenin, Bukharin, Luxemburg, Steinberg, and Grossman it leaves something to be desired.[68] In short, Harvey is an eclectic—or perhaps it would be more accurate to say that he has *become* an eclectic as his work has become more concrete: his earlier, more abstract writings show far greater theoretical consistency.[69] In any event, pluralism does not necessarily involve him in a major theoretical problem. It does however mean that his position is quite compatible with—indeed is an unacknowledged example of—a neo-Weberian separation of different types of power. "The territorial logic dominated and frustrated the capitalist logic," Harvey writes of the Second World War, "thus forcing the latter into an almost terminal crisis through territorial conflict."[70] Harvey sees something similar occurring for the US now, but so, for example, does Mann.[71] The terminology is different, the analysis broadly similar. Weber himself was clear that capitalism and states had entered an "alliance," following the revival of the cities under feudalism and their subsequent deprivation of power:

> Everywhere the military, judicial, and industrial authority was taken away from the cities. In form the old rights were as a rule unchanged, in fact the modern city was deprived of its freedom as effectively as had happened in antiquity with the establishment of the Roman dominion, though in contrast with antiquity they came under the power of competing national states in a condition of perpetual struggle for power in peace and war. This competitive struggle created the largest opportunities for modern western capitalism. The separate states had to compete for mobile capital, which dictated to them the conditions under which it would assist them to power. Out of this alliance of the state with capital, dictated by necessity, arose the national citizen class, the bourgeoisie in the modern sense of the word. Hence it is the closed national state which afforded to capitalism its chance for development—and so long as the national state does not give place to a world empire capitalism will endure.[72]

Callinicos is of course aware of the danger of "surreptitiously embracing" Weberian positions.[73] In a review of Harvey's *The New Imperialism* he and Samantha Ashman reject treating "economic and geopolitical competition" as "separate spheres," because the "interdependence" of state managers and capitalists impels each to intrude on the other's domain: managers attempt to strengthen the economic position of the state "relative to its actual and potential competitors"; capitalists engage in "corporate lobbying."[74] This is true, but in the context of the "two logics" approach is possible to interpret in a way that suggests a mere conjunctural coincidence of interests, whereas what is involved are two sets of interests *both* of which are generated by different moments within the capitalist system.

FOR MEDIATED TOTALITY

Arguments from contingency and twin logics both invoke the same reason for denying any necessary connection between capitals and states, although it is expressed in different terminology. Callinicos, for example, treats the states system as "a set of determinations" with "specific properties that are irreducible to those of previously introduced determinations."[75] Lacher supports his argument for a purely contingent relationship between capitalism and territoriality by claiming that the alternative is to treat everything that exists under capitalism as an emanation from the capitalist relation and to thus treat capitalism as an "expressive totality."[76] This term was first used by Althusser, who associated it with Hegel and contrasted it with his preferred alternative: the unity of a "structure articulated in dominance."[77] According to Nicos Poulantzas, many Marxists—above all Georg Lukács—have also mistakenly embraced expressive totality.[78]

The concept of totality was in fact one of the fundamental components of classical Marxism. And while there were certainly problems with Lukács's elevation of totality to the single most important aspect of Marx's analysis of capitalism, notably his neglect of internal contradiction, the concept itself is indispensable.[79] In any case, Lukács did not himself refer to an "expressive totality"—that expression has been ascribed to him by the Althusserians and political Marxists—but rather to a "*mediated* totality." To be part of a totality is to be part of "a total social situation caught up in the process of social change," and to say that a totality is mediated is to overcome what Lukács calls "the mere immediacy of the empirical world," in which moments are "torn . . . from the complex of their true determinants and placed in artificial isolation."[80]

To what extent is Lukács following Marx here? Callinicos reminds us that Marx begins *Capital* with the commodity, and as the work proceeds he introduces a series of ever more complex and irreducible freestanding determinations, each resolving problems posed earlier in the process of explanation, until a full picture of the capitalist mode of production emerges. The explanatory power of the successive determinations, of which the states system is one, is therefore derived precisely from their externality to the original starting point.[81] Callinicos has consistently contrasted this methodology with that used by Marx in the introduction to the *Grundrisse*, where these additional determinations are generated precisely by the original starting point, thus remaining in classical Hegelian style mere emanations of "capital-in-general."[82]

Now, it is unclear whether *Capital* is as radically anti-Hegelian as Callinicos claims. Marx himself noted in a letter to Engels during 1858 that his "demolition" of the existing theory of profit was methodologically inspired by a rereading of Hegel's *Logic*.[83] In any case, it is possible to establish a genetic connection between determinations while avoiding unreconstructed Hegelianism. Derek Sayer argues that determinations form "a hierarchy of conditions of possibility." So Marx analyzes the commodity before money, because the first is "a condition of the second."[84] But while a determination like money cannot be explained without recourse to the commodity, nothing in the chain of concepts of which they are both part is a "condition of possibility" for the states system. The states system enters stage left, as a fully formed determination whose origin is unexplained. What seems to be involved here are tendencies criticized long ago by Lukács for "tak[ing] over . . . determinations without either analyzing them further or welding them into a concrete totality" or for "forg[ing] arbitrary unmediated connections between things that belong together in an organic union."[85] Nor can the states system itself be explained by the separate application of this methodology, for what could be the starting point analogous to the commodity?

Part of the problem here seems to be the confusion of two types of methodology. In *Capital* Marx sets out a mode of conceptual *presentation*, not one of historical explanation or logical interconnection.[86] For this purpose it need not explain the origin of the determinations, which can be taken as pre-given. But this is different from Marx's actual method of historical and social *analysis*. As Bertell Ollman writes, Marx conceives of reality "as a totality composed of internally related parts," where each of these parts "in its fullness can represent the totality." This involves more than simply affirming that the different aspects of social life are related to each other—a position from which few people would dissent. It means that for each aspect "the conditions of its existence are taken to be part of what it is."[87]

In his mature work Marx argued that there were three different forms of human practice, which together explain how societies emerge, develop, and transform themselves. One form of human practice involves those activities that bring together natural and technological capacities and qualities to directly produce and reproduce human existence. These activities set the conditions of possibility for the social relationships of cooperation, exploitation, and conflict within which they take place. These relationships in turn set the conditions of possibility for the institutions—of which the states system is fundamental—and ideologies by which they are justified, defended, and challenged.[88] Marx famously summarizes this perspective in the 1859 "Preface" to *A Contribution to the Critique of Political Economy*, but its most illuminating expression occurs in an equally familiar passage from *Capital* itself: "It is in each case the direct relationship of owners of the conditions of production to the immediate producers—a relationship whose particular form naturally corresponds always to a certain level of development of the type and manner of labor, and hence to its social productive power—in which we find the innermost secret, the hidden basis of the entire social edifice, and hence also the political form of the relationship of sovereignty and dependence, in short, the specific form of the state in each case." As we shall see, "the direct relationship of owners of the conditions of production to the immediate producers" can explain "the innermost secret, the hidden basis" not only of the state but of the *system* of states.[89] It is true, as Gonzalo Pozo-Martin reminds us, that the states system cannot be "deduced from the concept of capital," but to then argue that "it exerts its own set of determinations, quite independently of capital," is to abandon the notion of totality central to Marx's method.[90] The problem can be illustrated by looking at two central claims associated with, respectively, arguments from contingency and arguments from two autonomous logics. The first is that there is a separation of *function* between the economic and the political under capitalism. The second—which in some respects is a specific example of the first claim—is that there is a divergence of *interest* between those who run the state and those who embody capital.

"The separation of the economic and the political under capitalism"

Under all precapitalist modes of production, exploitation took place visibly through the extraction of a literal surplus from the direct producers by the threat or reality of violence: economics and politics were fused in the power of the feudal lord or the tributary state. Under the capitalist mode of production, exploitation takes place invisibly in the process of production itself, through the creation of surplus value over and above that required in reproducing the labor force. Wood identifies a resulting "division of labor in which the two moments of capitalist exploitation—appropriation and coercion—are allocated separately to a 'private' appropriating class and a specialized 'public' coercive institution, the state: on the one hand, the 'relatively autonomous' state has a monopoly of coercive force; on the other hand, that force sustains a private 'economic' power which invests capitalist property with an authority to organize production itself." Furthermore, unlike previous exploiting classes, capitalists exercise economic power without "the obligation to perform social, public functions": "Capitalism is a system marked by the complete separation of private appropriation from public duties; and this means the development of a new sphere of power devoted completely to private rather than social purposes."[91]

The implications of this division for capitalists as a ruling class were noted by some of the earliest social theorists to concern themselves with the emergent system (which they tended to refer to as "commercial society"). Since Adam Smith is—quite unfairly—treated as the patron saint of neoliberalism, it may be worth reminding ourselves of his actual views on capitalists and the narrowness of their interests:

> As their thoughts . . . are commonly exercised rather about the interest of their own particular branch of business, than about that of the society, their judgment, even when given with the greatest candor (which it has not been upon every occasion), is much more to be depended upon with regard to the former of those two objects than with regard to the latter. . . . The proposal of any new law or regulation of commerce which comes from this order ought always to be listened to with great precaution, and ought never to be adopted till after having been long and carefully examined, not only with the most scrupulous, but with the most suspicious attention. It comes from an order of men whose interest is never exactly the same with that of the public, who have generally

an interest to deceive and even to oppress the public, and who accordingly have, upon many occasions, both deceived and oppressed it.[92]

For the purposes of our discussion, the interest in this passage lies not in Smith's still refreshingly candid views about the capacity of business interests for deception and oppression, but in what he says about their inability to see beyond their own immediate interests. This was one of the reasons why he also wrote (thinking of the East India Company): "The government of an exclusive company of merchants is, perhaps, the worst of all governments for any country whatsoever."[93]

Nearly a century later in the 1860s, Smith's greatest successor, Marx, was able to point in *Capital* to the example of the British Factory Acts as an example of how the state had to intervene to regulate the activities of capital in the face of initial opposition from the capitalists themselves:

> The [Factory] Act had hardly received the sanction of Parliament when the manufacturers also discovered this: "The inconveniences we expected to arise from the introduction of the Factory Acts into our branch of manufacture, I am happy to say, have not arisen. We do not find the production at all interfered with; in short, we produce more in the same time." It is evident that the British Parliament, which no one will reproach with being excessively endowed with genius, has been led by experience to the conclusion that a simple compulsory law is sufficient to enact away all the so-called impediments opposed by the nature of the process to the restriction and regulation of the working-day.[94]

Reflecting on the entire legislative episode, Marx noted: "But for all that, capital never becomes reconciled to such changes—and this is admitted over and over again by its own representatives—except 'under the pressure of a General Act of Parliament' for the compulsory regulation of the hours of labor."[95] In fact, the most irreconcilable positions were expressed not by employers but by their ideologues, the most important of whom was Herbert Spencer, who saw—and here we can detect the genuine ancestry of contemporary neoliberalism—the specter of socialist slavery in any form of state intervention.[96]

The thesis concerning bourgeois incapacity was not only restricted to critics like Marx but also shared by supporters of capitalism, and even of Fascism. Carl Schmitt, for example, complained after the First World

War that, unlike working-class ideologues, members of the bourgeoisie no longer understood the friend/enemy distinction, which was central to his concept of "the political"; the spirit of Hegel, he thought, had moved from Berlin to Moscow.[97] Joseph Schumpeter argued a more general case during the Second World War. Yielding to no one in his admiration for the heroic entrepreneur, he nevertheless also noted that, with the possible exception of the United States, "the bourgeois class is ill equipped to face the problems, both domestic and international, that normally have to be faced by a country of any importance"; the bourgeoisie needs "protection by some non-bourgeois group"; ultimately, "it needs a master": "In breaking down the pre-capitalist framework of society, capitalism thus broke not only barriers that impeded its progress but also flying buttresses that prevented its collapse. That process, impressive in its relentless necessity, was not merely a matter of removing institutional deadwood, but of removing partners of the capitalist stratum, symbiosis with whom was an essential element of the capitalist schema."[98] Thus, as Eric Hobsbawm remarks, "a plainly bourgeois society—nineteenth-century Britain—could, without serious problems, be governed by hereditary peers."[99] Without the kind of constraints provided by this precapitalist framework, the more sober instincts of the bourgeois would be overcome by the impulse toward what Schumpeter called "creative destruction."

The delegation of power to the state therefore exists because of what Draper calls "the political inaptitude of the capitalist class" compared to other ruling classes in history. It is not only that feudal lords combine an economic and political role while capitalists perform only the former; it is also that the necessity for capitalists to devote their time to the process of accumulation and their own multiple internal divisions militates against their functioning directly as a governing class.[100] More broadly, Bernard Porter notes that capitalists "tend to be hostile to 'government' generally, which they see mainly as a restraint on enterprise, and on a personal level don't find 'ruling' half so worthwhile or satisfactory as making money."[101] This arrangement is quite compatible with the exercise of bourgeois hegemony over society as a whole, although even in this respect some sections of the bourgeoisie tend to play a more significant role than others; but politically, as Fred Block has written, "the [capitalist] ruling class does not rule."[102]

Claims for the separation of the political and the economic do therefore have scientific validity and highlight a central distinction between the process of exploitation under capitalism and under other modes of production. This clearly has implications for inter-state relations, but what are they? According to Teschke, there is a "complete separation" between the political and the economic under capitalism: "Capitalism's *differentia specifica* as a system of surplus appropriation consists in the historically unprecedented fact that the capital circuits of the world market can in principle function without infringing on political sovereignty. As a rule, capitalism can leave political territories intact. Contracts are concluded, in principle, between private actors in the pre-political sphere of global civil society."[103] The qualifiers introduced by Teschke here—"as a rule" and "in principle" (twice)—suggest a certain conceptual unease, as if these rules and principles might not actually apply in reality, which is indeed the case. "Capital circuits" do operate outside the control of states insofar as they involve money capital, but money capital is ultimately dependent on the moment of production, which cannot escape territoriality and consequently a relationship with state power. Failure to distinguish between the logical development of categories in theory and their development in history leads to the danger of working with platonic or "ideal" conceptions of the capitalist economy and capitalist states that do not correspond to the operation of any actual capitalist economies or capitalist states. In this case, the danger is compounded by convergence with one of the key ideological positions of the bourgeoisie, now attaining something like its purest expression under neoliberalism, which is precisely that politics and economics are, or at least should be, separate realms.[104] As China Miéville remarks, Political Marxists such as Teschke err in both of these respects, first by erecting an abstract model of capitalism and then by taking "capitalism at its own word": "Rather than conceptualizing the separation of politics and economics as a tendency, with an ideological component, he has understood it to be an absolute truth more important to the definition of capitalism than the actual composition of capitalism at any particular time."[105]

Throughout the history of the system, capitalists have employed extraeconomic means to recruit, retain, coerce, and control labor. The self-expansion of the total social capital can never be completely based on unfree labor, of course, because it assumes and requires *general* labor

mobility; but "general" does not mean "universal," and individual capitals can employ, have employed, and continue to employ unfree labor.[106]
As Chibber has noted, even the extent to which these supposed devi-
ations from the capital relation have been discarded has not been because the system grows nearer to some abstract model but because of
successful resistance: "These practices were only abandoned once labor
movements made their continuation impossible."[107] In many cases the
type of controls exercised by capitalists relate specifically to the use of
violence, and only adherence to Weberian definitions of the state can
explain failure to recognize this fact.[108] From the use of private armies
by J. D. Rockefeller in America after the Civil War through to the current universal expansion of private security firms, violence has never
been the monopoly of the capitalist state, for, as Timothy Mitchell argues, violence is not "contingent or external to the logic of history"
but is "constitutive of both markets and monopolies."[109]

In terms of *external* relations, of course, states have always fought to
retain the sole right to exercise violence (civil wars are ultimately struggles to control this right), but now even this is challenged. "With the eas-
ing of state monopolies on violence and the proliferation of acquisitive
private military and mercenary corporations, the brutal 'urbicidal' violence and dispossession that so often helps bolster the parasitic aspects of
Western city economies, as well as feeding contemporary corporate capitalism, is more apparent than ever."[110] The rightly derided notion of the
global War on Terror is an ideologically refracted recognition of this fact.
As Hobsbawm writes: "Over the past thirty years or so . . . the territorial
state has, for various reasons, lost its traditional monopoly of armed force.
. . .The material equipment for warfare is now widely available to private
bodies, as are the means for financing non-state warfare. In this way the
balance between state and non-state organizations has shifted."[111]

In the context of this discussion, however, the key issue is not simply
that non-state actors in general can carry out state functions but that
capital in particular can acquire the characteristics of a state. Take, for example, the free trade or export processing zones in at least some areas of
the developing world. In the Philippines, for example, these are in many
respects "sovereign territory" of the multinationals, from which agents
of the local state are excluded.[112] Nor is the scope of capitalist activity
restricted to coercion. In the US in particular, the most all-embracing

forms of welfare during the twentieth century were provided not by the state but by capital, in the form of deferred wages, agreed upon by private contract on the basis of collective bargaining with the unionized minority of the workforce.[113]

The separation of the economic and the political is not simply unsustainable from the perspective of capital but from that of states themselves. In certain cases states act *as* capital, and in such situations the vaunted separation ceases to exist. Virtually every contributor to the renewed debate over the state and capital has referred to Colin Barker's contribution to the state-derivation debate of the 1970s—the last occasion on which the issue of the states system was seriously discussed before the 2000s—yet very few seem to have understood his point.[114] Barker does not of course argue that all activities undertaken by states are examples of capitalist activity, but in some aspects states can be productive capitalists, exploiting wage labor and producing surplus value, most obviously in the case of the integral "bureaucratic state capitalisms" (established under Stalinism), but also in the nationalized industries and the state-subsidized sectors of the West.[115] Given that the ideology of neoliberalism has in any case attempted to conceal rather than reveal the actual role of states in reorganizing capitalism since the 1970s, it should come as no surprise to find, following the financial crisis that opened in August 2007, an open return to direct state regulation and control, and even to traditional strategies of nationalization (which neoliberal politicians had previously claimed were either impossible or at least damaging to the free operation of markets). But even before the extent of the state response to the credit crunch became apparent, Jeffrey Garten, a professor of international trade and finance at the Yale School of Management, had already lamented what he calls "the rise of state capitalism" as signaled by the increase of regulation, particularly in the environment, the public ownership of natural resources, particularly in energy, and the activist role of state banks, particularly in China.[116]

Professor Garten's reaction to the subsequent nationalization of the insurance company AIG and the mortgage institutions Freddie Mac and Fannie Mae, by one of the most right-wing administrations in US history, has not been recorded but was presumably disapproving. Yet this episode simply demonstrates that state managers will usually act in what they perceive to be the interests of capital, rather than according to the dictates of whatever version of capitalist ideology currently happens to be dominant. Ideology will adapt in due course. Less than a year after Garten expressed his concerns, Andrew Graham, the Master of Balliol College, Oxford, reflected with equanimity that "the Anglo-Saxon model of unfettered capitalism" might be replaced by "a form of state capitalism" resembling the contemporary Chinese model.[117] I will return to the implications of the nonseparation of state and capital for the states system below. For the moment, however, I simply note that under capitalism, the economic and the political overlap and interpenetrate to such a degree that the distinction should be maintained mainly for conceptual purposes, rather than because it directly corresponds to reality.

Capitalists and state managers

The argument from the twin logics of state and capital is nevertheless more concrete and, at first sight, more plausible than unfounded assertions about the separation of functions under capitalism, not least because it discusses actual social groups rather than reified abstractions like "the economic" and "the political." Schumpeter was too pessimistic in imagining that the end of the precapitalist classes who had acted as the shepherds of capital would threaten the existence of the system. From the First World War in particular, they were increasingly replaced by state managers: the professional politicians and civil servants respectively responsible for the legislative and executive wings of the state. Block, who popularized the term "state managers" in the first place, writes that "since the bourgeoisie or other propertied classes cannot survive without a state, those classes have little choice but to seek a *modus operandi* with the state managers."[118] Callinicos follows Block on the grounds that his position "has the great merit of starting from the non-identity of interests between capitalists and state managers."[119] Callinicos is rightly concerned not to succumb to economic reductionism or to display what, following Chibber, he calls a "soft functionalism," and he sees this as a way of avoiding it.[120] Nevertheless, claims for the "non-identity" of state-managerial and capitalist interests are a specific form of the ideal separation of the political from the economic under capitalism. If the latter is nowhere near as total as has been claimed, then there are also reasons for doubting the completeness of the former.

At the most fundamental level, the common interest between capitalists and state managers stems from their common class position. Both are part of the bourgeoisie: departmental permanent secretaries in the British home civil service as much as, say, the chief executive officers of major companies. I argued earlier in this book that we should visualize the bourgeoisie as a series of concentric circles, with the capitalist class as such occupying the center and other layers radiating outward. Those closer to the periphery are progressively less directly connected to the core economic activities of production, exploitation, and competition, and more directly involved with those of an ideological, administrative, or technical nature, but the latter are nevertheless essential to the repro-duction of capitalism.[121] The incomes that state managers are paid from state revenues ultimately derive from the total surplus value produced by the working class, as do the profits, interest, and rent received by dif-ferent types of private capitalist.[122] And this applies not only to the source of their income but also to its level, since the relatively high levels of re-muneration, security, and prestige enjoyed by these officials depend on the continued exploitation of wage labor. In this respect the interests of state managers and capitalists are the same.

But if we expand the notion of "interests" to encompass a broader sense of shared ideological commitment, even here the interests of state managers and capitalists are not dissimilar. A shared background in insti-tutions like schools, universities, and clubs helps to consolidate a class consciousness that articulates these interests in both groups, but a more fundamental source of convergence is that the activities of states are, to use Draper's term, subordinated to the accumulation of capital. In the British case the state may not do this as successfully as the capitalist class might wish, but that is an indication of the problems of managing long-term relative decline, not a sign that the state managers have different goals. In fact, no state managers above a certain level—in Britain, entry level to the Senior Civil Service—can survive long in post without com-mitting themselves to capital's goals. This tends to mean that, regardless of their class origins, state managers and capitalists are drawn together into a series of mutually supportive relationships: the former need the resources provided by individual national capitals, principally through taxation and loans, in order to attend to the needs of the national capital as a whole; the latter need specific policy initiatives to strengthen the competitive position of their sector of the national capital within the global economy.[123]

Two apparently contradictory aspects of the relationship between state managers and politicians are particularly important. First, in order to maintain links to capital in all its multiple incarnations, the state must partly mirror capital's fragmentation. Joachim Hirsch once noted that "the state apparatus in the functional sense ... but also the actual administration cannot be understood as a closed formation, but represents in reality a heterogeneous conglomerate of only loosely linked part-apparatuses." Yet what Hirsch calls the "increasingly chaotic structure of the bourgeois state apparatus"—chaos that has increased still further since these words were written in 1974—is a necessary feature of its operation: "It must be open to the divergent interests and influences of individual capitals, which always encounter each other as 'hostile brothers,' and in order to secure the political domination of the bourgeoisie and keep class conflict latent, it must maintain links with other classes and strata not to be counted as part of the bourgeoisie."[124]

Second, if policies were nevertheless being framed for the benefit of particular sectional capitalist interests, this would constitute a problem for the local capitalist class as a whole. In the US particularly, the penetration of the higher reaches of government by executives, notably those associated with the oil and automobile industries, has in some respects overtaken even the most deranged imaginings of vulgar Marxism.[125] There is some evidence that this represents a general and self-destructive tendency within neoliberal capitalism.[126] Until relatively recently, however, state managers might see their interests as being distinct from *specific* national capitals or even specific *sectors* of national capital, but not from the national capital as a whole. Indeed, the reason why the first capitalist state, the United Netherlands, was unable to sustain its preeminent position was not simply because it was territorially fragmented into an unwieldy compromise between a federal and a confederate structure.[127] It was also because the government of each province was too closely aligned with particular capitalist interests for the central apparatus of the States General to make decisions that could advance their collective interest.[128] The English and subsequently British state did not suffer from this disadvantage.

It could be argued that I am ascribing too great a level of class consciousness to state managers. They may well share a class location with capitalists (in the developed world at least they almost certainly do), but this does not mean that their actual motivations are inspired by the same economic considerations. Indeed, the behavioral mechanisms driving the actions of state managers certainly involve noneconomic considerations, even the achievement of what one might call reformist objectives, in which support for national capitals is merely a means to an end. Oliver James, for example, recounts the response of one senior civil servant to the argument that economic growth does not necessarily increase human happiness. The official in question (after "sighing as if I were a tiresome four-year-old who had asked what God is") replied that "if economic growth was no longer the goal, unemployment would increase and there would be less funding for projects such as child poverty, and people would be *un*happier."[129]

But does a concern for noneconomic outcomes matter? Take one society in which there were no individual capitalists and the state managers collectively performed the role of this absent class: the USSR between 1928 and 1991. In one of the debates on the nature of the USSR, the late Ernest Mandel claimed that Stalinist bureaucracy was not compelled to accumulate, yet it sought to retain its collective managerial position "as a means of achieving the optimum standard of consumption available under given conditions. . . . *The consumption desires of the bureaucracy* (like the consumption desires of pre-capitalist classes), *and not the need to maximize accumulation and output*, are the motive force behind bureaucratic management."[130] The answer to this, from those like Barker, Callinicos, and myself who believe that the USSR was a form of bureaucratic state capitalism, is that whatever motivations brought individual members of the bureaucracy to seek those roles (and the material benefits of a place among the ruling class would have exercised attractions, regardless of the risks), and whatever post hoc justifications they may have used to rationalize their behavior, once in post they were indeed compelled to behave in such a way as to enable Russia to match American military spending, or else face being overwhelmed by their Western imperial rival.[131] Even allowing for the exceptional fusion of state and capital under Stalinism, however, is the situation of Stalinist bureaucrats different *in principle* from that of state managers in situations where multinational capital is still dominant?

Nor are the motivations of state managers and capitalists as different as might be thought. Michael Kidron once noted that accumulation did not take place automatically but through decisions taken by individuals and groups who had both criteria for success and incentives to pursue it. From the point of view of the system, however, the nature of these incentives and the motives of these actors are irrelevant except insofar as they contribute to the expansion of capital.[132] In other words, once capitalists enter the system as competitors, they are compelled to accumulate, but their reasons for entering the system are not, generally speaking, because they want to become the living embodiments of capital. They want money with which to buy commodities, certainly, but also so they can allay their status anxiety, have revenge on the people who bullied them at school, ensure that their memory is preserved by endowing a university chair, enhance their reputation by posing as the benefactor of picturesquely poverty-stricken children in Central Africa, or any number of other reasons. But whatever the motivations, it is only by submitting to the imperatives of accumulation and successfully competing with other capitals that they stand any chance of fulfillment.

Is this so very removed from the motivations of state managers? Like capitalists, state managers can be motivated to act in the interest of capital accumulation as a means to quite other ends; they simply do so from a position of greater distance from the process of capital accumulation and of less concern with the fate of individual capitals. After all—to take one of Callinicos and Ashman's examples—why do state managers have an "interest" in developing the military capacities of their state, if not in their capacity as representatives of capital? And they do so not only in preparation for war but for economic reasons. Liah Greenfield quotes one Indian economic commentator as saying: "A soft state that yields on vital national security issues cannot project an image of a tough negotiator on trade and commerce."[133] But arms need not be involved in any sense. As Edward Luttwak notes, "investment capital for industry provided or guided by the state is the equivalent of firepower; product development subsidized by the state is the equivalent of weapon innovation; and market penetration supported by the state replaces military bases and garrisons on foreign soil as well as diplomatic influence." These are not simply analogies; war is "different from commerce, but evidently not different enough," as the response to a perceived threat is similar: "In particular, an action-reaction cycle of trade restrictions that evoke retaliation has a distinct resemblance to crisis escalation that can lead to outright war."[134] Greenfield notes of one development in the US during the late 1990s that could be taken as preparatory for such escalation:"The establishment of the National Economic Council raised economic interests ... to the significance of security concerns—that is, concerns with national defense and independence itself—a symbolically striking gesture."[135] It *is* symbolic—of a ruling class that understands the unified nature of its own interests.

There are, however, areas where there are genuine differences of interest between capitalists and state managers, but to understand them we need to make finer distinctions among the latter group than we have until now. In two respects at least, there are central differences between politicians and civil servants.

First, their importance for capital occurs in different historical situations. The virtues of civil servants for capital are those associated with a consolidated regime: stability, continuity, and predictability. In such periods, these are also expected of political actors. In times of crisis, however, the significance of the latter is quite different, and this has been the case from the bourgeois revolutions onward. In these periods of crisis, political leadership was rarely provided by merchants, industrialists, or bankers, but rather by journalists, lawyers, or priests, groups whose boldness was in inverse proportion to their ownership or control of capital and who consequently had less to lose.[136] Like Hirsch, Barker sees the capitalist state not as "a permanently structured bloc of interests" but rather "a field of intra-capitalist conflict, through which only temporary and shifting determinations and enforcements of the 'national interest' are made."[137] At certain points, however, one view of the "national interest" must prevail and one strategy to achieve it be followed, if military defeat, economic relegation, or successful working-class insurgency is to be avoided. In contemporary terms, then, the importance of the elevation of political actors above the economic core of the bourgeoisie comes in periods of crisis where major restructuring of capital is required, when the intra-capitalist conflicts have to be resolved, at least until the immediate danger is past. Throughout the Social-Democratic era, capital always acted to discipline politicians who were perceived to be acting against its interests, by organizing runs on currency, withdrawing investment, or moving production. But such actions were a blunt instrument, capable of reversing one set of decisions and making others more likely, but not of bringing about a complete reorientation in state economic policy: that requires political action.

The establishment of neoliberal hegemony was one such reorientation. Antonio Gramsci discussed this type of ruling-class response to crisis in his prison notebooks as "an organic and normal phenomenon": "It represents the fusion of an entire social class under a single leadership, which alone is held to be capable of solving an overriding problem of its existence and of fending off a mortal danger."[138] The neoliberal response was not originally articulated in any systematic way by the capitalists who ultimately benefited from it. It was rather the obsession of peripheral ideologists employed mainly as academics and journalists, later taken up by politicians who accepted these ideas as a means of restoring profitability and only then by the majority of capitalist owners and managers, even in the US, which had the most developed tradition of business activism. As Al Campbell points out, the representatives of finance capital were the only ruling-class fraction to consistently uphold free-market principles throughout the so-called Keynesian era. But the fact that the capitalist class eventually adopted these principles more or less universally does not mean that "the interests of finance capital" are now dominant, only that in circumstances of economic crisis this class has come to accept that the reorganization of capitalism along such lines is in its overall interest.[139] The Thatcher government directly represented capital insofar as it was opposed to the working-class movement ("vertically") but could not represent every component of capital ("horizontally"), because there was no general agreement on strategy during the late 1970s—not least because individual capitals would and did suffer from the strategy eventually adopted, from 1979 onward.[140] In this sense the state under the minority Thatcherite wing of the Tory Party acted as the vanguard of the British capitalist class. It is in these situations where there is most likely to be conflict between the political and civil-service wings of the state managers, since the former can regard the latter—quite unjustifiably—as being less committed to capitalism because they are more committed to the current regime within the state. As Tory Douglas Hurd wrote immediately prior to his party returning to office under Thatcher in 1979:

> I do not believe that in any important respect the civil service is a natural ally of the Conservative Party. I did not know the voting habits of the

civil servants with whom I worked, though sometimes I could guess. What is certain is that these voting habits were far less important than the traditions of public service in which they were trained. That tradition made them scornful of the political struggle, though often fascinated by it. It was the Ministry rather than the Minister that mattered, the general administration of the country rather than the ambitions of each fleeting group of politicians. Indeed this attitude works in practice to the advantage of Labor Governments because allied to it is a firm belief in the merits of action by the state.[141]

The second major difference between civil servants and politicians is that the latter have to some extent to reflect the interests of their electoral supporters, which is easier when those interests are coincident or at least compatible with those of capital. As I noted above, politicians of all the main parties increasingly converge on openly capitalist notions of the national interest, but in some cases, the beliefs of their supporters may inadvertently cause difficulty for the accumulation process. I refer here not to Social-Democratic reforms or reforms beneficial to the working class but to right-wing populism, which I discuss later in this book.[142]

If mediation is indeed a preferable alternative explanation for the continuation of the states system than either historical contingency or interpenetrative logics, what does this actually mean in concrete terms? Marx wrote that "the anatomy of . . . civil society . . . has to be found in political economy."[143] Civil society in its turn contains the anatomy of the state—the "concentration of bourgeois society in the form of the state."[144] Each is a different but interrelated moment in the totality of capitalism. As Henryk Grossman emphasized, Marx was attempting to understand social phenomena, not by focusing on their "superficial attributes . . . at any given moment or period" but "in their successive transformations, and thus to discover their essence."[145] For Marx, the essence of capitalism, its "inner nature," is competition.[146] And "competition on the world market" is the "very basis . . . of the capitalist mode of production."[147]

But competition has both a precondition and consequence: the precondition is the creation of a class of wage laborers; the consequence is the compulsion to accumulate.[148] Capitalism is a system of competitive accumulation based on wage labor, and these two defining aspects also point to the reasons for the persistence of the states system: on the one hand, the need for capitals to be territorially aggregated for competitive purposes; on the other, the need for that territory to have an ideological basis—nationalism—that can be used to bind the working class to the state and hence to capital. The problem in most discussions of the nation-state is that emphasis tends to fall on either one part of the term or the other, with the focus falling on internal nationalist politics or external geopolitical relationships depending on which is chosen. In the remainder of this chapter I will attempt to give each part equal weight and treat both as aspects of the totality of capitalism.

NATION-STATES AND COMPETITIVE ACCUMULATION

Fernand Braudel once argued that capital has *always* existed beyond the limits of "the state and its particular preoccupations."[149] But despite these complications, the capitalist class in its constituent parts continues to retain territorial home bases, presided over by states, for their operations.[150] Why? Capitalism is based on competition, but capitalists want competition to take place on their terms; they do not want to suffer the consequences if they lose. In one sense, then, they require from a state more than just an infrastructure; they need it to ensure that the effects of competition are experienced as far as possible by someone else. A global state could not do this. Indeed, in this respect it would be the same as having no state at all. For if everyone is protected, then no one is: unrestricted market relations would prevail, with all the risks that entails. The state therefore has to have limits; it has to be able to distinguish between those capitals who will receive its protection and support, and those who will not. But what sets the territorial limits of a state? Here Harvey's early writings are helpful.

The confines are set by the limits of what he calls "a *structured coherence* to production and consumption within a given space," a space within which "capital can circulate without [*sic*] the limits of profit within [*sic*] socially-necessary turnover time being exceeded by the cost and time of movement," a space where "a relatively coherent labor market prevails (the space within which labor power can be substituted on a daily basis)." It is this space of "territorial coherence" that is "formally represented by the state."[151] Two conclusions follow. First, capitalism would have produced a similar states system to the one that currently exists no matter what preceded it. Second, even if a global superstate were to come into being (and this hypothesis is extremely unlikely, given the catastrophic levels of inter-state violence that would be required to bring it into being), capitals within it would tend to group together to create new states or recreate old ones: it would be unsustainable as long as there were many capitals.

If the preceding argument is correct, then we should expect to find not only the persistence of many states but also that these many states will persist in competing with each other—that is, capitalist competition will find *expression* in geopolitical competition. Pozo-Martin claims that any attempt to show that the latter is "directly determined" by the former will "crash against reality time after time."[152] Quite a lot hinges here on the words "directly determined," since it is precisely in order to show the indirect routes by which economic competition is manifested politically that I have insisted on the need for the concept of mediated totality. In order to demonstrate this point it is not necessary to show that, say, France is likely to go to war with Germany in the near future—a scenario that I agree is unlikely—but that capitalist states are engaged in forms of competition that have the potential to end in war, whether or not that potential is ever realized.

The notion that capitalism is essentially pacific is an aspect of bourgeois ideology, intended to absolve the system of blame for the carnage it has caused and continues to cause. While the capitalist world system was still in the process of formation, Smith described the dominant mercantilist system as "a species of warfare."[153] He and other Enlightenment thinkers welcomed "commercial society" as a means of reducing the propensity of states to go to war. "For the *spirit of commerce* sooner or later takes hold of every people," wrote Kant in a work much quoted since 1989, "and it cannot exist side by side with war."[154] Unfortunately, like so many of the aspirations that the Enlightenment had for capitalism, this was not to be fulfilled, although Kant, and his predecessors and contemporaries like Montesquieu, Smith, and Paine, were at any rate dealing with a new situation and may be forgiven for failing to foresee the future.[155] The public ideology of the bourgeoisie after the end of the Cold War revived precisely these assumptions. Neoconservative ideologist Robert Kagan has summarized the "dreams" engendered by the new world order: "Competition among nations might continue, but it would be peaceful commercial competition. Nations that traded with one another would be less likely to fight one another. Increasingly commercial societies would be more liberal both at home and abroad."[156] Kagan rightly points out that states do not need to choose between "commercial engagement and economic growth" on the one hand and "military strength and geopolitical confrontation" on the other: they can do both. Rather than present this as a general proposition, however, Kagan restricts it to what he calls the "autocracies," whose leading representatives are Russia, China, and Iran, as opposed to the liberal democracies that are forced into military competition by the actions of the former group. "It may not come to war, but the global competition between democratic and autocratic governments will become a dominant feature of the twenty-first century world."[157] The ideological content of these claims should be obvious. Now that market capitalism is dominant almost everywhere, new excuses will have to be found to explain continuing geopolitical rivalries.

Arguments like Kagan's convey the impression that geopolitical rivalry is entirely driven by the undemocratic political nature of certain regimes rather than being a function of capitalism. It is not the only argument of its kind, of course; another is that the errant regimes are insufficiently cap-italist or are based on the wrong sort of capitalism—anarcho-capitalism, mafia-capitalism, "wild"-capitalism, and so on. Alan Greenspan criticized the way in which Russia used its control over natural gas supplies to remove subsidies and demand higher prices from the Ukraine in 2006. It might have seemed that Russia was simply applying the capitalist lesson of charg-ing "what the market will bear" and exploiting "economic advantage for profit," but apparently not: "True capitalists protecting their long-term profitability would have sought a gradual adjustment in the name of good customer relations and maximum *long-term* profitability."[158] Given recent events in the world financial markets, Greenspan was perhaps unwise to draw attention to the supposed capacity of Western capitalists for long-term planning, but there is also a problem here for some on the left.

Marxist thinkers from Kautsky to Wood have emphasized a different aspect of the Kantian argument for "pacific capitalism": not the supposed ability of capitalism to channel aggressive energies from war to com-merce but what Kant called "mutual self-interest" that acts to prevent the self-destructive effects of internecine warfare.[159] However, there is a fairly obvious problem with this claim, namely that the most capitalist states—Britain and America—have historically also been the most warlike.[160] Furthermore, these "capitalist giants," as Luttwak calls them, had close economic relations with their enemies and entered into conflict knowing they were liable to suffer extensive economic damage.[161]

Two explanations are possible here. One is that wars took place previously because the world as a whole was not completely dominated by the capitalist mode of production: between 1914 and 1945, conflicts were between capitalist and precapitalist powers; between 1945 and 1989, conflicts were between capitalist powers and those that at least claimed to be postcapitalist. In neither period, therefore, were conflicts generated by the pure "imperatives" (to use Wood's favored term) of the system itself. I am less concerned here with the accuracy of this periodization of capitalist development (although I reject it) than with the implications of the fact that capitalist imperatives now operate unimpeded: "For the first time in the history of the modern nation state, the world's major powers are not engaged in direct geopolitical and military rivalry. Such rivalry has been effectively displaced by competition in the capitalist manner." As a result, Wood claims, conflict between the states at the core of capitalism is unthinkable: "The classical age of imperialism . . . is now long over."[162] This position is worryingly close to the pronouncements of neoliberal yea-sayers like Fareed Zakaria: "Since the late 1980s, the world has been moving toward an extraordinary degree of political stability. The end of the Cold War has ushered in a period with no major military competition among the world's great powers—something virtually unprecedented in modern history."[163]

Wood further argues that the separation of the economic and the political under capitalism has ceased to operate, at least at the international level, as a result of the universalization of capitalist imperatives. As the rise of capitalist globalization requires states to become more deeply involved in the management and organization of the economy, she writes, "the old capitalist division of labor between capital and the state, between economic and political power, has been disrupted."[164] Why then does Wood believe that the demarcation between the economic and the political has only broken down with the onset of neoliberal globalization? "Capitalist imperialism has become almost entirely a matter of economic domination," she writes, "in which market imperatives, manipulated by the dominant capitalist powers, are made to do the work no longer done by imperial states or colonial settlers." In this case we should surely expect the incidence of war to decrease, perhaps even cease completely. However, having identified the difference between capitalist imperialism and earlier commercial and territorial empires that depended on extra-economic power, Wood then tells us that "the universality of capitalist imperatives has not at all removed the need for military force." And what is this military force for? To impose the capitalist economic imperatives that we have previously been told are already universal! In the light of this rather circular reasoning, it is perhaps unsurprising that Wood discovers what she calls "paradoxes" in the current global situation, such as the fact that "while market imperatives may reach far beyond the power of any single state, these imperatives themselves must be enforced by extra-economic power," or that "the more purely economic empire has become, the more the nation-state has proliferated."[165] On this analysis, military and political pressure up to the level of warfare will continue to be exercised by the imperial powers against states of the global South, but not between those powers themselves.

The other explanation, advanced for example by Robert Brenner, is that while states generally act in support of capital, the system of multiple states that capitalism inherited from feudalism means that even the biggest cannot predict or control the outcomes of their actions, since every other state is also acting in a similar way; as a result, counterproductive outcomes can result.[166] At an extreme, these outcomes can involve catastrophes like the First World War, which is presumably why Brenner believes that a "global-state solution" would be in the best interests of capital. Now, if Brenner was simply pointing to the incommensurability of outcomes, it would be difficult to disagree. His position goes further than this, however, suggesting not only that the consequences of certain actions are unpredictable but that from the point of view of capitalism they are incomprehensible.

The theoretical difficulty behind these arguments is a conception of capitalism as essentially involving market competition on the basis of price, behind which lies the compulsion to achieve cost savings through technical innovation. Brenner famously distinguishes "horizontal" *competition* between capitals from "vertical" *conflict* between labor and capital, which is helpful up to a point, but intercapitalist competition does not take place only through the market.[167] In 1920 Bukharin described "the struggle for spheres of capital investment . . . for the very opportunity to expand the production process" as an example of capitalist competition by other means.[168] Chris Harman has argued that other nonmarket forms of competition involve "spending surplus value on ways of manipulating the market, advertising goods, creating a 'product image,' [and] bribing buyers in firms and state agencies."[169] Capitalist competition can be external to markets, but so too can the agents of competition be separate from capitals: they can be states, and competition between states tends to lead to *conflict*.

As Arrighi notes, there are two kinds of competition between capitals. The first amounts to a form of regulated cooperation in which all benefit from the expansion of trade. The second, however, involves "substantive" competition in which the profits of one capital are achieved at the expense of another; the situation ceases to be "positive-sum" and becomes "zero-sum." This type of competition is not restricted to firms, however, but involves states, beginning with the behavior of the Italian city-states during the Hundred Years' War.[170] Arrighi thus concludes that "inter-capitalist competition has indeed been the predominant influence" in causing contractions in profitability, "provided that we include intercapitalist wars among the most important forms of that competition." If we do not, then it can lead to "the virtual eviction of world politics from the analysis of capitalist dynamics."[171] In this context, the situations that state managers face are similar to those that face individual capitalists. When a firm invests in new labor-saving technology that will reduce its costs, rival capitalists ultimately must make similar investments, even at the risk that the initial cost of purchase, installation, and training will be so great as to threaten to force them out of business before the savings can be realized. Not investing means the virtual certainty of failure; investing means it is only a possibility. State managers and politicians behave similarly to capitalists in relation to national economies. They too have to take decisions that, on balance, are likely to result in disaster because the alternative exposes them to even greater risk in the long term. And this does not only apply to situations that are directly economic in nature, as can be demonstrated from both history and contemporary politics.

The example of the First World War illustrates both the inherently warlike nature of capitalism and the way in which seemingly irrational decisions were in fact unavoidable given the compulsions of competitive accumulation. All historians obviously recognize that the main players were established or aspirant imperial powers, but this fact is rarely given any explanatory power so long as imperialism is regarded as coextensive with colonialism. Yet the concept of imperialism, at least within classical Marxism, is not restricted to relationships of domination by the metropolitan powers over the colonial and semicolonial world but also includes—in this context, more importantly—relationships of rivalry between the metropolitan powers themselves, a rivalry that fuses economic and geopolitical competition.[172] Niall Ferguson's dismissal of the Marxist explanation therefore simply misses the point: "Inconveniently for Marxist theory … there is scarcely any evidence that these [capitalist] interests made businessmen *want* a major European war. In London the overwhelming majority of bankers were appalled at the prospect, not least because war threated to bankrupt most if not all of the major acceptance houses engaged in financing international trade." Ferguson then cites statements and actions by a range of mainly German business leaders indicating either their hostility to the prospect of war or their disbelief that it would occur.[173] The citations are accurate enough, but the relationship of the war to capitalism is not disproved because individual capitalists were not demanding it, and at least some individuals among the ruling classes of Europe understood this. The German chancellor Theobald von Bethmann-Hollweg was partly responsible for the outcome of the so-called "Potsdam consultation" of July 5–6, 1914, at the end of which Germany committed to support Austrian military action against Serbia. Nevertheless, at the beginning of 1918 he sent an extraordinary letter to Prince Max of Baden, in which he wrote: "Imperialism, nationalism and economic materialism, which in broad outline have governed the policies of all the nations during the past generation, set themselves goals that could be pursued by each nation only at the cost of a general collision."[174]

All the major participating states were either already capitalist or in the process of completing the transition. Their empires were important to the metropolitan centers for economic reasons: principally as captive markets, less so as a source of raw materials (except in the case of Britain), and least of all as the destination of investments. But even where colonies or "mandates" had no direct economic rationale, this did not mean they were detached from "the logic of capital." Once the race of imperial territory began in earnest during the closing decades of the nineteenth century, it became necessary for strategic reasons to seize territories that were often of no value in themselves—indeed, that were often net recipients of state expenditure—but that were necessary in order to protect those territories that *were* of economic value, like India.[175]

In some cases the diplomatic alliances that eventually plunged the world into catastrophe had direct economic origins. Russian grain exports and raw material imports for industry passed through the straits between the Black Sea and the Sea of Marmara, or the Dardanelles and the Aegean. Early in 1914 Russia and her allies forced the Ottoman Empire to grant autonomy to the partly Armenian provinces of eastern Anatolia in order to pull the Christian Armenians under Russian influence. As a result the Turks began to form an alliance with Germany in order to protect the integrity of their empire.[176] As for Britain (surely the most capitalist of all the European great powers), economic specialization and a consequent lack of self-sufficiency in food and raw materials made her dependent on these being constantly available from overseas, which in turn required the Royal Navy to protect the merchant marine. Challenged by the other European powers, above all Germany, in the naval arms race from the 1890s, Britain began to create the system of Continental alliances that would pull her into war.[177] In both cases the logic of conflict was set in motion by tensions between the metropolitan centers themselves, not what Wood describes as "relations between colonial masters and subject territories."[178] In this historical moment, threats to overseas markets and sources of raw materials would have been causes for war *even if the territories involved had not been actual colonies.* The generals, politicians, and civil servants in all the combatant states were trapped within a structural logic that first led to war and then determined their conduct of it. Seemingly irrational decisions were in fact inescapable given the compulsions of competitive accumulation. Rather than the "sleepwalkers" described by Christopher Clark, they were closer to being the "prisoners" invoked by Bernadotte Schmitt and Harold Vedeler:

> The system and the age were as responsible as the actors for the July crisis and its ending in war. We can hardly imagine that any of the statesmen in office during the decade before 1914 would have acted in a substantially different manner from those of the July crisis if they had been in power at the time. The men actually at the helm of affairs, given the preceding decade of events and all the other conditions and forces

of the time, would have been almost inescapably the prisoners of those factors in discharging the practical responsibilities of office.[179]

Now take the most obvious contemporary example: Iraq. Several historians of empire, both Marxist and non-Marxist, have expressed the view that US foreign policy under the Bush administration was inexplicable in terms of geopolitical or economic interest. Brenner has concluded that since US power is already undisputed and required no demonstration (such as the invasion of Iraq is taken to be), the strategy of the contemporary Washington neoconservatives is genuinely irrational.[180] For Hobsbawm, too, it has no rational basis, being "not for US imperial interests . . . and certainly not for the interests of US capitalism."[181] Porter grants that "madness (delusion, paranoia, etc.)" has only a "*slight* influence . . . on US foreign policy in particular"; far more significant is the "sheer scale and simplicity" of what he calls "ideologism," so different, in his eyes, from the sensible pragmatism of the men who ruled the British Empire.[182] Mann sees the invasion of Iraq as motivated by "revenge plus oil," which he describes as "not entirely rational."[183] Perry Anderson accounts for the "circumstantial irrationality" of the invasion of Iraq by referencing the influence of the Israeli lobby, although elsewhere in the same article he rightly points out that it was an "escalation" of the treatment of Iraq under the Clinton administration and, before it, that of Bush the Father.[184] Failure to ground analysis in the class basis of modern states (i.e., capitalism) leads to a restricted notion of what is rational for state managers and consequently a failure to understand why they take certain actions.

Take the question of Israel raised by Anderson. The problem with this analysis, which it shares with Realism, is that it is not realist enough. Mearsheimer and Stephen Walt argue that US policy in the Middle East is driven by a lobby acting in the interests of the Israeli state, which have been different from and sometimes opposed to those of the US, most recently in the Second Lebanon War.[185] Given the entirely predictable abuse that has been directed against the authors, it is important to say that their work is courageous and illuminating on many points. The two central premises are, however, completely misconceived. The US would support Israel even if no lobby existed, and, whatever disasters have occurred as a result of this support, it is ultimately in the US interest to do so, because in that most geopolitically vital of regions there is no other state upon which the US can rely to act on its behalf. The "Israeli lobby" has been successful precisely because virtually all American politicians are already predisposed to support its aims.[186] As the British journalist Jonathan Freedland has written: "American support for Saudi Arabia is incompatible with total subjection to Israeli wishes. Surely the interests the US has in the Middle East would be sufficient to make it act in these ways without the American-Israeli Public Affairs Committee: after all, the US acts in precisely the same ways in other parts of the world where there is no AIPAC to influence it."[187]

What then might be a rational explanation for the invasion of Iraq? Patrick Cockburn has identified much analysis of US motives as being "oversophisticated." After an initially swift victory in Afghanistan—a victory that has now unraveled—they thought Iraq would be similarly easy to conquer. That assumption was correct; the real gamble was that they would be able to control what they had occupied.[188] Why did they take such a gamble in the first place? Emmanuel Todd has argued that the new imperial strategic option was not—as is commonly thought— adopted by the American ruling class immediately after the collapse of the Russian Stalinist regime in 1991. At that stage the assumption was that a capitalist Russian Federation would continue to act as a global superpower, weakened, certainly, but still capable of strategically balancing total American military domination. The real shift occurred around 1995, when it became apparent that in terms of the economy, production and to an even greater extent investment had collapsed, and that in terms of territory, not only had Russia had lost economically vital former republics, it was threatened by secessionist movements within the Federation itself. The US ruling class gambled that Russia would continue to decline, perhaps to the point of complete disintegration, and that the US could therefore provoke it with impunity while maintaining its geopolitical position through the demonstration effect of overwhelming vulnerable (i.e., non-nuclear) states that could be, however implausibly, identified as threats. The very fact that US military strength could only be safely applied against weak regimes in the global South indicated how exaggerated was its putative dominance. Insofar as this strategy was temporarily effective, it meant that both the Clinton and Bush regimes could avoid confronting America's increasingly rentier position in the world economy by rebuilding the declining manufacturing base or introducing regulation to the financial sector.[189]

Why did the American ruling class choose to construct an external empire rather than conduct internal economic reform? Todd puts this down to a combination of incompetence and inertia, both of which tend to make the path of least resistance more attractive than undertaking difficult and uncomfortable decisions. In fact he exaggerates the decline of manufacturing in the US economy and underplays the ways in which the state has continued to enable corporate restructuring, not least in the computer industry, but he is right to emphasize the absence of any *systematic* industrial policy.

For this there are two reasons. One is that the entire neoliberal project was premised on the irreversibility of the process: the abolition of regulatory mechanisms, dismantling of welfare programs, ratification of international treaties for which there are no formal mechanisms allowing them to be either amended or annulled, and so on. All these could be reversed, but it would require new legal and administrative structures, which would in turn require planning and a will to do so that has not existed since the beginning of the neoliberal era.[190]

The second reason, which also explains why the will has not existed, is that to act in this way would be to encounter the hostility of the majority of a ruling class who have personally benefited from the transfer of wealth and resources that lie at the heart of neoliberalism. Iain Boal and his colleagues argue that what they call "military neoliberalism" emerged from the late 1990s as a response to a situation in which "a dominant capitalist core begins to find it harder and harder to benefit from 'consensus' market expansion or corporate mergers and asset transfers."[191] But this was true for all the major capitalist powers, as neoliberal globalization came under attack from mass opposition for the first time. Uniquely, the US had the military capacity to use force as a demonstration effect in two ways. The first was to show states in the global South what would befall them if they dared to flout imperial instructions or even undertake actions that were neutral in relation to the US but detrimental to other more pliant vassals. It was not enough for dissident regimes to learn the lesson of disobedience; loyal regimes had to be shown that they would be protected. The second was to show competitors in the core of the system that they had no need to assume the role of rivals to the US, because it was prepared to undertake the role of global policeman on behalf of the system as a whole, but also to show them what the costs would be of attempting to play a comparable role. This was not the first time that mass destruction had been used for diplomatic effect. The dropping of the atomic bombs on Hiroshima and Nagasaki was not intended to compel the Japanese to surrender, which could have been accomplished by other means, but, as Richard Seymour points out, to "prevent the USSR from having a post-war claim in Southeast Asia, which the USA planned to hegemonize" and "because of the beneficial effects it was likely to have on diplomacy with Russia in Europe."[192]

The destruction of Iraq was not, however, simply undertaken for educational purposes. As Greenspan has recently claimed, "everybody knows" that "the Iraq war was largely about oil."[193] But in what *sense* was it about oil? Here we need to avoid what Kevin Phillips calls a "vaguely Marxian mineral determinism," where the future of the US is solely determined by access to this crucial mineral.[194] The nature of this goal shows the difference between the relationship of state managers and that of capitalists to the system as a whole. As Mearsheimer and Walt note, most US-based oil companies did not lobby for an invasion and would have preferred sanctions to be lifted rather than war to be declared: "The oil companies, as is almost always the case, wanted to make money, not war."[195] The state managers were, however, not simply working for this specific sectoral interest but for what they perceived to be American interests as a whole. In this case, as the more perceptive analysts of US policy in the Gulf have argued, the goal was not to guarantee price or even supply for American use, but to control the supply in relation to competitors, whether these were allies or not.[196] In fact the key targets were those ascendant states, above all China, which can no longer be considered part of the global South as such, but which are not yet part of the developed world either—and perhaps never will be, though they have already attained regional power status.[197]

Was the invasion of Iraq solely driven by what one might call the geopolitical externalization of geoeconomic imperatives? There is one sense in which it was influenced by developments internal to the American political system. Generally, the search for internal determinants for the content of foreign policy (as opposed to the timing of initiatives) should be avoided, unless it can be demonstrated that a particular policy—in this case, invasion and occupation of a sovereign state—allowed the ruling bloc to accomplish domestic goals that it would have otherwise found difficult to achieve. One historic example of this would be Nazi war aims. Tim Mason argues that "*one* function" of Nazi military aggression and occupation was to "avoid internal dangers": "The weakness of the ruling system and its apparent reliance on a political outlook whose internal contradictions could be disguised only so long as it was bolstered by material success; the possibility of a 'decline of Germanism' and of 'sterility'; the political impossibility of lowering living standards—these became the proposed grounds for military expansion."[198] In the case of the US Republicans, the reasons are narrower. After 9/11 the Bush administration certainly used the rhetoric of national emergency to feed the military–industrial complex, cut taxation for the wealthy, reduce regulation for business, and attack social provision.[199] But all of these moves were continuations of policies that already existed and were in the process of being implemented. The war may have given them a blanket of patriotic cover, but they were not reasons for the war being launched. The exception was the need to retain the unified support of Republican voters, "to paper over divisions between factions in what Republicans call 'the base,' the inner network of organized new right groups, some of them with far-flung constituencies, that support conservative Republicanism." These constituencies are not only diverse but, in many respects, incompatible: "Christian fundamentalists are not libertarians; tax cutters are not natural allies of the military establishment."[200]

The invasions and occupations of Afghanistan and Iraq have turned into disasters for the US (they were always so for the Afghans and Iraqis), but this outcome was not preordained. A failed strategy does not become irrational simply because it fails. Politicians make calculated gambles, the results of which appear inevitable if they pay off and irrational if they do not. There is therefore no need to regard Dick Cheney and the other neoconservatives as insane or following a perverse political strategy in relation to American capitalist interests, which their actions have nevertheless undermined, with certain implications.[201] As Prem Shankar Jha notes, "hegemony cannot be built on failure."[202] As the catastrophe unfolded, Ferguson expressed concern at the prospect of apolarity, "a world without even one dominant superpower," by which he meant "a world without the US as the one dominant superpower."[203] Is it really possible for the US to be displaced from its position of sole dominance?

The assumption of both friends and foes of the US is that any challenge to its hegemony must come from either another individual power of comparable weight, at least in military terms, or a consciously constructed alliance. Since this is unlikely to happen in the foreseeable future, the prospect is usually dismissed.[204] But the challenge need not be singular, nor need it come from one of the established regional groupings of which the European Union (EU) is the most important. Callinicos accepts in principle that inter-imperialist rivalries (or geopolitical rivalries more generally) could occur, but argues—correctly, in my view—that the EU is unlikely to be the basis of an alternative to the US, since it does not transcend national antagonisms but rather acts as "the framework within which the leading continental states have pursued their interests." Furthermore, it is divided between "pro- and anti-American axes" that would prevent any unified response.[205]

But the challenge to the US need not come from a single source. If it were to be confronted on a number of regional fronts by a range of different states, by no means all of equivalent size or politically aligned in any way, the impact on the US would be similar. And this may be happening. The political challenge of the reformist governments in Latin America is one challenge; the stalemate in the Middle East and the rise to regional prominence of Iran form a second; the resurgence of Russia as a military and—as far as possession of energy reserves is concerned—economic power in Central Asia and Eastern Europe is a third; and the Chinese emergence as an economic, political, and military power in the Far East is a fourth. These all vary greatly in the scale and depth of their own ability to influence events, and none is capable of threatening the US on a global scale, not even China, despite some overexcited speculation to the contrary. Nor are they capable of uniting in any coherent way, although China has begun to sign trade and investment agreements with Iran and several of the Latin American states, and to set up a free-trade zone with the ten-member Association of Southeast Asian Nations, which came into effect on January 1, 2010.[206]

Future conflicts are therefore unlikely to be restricted to the attempted imposition of US dominance on recalcitrant states of the global South: they will involve the states of the developed world themselves. As Miéville has noted, "the struggle between capitalist states is more than the struggle between states that happen to have capitalist economies. It is a struggle *for* resources *for capital*. That is what makes the state a capitalist state." Consequently, the content of international law "is an ongoing and remorseless struggle for control over the resources of capitalism, that will often as part of that capitalist ('economic') competitive process spill into political violence."[207] It is not as if the pursuit of resources has ceased, as the Iraq war has demonstrated. And other potential conflicts are on the horizon. At the moment, at least forty-five countries with coastlines, including Australia, Britain, France, and Russia, are lodging claims with the UN Commission on the Limits of the Continental Shelf for "extended underwater territory rights" over an area thought to be 2.7 million square miles. States can set a "continental shelf outer limit" of up to 350 miles from shore. In the case of Britain these shores are situated on the Falklands and Ascension Island in the South Atlantic, and Rockall in the North Atlantic. The availability of oil, gas, and mineral deposits is investing these almost uninhabited rocks with an increasing strategic significance.[208] A Russian national security strategy document published in 2009 and intended to remain in force until 2020 saw potential conflict as arising from the struggle for resources, above all gas and oil, in the Arctic, the Middle East, Central Asia, and the Caspian Sea: "In the competition for resources, it can't be ruled out that military force could be used for resolving emerging problems."[209]

Does this mean that war is imminent between the core states of the world system? In the short term, of course not; but this is scarcely the only form of geopolitical rivalry. Since the end of the Cold War, one expression has been "war by proxy," where the dominant states jostle for influence by supporting different sides in inter- or intra-state conflicts. As Boris Kagarlitsky reminds us, the key opponents in the First World War had already been engaged in conflict-at-one-remove before 1914: "The Anglo-Boer War was in many ways a conflict between Britain and Germany who backed, encouraged, trained and supplied the Boers. The Russo-Japanese war was a clash between Germany (backing Russia) and England (supporting Japan)."[210] This is one of the many reasons why, as Thomas Otte writes, "the events of July 1914 are no quaint period drama": "It would be crass presentism to suggest that they offer neat 'lessons of history,' yet the concerns of the years leading up to 1914 are more immediate to us today than the seemingly closer events of the

1970s. In the 21st century, as multiple power centers compete for economic, military, and political influence, the contours of the 1914 international landscape look familiar again."[211]

The different sides supported by France, Germany, and the US during the disintegration of Yugoslavia was perhaps the first example of this strategy in the post–Cold War world; the conflict between NATO and Russia over Georgia (and the divisions within the NATO member states over attitudes to Russia), the most recent. It is tempting to see the former Soviet republics as playing the role once played by the Balkans, but the dangers are actually more geographically widespread. Similar situations are beginning to take shape in Central Africa, where France is already in the dominant position among the Western powers, but where China is rapidly extending its influence. In Asia itself, the growing rivalry between the US and China is channeled through their respective nuclear surrogates in India and Pakistan.[212] And then there is the growing tension between China and Japan. If the argument here is correct, then we may be entering not only a world situation that resembles in several important ways that of 1914 but also one in which the potential flashpoints are actually more numerous.

As the current crisis deepens, we can expect the first manifestations of renewed inter-state conflict to take the form of direct pressure by larger states on smaller states at the same point in the developmental spectrum: Britain threatens Iceland with the seizure of assets (under antiterrorist legislation) because the latter refuses to guarantee British deposits in Icelandic banks; Russia invades Georgia because the latter refuses to countenance the secession of areas with majority Russian populations. If the argument here is correct, then rather than being different kinds of events, such things would represent different points on a continuum, the end point of which is the escalation to violence. The moment of maximum danger for humanity will come when the capitalist great powers no longer express their different competitive interests by proxy in the global South or assert their interests over lesser states within the developed world—it will be the moment when they directly confront each other on the geopolitical stage.

NATION-STATES AND NATIONALIST IDEOLOGY

International relations specialists have been known to complain that the very concept of "the international" improperly draws attention away from the fact that their discipline is concerned with state relations, not national relations.[213] In fact, despite the presence of the term "national" within the title of the discipline, discussions of "the international" are almost always about inter-state relations, and the fact that states are usually also nation-states is simply not registered as significant. The terms "state" and "nation-state" are treated as virtually interchangeable. The difficulty is compounded if nations are also seen as predating capitalism, as they are by both Political Marxists and Althusserians, for whom nations are apparently a phenomenon with a purely contingent relationship to the dominant mode of production.[214] Callinicos, who is certainly aware of the modernity of nations, only writes in passing that "the formation and fission of national identities no doubt plays its part in producing the intense and exclusive nature of modern territorial sovereignty."[215] The issue is more central than these positions suggest. As Claudia von Braunmühl once noted, "the bourgeois nation state is both historically and conceptually part of the capitalist mode of production."[216] The prefixes "bourgeois" and "nation" are not simply terminological elaborations here; they indicate a key distinguishing feature of capitalist states that contributes to the survival of the states system.

The early theorists of commercial society assumed that capitalists would be rootless cosmopolitans. Smith wrote in *The Wealth of Nations*: "The proprietor of stock is properly a citizen of the world, and is not necessarily attached to any particular country. He would be apt to abandon the country in which he was exposed to a vexatious inquisition, in order to be assessed to a burdensome tax, and would remove his stock to some other country where he could either carry on his business, or enjoy his fortune more at his ease."[217] His great French admirer Condorcet had similar views, contrasting the behavior of the rich more generally with the greater rootedness of the classes that produced their wealth: "[Peasants] have an interest in the general happiness of the society which is the greater because it is more difficult for them to leave it. This interest diminishes in other classes because of the ease with which they can change their country. It ceases almost entirely for the owner of money who, by a banking operation, within an instant becomes English, Dutch, or Russian."[218] Both these great thinkers were wrong, in relation to their own time, but has neoliberalism rendered their perspectives correct in ours? One of the bankers interviewed by *Guardian* journalist Joris

Luyendijk in the 2010s thought so: "A highly educated professional in the City of London has much more in common with a peer in Hong Kong, New York City or Rio de Janeiro, than with a monolingual, mono-cultural teacher or nurse somewhere up in Birmingham or Manchester. Solidarity for the new global elite is not geography-based or tied up with a state. . . . It's quite ironic how postmodernists and many contemporary social thinkers on the left will tell you that all sense of belonging is a construct, tradition is invented and nations are simply fantasies or imagined communities. Well, the global financial elite agrees."[219] Even if members of the "global financial elite" are tempted to imagine themselves without ties to a particular nation-state, crisis—as we have recently seen—has a tendency to reintroduce a sense of reality, at least temporarily. As novelist André Malraux has one of his characters put it, with commendable cynicism: "There is nothing like approaching bankruptcy for awakening a financier's consciousness of his nationality."[220] The fact that this consciousness can fade so soon after the immediate crisis is passed is suggestive of the blind self-destructive nature of contemporary financial capital.

But for the majority of capitalists, their nation-states cannot simply be the site of particular economic functions, with no ideological attachment; for they, and to an even greater extent state managers, have at least to try to convince themselves that what they are doing is in a greater "national" interest, even if it is plainly in their own. Without some level of self-delusion, some "ethico-political" justification for their actions, the tendency would be for the legal rules and other structures put in place to organize the collective affairs of the bourgeoisie to be in constant danger of collapse, resulting in mere gangsterism. The nation is as much required here as the state. Therefore, when Greenfield describes the "spirit of capitalism" as "the economic expression of the collective competitiveness inherent in nationalism—itself a product of its members' collective investment in the dignity and prestige of the nation," she is turning history on its head.[221] It is the collective competitiveness of capitalism, expressed at the level of the state, that requires nationalism as a framework within which competitiveness can be justified in terms of a higher aspiration than increased profit margins. If "Britain" is to be collectively competitive, then this obviously means that individual British companies must be individually competitive, but they are in competition with each other as much as with foreign rivals. In the course of competition some will fail. Their failure is, however, a contribution to national survival, comparable perhaps to the sacrifice of soldiers in the field: competition is the health of the nation, just as—in Randolph Bourne's famous phrase—war is the health of the state.[222]

Nationalism does not merely unify territorially demarcated sections of the bourgeoisie; it plays an equally important role for capital in fragmenting the working class.[223] Lukács points out that one of the ways in which the bourgeoisie tries to prevent workers from achieving coherent class consciousness is by "binding the individual members of those classes as single individuals, as mere 'citizens,' to an abstract state reigning over and above them."[224] But it cannot be an "abstract state"; it has to be a very concrete, particular state founded on a sense of common identity. In historical terms, nationalism originally had two sources in individual working classes: one was the spontaneous search for a form of collective identity with which to overcome the alienation of capitalist society; the other was the deliberate fostering of nationalism by the bourgeoisie in order to bind workers to the state, and hence to capital.[225] Hence the absurdity of claims by Nairn that "what the extra-American world should fear is not US *nationalism* but the debility of the American *state*"—as if nationalism was not the means by which the American state mobilizes popular support behind imperialist adventures like Afghanistan and Iraq.[226] Appeals to a fictitious national interest can be partially successful, not only because they meet the need for community that capitalism has itself created but because it is not only politicians and state managers who make such appeals. The organizations of the working class themselves reinforce reformist class consciousness within a national context. At the most elementary level this is because trade unions and Social-Democratic parties are unwilling to challenge the nationalism within which political discourse is conducted, for fear of being labeled unpatriotic. More importantly, however, it is because they seek either to influence or to determine policy within the confines of the existing nation-state.

Ideologists of the free market have always been ambivalent toward nationalism. In a book first published in 1919, the leading Austrian neoclassical thinker Ludwig von Mises argued that it was natural for human groups, particularly those who shared a common language, to adopt national identities, although as the example of German speakers showed, these did not have to be coterminous with state boundaries.[227] Given the practical difficulties of establishing a world state to oversee the capitalist system, Mises thought that nation-states were the most effective basis for establishing the necessary legal framework for markets to operate. However, where nationalism was used to mobilize popular support for state activities that impeded competition, then it became a danger to economic rationality, at least as defined by representatives of the neoclassical school. Nationalism as the mobilizing principle with which to establish and maintain a market economy was acceptable to them; nationalism as an obstacle to or collective interference with a market economy was not. Indeed, Friedrich von Hayek claimed that collectivism in any form would inevitably involve the most militant forms of nationalism in order to unify an atomized population and provide it with a race or class enemy upon which to focus resentment and discontent.[228]

Neoliberalism follows neoclassicism in relation to nationalism, as in so much else. Turn to any of the contemporary works that extol the benefits of capitalist globalization and we find nationalism indicted for an extensive litany of crimes, which include making militarist threats to peace, erecting protectionist barriers to free trade, and expressing racist hostility to migrants. The movement for an alternative globalization that emerged in Seattle during the 1999 demonstrations against the World Trade Organization is routinely accused of wanting to prevent Third World development for selfish nationalist reasons.[229] Yet if we look beyond the rhetoric of neoliberal ideologues to the actual behavior of the capitalists, politicians, and state managers responsible for imposing the neoliberal order, we find a different attitude toward nationalism, one that sees it as being quite compatible with free-market beliefs. Enoch Powell, in many ways the founding father of British neoliberalism, once wrote: "The collective wisdom and collective will of the nation resides not in any little Whitehall clique but in the whole mass of the people—expressing [itself] through the complex nervous systems of the market."[230] In other words, it is not simply that neoliberalism needs the state but, as Harvey has noted, that the neoliberal state itself "needs nationalism of a certain sort to survive."[231] Why?

The neoliberal organization of capitalism heightens three existing tendencies: the transformation of human relationships into market transactions, the reduction of human capacities to mere factors of production, and the self-identification of human beings primarily as consumers. The result is to increase atomization and alienation to previously unimaginable levels, with potentially dangerous consequences for capital, which still has to achieve the tacit acceptance, and preferably the active support, of the working class in the process of its own exploitation. Otherwise, the system is potentially threatened, either by social breakdown, as individualized consumers transfer the competitiveness of the market to all other areas of life, or by social conflict, as workers begin to discover or rediscover their class consciousness and mobilize in their own collective interest. "Capitalism needs a human being who has never existed," writes Terry Eagleton, "one who is prudently restrained in the office and wildly anarchic in the shopping mall."[232] Precisely because these human beings do not exist, however—because the economic and the social are not as separate in life as they are in academic disciplines—it is the anarchic element that has tended to predominate, the emphasis on self-gratification, self-realization, and self-fulfillment through commodities, permeating all relations, with uncertain consequences requiring repression.[233] But repression on its own will not produce the degree of willing acceptance that the system requires.

In these circumstances nationalism plays three roles. First, it provides a type of psychic compensation for the direct producers, which is unobtainable from the mere consumption of commodities. It is, as they say, no accident that the nationalist turn in the ideology of the Chinese ruling class became most marked with the initial opening up of the Chinese economy to world markets in 1978 and the suppression of the movement for political reform in 1989, which was followed by a "patriotic education campaign," the general tone of which continues to this day.[234] Second, it acts as a means of re-creating at the political level the cohesion that is being lost at the social level. Third, it uses this sense of cohesion to mobilize populations behind the performance of national capitals against their competitors and rivals.

This occurs most sharply in cases of actual military conflict: "In an age of mass politics all interstate wars are nationalist wars, conducted in the name of nations and purportedly in their interests."[235] But war is scarcely the only or even the most common form of geopolitical rivalry; there is also what Luttwak describes as "geo-economics" or "warfare by other means." Recall the passage cited above: "In [geo-economics], in-

vestment capital for industry provided or guided by the state is the equivalent of firepower; product development subsidized by the state is the
equivalent of weapon innovation; and market penetration supported by
the state replaces military bases and garrisons on foreign soil as well as
diplomatic influence." But what Luttwak calls the "adversarial attitudes"
mobilized by states can of course escape the control of those who initially
fostered them.[236] Ian Kershaw suggests that one of the reasons the Japanese
military elite was forced into the Second World War was that it had encouraged levels of mass chauvinism and expectations of military-territorial
expansion from which it could not retreat without provoking popular
hostility: the generals were trapped in a prison of their own devising.[237]
Norman Stone argues more generally that the First World War could not
have been brought to a negotiated conclusion by the end of 1916 no
matter what the politicians and generals may have wished, because the
nationalist hatreds they had encouraged, now amplified by deaths, injuries,
and destruction, had acquired their own momentum and called forth
leaders committed to victory.[238]

Similar outcomes can be found in the neoliberal era. The Conservatives did not unleash imperial nationalism before 1997 in relation to
"Europe" because the EU was in any sense hostile to neoliberalism but
rather as an ideological diversion from the failure of neoliberalism to
transform the fortunes of British capital. The nationalism invoked for this
purpose is now a major obstacle for British politicians and state managers
who want to pursue a strategy of greater European integration, however
rational that may be from their perspective.[239] But there is another danger
for the ruling classes too, namely that neoliberal nationalism will lead to
the fragmentation of neoliberal states. Harvey writes: "Margaret Thatcher,
through the Falklands/Malvinas war and in her antagonistic posture toward Europe, invoked nationalist sentiment in support of her neoliberal
project, though it was the idea of England and St George, rather than
the United Kingdom, that animated her vision—which turned Scotland
and Wales hostile."[240] But would the hostility of (some) Scottish and
(some) Welsh people have been less, had Thatcher conveyed a sense of
Britishness rather than Englishness? The difficulty here is a deeper one.
Because nationalism is such an inescapable aspect of capitalist development, the first response to intolerable conditions is to seek to establish a
new nation-state, although this is usually only possible where some level

of national consciousness already exists, as it does, for example, in Scotland. In other words, neoliberalism may require nations, but it does not require particular nations. And invoking nationalism as a counterweight to neoliberal social and economic policy can involve a different set of problems for individual ruling classes: not problems on the order of class war or the war of each against all, but those involving the uncertainties and inconveniences caused by the potential fragmentation of the nation-state. This outcome is generally only possible where an alternative national consciousness is available and associated with a distinct territory within the state.

In spite of the risks, however, it is not clear what could replace nationalism as a means of securing even the partial loyalty of the working class to the capitalist state and preventing the formation of revolutionary class consciousness. Early in the neoliberal era, Raymond Williams noted that "a global system of production and trade" also required "a socially organized and socially disciplined population, one from which effort can be mobilized and taxes collected along the residual but still effective national lines; there are still no effective political competitors in that."[241] Could loyalties be transferred upward to a global or even regional state? Montserrat Guibernau has argued that the EU will ultimately require "European national consciousness" to give coherence to the otherwise uneven group of nations that comprise that body.[242] But as Benedict Anderson writes, "*in themselves*, market-zones, 'natural'-geographic or politico-administrative, do not create attachments. Who would willingly die for Comecon or the EEC?"[243]

Nor could loyalties easily be transferred downward to individual capitals. Workers have been known to support their company, even to make sacrifices to keep it in business. But this tends to happen where firms are local and well established, and where workers are employed on a long-term basis. Where workers make sacrifices in terms of job losses, worsened conditions, and—as happened in the US during the 1980s— real cuts in pay, they do not do so because of loyalty to the firm but because they see no alternative that does not involve the even worse fate of losing their job entirely. Individual managers or "team leaders" may internalize the ethos of McDonald's or Wal-Mart, but workers cannot: the reality of the daily conflict between themselves and the employer is too stark to be overcome. Beyond this, even those companies that still retain health insurance and pension arrangements come nowhere near providing the integrative functions of even the weakest nation-state. It is of course possible for workers outside a company to celebrate its achievements—but only because it is *national*, as, for example, in the reaction of German workers to the merger of Daimler and Chrysler, which effectively saw the German company acquire the American.[244] Worker acquiescence in the "dull compulsion to labor" at the workplace is not the basis for mobilizations to defend the interests of Capital. The oil millionaires and media celebrities who respectively fund and front the Tea Party in the US may intend to make that country even safer for Wal-Mart and Wall Street, but their free-market rhetoric always has to be expressed in terms of reclaiming the nation from the Marxist Antichrist in the White House and the liberal elites who threaten American freedom, not restoring the rate of profit.

CONCLUSION

Capitalism did not inherit the feudal-absolutist states system. Instead it destroyed and rebuilt the internal structures of the constitutive states, and then reconfigured their external relationships on a different basis. Once the new system emerged, the dynamics of competition between the component states assumed a distinctive logic, but it is the geopolitical expression of the same logic that impels the most rudimentary moments of competitive accumulation involving commodities. There are not two logics. As Father Merrin says in *The Exorcist*, "there is only one," although our demon is called Capital rather than Pazuzo.[245] What are the implications of this for the classical Marxist theory of imperialism?

Critics of the theory are fond of listing its supposed inadequacies, not only as a guide to the current situation but even in relation the period in which it was formulated.[246] Inadequacies there certainly were: Lenin overgeneralized from the German fusion of banking and industrial capital, and was empirically wrong about the destination of overseas capital investment; Bukharin gave too one-sided a picture of the tendency toward state capitalism; and so on. But when all these criticisms have been registered, there remains the fact that the theory identified aspects of the system that have largely been lost by subsequent generations of Marxists.

As we have seen, the theory involved two sets of relationships: those of domination by the metropolitan powers over the colonial and semicolonial world and those of rivalry between the metropolitan powers themselves. The former came popularly to define "imperialism," not least because during the Cold War intercapitalist economic rivalries were held in check—not abolished—by enforced political and ideological solidarity against the Eastern Bloc. The Cold War further obscured this aspect of the system by appearing to make geopolitical rivalry an aspect of inter-systemic conflict rather than a function of the system itself. National Se-curity Council Report 68 (NSC-68), delivered to President Truman in 1950, is usually considered to be the foundation of the ideology of total mobilization against the USSR and its allies. It is, but within this text is a statement that speaks of a wider consideration:*"Even if there were no So-viet Union we would face the great problem of the free society of reconciling order, security, the need for participation, with the requirement for freedom.* We would face the fact that in a shrinking world the absence of order among nations is becoming less and less tolerable."[247] In these circumstances, outside of the very few socialists who regarded the Stalinist regimes as being bu-reaucratic state-capitalist, and consequently the Cold War as being a form of capitalist inter-state competition, the identification of imperialism with opposition to the anticolonial and liberation movements was understand-able. But it was capitalist inter-state competition that most concerned the theorists of classical Marxism. During the interwar period several ar-gued that the next world war would be between the Britain and US, the declining and rising world powers.[248] They were right that these very different empires could not coexist but wrong about the means by which the latter would achieve its ascendancy. In 1930 Douglas MacArthur and other US generals drew up plans to invade Canada and other British ter-ritories in the Americas, part of a design to "liquidate the British empire which would only reach fruition during and after the Second World War."[249] But as Arrighi points out, the US "had no need to challenge Britain militarily to consolidate its growing power." During the Second World War the US used three tactics:"one, let Britain and its challengers exhaust one another militarily and financially; two, enrich itself by sup-plying goods and credit to the wealthier contestant; and, three, intervene in the war at a late stage so as to be in a position to dictate terms of the peace that facilitated the exercise of its own economic power on the largest possible geographical scale.[250] The final stage in the transfer of hegemonic status occurred, however, during Britain's imperial self-immolation at Suez, which the US hastened by pressurizing the pound and refusing to allow the IMF to offer support.[251] It is less often remembered that Eisenhower also instructed the Sixth Fleet, then permanently based in the Mediterranean, to harass and obstruct the Anglo–French expedition between Malta and Port Said.[252]

I am not suggesting that the end of the Cold War has simply seen a reversion to the situation that existed between 1914 and 1945, and that the classical theory of imperialism can be reapplied as if there had been no developments in the intervening decades. On the contrary, I want to suggest that the aspect of the theory that deals with conflict between the capitalist states is relevant precisely because it transcends the issue of imperialism. If there is a general problem with the classical theory, it is not, as critics suggest, that it is irrelevant because imperialism has changed into new forms. *It is rather that the theory is not a theory of imperialism at all, except insofar as it dealt with relations between the metropolitan powers and the colonial and semicolonial world; it is instead a theory of how capitalism itself would work in a world where all the major economies were dominated by the capitalist mode of production.* In other words, the "inter-imperialist rivalry" aspects of classical imperialism should be seen as simply the first manifestation of the type of geopolitical conflict between capitalist states that is the *normal* condition of the system. Capitalist states have always competed with each other, in military as well as market terms, from Italian city-state and Anglo-Dutch rivalries onward, but until the later decades of the nineteenth century there were simply too few states dominated by the capitalist mode of production for any generalizations about their conduct to be made—indeed, this was precisely why many early theorists of capitalism could assume that a world of capitalist states, happily trading with each other, would be one of peace. From some point in the last third of the nineteenth century, it became apparent that capitalism in fact meant war, but this was theorized as an aspect of a special stage in capitalist development rather than a permanent aspect of the system at full maturity.

There will be many capitalist states as long as there are many capitals; and as long as there are many capitalist states they will behave as capitals. The trajectory of geoeconomic competition ultimately ends in geopolitical rivalry. This is why explaining the persistence of the states system is more than an academic issue: it is central to a realistic assessment of what we can expect from the capitalist system in terms of its destructive capabilities, which we should not complacently assume will only ever be directed toward the global South. And that in turn should give added urgency to our considerations on how we might bring it to an end.

$\ll$ Chapter 8 $\gg$

Far-Right Social Movements as a Problem for Capital*

INTRODUCTION

There was originally only one social movement: the movement for social-ism. The first socialists, from Babeuf to Marx and Engels, looked forward to what they called a "social revolution," which they argued would be the

---

* Previously unpublished in this form, but drawing on: "Right-Wing Social Move-ments: The Political Indeterminacy of Mass Mobilization," in *Marxism and Social Movements*, edited by Colin Barker, Lawrence Cox, John Krinsky, and Alf Gunvald Nilsen (Leiden: E. J. Brill/Historical Materialism, 2013); "The Far-Right and the 'Needs of Capital,'" in *The Longue Durée of the Far-Right: An International Historical Sociology* (London: Routledge, 2014); and "Neoliberal Regimes, the Far-Right, and the Implications for Capital," in *Researching the Powerful: Public Sociology in Ac-tion*, edited by Lucy Brown, William Dinan, David Miller, and Ludek Stavinoha (London: Routledge, 2016).

first in history, earlier revolutions like the French having been merely political in nature.[1] This social revolution would, appropriately enough, be
carried out by the "social movement," another term widespread throughout
socialist and Communist circles in the first half of the nineteenth century.
In one of the notes eventually published as *The German Ideology* (1845–46)
there is an acerbic review by Engels of Karl Grün's 1845 book *The Social
Movement in France and Belgium*, but Engels himself uses the same term—
"the French social movement"—indicating that he recognizes its existence,
and his quarrel is rather with Grün's views on the subject.[2]

By the mid-1840s Marx and Engels had identified the proletariat as
the only force capable of achieving the social revolution, but they did
not regard it as acting entirely alone—the minority position of the working class on a global scale, even at the time of Engels's death in 1895, pre-
cluded that. Their position seems rather to have been that workers would
act as both the political leadership and the organizational core of the social movement as a whole. Indeed, toward the end of his life Marx
claimed that in some situations, above all that of British rule in Ireland,
it might be the colonial peoples who would initiate the process of social
revolution; this was why, he wrote in a letter to Engels at the end of 1869,
"the Irish question is so important for the social movement in general."[3]

This notion of "the" social movement as all those forces seeking to
establish socialism, with the working class at their center, had fallen into
disuse by the formation of the Second International in 1889, at least in
Western Europe and North America. In its place a more fragmented set
of notions began to be used, each capturing different aspects of what had
once been a unified conception: the terms "trade union," "labor," "working class," and "socialist" all referred to different, if overlapping, movements,
and only the last was unambiguously associated with the complete tran-
scendence of capitalism. These new usages were both more specific than
the one originally used by Marx and Engels, in that they referred directly
to the working class and its institutions, and narrower, in that they excluded any other forces. The split in the socialist movement that became
apparent at the outbreak of the First World War, and that was formalized
by reactions to the Bolshevik Revolution and the establishment of the
Communist International, added yet another division, in the shape of a
"revolutionary" movement distinct from the "reformist" movement associated with Social Democracy.

When the term "social movement" reentered widespread use during the 1970s, it was generally in connection with what were termed the "new social movements"—attempts to end various forms of oppression or to achieve other goals that were not specific to a single social group, such as banning nuclear weapons or defending the environment. Some of these, the most important being the movement for black civil rights in the US, had actually emerged as early as the 1940s, but most were products of the following two decades. Nevertheless, the adjective "new" was always something of a misnomer: any surviving suffragettes would have been surprised to learn that the women's liberation movement had begun in the 1960s. In practice, however, the supposed novelty of these movements was not based on the historical absence of mobilization but on three contemporary characteristics that distinguished them from their predecessors. First, these new formations were not based on the working class or its organizations. They tended instead to be led by individuals from the middle classes—specifically from the new middle class—although they all had working-class members and often sought trade-union affiliations.[4] Second, they distinguished between their methods of organization and those of both the trade-union movement and the political left, which "new movement" figures accused of being hierarchical and authoritarian.[5] Third, insofar as they recognized predecessors, their methods of campaigning had shifted from an earlier emphasis on lobbying to one on direct action.[6] In retrospect, it can be seen that by the time the various movements were classified as "new," a shift from resisting oppression to merely asserting identity was underway, as part of the general retreat of the left that began in the mid-1970s in the face of the neoliberal ascendancy: the shortening of "women's liberation movement" to "women's movement" had more significance than the dropping of a word might suggest.

Although social movements are one of those phenomena that are easier to identify than to define, some generalizations about their nature are possible. Social movements tend to be broader than a specific campaign. Thus, campaigns for equal pay or the legalization of abortion were components of the women's liberation movement but did not in themselves constitute distinct social movements. In the British context, a handful of campaigns have some of the quality of social movements because of their deep and lasting impact on public life, above all those associated with the Campaign for Nuclear Disarmament, the Vietnam Solidarity

Campaign, the Anti-Nazi League, the Anti–Poll Tax Federation, and the Stop the War Coalition. At the same time, social movements tend to be more diffuse than political parties—partly because of the relative permanence of "political" as opposed to "movement" organization, partly because political parties have to take positions on the entire range of issues that concern their supporters. A social movement concerned with, say, opposing racism need not have a position on global warming—indeed, would not survive very long if it insisted that its members adhere to one—while a party can scarcely avoid doing so. In practice, social movements can involve a range of different parties, in the way that "the socialist movement" in Britain before the First World War included, among others, the British Socialist Party, the Independent Labour Party, the Socialist Labour Party, and the Socialist Party of Great Britain.

If there is one dominant assumption concerning the politics of social movements, it is that expressed by Paul Byrne: "Social movement supporters are clearly located on the left of the political spectrum."[7] Indeed, it is not unusual for the terms "popular movement" and "social movement" to be treated as virtually synonymous. Since the majority of people by definition do not belong to the ruling class, social movements will tend to be composed of members of the oppressed groups and exploited classes that do constitute that majority, and they will also tend to be directed toward goals that are in the interest of these groups and classes. We cannot, however, equate all social movements with what the Stalinist tradition used to call "progressive" politics. Attempts to do so depend either on a self-confirming definition by which only left movements are designated as social, or on the indefensible assumption that popular movements cannot be oppressive or act against their own long-term interests. The historical record does not support such definitions or assumptions. The new social movements have both "right" as well as "left" predecessors. Consideration of these earlier examples may help us to understand, in general terms, why the former are also possible today, as well as the contradictory nature of their politics in relation to capital.

RIGHT-WING SOCIAL MOVEMENTS IN HISTORY

During the Napoleonic Wars the French occupying armies attempted to impose bourgeois revolution "from above and outside" on the absolutist regimes of Western and Southern Europe, in alliance with local liberals. Yet in at least two important cases, those of Spain and Naples, the republics established by Napoleon were resisted not merely by representatives of the feudal ruling class, using conscripts and mercenaries, but by popular uprisings dedicated to restoring church and king. These often operated completely outwith the command or control of the elites. It is meaningless to describe these revolts as nationalist in inspiration, since the kingdoms of Spain and Naples that the insurgents sought to defend were, in their different ways, the antithesis of modern nation-states. Indeed, in both cases modern nation-states were precisely what the hated liberals were attempting to construct. Yet the mass of the population, who might have benefited from the overthrow of feudalism, were isolated from the liberals by the latter's bourgeois status and relative wealth: "a liberal is a man in a carriage," as the Spanish saying went. The liberals heightened their social distance from the masses by relying on a foreign power and by offering no positive reforms to the peasantry. As Jaume Torras writes of the Spanish Jacobin experiment: "The anti-feudalism of the liberal project was not generic; it pointed in a clearly defined direction. It did not aim to suppress nor relax the exaction of peasant surplus labor embodied in feudal rent, but to transform it into ground-rent founded on private property and insert it in a pattern of social relations under the hegemony of capital (by disentailment measures a free market of land and rents was created)." Presented with a mere change in the mechanism of exploitation, but one that would nevertheless destroy the only aspects of society that offered stability and consolation, the masses rejected the new order arms in hand:

> To oppose the [liberal] Constitution would signify, rather than supporting the old order, preferring an alternative that was defining itself solely by its incompatibility with the concrete development of the liberal program: a program which, seen from below and from the countryside, could be viewed as a mere variant of the Old Regime; rather an undesirable variant, in which some already known and hated subjects would be preponderant, and in which the church's role would be weakened— this church which the poorest peasants believed was their only defense in a hostile society organized to spoil them.[8]

In Spain, the deep contradictions within a popular resistance dedicated to restoring one of the most reactionary regimes in Europe were captured by Francisco Goya in *The Disasters of War*, expressing both his awareness of the tragedy and his ambivalence toward the forces involved. Yet if the meaning of the movement was ambiguous, the outcome—the restoration of church and king—was not in doubt: "It was the greatest irony of the war—a conflict replete with ironies—that at an enormous cost of lives and destruction and the almost certain loss of its colonies, patriot Spain had in the end fought to restore an absolutist monarchy. The people had risen to defend king, religion and fatherland; the liberals' attempt to create a parliamentary monarchy out of the conflict had not counted on the lower classes' necessary support, offering them little but the panacea of a market economy which would further destroy their traditional 'moral economy.'"[9]

A similar story could be told of events in Naples: "The Neapolitan Republic, which emerged under the tutelage of the French forces, never succeeded in winning popular support." It failed to abolish feudal relations on the land but instead raised taxes on the peasants and urban poor, with the result that "accordingly the Republic soon became synonymous with the interests of the propertied, and opposition to it dovetailed with old class hatreds." The retaking of Naples by Calabrian forces and the British involved a slaughter that continued for two weeks: "The *lazzaroni* [i.e., the lumpen-proletariat] joined in, roaming the streets with the Calabrians to cries of 'Long live the King,' hacking down Trees of Liberty, ransacking and burning the houses of the rich, looting monasteries and churches, and murdering anyone who looked like a supporter of the Republic." Even after the city had been retaken with the aid of the British, the killing continued: "[King] Ferdinand returned to his capital on 10 July, greeted by rapturous crowds shouting: 'We want to see our father,' and in the weeks that followed dozens of patriots were tracked down then hanged or decapitated."[10]

The Spanish peasants and Neapolitan urban masses, facing a choice of two evils, actively embraced the one that was familiar to them and that at least preserved their existing lifeworld. Nevertheless, these struggles, the Spanish in particular, involved self-sacrifice and collective organization linked to overt forms of class hostility, albeit focused almost entirely on the external foreign enemy and its internal supporters, who were seen as both betraying the kingdom and seeking to impose new forms of exploitation. The liberal revolutionaries could offer the masses nothing, and the resulting absence of popular opposition to the existing regimes was one reason why bourgeois revolutions in both Spain and what would eventually become Italy were delayed for so long after these initial top-down attempts.

There were other circumstances, too, where a combination of independent small producers and workers could be mobilized for entirely reactionary ends. Unlike the Spanish or Neapolitan events, the American Civil War was a successful bourgeois revolution, in that it removed from the federal capitalist republic the threat posed by an expansionist Confederate slave society. The Northern triumph was made possible by the abolition of slavery, but the victors' attempts to democratize the South, above all by supporting the black population's claims to political equality, were inconsistent and uneven. They ceased entirely in 1877, when federal troops were withdrawn from the former Confederate states. Long before that point, indeed almost from the end of the war, the former slave owners had unleashed a movement to impose new forms of labor discipline and social control on the now-free blacks, above all through the Ku Klux Klan. This was certainly initiated and led by members of the Southern elite, rather than reflecting a spontaneous movement from below of poor whites. As Eric Foner writes:

> Some historians attribute the Klan's sadistic campaign of terror to the fears and prejudices of poorer whites. The evidence, however, contradicts such an interpretation. Ordinary farmers and laborers comprised the bulk of the membership, and energetic "young bloods" were more likely to conduct midnight raids than middle-aged planters and layers, but "respectable citizens" chose the targets and often participated in the brutality. . . . Personal experience led blacks to blame the South's "aristocratic classes" for violence, and with good reason, for the Klan's leadership included planters, merchants, lawyers, and even ministers.[11]

The former slave owners were not numerous enough to carry out the levels of repression exercised against the black population after 1865 and had therefore to rely on support from white yeoman farmers and the petty bourgeoisie. Why did these two groups align themselves with their ruling class?

The majority of Southerners had not been slave owners, and there were major class differences between slave owners and yeoman farmers.

According to Elizabeth Fox-Genovese and Eugene Genovese, the latter class accepted the system "not because they did not understand their position, or because they were panicked by racial fears, and certainly not because they were stupid, but because they saw themselves as aspiring slaveholders or as non-slaveholding beneficiaries of a slaveholding world that constituted the only world they knew."[12] The problem for the ruling class was not so much with the yeomen, however, as with the whites below them in the social structure, those who did not own slaves and who had little chance of ever owning them. As Theodore Allen has pointed out, it was in order to prevent the emergence of solidarity between this group and black slaves that the condition of racialized slavery had to be absolute: "If the mere presumption of liberty was to serve as a mark of social status for masses of European-Americans without real prospects of upward social mobility, and yet induce them to abandon their opposition to the plantocracy and enlist them actively, or at least passively, in keeping down the Negro bond-laborer with whom they had made common cause in the course of Bacon's Rebellion, the presumption of liberty had to be denied to free African-Americans."[13] The decisive issue was whether, once slavery had been abolished, the former slaves could form an alliance with the exploited majority of whites, both groups then allying with the organized working class in the North. Obviously the Southern ruling class did everything they could to prevent such an outcome and were largely successful in doing so. The question is whether this was preordained by the strength of a racism that was impossible to dislodge in the decade following Lee's surrender, or whether a different strategy, either on the part of the Radical Republicans or the Northern trade-union movement, could have overcome it.

The actual outcome after 1877 was a social structure in which, across large areas of the South, the petty bourgeoisie and white workers were complicit in an institutionalized regime of terror against the black population that led between 1890 and 1930 to three thousand black Americans being tortured and killed, often as part of a public spectacle.[14] Yet none of this actually improved conditions for the white population below the level of the ruling plantocracy and the social layers immediately surrounding it. A careful paper by Albert Szymanski, published a hundred years after the end of Reconstruction, showed that "the more intense racial discrimination is, the lower are white earnings *because* of the effect of the intermediate variable of working class solidarity." He concluded: "No matter how measured, whites do not benefit economically by economic discrimination [against nonwhites]."[15] Why then did they not ally with the blacks?

In his pioneering study of Reconstruction, W. E. B. Du Bois asked why it was that "the South reached the extraordinary distinction of being the only modern civilized country where human beings were publicly burned alive," and noted: "The political success of the doctrine of racial separation, which overthrew Reconstruction by uniting the planter and the poor white, was far exceeded by its astonishing economic results." By this Du Bois meant the way in which structural racism prevented the poor whites from uniting with the blacks, to the economic benefit of their rulers. But this was not the whole story:

> It must be remembered that the white group of laborers, while they received a low wage, were compensated in part by a sort of public and psychological wage. They were given public deference and titles of courtesy because they were white. They were admitted freely with all classes of white people to public functions, public parks, and the best schools. The police were drawn from their ranks, and the courts, dependent on their votes, treated them with such leniency as to encourage lawlessness. Their vote selected public officials, and while this had a small effect upon the economic situation, it had a great effect upon their personal treatment and the deference shown to them.[16]

The typical situation of the white Southern petty bourgeoisie and working class was therefore that they had marginally superior material conditions to their black neighbors, but significantly inferior material conditions to whites who lived in areas where blacks were not subject to the same degree of systematic oppression. The marginal material superiority therefore acquired a quite disproportionate social significance compared to its economic value, allied as it was to the noneconomic, psychosocial compensation whites received from occupying a position of absolute ascendancy over blacks. The majority of Southern whites, most of the time, appear not to have considered what conditions existed elsewhere or how their own might be raised to that level, let alone surpass it.

My final example, Ulster prior to the partition of Ireland in 1922, resembles the situation in the Southern states of the US in that the protagonists were almost entirely members of the Protestant industrial working class and their families. Protestant industrial workers enjoyed a higher standard of living than Catholics, since they had access to more skilled, better-paying jobs, and marginally better housing. The relative differences were probably no greater than the differences between poor whites and blacks in the South after 1865, but in this case both groups were *better* off than their respective counterparts in southern Ireland. Although the Orange Lodges embedded the ideology of Ulster Loyalism in a strong organizational base, material self-interest played a stronger role. The comparison that Protestant workers made was not primarily with their Catholic coworkers but with the peasant Catholic population of the rest of Ireland, whose fate they would supposedly have to share following Irish independence; this provided the element of rationality in the decision of most Protestants to remain Unionists. As Eamonn McCann writes of this period:

> The protectionist policies of Sinn Fein, had they been applied in the North, would have bid to destroy all the Northern industrial structure. The ship-building and linen industries, cut off from the sources of raw materials or markets, or both, would have gone to the wall. . . . It is not true that the Protestants, blinded by propaganda, made a crazy choice. They made a perfectly rational economic decision between the alternatives offered. This is not to say that their conscious decision was based on cold economic calculation. It is to say that there was a curious economic rationality underpinning all the quasi-religious jingoism with which the Unionist case was expressed, a rationality that was not being challenged in the existing working-class movement. . . . This is not to argue that that in 1921 the Protestants were "right" to choose to fight for the link with Britain; insofar as such monolithic concepts are applicable they were wrong. It is to argue that in the absence of the left it was inevitable.[17]

Each of these cases involves subordinate classes and groups willingly participating in, and sometimes providing the main social basis for, movements in support of Catholic absolutism, white supremacy, or the Protestant Ascendancy. In the American and Irish cases at least, left-wing alternatives did emerge and sought to address the concerns of those sections of the oppressed who had been harnessed behind reaction. This happened in the South during the era of populism in the 1890s, and in Ulster immediately before the First World War and again during the

Great Depression of the 1930s. These alternatives failed to produce lasting unity; but if their lack of success was not inevitable, it does testify to the ideological strength of the movements they opposed. Are these examples peculiar to their own times and circumstances? Or can they also illuminate the nature of contemporary right-wing social movements under neoliberal capitalism?

FAKE AND AUTHENTIC RIGHT-WING SOCIAL MOVEMENTS

The capitalist ruling class does not generally require social movements to achieve its objectives, least of all in the developed West. Unlike most previous ruling classes, it does not tend to directly control states, but it can usually rely on them to act in its collective interest, if not always the interest of individual firms or sectors.[18] Where social movements apparently supportive of business objectives do emerge, it usually transpires that they are in fact modern examples of the type of public relations offensive familiar since the beginning of the twentieth century: they are astroturf rather than genuine grassroots mobilizations. Astroturf campaigns usually involve PR agencies hired by industry-wide corporate coalitions to argue that, in the title of one exposé, "toxic sludge is good for you"—as apparently are cigarette smoking, deforestation, and abolishing the minimum wage.[19] Front organizations staffed by agency employees create the illusion of a movement by bombarding politicians with telephone calls, letters, and emails, usually to prevent regulatory legislation from being enacted or to exert pressure for its repeal. The expansion of electronic media has taken astroturfing into the blogosphere, enabling more general campaigns to alter public perception, often—as in the case of climate change—by creating an atmosphere of doubt or controversy that does not exist within the scientific community but makes it easier for politicians to succumb to corporate pressure while claiming to be responsive to public opinion.

Similar pseudomobilizations in defense of political regimes rather than corporate interests can appear more plausible as social movements, if only because they involve the physical presence of demonstrators on the streets rather than in the virtual sphere. No less fraudulent, they take a wider range of forms and are usually found in the global South, especially where representative democracy is weakly embedded. One variant, seen most recently across the Middle East and North Africa during the revolutions of 2011, simply involves state employees and hired criminal elements being organized by the police to attack opposition forces. One report from Yemen, for example, describes how the regime of Ali Abdullah Saleh responded to student and other activist attempts to occupy an area outside Sana'a University: "At least ten trucks carrying dozens of men dressed as civilians soon arrived. Hundreds of reinforcements carrying sticks, knives, automatic weapons and pictures of Saleh turned up, too. These were the *balatanga*, thugs paid by the state to crush dissent. In a series of skirmishes, the *balatanga* charged the youth, forcing them to flee, then sang, banged drums and danced. It was a symbolic victory: the regime had no intention of letting them occupy Tahir, unlike Egypt."[20] The final sentence in this report indicates the lack of autonomy of the *balatanga* and comparable groups.

The people taking part in these operations, even if they lack autonomy, do share a material interest in their actions, since they rely on the state for their living. Members of the security forces in particular are concerned to preserve whatever dictatorship they happen to serve, since any serious revolution would threaten a purging of the state apparatus, an end to their relatively privileged position, and possible retribution for their many crimes and violations. Their slogans do not of course focus on these vulgar personal concerns but on the indispensability of the Great Leader and the need to repel traitorous foreign-funded attempts to undermine the Unity of the People. Such forces do not constitute genuine counter-movements, since they are not merely dependent on the state but are mobilized by the state and have no independent organizational life outside it.

Even the most dictatorial regimes have a class basis of support beyond paid officials—the petty-bourgeois trader deploring the breakdown of order and stability is the characteristic figure here. But these are not the forces that regimes rely on for their salvation in extremis. They tend to be activated only in two ways. One is through one-off events like the pro–de Gaulle demonstration that marked the end of the events of May 1968 in France. The other is through short bursts of protest like those directed against the Salvador Allende government in Chile during the early 1970s or the Hugo Chavez government in Venezuela now. These manifestations lack the organizational structures and long-term objectives of social movements. Is it possible then for there to be genuine right-wing social movements, whose members have not simply been hired to promote or defend the interests of corporations and regimes?

There are certainly fewer right-wing than left-wing social movements, although there have certainly been mobilizations against left-wing governments.[21] Examples of right-wing mobilization in this sense are most commonly found where reformist governments in the global South have faced opposition from middle-class opponents hostile to redistributive policies toward the poor or the working class. These have involved elements of self-organization, as with the Thai People's Alliance for Democracy (the "yellow shirts") who forced the resignation of Prime Minister Thaksin Shinawatra in 2006—although the key factor in achieving this result was that their demonstrations allowed the army to intervene to "restore order." However, "right-wing" should not be understood in too narrowly a party-political sense. The very notion of the social means that mobilizing issues will tend to be not particular government policies or even particular governments but longer-term developments that may have been supported by governments of different political persuasions and that the movement wants to stop or restrict, like abortion, immigration, or welfare spending. We can therefore distinguish between the common objectives of the global ruling class as pursued by the various components of the states system on the one hand, and of "right-wing" or "conservative" social movements on the other. What is the relationship of the latter to capitalism?

FAR-RIGHT SOCIAL MOVEMENTS AND "THE NEEDS OF CAPITAL"

The very notion of capitalist "needs" has been criticized for ascribing to impersonal systems a characteristic that is only possessed by living organisms.[22] But, as Gregor McLennan writes, "if complex systems evolve as a way of meeting various basic human needs—as they surely do—then it is not inappropriate to speak of the resulting systems themselves as having needs. . . . Transport systems, computer networks, economic models—these 'instrumental' systems are obviously designed to meet needs, and themselves will have certain 'needs' if they are to function effectively." If we avoid what he calls "looking ex post facto for functional fits," then this notion of needs can be helpful.[23] Given that one central characteristic of the capitalist mode of production is *competition* between capitals, any specific discussion about needs must refer to those of national capitals, demarcated by their position within the states system. As I discussed earlier in this book, these needs primarily involve nation-states in providing the necessary conditions for the reproduction of capital and in representing the collective interests of capital (against the working class on the one hand and against other national capitals on the other).[24]

The needs of capital are, however, not always aligned with the issues that concern groups who in most other respects are supporters of the system. Right-wing social movements can relate to the accumulation strategies of capital in three ways: 1) They are directly supportive; 2) They are compatible and/or indirectly supportive, mainly through strengthening ideological positions that are associated with capitalist rule but may not be essential to it; or 3) They are indirectly (and possibly unintentionally) destabilizing. Until recently, examples of type 1 have been very rare indeed, since, for reasons set out in the previous section, capitalists prefer to use corporate pressure rather than popular support to achieve their political goals. Examples of type 2 are the most frequent. But as I will argue below, we are currently seeing and are likely to see more examples of type 3, which raises a question: what is the relationship between far-right politics and capitalism?

I want to begin answering this question by considering what different theoretical traditions have said about the most extreme form of the far right, Fascism, in its most extreme form, German National Socialism. But this is not because it should be regarded as the model against which all other examples of far-right politics must be measured. It is rather because the very extremity of Nazism highlighted the ongoing tensions between the far right and capital, in their most acute form. The examples given below were all written while the Nazi regime either was still in power or had only recently fallen.

The first is what might be called the dominant left-wing conception of the relationship between the two, expressed here by Rajani Palme Dutt: "Fascism . . . is a movement of mixed elements, dominantly petit-bourgeois, but also slum-proletarian and demoralized working class, financed and directed by finance-capital, by the big industrialists, landlords and financiers, to defeat the working class revolution and smash the working class organizations."[25] The decisive word here is "directed." Fascism as a movement consists of members of the petty bourgeoisie and the lumpen-proletariat, but these forces are actually organized and mobilized by representatives of the capitalist class. Palme Dutt was voicing the Stalinist orthodoxy of the time, but it is interesting to compare his position with that of Stalinism's greatest opponent within the socialist movement. Trotsky was considerably more subtle, understanding that, far from being the political expression of monopoly capitalism, ruling classes regarded Fascism only as a last resort:

> The barons, the magnates of capital, and the bankers have made an attempt to safeguard their interests by means of the police and the regular army. The idea of giving up all power to Hitler, who supports himself upon the greedy and unbridled bands of the petty bourgeoisie, is a far from pleasant one to them. They do not, of course, doubt that in the long run Hitler will be a submissive instrument of their domination. Yet this is bound up with convulsions, with the risk of a long and weary civil war and great expense.[26]

He also rightly argued that Fascist organizations were independent of the state and capital before the seizure of power; that is precisely why they were able to act as a final recourse for the ruling class. According to Trotsky it is only *after* the regime is in place that the interests of monopoly capital are asserted: "After fascism is victorious, finance capital gathers into its hands, as in a vice of steel, directly and immediately, all the organs and institutions of sovereignty, the executive, administrative, and educational powers of the state: the entire state apparatus together with the army, the municipalities, the universities, the schools, the press, the trade unions, and the cooperatives."[27] Fascism in power is "least of all the rule of the petty bourgeoisie"; it is rather "the most ruthless dictatorship of monopoly capital."[28] I have quoted Trotsky at length precisely because he was responsible for some of the most brilliant insights into the class basis of Fascism in the Marxist tradition, and for developing strategy to prevent its coming to power. Yet his analysis of the relationship between Fascism *in* power and capitalism is relatively orthodox.[29]

A second, essentially liberal position sees Fascism not as ultimately supportive of capitalism but, on the contrary, as its negation. "While 'progressives' in this country and elsewhere were still deluding themselves that communism and fascism represented opposite poles," wrote Friedrich von Hayek in 1944, "more and more people began to ask themselves whether the new tyrannies were not the outcome of the same tendencies." According to Hayek, Nazism was not, "as so many people wish to believe, a capitalist reaction against the advance of socialism. On the contrary, the support which brought these ideas to power came precisely from the socialist camp."[30] Hayek was not of course concerned with the suppression of democracy under Fascism so much as with the degree to which it interfered with markets, even expressing his opposition to making what he called a "fetish" of democracy.[31] These views were most clearly expressed, however, not during the Second World War but much later and in relation to a different type of far-right regime. In a justly infamous letter to the *Times* in 1978, he wrote: "I have not been able to find a single person even in much-maligned Chile who did not agree that personal freedom was much greater under Pinochet than it had been under Allende."[32] Leaving aside Hayek's characteristic hypocrisy, the problem here is his conception of capitalism. Friedrich Pollock had in 1941 already begun to talk about a "state capitalism," which could exist in either democratic or totalitarian forms: "The closest approach to the totalitarian form . . . has been made in National Socialist Germany."[33] But variants could be found even in the democracies opposed to Nazi Germany. Robert Brady wrote, of the influence of John Maynard Keynes's ideas, that "how far State control was to reach in this British version of National Socialism is hard to gather," but that it "is en route to the goal."[34] In other words, it was possible to conceive of the Nazis as acting in the interests of capital, but only if capital were conceived of in wider terms than the market order beloved of Hayek and other proto-neoliberals.

A third and final position, most often associated with social and liberal democracy, was perhaps the most widely held at the time and has been since: Fascism is essentially an autonomous political phenomenon. For G. D. H. Cole, capitalism was merely an "aspect" of Fascism, and by no means the most important aspect: "Fascism . . . was not in essence an economic movement, but a nationalist, imperialist and militarist movement using economic inducements to reinforce its primary appeal."[35] There is, in other words, a *coincidence* of interests between Fascism and capital, rather than those of the former being subordinated to those of the latter. The point was made in more theoretical terms, from a Marxist position otherwise close to that of Pollock, by Franz Neumann in his classic *Behemoth*. In Nazi Germany, he wrote,

> the automatism of free capitalism, precarious even under a democratic monopoly capitalism, has been severely restricted. But capitalism remains.

> ... National Socialism and big business have identical interests. ... National Socialism utilized the daring, the knowledge, the aggressiveness of the industrial leadership, while the industrial leadership utilized the anti-democracy, anti-liberalism and anti-unionism of the National Socialist party, which had fully developed the techniques by which the masses can be controlled and dominated.[36]

Essentially then we have three positions about the relationship of Fascism to capital. In the first, Fascism is brought about by movements of the petty bourgeoisie and lumpen-proletariat, who, lacking any coherent alternative of their own, are then forced to either carry out the wishes of, or be replaced by direct representatives of, monopoly capitalism. In the second, Fascism represents an alternative system to capitalism, either socialism or a more generalized "totalitarianism" in which the supposedly shared antimarket economies of Stalinist Russia and Nazi Germany override any other differences between them. In the third, Fascism is interested in economic structures only to the extent that they can support its political and social goals, but since capitalism can do so, Fascism is prepared to provide reciprocal support in turn. All three positions have contemporary supporters.[37]

Of these alternatives, the first, at least in its Trotskyist version, has some important observations to make about the class nature of Fascism as a mass movement prior to the seizure of power, but then it lapses into a more or less functionalist position. The second is theoretically and empirically bankrupt: even if capitalism requires markets—and there is no reason why they should always be fundamental to a system of competitive accumulation based on wage labor—neither Italian nor German Fascism came anywhere near abolishing them. The third corresponds most closely to reality but is weakened by a failure to establish any connection between the goals of Fascism and the capitalist society from which they emerged—or, indeed, to even see this as a problem. The third interpretation does, however, raise an interesting question with some bearing on our current concerns. What if the coincidence of Fascist and capitalist needs was itself, so to speak, a coincidence? What if a Fascist or far-right movement came to power that implemented policies against the needs of capital—not because they were "anticapitalist" in the way that the Strasserite wing of the Nazi Party was (falsely) supposed to be, but simply because their interests lay elsewhere? Is such a scenario conceivable? Before turning to the contemporary far right we need first to identify what the needs of capital are, and to what extent the Nazi regime actually met them.

RATIONALITY AND IRRATIONALITY IN NAZI GERMANY

"To him who looks upon the world rationally," wrote Hegel, "the world in turn presents a rational aspect."[38] As we saw in chapter 5, Max Weber, one of the most able (albeit one of the most pessimistic) intellectual defenders of the capitalist system, distinguished between two types of rationality. Of one, "instrumental rationality," he wrote: "Action is instrumentally rational when the end, the means and the secondary results are all rationally taken into account and weighed." Central to this type of rationality is the fact that it involves *alternatives*: "alternative means to the end, of the relation of the end to secondary consequences, and finally, of the relative importance of different possible ends." In the case of the other, "value-rationality," ends are decided in advance: "Examples of pure value-rational orientation would be the actions of persons who, regardless of possible cost to themselves, act to put into practice their convictions of what seems to them to be required by duty, honor, the pursuit of beauty, a religious call, personal loyalty, or the importance of some 'call,' no matter in what it consists." From the perspective of instrumental rationality, "value-rationality is always irrational": "For, the more unconditionally the actor devotes himself to this value for its own sake ... the less is he influenced by consideration of the consequences of his actions."[39] For Weber, values (ends) are fundamental beliefs, which may themselves be irrational (the "warring gods" between whom he believed we all have to choose), but to which adherence can be given by rational means.

Zygmunt Bauman has argued, rightly, that the Holocaust was the product of modernity, not irrational premodern residues. But he has also argued, wrongly, that the Holocaust was equally the product of instrumental rationality: "it was the spirit of instrumental rationality, and its modern, bureaucratic form of institutionalization, which has made the Holocaust-style solutions not only possible, but eminently 'reasonable'— and increased the probability of their choice."[40] But the roots of the Holocaust ultimately lie in the anti-Semitism at the heart of Nazi ideology (a *value* rationality). Once it had been assumed that this belief demanded a particular end—that the Jewish people be exterminated—its logic was only then implemented with all the bureaucratic efficiency that Eichmann defended at his trial (an *instrumental* rationality). As Stephen Bonner writes: "Instrumental reason did not bring about Nazism or destroy the ability of individuals to make normative judgments. . . . Instrumental reason and bureaucracy may have been the necessary, but they were not even the remotely sufficient conditions for totalitarianism."[41] Racism and anti-Semitism were *value* rational for the Nazis, notes Ulrich Herbert, but not for German national capitals:

> Any attempt to reduce the Nazi policy of mass annihilation solely or largely to underlying economic, "rational" interests, however, fails to recognize that, in the eyes of the Nazis, and in particular the advocates of systematic racism among them, the mass extermination of their ideological enemies was itself a "rational" political goal. It was supported by reference to social, economic, geopolitical, historical and medical arguments, as well as notions of "racial hygiene" and "internal security." Racism was not a "mistaken belief" serving to conceal the true interests of the regime, which were essentially economic. It was the fixed point of the whole system.[42]

Several leading Marxists have failed to understand this. Ernest Mandel, for example, sees the "germ" of the Holocaust in the "extreme racism" generated by colonialism and imperialism, which only produces the disease "in its worst form" when "racist madness has to be combined with the deadly partial rationality of the modern industrial system." He continues for several empty paragraphs, adding yet more enabling conditions—a "servile civil service," "consistent disregard of individual critical judgment . . . by thousand[s] of passive executive agents," "the conquest of power by desperado-type political personnel of a specific bourgeoisie," and so on—which explain precisely nothing.[43] Racism emerged and evolved to justify different aspects of capitalist global expansion signaled by the eras of slavery, settler colonialism, and postcolonial immigration. The racial crimes of imperialism were all committed for rational motives: the massacre of indigenous peoples in Australasia and North America was undertaken to clear land for white settlers; the famines that devastated Ireland in the 1840s and Madras in the 1870s were allowed to take place in accordance with Malthusian tenets of political economy. More directly relevant is the attempted extermination of the Herero and Nama peoples of German South-West Africa between 1904 and 1907. But while this, the first genocide of the twentieth century, contributed to the repertoire of horror that was later brought home to Europe by the Nazis, including concentration camps and medical experiments, it too was the dominance of one instrumental rationality over another, in this case security from the resistance of native peoples to colonialism over the need for native labor.[44] All these examples were certainly justified by racism, but they were not the outcome of "racist madness," except perhaps at the level of individual participants. The epithet can with more justice be applied to the Holocaust, and by seeking to conceptualize it simply as an extension of earlier colonial genocides, Mandel risks either treating them as instrumentally irrational (which *they* were not) or treating the Holocaust as if it was instrumentally rational (which *it* was not).

These difficulties with Mandel's argument have driven even sympathetic critics to abandon rational explanation altogether in response. Norman Geras quotes Trotsky's description of how the perpetrators of a pogrom in tsarist Russia were "drunk *on the smell of blood*" and asks: "What specifically Marxist category is there for that? ...There is something here that is not about modernity; something that is not about capitalism either. It is about humanity."[45] There are strong echoes here of Ernst Nolte, who argued that Fascism emerged from "something unique and irreducible in human nature": "It is no blossom of the capitalist system, although at the present time it could only arise on the foundations of the capitalist system, specifically, at certain times when the system is in jeopardy."[46]

Irrationality is not, however, challenged by declaring it inexplicable and collapsing into arguments from fallen human nature. It is true, as Alex Callinicos points out, that "the extermination of the Jews cannot be explained in economic terms." He sees the connection between the Holocaust and German capitalism as an example of an interpenetration of interests, in this case between "German big business" and "a movement whose racist and pseudo-revolutionary ideology drove it toward the Holocaust."[47] The position that Callinicos is articulating here was first expressed by Peter Sedgwick in 1970: "German capitalism did not need Auschwitz; but it needed the Nazis, who needed Auschwitz."[48] But where did the Nazi "racist and pseudo-revolutionary ideology" come from in the first place? Callinicos only sees a connection with capitalism as arising from the immediate needs of the economy at a time of crisis.

But the ideological formation of the Nazi worldview took place over a much longer period, which saw the combination of a series of determinations arising from the contradictions of German and European capitalism, including the authoritarian character of a subordinate middle class that had never successfully developed its own political identity, extreme right-wing nationalism first formed in response to the French Revolution, racism in its anti-Semitic form, disappointed imperialism, a taste for violence acquired in the trenches, and so on.[49]

Adapting Sedgwick, then, we might say that German capitalism did not need the Holocaust, but the long-term development of German capitalism produced, through a series of mediations, the ideology of Nazism, which did contain the possibility of a Holocaust, and when German capitalists turned to the Nazis in its moment of crisis, they were given the opportunity to realize that possibility, however irrelevant and outright damaging it was to German capital's more overarching imperial project. In other words, the barbaric ideology of Nazism and the socioeconomic crisis of Germany to which it provided one solution were already connected as different moments in the mediated totality of capitalism.

But if the Holocaust was a barbaric irrelevance—except incidentally—for German capital, the Nazi regime also presents us with examples of policies that were instrumentally irrational from the perspective of the capitalist state. As Detlev Peukert writes: "To see fascism as an effective answer to the weakness of the bourgeois democratic state, i.e., as a functional solution to the crisis in the interests of capital, is to be taken in by the self-image of National Socialism created by its own propaganda." For one thing, it led to the creation of a deeply fragmented and incoherent institution:

> The equipping of state bodies with economic functions, and of business enterprises with quasi-state powers, led not to a more effective and rationally functioning "state monopoly capitalism," but to a welter of jurisdictions and responsibilities that could be held in check only by short-term projects and campaigns. The splintered state and semi-state managerial bodies adopted the principle of competition. The "nationalization" of society by Nazism was followed by the "privatization" of the state. This paradox meant that, on the one hand, there were huge concentrations of power as a result of internal and external Blitzkrieg campaigns, while, on the other hand, inefficiency, lack of planning, falling productivity and general decline prevailed.[50]

The distinctiveness of the Nazi state can be illustrated by comparing it to the other "classic" Fascist regime, Italy: "In Italy, the traditional state wound up with supremacy over the party, largely because Mussolini feared his own most militant followers. . . . In Nazi Germany, the party came to dominate the state and civil society, especially after war began."[51] This had the most serious implications in relation to German war making. Götz Aly claims that the plundering of conquered territories and externalization of monetary inflation undertaken by the Nazis as the Second World War progressed served to bind the German masses to the regime by raising their living standards.[52] The thesis is massively exaggerated and ignores the opposition and resistance that did take place.[53] Nevertheless, it inadvertently identifies a central problem for the regime: the provision of material resources for German industry and the German population would have been impossible without territorial expansion through war, yet the ability of the German state to carry out this type of expansion was undermined by the nature of the regime. As Tim Mason has noted, "the racial-ethical utopia . . . was taken so seriously by the political leadership, in particular by Hitler and by the SS, that in decisive questions even the urgent material needs of the system were sacrificed to it."[54] Germany had higher rates of female participation in the workforce than either Britain or the US at the beginning of the war, although many of these jobs were in roles considered suitable for women, which would not be detrimental to their roles as wives and mothers.[55] Yet, despite a desperate shortage of labor, Hitler resisted female conscription until after German defeat at the Battle of Stalingrad, apparently due to ideological concerns over the potential decline in the birth rate (and hence the strength of the "Aryan" race) and the perceived threat to female morals; but even after Stalingrad it was implemented half-heartedly and was widely evaded.[56] Thus there can be situations where there is a genuine nonidentity of interest between capitalists and what are from their point of view the irrational demands made by the social base of a political party, even if that party is in other respects the one they would prefer to have custody of the state.

The Nazi regime performed two services for German capital: crushing an already weakened working class and launching an imperial-expansionist drive to conquer new territory. The contemporary relevance of this experience is limited in both respects: the working class is not currently combative enough to inspire fear in the bourgeoisie, and the states in which the Fascist far right is closest to achieving power—above all, Greece—are not imperialist powers capable of attempting continental domination in the way that Germany or even Italy could. In the contemporary situation, all that may remain are those aspects of the far-right program that are irrational for capital, particularly in its current neoliberal manifestation. Before turning to these aspects, however, we first need to identify the present-day far right and the basis of its support.

THE CONTEMPORARY SPECTRUM OF THE FAR RIGHT

Roger Eatwell has claimed that "Marxists are capable of arguing both that capitalism in crisis can bring dictatorship, and that it can lead to a revival of free market principles." He is right, but fails to notice that Marxists are capable of doing so because the crises of 1929, 1973, and 2007 belonged to different periods in the history of capitalism and produced different responses from capital, in which the far right did not necessarily play the same role.[57] Historically, far-right regimes have tended to adapt to whatever the dominant organizational forms of capital have been at any time. Between 1929 and 1973, for example, right-wing military dictatorships—historically the most common type of far-right regime—in Latin America were as committed to state-led interventionist strategies for development as were nominally left-wing postcolonial regimes in Africa and the Middle East. Brazil is a case in point, particularly between 1964 and 1968.[58] In the later case of Chile, however, the generals initially had little idea what economic policies to introduce and in an earlier period might well have looked to the Catholic Corporatist model introduced by Franco to Spain after 1939, which had been followed more or less faithfully by almost every Latin American dictatorship since the Second World War. In fact, as Karin Fischer points out, "it took about two years before the neoliberal faction ascended to positions of authority, which enabled technocrats to advance their far-reaching organizational program." Far from there being "a prior decision to establish a new type of institutional order" as has been retrospectively assumed, "the insurrection only determined that the future of the country would be decided by some combination of different forces represented in the junta."[59]

The Brazilian and Chilean juntas both belonged to the same genus, even if the brutality of the latter was greater, but they had quite different attitudes toward the role of the state in relation to ownership, control, and regulation of the economy. Differences in far-right economic policy are not simply reflective of the different historical periods in which parties, movements, and regimes have arisen. The contemporary far right occupies a spectrum ranging from Fascism at one end to extreme conservatism at the other: in other words, the span of positions between the British National Party (BNP) and the United Kingdom Independence Party (UKIP) in Britain, or between the American Nazi Party and the Tea Party in the US. It is, however, possible for Fascist regimes to move toward a more conventionally authoritarian position on the far right, indicating elements of commonality that I will address below. In the case of Spain after the Civil War this was partly because Franco took power by military means, rather than by the combination of paramilitary violence and electoralism that installed Mussolini and Hitler. The actual Fascist movement in Spain, the Falange, was used by Franco but played no part in determining policy and was completely sidelined after the Second World War.[60] Roger Griffin describes regimes like Franco's as "parafascist," indicating their defense of existing conservative elites despite the adoption of the "external trappings" of Fascism.[61]

What then is it that unites the Fascist and non-Fascist far right? It is not their attitude to economic policy, for the simple reason that they do not possess a consistent attitude toward it. Deep in the fourth decade of the neoliberal era, there are marked differences between the demands for less welfare and lower taxation made by supporters of the Tea Party or the Dutch People's Party, and the demands for greater state intervention to mitigate the effects of globalization made by supporters of Jobbik in Hungary and Golden Dawn in Greece.[62] All wings of the far right are in fact united by two characteristics.

One is a base of membership and support in one or more fractions of the middle class (such as the petty bourgeoisie, traditional middle-class professionals, or the technical-managerial new middle class). Some regimes that are occasionally labeled as Fascist or parafascist have not had the petty-bourgeois base that they require in reality, as was the case in Argentina after the coup of 1943, when the Peronists found that they had to rely on the trade unions in order to survive.[63] Fascist movements cannot *base* themselves on working-class organizations, since one of their defining characteristics is to seek the destruction of such movements. This is why not only Peronism but also a movement like Ulster Loyalism, based as it was on the skilled Protestant working class, cannot be described as Fascist, however reactionary and divisive it may otherwise have been. But if Fascist movements are incompatible with working-class *organization*, they can and do draw support from individual *members* of the working class, as can the far right more generally.

The other common characteristic is an attitude of extreme *social* conservatism, always in relation to race and nation, sometimes in relation to gender and sexual orientation: far-right politicians in the Netherlands, for example, have rhetorically invoked the relative freedoms of women or gays in the West as a way of denouncing the supposedly oppressive beliefs of Muslims. The political goal is always to push popular attitudes and legal rights back to a time before the homogeneity of "the people" was polluted by immigration, whenever this Golden Age of racial or cultural purity is deemed to have existed, which is usually at some undetermined period before the Second World War.

There are nevertheless large differences between these two types of organization. Michael Mann argues that non-Fascist far-right parties are distinguished from Fascism by three characteristics: 1) They are electoral and seek to attain office through democratic means at local, national, and European levels; 2) They do not worship the state, and while they seek to use the state for welfare purposes for their client groups, some (e.g. the Austrian Freedom Party or the Tea Party) have embraced neoliberal small-state rhetoric; 3) They do not seek to "transcend" class: "These three ambiguities and weaknesses of principle and policy make for instability, as either extremists or moderates seek to enforce a more consistent line that then results in splits and expulsions, such as the makeover of the Italian MSI and the disintegration of the German Republikaner in the mid-1990s."[64]

The first of these characteristics, adherence to bourgeois democracy, is crucial since it indicates the fundamental distinction between the Fascist and non-Fascist far right: the latter, as Peter Mair notes, "do not claim to challenge the democratic regime as such."[65] Activists and commentators often draw an absolute distinction between Fascism and other forms of right-wing politics based on the way the former rely on paramilitary organization and violence as part of their strategy for attaining power. In that sense Golden Dawn in Greece is a classic Fascist formation in a way that the Northern League in Italy is not. The distinction is important, not least in determining the tactics of their opponents, but Fascism is not defined simply by its recourse to extraparliamentary or illegal activity. Here, Trotsky's analysis remains relevant: "When a state turns fascist . . . it means, primarily and above all, that the workers' organizations are annihilated; that the proletariat is reduced to an amorphous state; and that a system of administration is created which penetrates deeply into the masses and which serves to frustrate the independent crystallization of the proletariat. Therein precisely is the gist of fascism."[66] Fascism then is revolutionary and the non-Fascist far right is not; but what does "revolutionary" mean in this context? Many Marxists are reluctant to use this term in relation to any modern political movement not of the left, with the possible exception of nationalisms in the global South. But if we consider Fascist seizures of power as political revolutions—changing the nature and personnel of the regime without changing the mode of production—then there is no reason why the term should not be applicable.[67] Reinhard Heinisch notes the dilemma of the Austrian Freedom Party, a dilemma that occurs for all populist parties of the far right that achieve office as part of a coalition: "If they adapt too quickly to their new role and show moderation and compromise, they become like any other center-right party and lose their *raison d'être*. If, on the other hand, they maintain their radical posture, they are likely to be deemed unsuitable for high public office [by likely coalition partners]."[68]

The second major difference, which flows directly from the first, lies in their respective attitudes to the society that they are trying to build. As Griffin points out, the "revolution from the right" in both Fascist Italy and Nazi Germany claimed to be using the state to socially engineer a "new man and woman" with "new values."[69] This is a project of *transformation*. The non-Fascist far right, however, insists that the people are *already* the repositories of homogeneity and virtue: "By contrast, the enemies of the people—the elites and 'others'—are neither homogeneous nor virtuous. Rather, they are accused of conspiring together against the people, who are depicted as being under siege from above by the elites and from below by a range of dangerous others." The purpose of the non-Fascist far right is to return the people to their formerly happy condition before these twin pressures began to be applied: "This is not a Utopia, but a prosperous and happy place which is held to have actually existed in the past, but which has been lost in the present era due to the enemies of the people."[70] This is a project of *restoration*.

The third and final major difference concerns social class. At one level, this may seem to be a nonissue, since, as I have just noted, both wings of the far right invoke "the people" as the basis for their politics. Fascists, however, tend to argue that social class is illusory, a Marxist fiction intended to cause divisions within what would otherwise be a unified national body. Fascists have sought to recruit individual workers, of course, but have never appealed to them *as* workers. This remains the case today. In a British context, for example, Daniel Trilling has noted the concerns expressed by BNP leaders in one of the party's publications: "As an editorial in *Identity* warned in early 2009, there was a danger of being perceived as a 'class party': 'Since its foundation the BNP has transcended the divisions of class.'"[71] The non-Fascist far right, on the other hand, precisely because they are not committed to visions of an organic national community, can focus on specific working-class grievances that traditional parties of the left no longer address. Interviewed by Robert Ford and Matthew Goodwin, UKIP leader Nigel Farage was insistent—and factually accurate—in pointing out that his party was not "populated only by disillusioned Tories," noting that "the numbers are perfectly clear. There is now a huge class dimension to the UKIP vote."[72] But discussion of class raises the issue of where the contemporary far-right parties draw their support, and it is to this question that we now turn.

THE FAR RIGHT IN THE CONTEMPORARY NEOLIBERAL ORDER (I): POPULAR SUPPORT

Chip Berlet and Matthew Lyons observe that, in the context of the US, there are "two versions of secular right-wing populism," each drawing on a different class base: "one centered around 'get the government off my back' economic libertarianism coupled with a rejection of mainstream political parties (more attractive to the upper middle class and small entrepreneurs); the other based on xenophobia and ethnocentric nationalism (more attractive to the lower middle class and wage workers)."[73] As the reference to "wage workers" suggests, the reactionary role played by sections of the middle classes does not exhaust the social basis of right-wing social movements. Since the majority of the population are exploited and oppressed, such movements must draw at least some support from their ranks.

It is nevertheless extremely unlikely that a right-wing social movement could be entirely composed of working-class members. Those that are not simply social movements of the middle classes aimed at essentially economic ends will tend to combine workers in unstable alliances with sections of the traditional petty bourgeoisie. In these cases interclass tensions are temporarily overridden by the mobilizing issue, a process made easier by the fact that in relatively superficial cultural terms—in other words, everything that does not immediately relate to the workplace— the traditional petty bourgeoisie and the working class can often be indistinguishable in terms of language, dress, and leisure activities. A self-employed electrician and a city garbage collector will drink in the same bars; a lawyer and a postman will not. But the working-class presence will also tend to produce expressions of misdirected hostility toward perceived ruling-class interests. Consequently, as Berlet and Lyons argue, the contradictory nature of right-wing social movements "challenge[s] us to go beyond binary models of power and resistance": "It is oversimplified and wrong to treat such movements simply as attack dogs for bigoted elites. It is also a serious mistake to gloss over these movements' oppressive politics just because they threaten certain kinds of elite interest."[74] Unfortunately, the spectacle of the working class or the oppressed more generally mobilizing against their own interests alongside members of other social classes has produced a number of inadequate responses from socialists.

One is the claim that working-class demands or actions that might appear reactionary actually contain a rational core, which renders them defensible by the left. There was more than a flavor of this during the Lindsey Oil Refinery strike of 2009, in which the slogan "British jobs for British workers" was raised with clear xenophobic if not actually racist intent against Eastern European migrant laborers. It is true that non–British nationals are hired by businesses on lower wages and worse conditions, with the effect of these being extended across industry as a whole; but the solution is to unionize migrant workers, not blame them for their employers' cost cutting. Similar exculpatory attitudes have been displayed in relation to vigilante violence against, for example, suspected drug dealers and pedophiles, on the grounds that this represents "people's justice," autonomous actions of self-policing outwith the parameters of the bourgeois state. Of course, there are situations where workers effectively impose their own "legality," most obviously in relation to strike breakers during industrial disputes, but these are quite different from ones where members of a community turn on each other at the behest of media-inspired moral panics.

The other inadequate response is the argument that even if working-class people participate in them, right-wing movements are illegitimate because they are funded or led by wealthy corporations or individuals. This argument inverts the classic conservative theme that popular unrest against the established order is never, as it were, natural, but always orchestrated by external forces ("outside agitators") who invent or manipulate grievances in order to further their own ends.[75] Glenn Beck, the Fox News ideologue, was heavily involved in launching the Tea Party movement in the US, and oil magnates, the Koch Brothers, supplied the funding. For commentators like George Monbiot, these facts are decisive:

> The Tea Party movement is remarkable in two respects. It is one of the biggest exercises in false consciousness the world has seen—and the biggest Astroturf operation in history. These accomplishments are closely related. An Astroturf campaign ... purports to be a spontaneous uprising of concerned citizens, but in reality it is founded and funded by elite interests. Some Astroturf campaigns have no grassroots component at all. Others catalyze and direct real mobilizations. The Tea Party belongs in the second category. It is mostly composed of passionate, well-meaning people who think they are fighting elite power, unaware that they have been organized by the very interests they believe they are confronting.[76]

It is not clear why this disqualifies the Tea Party from consideration as a social movement. According to Donatella della Porta and Mario Diani, members of social movements display three characteristics: they are "involved in conflictual relations with clearly identified opponents," "linked by dense informal networks," and "share a distinct collective identity."[77] Members of the Tea Party and those of earlier right-wing insurgencies in the US display all of these characteristics.

Thomas Frank describes one conservative organizer in Kansas who led a prolonged and ultimately successful campaign throughout the eighties and nineties to gain majority support for the Republicans in formerly Democratic Wichita: "[Mark] Gietzen was building a social movement, one convert at a time. On the left it is commonplace to hear descriptions of the backlash as a strictly top-down affair in which Republican spellbinders rally a demographically shrinking sector of the population for one last, tired fight. What the Wichita Republicans have accomplished, though, should dispel this myth forever." Frank acknowledges that the "conservative 'movement culture'" depends on "lobbyists . . . magazines and newspapers . . . [and a] publishing house or two," but it also depends, "at the bottom, [on] the committed grassroots organizers like Mark Gietzen . . . going door-to-door, organizing their neighbors, mortgaging their houses, even, to push the gospel of the backlash."[78] The people organized by the likes of Gietzen may well be morally wrong and politically misguided, but it is patronizing—and above all politically useless—to pretend that they are simply being manipulated by elite puppetmasters. Sara Diamond is therefore correct when she argues that left critics of the US Christian right are wrong to adopt what she calls "a view of conspiracies by small right-wing cliques to stage-manage what was truly a mass movement." She is also right to emphasize the complexity of right-wing populism's attitude toward "existing power structures," being "partially *oppositional* and partially . . . *system supportive*."[79]

Mike Davis has argued against Frank that in fact the capture of working-class consciousness by social conservatism is more apparent than real: "the real Achilles' Heel" of the Democrats in 2004 was "the economy, not morality." While "Kulturkampf may have played an important role at the margin," Davis points out that there are real class issues involved, in that "visceral blue-collar contempt for the urban knowledge-industry elites . . . is, after all, grounded in real historic defeat and class humiliation."[80] This suggests two different processes, both of which Frank refuses to consider: one is that working-class voters refused to vote for the Democrats because the party had essentially adopted the same neoliberal economic policies as the Republicans; the other is that working-class hostility to elite views is a legitimate expression of class anger. Both these positions are true, although in relation to the second it is not clear why hostility to elites would most focus on their socially liberal wing. In fact, Davis does concede that there is an element here that is not explicable in terms of genuine class interest: "With union halls shut down and the independent press extinct, it is not surprising that many poor white people search for answers in their churches or from demagogues like Limbaugh and Dobbs on the radio."[81] It is possible to accept the reality of this process without, as Frank does, regarding it as incomprehensible. The real issue is surely why working-class people might be predisposed to respond positively to right-wing arguments. There are both general reasons for this, true at all periods in the history of capitalism, and specific reasons relevant to the present neoliberal conjuncture.

It is a Marxist truism dating back to the very formation of historical materialism in *The German Ideology* that the ideas of the ruling class tend to be the ruling ideas.[82] Marx and Engels subsequently revised this potentially elitist proposition in more dialectical terms, both elsewhere in the same notes and in other works of the same period.[83] Later Marxists, above all Gramsci, showed that most members of the subordinate classes have highly contradictory forms of consciousness.[84] Nevertheless, the capitalist system could not survive unless it was accepted at some level, most of the time, by the majority of the people who live under it. The implications of this are darker than is sometimes supposed.

The consciousness of the subaltern classes is, as Gramsci says, typically contradictory. A characteristic form involves a reformist inability to conceive of anything beyond capitalism, even while opposing specific effects of the system. But the alternatives are not restricted to active rejection at one extreme and passive acceptance at the other. There can also be *active* support, the internalization of capitalist values associated with the system, to the point where they can lead to action. Marxists and other anticapitalist radicals frequently point out that, rather than men benefiting from the oppression of women, whites from the oppression of blacks, or straights from the oppression of gays, it is capitalism and the bourgeoisie that do so. This is a useful corrective to the argument, common in many left-wing movements, that each form of oppression is separate from the others and that none has any necessary connection to the capitalist system. Nevertheless, it fails to take seriously the distinction made by Lukács between "what men *in fact* thought, felt and wanted at any point in the class structure" and "the thoughts and feelings which men would have in a particular situation if they were *able* to assess both it and the interests arising from it in their impact on immediate action and on the whole structure of society."[85] For we cannot just assume that members of the working class are not only capable of having but in fact do *actually* have the thoughts and feelings "appropriate to their objective situation." What if workers do not attain this level of consciousness? As John Rees writes:

> There are often large sections of the working class—Tory voters, strike breakers, racists, volunteers for the First World War—whose actions cannot

be explained simply by claiming that they are begrudgingly going along with ruling-class ideology. To support the party that openly champions the ruling class, to scab on a strike, to shoot or physically attack fellow workers requires more than a passive feeling that "nothing can be changed."... Certainly alienation plays its part, but the result of alienation is not merely surly submission. It often takes the form of workers trying to overcome their exclusion from official society by conforming all the more completely, in action as well as thought, to its values.[86]

Socialism became possible on a world scale at some point in the early decades of the twentieth century, but several generations have lived and died since then. Many of those people have either been unaware of "the standpoint of the working class" or have simply refused to adopt it. Instead, as we saw in relation to the post–Civil War US South, a significant minority have taken positions supportive of, for example, racial oppression, even though this was not to their benefit when compared with the benefits they would have received by struggling for racial equality, let alone full social equality. Without some degree of class consciousness, however, they need not ever consider this alternative: in the immediate context of their situation, a stance that is detrimental to working-class interests as a whole may make sense to particular individual members of the working class. Lukács once wrote of revisionism, which in this context can be taken to mean reformism more generally, that "*it always sacrifices the genuine interests of the class as a whole ... so as to represent the immediate interests of specific groups.*"[87] Working-class people who participate in right-wing social movements have, in effect, taken this a stage further, by sacrificing even the interests of specific groups in favor of their immediate individual interests, usually equated with a supraclass national interest.[88]

The victories of neoliberalism have left the working class in the West increasingly fragmented and disorganized, and, for some workers, its appeals to blood and nation appear as the only viable form of collectivity still available, particularly in a context where the only systemic alternative to capitalism—however false it may have been—apparently collapsed in 1989–91. Dismissing their views on grounds of irrationality is simply an evasion. As Berlet and Lyons write: "Right-wing populist claims are no more and no less irrational than conventional claims that presidential elections express the will of the people, that economic health can be measured by the profits of multimillion-dollar corporations, or that US military interventions in

Haiti or Somalia or Kosovo or wherever are designed to promote democracy and human rights."[89] Yet these beliefs, which are accepted by many more people than those who believe in, say, the literal truth of the Book of Genesis, are not treated as signs of insanity. The issue, as Berlet has argued elsewhere, is not "personal pathology" but collective "desperation."[90]

It is more illuminating to ask how such movements come into existence and how far they offer false solutions to genuine problems. In fact, as Joe Bageant writes of the US, "the New Conservatism arose in the same way left-wing movements do, by approximately the same process, and for the same reasons: widespread but unacknowledged dissatisfaction, in this case with the erosion of 'traditional' life and values in America as working people perceive them."[91] More generally, Paul Taggart has plausibly suggested that far-right movements do not simply deploy similar methods to the left in building support; their very emergence was in some respects a reaction to that of the 1968 far left:

> The waves of crisis that hit Western Europe in the 1970s provided the momentum for the tides of protest that have characterized the 1980s and 1990s. This protest first came from the left with the Green parties, the alternative politics and what was to crystallize into the New Politics. We are only now witnessing the equivalent protest on the right. Melding together issues of taxation, immigration, and radical regionalism, across Western Europe new parties of the right are protesting not only the policies but the politics of the old parties. This New Populism is, in many respects, the mirror image of the New Politics [and derives] from the same deep wellsprings of change that have come about with the crises of the postwar settlement.[92]

The increasing interchangeability of mainstream political parties, including those on the Social-Democratic left, gives the far right an opening to voters by positioning it as outside the consensus in relation to social policy.[93] Magnus Marsdal notes the decline in Danish public anger between the introduction of pension cuts by the Social Democrats in 1998 and the general election in 2001 because of the almost total agreement between different parties and commentators about their necessity: "This *depoliticizing of economics* leads to the politicizing of everything else."[94]

The roots of the US militia movement, for example, lay in the crisis of farming communities during the 1980s. During the previous decade, the Nixon administration had encouraged farmers to take out loans, on floating interest rates, in order to expand agricultural production. The loans were arranged through one US state body, namely the Farm Home Administration (or, as militias would say, "the government"); but from 1979 the now-heavily-indebted farmers were subjected to several interest rate rises in succession at the hands of another state (or "government") body, the Federal Reserve, as Chairman Paul Volcker instituted the famous economic "shock" associated with his name. Foreclosures by the banks and consolidations at the hands of agricultural corporations inevitably followed. As Carolyn Gallaher reports: "In such a context farmers became ripe for mobilization. Many formed private militias—usually formed to defend local farms on foreclosure day—while others filed illegal liens against bankers, judges, and government officials involved in the foreclosure process. And . . . desperate farmers found help from far-right activists (from Klansmen to neo-Nazis) who viewed the devastation in farm country as an opportunity to expand their political base outside the traditional supremacist circles."[95] In this case, a particular explanation for the farmers' economic grievances became an entry point for the full range of far-right politics. Why do these politics so often center around questions of race, gender, and sexuality?

Michael Kimmel points out that, although it would be absurd to claim that "women or gay people or people of color *are* being treated equally," it is true that "we have never been *more* equal than we are today"; but "at the same time . . . economically we are more *unequal* than we have been in about a century": "So it's easy to think these phenomena are related—that the greater class inequality is somehow attendant upon, even caused by, greater social equality. Perhaps we can be convinced that the reason for the dramatic skewing of our country's riches is somehow that these newly arrived groups are siphoning off the benefits that were supposed to be trickling down to middle- and lower-middle-class white men." Kimmel follows the characteristic everyday discourse in the US, in which working-class people are described as, or contained within the categories of, "middle and lower-middle class," but his conclusion is apt: "To believe that greater social equality is the cause of your economic misery requires a significant amount of manipulation, perhaps the greatest bait and switch that has ever been perpetuated against middle- and lower-middle-class Americans."[96] Lisa Mc-Girr's study of right-wing politics in Orange County, California, gives a concrete example of how anger at the economic uncertainty created by neoliberalism can be deflected into a deep social conservatism:

> Orange Countians lamented the decline of family authority, the emphasis on change and innovation, the undermining of community, and the decline of the importance of locality—all of which resulted from the growth of large-scale institutions and the concentration of economic and political power that are part of the functioning of a free-market economy. Their strong stakes in this capitalist order, however, caused them to elide the very real market forces that often undercut family values and community stability, since such a knowledge would have challenged the material base on which their lives were built. Instead, they argued that it was the deviation from a true laissez-faire capitalism, one without a strong role for the state, that was at the heart of America's problems. The strong emphasis on a market order combined with socially conservative values that celebrated family values, morality, and religion validated conservatives' own lives and success, provided an explanation for their discontents, and gave them a strong sense of cohesion and community. They thus were able to avoid examining the internal contradictions within their own ideology, the ambivalence and tensions between a strong embrace of the free market and the way in which free markets often assaulted family, community, and neighborhood norms.[97]

So, while Davis is undoubtedly right that a majority of the people who become involved in right-wing social movements do so because of underlying economic concerns, the more relevant point is whether, in the absence of a left-wing solution to those concerns, they continue to demand the implementation of their social program as a condition of support for politicians who claim to represent them. In these circumstances a deeper problem for the stability of the capitalist system than the less likely possibility of far-right parties themselves coming to power, with a program destructive to capitalist needs, might be their influence over the mainstream parties of the right, when the beliefs of their supporters may inadvertently cause difficulty for the accumulation process.

THE FAR RIGHT IN THE CONTEMPORARY NEOLIBERAL ORDER (2): INADVERTENT ANTICAPITALISM

The clearest examples of this type of inadvertency are to be found in the Anglo-Saxon heartlands of neoliberalism: the US and Britain. Take an important area of Republican Party support in the US. Since the late sixties, Republicans have been increasingly reliant on communities of fundamentalist Christian believers, whose activism allows them to be mobilized for voting purposes. Kevin Phillips has argued that this strategy benefits not only the Republican Party but the ruling class whose interests it represents: "The financial sector—and a large majority of the richest Americans—understandably finds the alliance convenient," as the faithful "are easily rallied for self-help, free enterprise, and disbelief in government." As a result: "With much of the [Republicans'] low- and middle-income electorate listening to conservative preachers, the corporate agenda has widely prevailed."[98] But this religious core vote, or at any rate its leadership, naturally also demands the implementation of policies in return for its support. Some writers, notably Frank, have argued that this is precisely what never happens: the demands of popular conservatism are precisely those that are never met, while those of the elites always are: "Values may 'matter most' to voters, but they always take a back seat to the needs of money once the elections are won. . . . Abortion is never halted. Affirmative action is never abolished. The culture industry is never forced to clean up its act."[99] He describes "the backlash" as being "like a French Revolution in reverse—one in which the sans-culottes pour down the street demanding more power for the aristocracy."[100]

Frank underestimates the way in which fundamentalist demands have in fact been implemented in relation to, for example, sex education or reproductive rights. This is a problem for the Republicans not only because the extremism of fundamentalist Christianity may alienate the electoral "middle ground" on which the results of American elections increasingly depend, but also because politicians are constrained from undertaking policies that may be necessary for American capitalism: "The Book of Genesis and the *Left Behind* series get in the way. We cannot be running out of oil; God made the climate; and the White House explanations about what the United States is doing in Iraq or elsewhere in the Middle East have to square with the fight between good and evil as the end times draw nigh. Much like intervention in Iraq, national energy policy takes weak shape in a vacuum of candor." The constraints imposed by the need to placate a religious base also affect the US's position in relation to other advanced states: "Realistically, these events and circumstances hardly encourage foreign central bankers, diplomats, or political leaders to buy and hold U.S. Treasury Bonds, support American energy profligacy, join U.S. ventures in the Middle East, or believe that young people unskilled in mathematics, addled by credit cards, and weaned on so-called intelligent design instead of evolution will somehow retool American science for another generation of world industrial leadership."[101]

As this example suggests, unwanted outcomes for capital need not be the product of a coherent religious worldview, simply one that no longer believes anything produced outwith its own experience—or the way in which that experience is interpreted by their trusted sources of information. Consequently, as Mark Lilla points out, precisely because the Tea Party is not a wholly owned subsidiary of the Republican Party, it is "transforming American conservatism.... The more it tries to exploit the energy of the Tea Party rebellion, the cruder the conservative movement becomes in its thinking and its rhetoric. ... Today's conservatives prefer the company of anti-intellectuals who know how to exploit non-intellectuals, as Sarah Palin does so masterfully."[102] Jonathan Raban confirms this in a report from one Tea Party Convention:

> The Tea Partiers I met at Nashville felt bamboozled by policies that made no sense to them at all, presented in language whose most basic terms (such as "quantitative easing") were beyond ordinary comprehension. When Palin rails against "so-called experts" and the "East Coast elites" and pitches her brand of "commonsense conservatism," she speaks for a vast congregation of the mystified and fearful. Palin and her kind have put heart into people who previously imagined themselves merely confused or ill-informed, and now see themselves as proud skeptics, resisting the tide of received professional opinion. "Skepticism"— of economists, paleontologists, and climate scientists alike—has become the mark of the stoutly independent citizen who knows that debt is debt, and must be promptly repaid, that God's world was created in six days, and that global warming is a left-wing conspiracy.[103]

This seems to be another example of a situation where there is genuine nonidentity of interest—not between capitalists and state managers, exactly, but between capitalists and the political party that happens to have control ("custody" would perhaps be a better term) of the state at a particular time. Of course, the reason why fundamentalist Christians have these irrational beliefs in the first place can be rationally explained in Marxist terms, with reference to the psychic wounds inflicted by capitalism.

But it is not only religious belief that can cause difficulties for US capital; so too can overt anti-migrant racism. One concrete example of this is the Tea Party–inspired Beason-Hammon Alabama Taxpayer and Citizen Protection Act—HB 56, as it is usually known—which was passed by the state legislature in June 2011, making it illegal not to carry immigration papers and preventing anyone without documents from receiving any provisions from the state, including water supply. The law was intended to prevent and reverse illegal immigration by Hispanics, but the effect was to cause a mass departure from the many agricultural businesses that relied on these workers for the bulk of their labor force: "In the north of the state, the pungent smell of rotting tomatoes hangs in the air across huge tranches of land that have been virtually abandoned by workers who, through fear or anger, are no longer turning up to gather the harvest."[104] But the effects went deeper. Before the law was introduced, it was estimated that 4.2 percent of the workforce, or 95,000 people, were undocumented but paying $130.3 million in state and local taxes. Their departure from the state or withdrawal to the black economy threatened to reduce the size of the local economy by $40 million. Moreover employers had to spend more money on screening prospective employees, on HR staff to check paperwork, and on insuring for potential legal liabilities from inadvertent breaches of the law.[105]

These developments are *not* equivalent to the type of policies with which Social Democracy occasionally (and decreasingly) attempts to ameliorate the excesses of capitalism. One the one hand, Social-Democratic reforms are usually intended to enable the system as a whole to function more effectively for capitalists and more equitably for the majority, however irreconcilable these aims may be. But far-right reforms of the type just discussed are not even intended to work in the interests of capitalists, nor do they: they really embody irrational racist beliefs that take precedence over all else.

It is important to note that the trumping of economics by ideology is not a universal trend. In Arizona a Republican mayor vetoed a bill discriminating against gays that had been introduced by members of her own party, and similar outcomes have occurred even in the Deep South. In Georgia, for example, bills allowing discrimination on the basis of sexual orientation that were introduced into the state House and Senate by Republican ultras died without even going to the vote. Why? "Here, in microcosm, was a big reason why gay rights campaigners scored a big victory across America last week: money. The power of the gay dollar, as well as cultural shifts, prompted local and international companies such as Delta, Home Depot, Apple and Coca-Cola to face down conservative challenges."[106] A similar picture emerges at the national level when we consider the shutdown of the US government in September and October 2013, which happened at the behest of Tea Party and other far-right elements of the Republican Party and provoked an unusual degree of hostility from the representatives of US capital. The *New York Times* noted: "Long intertwined by mutual self-interest on deregulation and lower taxes, the business lobby and Republicans are diverging not only over the fiscal crisis, but on other major issues like immigration reform, which was favored by business groups and party leaders but stymied in the House by many of the same lawmakers now leading the debt fight." As Dan Danner, head of the National Federation of Independent Business (NFIB) and a key opponent of Obama's health-care law, said of the Tea Party caucus: "They don't really care what the N.F.I.B. thinks, and don't care what the Chamber [of Commerce] thinks, and probably don't care what the Business Roundtable thinks."[107] As one candidate for the Republican presidential nomination wrote of the government shutdown: "Besides alienating mainstream voters, the party has come close to alienating its most traditionally loyal constituency—business. . . . Boardrooms and entrepreneurs by and large want a commitment to stable markets."[108]

The British Conservative Party has encountered similar problems to the Republicans in relation to Europe. Chris Gifford argues that there are four "distinctive features of a populist Eurosceptic mobilization":

> First, it was a profound attack on the governing elite that could not be contained by traditional forms of party discipline. Second, the strength of this attack stemmed from the establishment of Euroscepticism as a national movement with mass appeal. . . . Third, the discourse of this movement was characterized by an appeal to the people based upon the cultural and symbolic construction of British exceptionalism. Finally, this mobilization had a significant and negative impact on the governing elite's European policy. It helped to secure a dominant Thatcherite approach to the EU

that has involved a re-assertion of British national exceptionalism. . . . The hardening of Euroscepticism on the right of British politics could be seen as part of the opposition to a Labour Government that first came to power in 1997 with an explicitly pro-European policy agenda.[109]

As we saw in the previous chapter, the nationalism invoked by the Conservatives against the EU is now a major obstacle for British politicians and state managers who want to pursue a strategy of greater European integration, however rational that may be from their perspective.[110] A 2013 British Chambers of Commerce poll of 4,387 companies showed only 18 percent agreeing that full withdrawal from the EU could have a positive impact, while a majority of 64 percent supported remaining inside the EU while repatriating some powers.[111] Unsurprisingly, the real source of anti-EU feeling is small business, for which increased regulation and improved worker rights—even of a minimal sort—pose a far greater threat to profit margins than they do for large corporations.[112]

The key beneficiary of the anti-European hysteria has been UKIP, and its success has in turn emboldened the right within the Conservative Party, even though the policies associated with both are incoherent. As one columnist noted in the *Observer*, the sensible Sunday voice of the British liberal middle classes: "The UKIP manifesto is a nonsense of contradictions. . . . Mr Farage promises tax cuts for everyone and spending increases on just about everything from building more prisons to restoring the student grant to more generous pensions. But strategists from the main parties tell me that they get nowhere when they try to discuss policy with sample groups of UKIP supporters. Even when they agree that the UKIP prospectus doesn't make sense, reports one party pollster: 'they just don't care about that.'"[113]

These contradictions may not matter in terms of the political struggle for power. UKIP has successfully created a scapegoat in the shape of a quasi-imaginary institution called the "European Union"—just as the Tea Party did in the shape of another quasi-imaginary institution called "government." The main difference is that in the case of the former, the institution is foreign rather than domestic, the crime of local elites being their compliance. The basis of at least part of UKIP's popular support is, however, drawn from a comparable constituency. As the authors of the most thorough study of the party note, one might expect that "at a time of falling real incomes and unprecedented economic uncertainty, voters from poorer and more insecure groups should rally behind the party who can offer them the best prospect for economic support and assistance," not "a party with a barely coherent or credible economic policy, no track record in helping the disadvantaged, and a libertarian activist base who openly favor free markets over the support for the disadvantaged." The explanation for this paradox is depressing but relatively simple: "UKIP voters, who are by some margin the most politically disaffected group in the electorate, have lost faith in the ability of traditional politics to solve their everyday problems and have instead turned their anger toward groups they feel are responsible for the decline in their standards of living and their loss of control over their lives."[114]

CONCLUSION

Shortly before his death, Eric Hobsbawm reasserted the necessity of both value and instrumental rationality for capitalist state managers and politicians:

> No government that funds nuclear research can afford to care a damn what the Koran or the Mahabharata or Marxism-Leninism has to say about the nature of matter, or the fact that 30 per cent of the voters in the USA may believe that the world was created in seven days. And why can they afford not to care? Because, since the early seventeenth century, fundamental research in the natural sciences has been essential to the holders of political power in a way that the arts and humanities have not. It has been essential for war. To put the matter with brutal simplicity: Hitler learned the hard way that he lost little by driving out Jewish musicians and actors. However, it proved fatal to have driven out Jewish mathematicians and physicists.[115]

This is not the most reassuring of arguments. Hitler may have failed to develop nuclear weapons partly as a result of his genocidal hatred of Jewish people, but he had unleashed the most destructive war in human history using those scientific methods that were available to him. Future lunatics in power will be perfectly capable of distinguishing between those aspects of rational thought that are useful to them, for which doctrinal exemptions can always be found, and those for which the prohibitions of the Bible (for example) must be followed to the letter. For even if I am right that certain aspects of far-right politics are detrimental to the needs of capital, it does not follow that the increased chaos resulting from the implementation of these policies would necessarily benefit the left, even indirectly. Defense of the system is always the principal objective of the bourgeoisie, even at the expense of temporary system malfunction. In a situation where economic desperation was leading to mounting disorder, far-right parties would be brought into play to direct attention from the real source of social anguish onto already-identified scapegoats, no matter what price they exacted in terms of policy. As several very different authors have noted, a market that entrenches personal fulfillment through consumer choice as the ultimate value not only destabilizes those forms of identity that have traditionally helped support the capitalist system, like the family and the nation, but the very personal constraints that allow accumulation to take place.[116] The political implications are ominous. Alan Sinfield once wrote that "the larger danger of Thatcherism," which can here be taken as a surrogate for neoliberalism as a whole, was not so much its victories over trade unions or Social Democracy, but "its eventual failure to satisfy or control the emotions it arouses": "The rhetoric of Law and Order and victimization of subordinate groups, with which it attempts to make plausible its social and economic policies, provoke forces of retribution and stimulate expectations that may find terrible kinds of satisfaction."[117]

Is there an alternative to this outcome? Marco D'Eramo has pointed out that the term "populism" is now invoked to indicate, with disapproval, any politics of left or right that deviate from the neoliberal consensus in any respect. As he argues, in contemporary usage "populism" is an ideological term designed to elide the difference between the far right and the radical left.[118] But right- and left-wing populism are not, alas, of equivalent weight. "Unfortunately, political 'polarization' is unidirectional," notes Davis.[119] As I have suggested here, the parties of the neoliberal "center" would cooperate, and in several countries already have cooperated, with electorally successful parties of the far right, while the parties of the radical left have tended to fragment even where they have achieved some degree of support. Given that a return to the halcyon days of "rational" capitalism looks remote—the Great Boom increasingly looks like an exceptional period in its history—the only hope of avoiding the scenario outlined here is for the left to mobilize around an alternative program that is genuinely against the "needs of capital"—not by accident or coincidence, but by conscious design. The preceding discussion suggests three conclusions.

First, right-wing social movements have existed since the later stages of the transition to capitalism, although they have been less frequent than those of the left. Their incidence is likely to increase under current neoliberal conditions, as the withdrawal of state provision will lead groups to defend their access to increasingly scarce resources using methods hitherto associated mainly with the left.

Second, the last real possibilities of socialist revolution in the West appeared during the years between 1968 and 1975, and even then nowhere progressed beyond the preliminary stages. Consequently, today's left has little conception of what revolution might require, apart from some very general if formally correct observations. In particular, there is a problem with the idea that revolution will simply involve revolutionary masses on the one side and the capitalist state on the other, with vacillating reformists occupying the space between: in other words, workers will only side with the ruling class if they are directly employed within the apparatus of repression. This seems unduly optimistic. There is a famous discussion by Lenin, part of which reads as follows: "The socialist revolution in Europe *cannot* be anything other than an outburst of mass struggle on the part of all and sundry oppressed and discontented elements. Inevitably, sections of the petty bourgeoisie and of the backward workers will participate in it—without such participation, *mass* struggle is *impossible*, without it no revolution is possible—and just as inevitably will they bring into the movement their prejudices, their reactionary fantasies, their weaknesses and errors. But *objectively* they will attack *capital*."[120] The last clause in this passage is open to doubt. Why should forces that have been mobilized by "their prejudices [and] their reactionary fantasies" necessarily be "objectively" opposed to capital? If the preceding arguments are correct, we should just as easily expect movements to arise that will attempt to defend the existing order, or their members' place in an idealized version of it, independently or in parallel with the state. The ruling classes would surely overlook any longer-term difficulties these movements might cause for capital, so long as they contributed to the immediate goal of suppressing revolutionary possibilities.

Third, the working-class movement is unlikely to find alliances in those sections of the professional and new middle classes that have a material interest in preserving the capitalist system. There are, however, far greater possibilities among the petty bourgeoisie and the "public-sector" new middle class. The ability of some of the members of these groups to mobilize, even in right-wing social movements, should be seen in a potentially positive light, since the focus of their frustration or discontent need not be decided in advance. Here Lenin's argument retains its relevance, when he writes that "the class-conscious vanguard of the revolution, the advanced proletariat, expressing this objective truth of a variegated and discordant, motley and outwardly fragmented mass struggle, will be able to unite and direct it, capture power, seize the banks, expropriate the trusts which all hate."[121] After all the disappointments of the century since these words were written, we might want to render the argument in more conditional terms. Nevertheless, the central point remains valid: the indeterminacy of social movements means that their ultimate direction will always depend on the availability of a persuasive socialist politics.

❧ Chapter 9 ❧

A Scottish Watershed*

INTRODUCTION

The odds were huge. On one side, the might of the British state, the three parties of government, Buckingham Palace, the BBC—still by far the most influential source of broadcast news and opinion—plus an overwhelming majority of the print media, the high command of British capital, and the liberal establishment, backed up by the international weight of Washington, NATO, and the EU. On the other, a coalition of the young and the hopeful, including swathes of disillusioned Labour voters in the council estates—the "schemes"—of Clydeside and Tayside, significant sections of the petty bourgeoisie, and Scotland's immigrant communities, mobilized in a campaign that was at least as much a social movement as a national one. Starting from far behind, this popular-democratic upsurge succeeded in giving the British ruling

---

* Originally published in *New Left Review* II/89 (September/October 2014).

class its worst fit of nerves since the miners' and engineering workers' strikes of 1972, wringing panicked pledges of further powers from the Conservative, Labour, and Liberal leaders. By any measure, the Yes camp's 45 percent vote on a record-breaking turnout in the Scottish independence referendum was a significant achievement. How did we arrive at this point—and where does the September 18 vote leave UK and Scottish politics?

The institutional origins of the 2014 Scottish referendum can be traced to 1976, when British prime minister James Callaghan's minority Labour government was struggling to cement a parliamentary majority while implementing draconian IMF cuts—the onset of neoliberal restructuring in Britain. The support of the minority nationalist parties— the Scottish National Party had won eleven Westminster seats in the October 1974 election, its best result ever, while Plaid Cymru had three MPs—was bought with the promise of referendums about devolving limited powers to new Scottish and Welsh assemblies. In the event, though the Yes vote won the 1979 Scottish referendum by 52 to 48 percent, turnout didn't reach the high bar set by Westminster, so devolution fell by the wayside. Under the Thatcher government, Scotland underwent the same drastic social engineering as the rest of the UK: high unemployment, deindustrialization, hospital closures, council-house sell-offs. Tory unionism had traditionally been the largest electoral force in Scottish politics; in 1955 it had won an absolute majority of seats and votes. By 1997, after eighteen years of Conservative rule at Westminster, its vote north of the border had dropped to 18 percent and it held not a single Scottish seat.

A second chance for devolution came in the 1990s, when Labour's fourth crushing electoral defeat led Blair and Brown to begin a desperate search for Liberal Democrat and SNP support to build an anti-Tory coalition. This short-lived alliance accounted for the only reformist measures— Scottish and Welsh devolution, an appointee-only House of Lords, a referendum on the voting system, a Freedom of Information bill—in New Labour's 1997 manifesto, otherwise devoted to boosting economic competition and cracking down on crime. The aim of devolution, Blair underlined, was a limited delegation of responsibilities through which "the Union will be strengthened and the threat of separatism removed." The Scottish Parliament was duly established in 1999 on a modified first-past-the-post voting system, which was intended to deny a majority to any party—especially the SNP—and guarantee a Labour–Liberal Democrat coalition, which was indeed the outcome between 1999 and 2007.[1]

RISE OF THE SNP

Yet, masked by the rotten-borough effect of the first-past-the-post system, the years of war and neoliberalism under the Blair–Brown governments steadily sapped support for New Labour. In the '90s and '00s, Scotland had again followed UK growth patterns, with the expansion of a low-end service sector—one in ten of the Glaswegian labor force works in a call center—and the growth of household debt. On a smaller scale, Edinburgh played the role of London as a center for booming, deregulated financial government, services, and the media, while inequalities gaped—the run-down housing scheme of Dumbiedykes lies just streets away from Holyrood Palace and the state-of-the-art Scottish Parliament building. After the financial crisis, Labour-led councils avidly implemented the mandated public-spending cuts, closing care homes, squeezing wages, and sacking workers. In successive Scottish Parliament elections Labour's share of the popular vote fell from 34 percent in 1999 to 26 percent in 2011, with ex-Labour voters passing first to the Greens and the Scottish Socialist Party in 2003, and then, after the SSP's collapse, to the SNP in 2007. In local elections Labour lost overall control almost everywhere except Glasgow and neighboring North Lanarkshire. Labour Party membership plummeted from 30,000 in 1998 to under 13,000 in 2010. Meanwhile the Liberal Democrat vote in Scotland collapsed after 2010, when the party entered government with the Tories in Westminster, once again to the benefit of the SNP. The result was to give the SNP an overall majority of 69 seats out of 129 in the 2011 Scottish Parliament, with 44 percent of the popular vote—10 points more than Labour had ever won.

The SNP's manifestos had long included the commitment to hold a referendum on independence if it won a majority in the Scottish Parliament. After its sweeping 2011 victory, the SNP's leader Alex Salmond duly declared that this plan would go ahead. The SNP's preference was for a triple-option referendum: Scotland's voters would decide between full independence, the status quo, or "maximum devolution," meaning that the Holyrood Parliament would gain full fiscal and legislative powers, but Scotland would remain under the canopy of the UK state—the

Crown, Foreign Office, Ministry of Defence, and Bank of England—
with regard to diplomatic, military, and monetary affairs. "Devo Max"
was the option overwhelmingly supported by the Scottish people, with
some polls putting this as high as 70 percent. The SNP leadership recognized that there was not—or at any rate, not yet—a majority for independence, but hoped they could in the short-to-medium term achieve
Devo Max. With a triple-option ballot paper, Salmond would have been
able to claim victory if the result was either independence (unlikely) or
Devo Max (very probable).

Under Labour's 1998 Scotland Act, however, all constitutional issues
relating to the 1707 Treaty of Union between England and Scotland were
reserved to Westminster. The question therefore was whether the referendum would be duly legitimated and recognized by the British or whether
it would be an "unofficial" one, essentially a propagandistic device, conducted by the Scottish Parliament. On January 8, 2012, the British prime
minister took the initiative, announcing that his government would leg-
islate for a referendum to be held. But Cameron specified certain conditions: it would be an In–Out referendum, with no option to vote for Devo
Max. His reasons were simple enough: he wanted to see the decisive defeat
of the independence option, if not for all time, then at least for the foreseeable future, while simultaneously denying Salmond the easy victory of
Devo Max. The risks involved seemed small—polls consistently showed
minority support for independence, generally around 30 percent. Like
Blair, Cameron wanted to see "the threat of separatism removed."

The Tories were willing to pay a high price for the In–Out option
in the negotiations, however, conceding to the Scottish Parliament the
temporary right not only to hold the referendum but to decide on the
date, the franchise, and the wording of the question. Salmond and his capable deputy Nicola Sturgeon could thus plump for a long campaign, a
franchise extended to all voters registered in Scotland—regardless of
country of origin—with the voting age lowered to sixteen, and a positive
framing of the question. "Do you agree that Scotland should be an independent country?"—rather than, for example, "Should Scotland remain part of the UK?"—allowed the SNP to campaign for an upbeat
Yes instead of a recalcitrant No. These terms were sealed by the Edinburgh Agreement, signed by Cameron and Salmond for their respective
governments at St. Andrew's House on October 15, 2012.

WHY INDEPENDENCE?

At this stage it's worth briefly pausing to ask why and how the character of the UK state had become such a live political issue. Compared to the turbulent constitutional history of its European neighbors—France, Spain, or Germany, for example—the very durability of the multinational parliamentary monarchy founded by the 1707 Act of Union between England and Scotland might seem a brilliant success. Exploring these questions in early issues of *New Left Review*, Tom Nairn sought to explain the lateness of Scottish nationalism as an organized political force—it scarcely figured during the "age of nationalism" in the nineteenth century and attracted mass support only from the 1960s. Like England and France, he argued, Scotland had constituted itself politically as a nation very early, in the feudal period—hundreds of years before the late eighteenth-century invention of ideological nationalism as such. In the crucible of the Reformation, its late-feudal absolutism "collapsed as a vehicle for unity, and became a vehicle for faction."[2] But while Scotland lost its political state and national assembly in the elite bargain of 1707, henceforth sending its MPs to the Parliament of Great Britain at Westminster, it retained the legal, religious, cultural, and institutional forms of its civil society, as well as a distinctive "social ethos," all of which would go to make up a resilient "subnational" identity.

For Nairn, the key to the 1707 Union's longevity lay in the English revolutions that preceded it. The English magnates' "Crown-in-Parliament" settlement of 1688 had created a state in the image of the most dynamic section of the English ruling class—its precociously capitalist landed aristocracy. Rather than struggle against an ancien régime, the Lowland gentry could exploit an open political system and a fast-growing economy, then embarking on two centuries of overseas expansion. Sheltered by the British state, the Scottish industrial revolution seeded the Central Belt with its iron towns and engineering works, producing a vast new Scottish working class; gigantic shipyards spread along the Clyde. Nationalism for Nairn, as for Ernest Gellner, was closely associated with the unevenness of capitalist expansion and with latecomers' struggle to master industrial development, experienced as a powerful outside force. But the Scottish bourgeoisie had already achieved industrialization, without any need to mobilize its working class on the basis of a national project. Far from sharing the dynamism of its economic base, Scotland's political superstructure, as Nairn put it, simply collapsed, leaving the subnation merely a province.[3]

With the end of empire and the deepening economic crisis of the 1960s and '70s, the problems of Britain's archaic multinational state—"William and Mary's quaint palimpsest of cod-feudal shards, early-modern scratchings and re-invented 'traditions'"—began to surface.[4] In these conditions, Nairn argued, Scotland's "subnational" cultural identity, combined with the promise of far-north energy reserves, provided raw material that could be politicized by the SNP; he dated the rise of organized political nationalism to the party's 1974 election success on the slogan, "It's Scotland's oil!" Nairn speculated that late-emerging separatist tendencies ("neonationalisms") in economically advanced subnations like Catalonia, the Basque Country, or Scotland might be read as another type of response to uneven capitalist dynamics—in this instance, relative regional *over*development. The context for their emergence was the declining status of their own "great state," under US hegemony and the internationalization of capital, and the absence of any viable socialist alternative.[5] Ever optimistic, Nairn suggested that this neonationalism was becoming "the gravedigger of the old state in Britain," and as such "the principal factor making for a political revolution of some sort in England as well as the small countries."[6]

Respect for the pioneering nature of Nairn's achievement—in particular, his 1973 essay "Scotland and Europe" has more interesting insights into Scottish development than most of the notoriously untheoretical Scottish historical profession had collectively managed down to that date—must however also be tempered by critique, as is the case with any serious thinker. His historical account can be challenged on three main grounds.

First, rather than emerging during the medieval period, a unified Scottish nation only became possible *after* the Union of 1707, with the irrevocable defeat of Jacobite feudal-absolutist reaction at Culloden in 1746 and the overcoming of the 400-year-old Highland–Lowland divide, which had previously acted as a block to it. "Scottishness" certainly contributed to the formation of "Britishness," but the opposite is also true: a modern Scottish national consciousness, extending across the territorial extent of the country, was formed in a British context. For the working class in particular, it was also formed in the tension between participation in and support for British imperialism on the one hand, and the British labor movement on the other. As a result, fundamental political loyalties, for both major classes, lay until relatively recently at the British rather than the Scottish level: Scottish national *consciousness* was strong, but Scottish national*ism* was weak for the simple reason that it met no political need.[7]

Second, it was not "overdevelopment" that led to the rise of the SNP and the posing of the question of independence, but the determined push for neoliberal restructuring by successive Westminster governments—Tory, Labour, or coalition. Though the SNP is the palest of pink, it doesn't take much to be positioned to the left of New Labour. In contrast to the Blair–Brown governments, the SNP has safeguarded free care for the elderly, free prescriptions, and fee-less university education; it has resisted water privatization and the fragmentation—read: covert marketization—of the NHS. While the SNP leadership basically accepts the neoliberal agenda—happy to cut corporation tax or cozy up to Donald Trump—it has also managed to position itself as the inheritor of the Scottish Social-Democratic tradition. In addition, Salmond is one of the few UK politicians capable of defying the Atlantic consensus—standing out against the Anglo-American imperialist wars, for example. The arena of the Scottish Parliament has also highlighted the fact that the SNP is a more effective political machine than Scottish Labour, with substantial figures like Nicola Sturgeon, Fiona Hyslop, Kenny MacAskill, Mike Russell, John Swinney, and Sandra White. This contrasts starkly with Labour, where the focus remains Westminster—its Holyrood representation, with very few exceptions, involves a cohort of shifty election agents, superannuated full-time trade-union officials, and clapped-out local councilors.

YES AS A SOCIAL MOVEMENT

The third reason for dissenting from Nairn's view, however—and this is the point that needs to be stressed—is that for the majority of Yes campaigners, the movement was not primarily about supporting the SNP, nor even about Scottish nationalism in a wider sense. As a political ideology, nationalism—*any* nationalism, relatively progressive or absolutely reactionary—involves two inescapable principles: that the national group should have its own state, regardless of the social consequences; and that what unites the national group is more significant than what divides it, above all class. By contrast, the main impetus for the Yes campaign was not nationalism but a desire for social change expressed through the demand for self-determination. It was on this basis that independence was taken up by a broad range of socialists, environmentalists, and feminists.[8] In an era of weak and declining trade unionism, popular resistance to austerity will find other means of expression. As the late Daniel Bensaïd wrote: "If one of the outlets is blocked with particular care, then the contagion will find another, sometimes the most unexpected."[9] The Scottish referendum campaign was one of those outlets. Yes campaigners saw establishing a Scottish state not as an eternal goal to be pursued in all circumstances but as one that might offer better opportunities for equality and social justice in the current conditions of neoliberal austerity.

The official "Yes Scotland" campaign was launched on May 25, 2012. Even though Devo Max was absent from the ballot paper, the version of independence promoted by the SNP closely resembled it: the new Scottish state would retain the monarchy, NATO membership, and sterling, through a currency union with the rump UK.[10] The intention was to make the prospect of independence as palatable as possible to the unconvinced by proposing a form involving the fewest possible changes to the established order that would be compatible with actual secession. However, as became clear during the campaign, most Scots voting for Yes *wanted* their country to be different from the contemporary UK. Campaigning alongside tens of thousands of SNP members, many of them former Labour activists, was the Radical Independence Campaign, several thousand strong, which included the left groups, the Greens, and the SNP left, and played a key role in organizing voter-registration drives in working-class communities: "Because we recognized that the poorest, most densely populated communities must bear the most votes and the most ready support for a decisive political and social change, we canvassed these areas the hardest. . . . We recognized early that those voters who would buck the polling trend would be those voters who don't talk to pollsters and hate politicians; those voters who have told our activists: 'You are the only people to ever ask me what I think about politics.'"[11]

A *Sunday Herald* report described "two campaigns": one traditional and led by the suits, arguing in conventional media set-piece debates; the other a "ground war," "one-to-one, door-to-door, intentionally bypassing the media."[12] It was this "other" campaign that drew in previously marginalized working-class communities—and that suddenly flowered, over the course of the summer, into an extraordinary process of self-organization. Over three hundred local community groups sprang up, alongside dozens of other spontaneous initiatives—Yes cafés, drop-in centers, a National Collective of musicians, artists, and writers, Women for Independence, Generation Yes. They were complemented by activist websites like Bella Caledonia, loosely connected to the antineoliberal Common Weal think tank.[13] As the *Sunday Herald* report put it: "Yes staffers knew the grass-roots campaign was working when they learned of large community debates they had not organized, run by local groups they did not know existed." Even unionist opinion makers in the London press felt obliged to report the packed public meetings, the debates in pubs and on street corners, the animation of civic life.[14] Glasgow's George Square became the site of daily mass gatherings of Yes supporters, meeting to discuss, sing, or simply make visible the size and diversity of the movement. It was as if people who were canvassing, leafleting, or posting flyers—activities that tend to be carried out in small groups—had to return to the Square to refresh themselves in a public space over which they had taken collective control. In the summer of 2014, Glasgow came to resemble Greek and Spanish cities during the Movement of the Squares—to a far greater extent than in the relatively small-scale Scottish manifestations of Occupy. George Kerevan noted: "By the end, the Yes campaign had morphed into the beginnings of a genuine populist, anti-austerity movement."[15]

PROJECT FEAR

The No campaign, Better Together, with its focus-group-tested slogan, "No Thanks," was essentially run by the Labour Party. It was chaired by Alistair Darling, the ex-Chancellor of the Exchequer responsible with Brown for the deregulation of UK banks, and directed by Blair McDougall, who had organized David Miliband's failed Labour leadership bid—though its platform included local Tories and Liberal Democrats, to the embarrassment of many Labour functionaries, who preferred to claim that the whole referendum campaign was a waste of time.[16] The core concern of the UK's governing class was summed up by *The Economist*: "The rump of Britain would be diminished in every international forum: why should anyone heed a country whose own people shun it? Since Britain broadly stands for free trade and the maintenance of international order, this would be bad for the world." The point was amplified for a Washington audience by George Robertson, Blair's Secretary of State for Defence during the war on Yugoslavia, then NATO's Secretary General: Scottish independence would leave "a much diminished country whose global position would be open to question"; it would be "cataclysmic in geopolitical terms."[17]

The UK elite's sense of world entitlement was not, of course, foregrounded by Better Together, whose managers dubbed their strategy Project Fear.[18] Though the No campaign got off to an underwhelming start—Darling was a wooden performer, Brown was sulking and refused to participate—this did not really matter, since its real cadre was provided by the media, above all the BBC. An analysis of media coverage halfway through the campaign found that STV's *News at Six* and the BBC's *Reporting Scotland* typically presented the No campaign's scaremongering press releases as if they were news reports, with headlines such as "Scottish savers and financial institutions might be at risk if Scotland votes for independence" or "Row over independence could lead to higher electricity bills." In terms of running order, *Reporting Scotland* typically led with "bad news" about independence, then asked a Yes supporter to respond. Presenters put hard questions to Yes supporters, passive softballs to Noes. Yes campaigners were consistently referred to as "the separatists" or "the nationalists," even when, like the Scottish Green Party's Patrick Harvie, they explicitly denied the label. "Expert opinion" from the UK government side—the Office for Budget Responsibility, Institute for Fiscal Studies, Westminster committees—was treated as politically neutral, while Holyrood equivalents were always signaled as pro-SNP. The Yes campaign was repeatedly associated with the personal desires of Alex Salmond—"Salmond wants"—while no such equation was made for No figures. The airtime for the No campaign was bumped up by responses from all three unionist parties to any statement from Salmond. Television news reports often ended with particularly wild and unsubstantiated statements—that GPs and patients were planning to move to England (*Reporting Scotland*); that the SNP's antinuclear policy would bring "economic disaster" (STV); that insurance companies were looking at "billions in losses" and "potential closures" (*Reporting Scotland*).[19] The result was to radicalize Yes campaigners' understanding of the media, since the experience of their own eyes and ears was so fundamentally at odds with what they saw on TV. One example out of hundreds is the way the

BBC ignored a September 13 Yes demonstration of ten thousand people at the top of Glasgow's Buchanan Street, yet filmed Labour No supporters Jim Murphy and John Reid with perhaps thirty supporters at the bottom of the same street.

The print media was less homogeneous. In addition to Scottish editions of the London press—*Guardian, Independent, Telegraph, Mail, Express*, and the Murdoch stable—the "native" Scottish press consists of the *Scotsman*, the *Herald*, the *Daily Record*, and their separately edited Sunday editions. Only the *Sunday Herald* called for a Yes vote, and that quite late in the day, although the *Herald* itself and, to a lesser extent, the *Daily Record* were relatively balanced; both Darling and Salmond edited special editions of the latter, for example. But even so, No campaign themes were given overwhelming prominence. Foremost among these were the currency, job losses from companies flocking south, budget deficits leading to cuts in the NHS (a *Record* favorite), anxiety about pensions (particularly for the *Express*, whose readership is mostly over sixty-five), increased taxes (*Scottish Daily Mail*), and rising prices in supermarkets. A subtheme was security: would NATO still want us? Would Russia invade? Would the Da'esh group blow up the oil platforms? Finally, there was the "proud Scot" theme—you can be patriotic and still vote No.

While the Scottish press kept up the relentless drumbeat of Project Fear, London's left-liberal unionists painted the Yes campaigners as semi-Nazis, bringing "darkness" upon the land. For Will Hutton, Scottish independence meant "the death of the liberal enlightenment before the atavistic forces of nationalism and ethnicity—a dark omen for the 21st century. Britain will cease as an idea. We will all be diminished." For the editor of the *New Statesman*, "the portents for the 21st century are dark indeed." For Martin Kettle, the "dark side" of the Yes campaign—"disturbing," "divisive"—must not be ignored. For Philip Stephens, Salmond had "reawakened the allegiance of the tribe."[20] *Guardian* readers were treated to Labourist unionism in a variety of modes, from an upbeat Polly Toynbee—"It's no time to give up on a British social-democratic future"—to a doom-struck Seumas Milne: "The left and labour movement in Scotland, decimated by decades of deindustrialization and defeats, are currently too weak to shape a new Scottish state."[21] This was the argument parodied decades ago by Nairn: "The essential unity of the UK must be maintained till the working classes of all Britain are ready."[22]

Darling and McDougall had early on identified the SNP's position on sterling as a weak point. Chancellor George Osborne came to Edinburgh in February 2014—a rare visit by a Tory government minister, since they themselves agreed their presence would be unhelpful—to announce that all three unionist parties had agreed to refuse to allow Scotland to join a currency union with sterling.[23] The SNP's unspoken preference for Devo Max was a major handicap here: a really determined new-state project would have developed and costed plans for an autonomous currency. The No campaign seized on Salmond's unwillingness, in the first televised debate with Darling on August 5, to say what his Plan B would involve if London refused to agree to a currency union. His only argument was that this would be irrational and self-defeating for the rest of the UK. As he pointed out subsequently, and as Sturgeon might have said straightaway, there were at least three other options: using the pound as a floating currency, adopting the Euro, or establishing a Scottish currency. The problem with Salmond's position was precisely the danger that London *would* have agreed to a currency union: a nominally independent Scotland would have remained under the tutelage of the Bank of England and the Treasury, which would have imposed a European Central Bank–style fiscal compact—a recipe for permanent subjection to the neoliberal regime.

THE PANIC

By the end of August, the groundswell for independence was starting to make itself felt in the polls. On September 7 a YouGov poll in the *Sunday Times* put Yes in the lead for the first time with 51 percent. Two days later a TNS poll put it just one point behind. The reaction was nicely captured by a *Financial Times* headline: "Ruling Elite Aghast as Union Wobbles."[24] Darling's leadership of the Scottish No campaign came in for scathing comment. Project Fear was ramped up from headquarters in Downing Street.[25] The press let it be known that the Queen was anxious. Big companies started warning their Scottish employees that independence would put their jobs at risk: Shell and BP suggested there could be redundancies in Aberdeen and Shetland; Royal Bank of Scotland (RBS), Lloyds, Standard Life, and Tesco Bank announced that they might shift jobs from Edinburgh to London; Asda, John Lewis, and Marks & Spencer warned of rising prices. Some firms wrote to individual staff members, stressing the threat to their employment—a none-too-subtle hint about how they were expected to behave in the polling booth. Ever eager to do its bit, the BBC broadcast the news of RBS's decision to relocate its registered office to London on the evening of September 10, on the basis of an email from Osborne's flunkeys at the Treasury, though RBS itself didn't make the announcement until the following morning.[26] Scotland's trade-union bureaucrats also put their shoulders to the wheel. Most full-time officials were hostile to independence, though few unions could openly align themselves with the No campaign without consulting their members, many of whom had voted SNP in 2011.[27] At branch level, things were different. In the case of Unite (transportation and general workers), union officials in aerospace and ship-building actively courted Tory ministers and Labour No MPs for meetings to "defend the defense industry." In some workplaces CEOs and managers organized "employee briefings," in effect mass meetings to agitate for a No vote, with the union representatives backing up the employers.

With great fanfare, Gordon Brown also lumbered into the campaign, giving a verbose and barely coherent speech at a rally in the Glasgow district of Maryhill, intended to staunch the flow of Labour voters to Yes. Having backed five wars, pioneered Private Finance Initiative handouts, and presided over a steep increase in inequality during his thirteen years in office, he now maundered about "solidarity and sharing" as defining features of the UK state.[28] Brown has a tendency to think that only he can save the world, as he revealed in October 2008 when he pledged the entirety of the British GDP, if needed, to bail out his banker friends in the City of London. With no mandate—he is a backbench opposition MP—he announced a fast-track timetable toward greater devolution to reward a No vote. In fact, this was merely consolidating the promises made by all three unionist party leaders after the September 7 poll had showed Yes in the lead.

Two days before the vote, Cameron, Clegg, and Miliband appeared on the front of Labour's loyal Scottish tabloid, the *Daily Record*, their signatures adorning a mock-vellum parchment headed "The Vow," affirming that the Scottish Parliament would be granted further powers if only the Scots would consent to stay within the Union.[29] Cameron had been so determined to exclude the Devo Max option from the ballot paper that he gave way to the SNP on everything else. Now the UK leaders had unilaterally changed the nature of the question: from being a choice between the status quo and independence, it had effectively become a choice between independence and some unspecified form of Devo Max. Exit polls would suggest that "The Vow" had a relatively limited effect: according to Lord Ashcroft's polling organization, only 9 percent of No voters made up their minds during the last week of the campaign, compared to 21 percent of Yes voters. The undecideds were still breaking two to one for Yes in the last days of the campaign, although this couldn't overcome the massive initial advantage of the unionists.[30] As for Brown's intervention: on the best estimates, around 40 percent of Labour voters just ignored him.

THE VOTE

By the time the electoral rolls closed on September 2, 2014, some 97 percent of the Scottish population had registered to vote: 4,285,323 people, including 109,000 of the 16- and 17-year-olds specially enfranchised for the occasion. This was the highest level of voter registration in Scottish or British history since the introduction of universal suffrage. By the time the ballot closed at 10:00 p.m. on September 18, 3,619,915 had actually voted, an 85 percent turnout, compared with 65 percent in the 2010 British general election. The popular vote was 2,001,926 for No, 1,617,989 for Yes, or 55 to 45 percent against Scotland becoming an independent country. The demographics were telling. The No vote was heavily weighted toward the elderly: a clear majority of over-55s voted No, including nearly three-quarters of over-65s, many citing pensions or fears about savings and the currency as the main reason. Women were slightly more inclined to vote No than men, though that may partly reflect female predominance in the older age groups. Among under-40s there was a clear majority for Yes, with the strongest showing among 25- to 34-year-olds, 59 percent of whom voted for independence.[31] Based on pre-referendum polling, a significant majority of Scots of Asian descent voted Yes. In general, the No vote was correlated with higher income and class status; in the poorest neighborhoods and peripheral housing schemes, the Yes vote was 65 percent, and it was from this group that most of the new voters had emerged. One striking feature was the clash between the referendum results and regional party loyalties. The working-class Yes vote was concentrated in what were formerly the great heartlands of Labour support, above all in Dundee (57 percent Yes) and Glasgow (54 percent Yes), with similar results in North Lanarkshire and West Dumbartonshire;

Inverclyde came within 88 votes of a Yes majority. On the other hand, Aberdeenshire, "Scotland's Texas" and an SNP stronghold that includes Salmond's Holyrood constituency, voted against independence.

In some respects the closest comparison would be the Greek election of June 2012, in which New Democracy (ND), the Panhellenic Socialist Movement (PASOK), and the Democratic Left (DIMAR) won by two points over the Coalition of the Radical Left (Syriza) by mobilizing the financial anxieties of pensioners, housewives, and rural voters, while the young and the cities voted to resist the predations of the European troika.[32] One difference lies in the Scottish legacy of a larger "formal" working class, now aging and mortgage-paying, with understandable fears for their jobs and pensions in conditions of crisis and austerity. For the vote of the working class—still the majority of the Scottish population—was deeply divided. Personal testimony from a Yes campaigner in Edinburgh on the day of the referendum gives a vivid sense of this:

> I visited two areas to get the Yes vote out. The first one was Dryden Gardens [in Leith] which was made up of mainly well-paid workers and pensioners living in terraced houses. On the knocker, half of them had changed their vote or were not prepared to share their intentions with me.... Following this, I walked round the corner to Dryden Gate, a housing scheme of predominantly rented flats that were more blue-collar, with a large number of migrant families. Every Yes voter I spoke to had held firm and had already voted or were waiting on family to go and vote together.[33]

The social geography of the vote bears this out. The No heartlands lay in the rural districts—Dumfries and Galloway (66 percent No), Aberdeenshire (60 percent No)—and in traditionally conservative Edinburgh (61 percent No). The only town of any size in Dumfries and Galloway is Dumfries itself, with a population of just over thirty thousand. The economy is dominated by agriculture, with forestry following, and—some way behind—tourism. Two relationships are crucial: one with the EU through the Common Agricultural Policy, which meant that the threat of exclusion, even for a limited time, had obvious implications for farmers and their employees; the other with England—Carlisle is closer than any Scottish city, and many have closer family and business links with Cumbria than with other areas in Scotland. Aberdeenshire, too, is a conservative rural area with relatively small towns, in which the Tories were the main political force before the rise of the SNP (the Conservatives are still the second-biggest party in the council). The main source of employment is the public sector—the local council, education, and health—but the second biggest is energy, with the majority in jobs related to North Sea oil; the gas terminal at St. Fergus, near Peterhead, handles around 15 percent of the UK's natural gas requirements. Understandably, the threat of the oil companies relocating was a major issue here, as it was in Aberdeen itself. The third biggest sector by employment, agriculture and fishing, has a complex relationship with the EU, but as in the case of Dumfries and Galloway, the uncertainties over continued membership would have had an effect for farmers receiving subsidies. Finally, Aberdeenshire has the highest growth rate of any local council area and the fastest-growing population in Scotland, which might have been seen as vindicating current constitutional arrangements. Edinburgh, the historic capital of Scotland, has a long history of Toryism and elected a Labour-majority city council for the first time only in 1984 (it is currently run by an SNP–Labour coalition). Outside London, it has the highest average gross annual earnings per resident of any city in the UK, and the lowest percentage of those claiming Jobseeker's Allowance (the typically New Labour term for unemployment benefit). It has both a disproportionately large middle class and a significant section of the working class employed in sectors supposedly threatened by independence, including higher education—the University of Edinburgh is the city's third-biggest employer—and finance: RBS, Lloyds, and Standard Life are respectively its fourth, fifth, and sixth. The only parliamentary constituency here that came close to voting for independence was Edinburgh East (47 percent Yes), which contains some of the city's poorest schemes, such as Dumbiedykes.

The strongest Yes vote, meanwhile, came in Dundee (57 percent Yes). Scotland's fourth-largest city after Glasgow, Edinburgh, and Aberdeen, it has the lowest level of average earnings of them all and one of the highest levels of unemployment. The staple industries of shipbuilding, carpet manufacture, and jute export were all shut down in the 1980s; the city saw one of the most important British struggles against deindustrialization in the ultimately unsuccessful six-month strike to prevent the closure of the Timex plant in 1993. The biggest employers—as in most Scottish cities—are the city council and the NHS, although publisher (and anti-trade-union stalwart) D. C. Thompson, and the Universities of Dundee and Abertay, are also important. (The latter has carved a niche in the video-games sector: Rockstar North, which developed Grand Theft Auto, was originally founded in Dundee as DMA Design by David Jones, an Abertay graduate.) Although manufacturing has slumped, companies like National Cash Register and Michelin are still notable employers. Formerly a Labour stronghold, Dundee has sent an SNP MP to Westminster since 2005. In the aftermath of the referendum there was a particularly angry demonstration outside the Caird Hall there, which was ostensibly held to call for a revote but turned, by means of an open mic, into an all-purpose expression of rage at the conditions that had led a majority of Dundonians into voting Yes in the first place.

The Yes vote in the heart of the former Red Clydeside—straddling Glasgow, North Lanarkshire, and West Dunbartonshire—was the biggest catastrophe for Labour. As noted, the first signs of its eroding support came after the invasion of Iraq in 2003, when a left protest vote sent seven Green, six SSP, and three radical independent MSPs, including Dennis Canavan and Margo MacDonald, to Holyrood. The SNP began to make real inroads into the Labour vote in Glasgow only in 2011, after the council set about cuts and closures in the wake of Brown's pro-City handling of the financial crisis. It is not hard to see why. Though Liverpool and Manchester have similar levels of deprivation, premature deaths in Glasgow are over 30 percent higher; mortality rates are among the worst in Europe. Life expectancy at birth for men is nearly seven years below the national average; in the Shettleston area it is fourteen years, and in Calton twenty-four years, lower than the averages in Iraq and Bangladesh. What was once one of the most heavily industrialized areas in Europe is now essentially a services-based economy, dominated—the usual story—by the city council and NHS, but with significant low-paid employment in retail and "business services," that is, call centers. The city is growing again, but on a strikingly uneven basis—demonstrated by the heritage makeover of the Clyde Walkway area and the Merchant City.

A MOTTLED DAWN?

Though it is too early to take the full measure of this watershed vote, one paradox stands out. Scottish Labour has been drastically undermined by its victory, while the SNP and the radical independence movement have been strengthened in defeat. This is immediately clear at the party level. Within ten days of the referendum, the membership of the SNP had leapt from 25,642 to 68,200, while the Greens had more than tripled, from 1,720 to 6,235. When the Radical Independence Campaign announced it would be holding a "Where Now?" conference in Glasgow on November 22, seven thousand people signed up for it on Facebook and the venue had to be shifted to the Clyde Auditorium: all three thousand tickets subsequently sold out. A rally in George Square called by Tommy Sheridan's Hope Not Fear operation in support of independence pulled an estimated seven thousand on October 12. Post-referendum polls indicated the possibility of an SNP landslide at Labour's expense in the 2015 Westminster election. Meanwhile Scottish Labour has collapsed into fratricidal strife after the resignation of its leader Johann Lamont, who accused Miliband and his claque of being "dinosaurs," out of touch with how the Scottish political landscape had changed, and of treating the party north of the border as a "branch office." Lamont's long list of grievances included being elbowed aside during Miliband's Beria-style takeover of the Falkirk selection process in 2013,[34] having her general secretary sacked by London, and being told she must not open her mouth about the coalition's deeply unpopular Bedroom Tax until Miliband had made up his mind about it—a notoriously lengthy process. The many resignations from Scottish Labour include Allan Grogan, a convener of the Labour for Independence group, widely derided by the leadership. He described the party as being "in deep decline, and I fear it may be permanent."[35]

The SNP has submitted a 42-page document demanding that the Scottish Parliament have the right to set all Scottish taxes and retain the revenues, to determine all domestic spending, employment, and welfare policy, including the minimum wage, and to define Scotland's internal constitutional framework—in short, Devo Max. The unionist parties' proposals are set to fall well short of this. There is an obvious danger here into which Yes campaigners may be led by an understandable wish to see the unionist parties keep their promises: the danger is Devo Max itself. Under neoliberal regimes, the more politics is emptied of content, the more opportunities for pseudodemocracy are multiplied: citizen-consumers may take part in elections for local councilors, mayors, police commissioners, and so on, spreading responsibility to bodies whose policy options are severely restricted both by statute and by reliance on the central state for most of their funding. The upshot at local-council level has seen atomized citizens given a vote on which services they want to close. If this is to be the basis of "further devolution" in Scotland, it should be rejected. Devo Max will be of value only insofar as it involves the greater democratization of Scottish society, rather than tightly circumscribed "powers" for the Scottish substate. Labour and the Conservatives are also at loggerheads over Cameron's dawn pledge—at 7:00 a.m. on the morning after the referendum—of "English votes for English laws": if further powers are devolved to Holyrood. Since 41 of Labour's 257 MPs are from Scottish constituencies, this would slash its voting weight in the House of Commons. The obvious solution to the "West Lothian" question—the constitutional asymmetry introduced by devolution, whereby English MPs can no longer vote on aspects of Scottish policy, whereas Scottish MPs at Westminster still vote on legislation that will apply to England and Wales alone—is a fully democratic, therefore written, constitution. But this is just what both parties want to avoid at all costs, so increasingly baroque proposals for serial committee stages for "English laws" are being put forward by the Tories, desperate to keep UKIP at bay, while Labour refuses to discuss the matter.

Rather than securing a stable future for the UK state, the Scottish independence referendum has ensured the issue will be kept on the table. In 2013, a Westminster coalition spokesman said that a "crushing defeat" was needed: if 40 percent or more of the population backed calls for independence, "pressure could build."[36] In the absence of that crushing defeat the Labour leadership, seeing housing schemes like Northfield in Aberdeen, Fintry in Dundee, Craigmillar in Edinburgh, or Drumchapel in Glasgow awaken to political life, must be recalling the words of that archunionist Sir Walter Scott to Robert Southey, shortly before the Scottish General Strike of 1820: "The country is mined beneath our feet."[37] Indeed it is.

Notes

PREFACE

1. Hagen Schulze [1994], *States, Nations and Nationalism: From the Middle Ages to the Present* (Oxford: Blackwell Publishing, 1998), 3–302. This work is nevertheless one of the very few to examine both aspects of the nation-state.
2. See, for example, Daron Acemoglu and James A. Robinson, *Why Nations Fail: The Origins of Power, Prosperity and Poverty* (London: Profile Books, 2012). However ideological its typical usage tends to be, the notion of a "failed state" is at least comprehensible; the notion of a "failed *nation*" makes no sense at all.
3. Tom Nairn [1976], "The Modern Janus," in *Old Nations, Auld Enemies, New Times: Selected Essays*, edited by Jamie Maxwell and Pete Ramand (Edinburgh: Luath Press, 2014), 150.
4. For my critique of Nairn's position see Neil Davidson [1999], "Tom Nairn and the Inevitability of Nationalism," in *Holding Fast to an Image of the Past: Explorations in the Marxist Tradition* (Chicago: Haymarket Books, 2014).
5. For an interesting recent attempt to reconstruct Marx and Engels's views on nationalism from texts that are not usually cited in this context, see Mike Davis, "Marx's Lost Theory: The Politics of Nationalism in 1848," *New Left Review* 1, no. 93 (May/June 2015), 50–66. Davis rightly draws attention to two works on the same subject that have received insufficient attention: Solomon F. Bloom, *The World of Nations: A Study of the National Implications in the Work of Karl Marx* (New York: Columbia University Press, 1941); and Erica Benner, *Really Existing Nationalism: A Post-Communist View from Marx and Engels* (Oxford: Clarendon Press, 1995).

6. Quoted in Vladimir I. Lenin [1914], "The Right of Nations to Self-Determination," in *Collected Works*, vol. 20, *December 1913–August 1914* (Moscow: Progress Publishers, 1964), 430–31, and Rosa Luxemburg [1908], "The National Question and Autonomy: 1. The Right of Nations to Self-Determination," in *The National Question: Selected Writings by Rosa Luxemburg*, edited by Horace B. Davis (New York: Monthly Review Press, 1976), 107.

7. *Lenin's Struggle for a Revolutionary International: Documents: 1907–1916, The Preparatory Years*, edited by John Riddell (New York: Monad Press, 1984), 5–15.

8. Luxemburg, "The National Question and Autonomy," 110–11.

9. Lenin, "The Right of Nations to Self-Determination," 410.

10. Ibid., 423.

11. See Stephen Velychenko, *Painting Imperialism and Nationalism Red: The Ukrainian Marxist Critique of Russian Communist Rule in Ukraine, 1918–1925* (Toronto: University of Toronto Press, 2015). For a summary of Velychenko's argument see 3–18.

12. See, for example, the complaints of Niall Ferguson, *Colossus: The Rise and Fall of the American Empire* (London: Allen Lane, 2004), 290–302.

13. I have strong reservations about the term "ethnicity," which are set out below and in chapter 1.

14. For a discussion of all three "stateless nations," see Michael Keating [1996], *Nations against the State: The New Politics of Nationalism in Quebec, Catalonia and Scotland* (Second edition, Houndmills: Palgrave, 2001).

15. Lenin, "The Right of Nations to Self-Determination," 410.

16. For my objections to this compound term, see Neil Davidson [2005], "How Revolutionary Were the Bourgeois Revolutions?," in *We Cannot Escape History: States and Revolutions* (Chicago: Haymarket Books, 2015), 37–39.

17. Davidson, "Tom Nairn and the Inevitability of Nationalism," 37.

18. Andrew C. Bacevich, *American Empire: The Realities and Consequences of U.S. Diplomacy* (Cambridge, MA: Harvard University Press, 2002), 105; Peter Gowan, "The Euro-Atlantic Origins of NATO's Attack on Yugoslavia," in *Masters of the Universe: NATO's Balkan Crusade*, edited by Tariq Ali (London: Verso, 2000), 8–10.

19. Ferguson, *Colossus*, 147; Robin Blackburn, "Kosovo: The War of NATO Expansion," *New Left Review* I/235 (May/June 1999): 119.

20. See, inevitably, Niall Ferguson, *The War of the World: History's Age of Hate* (London: Allen Lane, 2006), and the more sober reflections in Michael Mann, *The Dark Side of Democracy: Explaining Ethnic Cleansing* (Cambridge: Cambridge University Press, 2005).

21. See, for example, Anthony D. Smith, *Nationalism and Modernism: A Critical Survey of Recent Theories of Nations and Nationalism* (London: Routledge, 1998), chapter 2, "The Rise of Classical Modernism."

22. Foster was virtually the only reviewer who would have described himself as a Marxist. Angus Calder, whom I knew and whose work I admired, was agnostic about Marxism but wrote an appreciative review for *Red Pepper* that remained unpublished until he included it in a book two years later. See Calder, "When Was Scotland?," in *Scotlands of the Mind* (Edinburgh: Luath Press, 2002); for a brief appreciation of his work, see Neil Davidson, "Angus Calder, 1942–2008," *Socialist Review* 327 (July/August 2008), 34.

23. A point made in different ways by both Luxemburg and Lenin in the debate over the national question: Rosa Luxemburg [1905], "Foreword to the Anthology *The Polish Question and the National Movement*," in *The National Question*, 77; Lenin, "The Right of Nations to Self-Determination," 434.

24. Richard Seymour, *The Liberal Defense of Murder* (London: Verso, 2008), 1–22, 165–269.

25. Terry Eagleton, *Reason, Faith, and Revolution: Reflections on the God Debate* (New Haven: Yale University Press, 2009), 2–3.

26. Harman was deeply suspicious of this argument, which he regarded as implying that certain societies were incapable of developing the productive forces, and I was accordingly rebuked by him for polluting the pages of *Socialist Review* with such heresies at a session on "Islam and Islamic Societies" at the Marxism 2006 conference. This was not, of course, what I was arguing. The misunderstanding probably arose through Harman's refusal to accept that the tributary mode of production was anything other than the discredited Asiatic mode in a new guise. See Davidson, *We Cannot Escape History*, xii–xv and chapter 2, "Asiatic, Tributary, or Absolutist? A Comment on Chris Harman's 'The Rise of Capitalism.'"

27. Ernest Gellner, *Muslim Societies* (Cambridge: Cambridge University Press, 1981), 7.

28. For my discussion of uneven and combined development, see Davidson, *We Cannot Escape History*, xvii–xxii and chapters 8 and 11.

29. "Yes: A Non-nationalist Argument for Scottish Independence," *Radical Philosophy* 185 (May/June 2014).

30. But see, in addition to the article cited in the preceding endnote, Neil Davidson, "Scotland: The Social Movement for Independence and the Crisis of the British State," November 21, 2014, available on the RS21 website at rs21.org.uk.

31. Robert Burns [1795], "A Man's a Man for a' That," in *The Canongate Burns: The Complete Poems and Songs of Robert Burns*, edited by Andrew Noble and Patrick Stewart Hogg (Edinburgh: Canongate Books, 2001), 512.

CHAPTER I: THE TROUBLE WITH "ETHNICITY"

1. Marcus Banks, *Ethnicity: Anthropological Constructions* (London: Routledge, 1996), 167–68. See also "Notes and Queries," *Guardian* (June 17, 1999).

2. Laura Silber and Alan Little, *The Death of Yugoslavia* (Harmondsworth: Penguin, 1995), 188–90.

3. See, for example, Michael Mann, "The Dark Side of Democracy: The Modern Tradition of Ethnic and Political Cleansing," *New Left Review* I/235 (May/June 1999), 31–32, 42–43.

4. Vladimir I. Lenin [1902], "What Is To Be Done? Burning Questions of Our Movement," in *Collected Works*, vol. 5, *May 1901–February 1902* (Moscow: Foreign Languages Publishing House, 1961), 423.

5. Pierre L. van den Berghe, "Race and Ethnicity: A Sociobiological Perspective," *Ethnic and Racial Studies* 1, no. 4 (October 1978), 404.

6. Susan Reynolds, "Medieval *Origines Gentium* and the Community of the Realm," *History* 68, no. 224 (October 1983), 379.

7. Linda Colley, *Britons: Forging the Nation, 1707–1837* (New Haven: Yale University Press, 1992), 15.

8. Michael Lynch, *Scotland: A New History* (Revised edition, London: Pimlico, 1992), 12. The origins of this process were famously mocked in the deathless prose of Sellar and Yeatman: "The Scots (originally Irish, but by now Scotch) were at this time inhabiting Ireland, having driven the Irish (Picts) out of Scotland; while the Picts (originally Scots) were now Irish (living in brackets) and vice versa. It is essential to keep these distinctions clearly in mind (and vice versa)." Walter C. Sellar and Robert J. Yeatman [1930], *1066 and All That: A Memorable History of England, Comprising All the Parts You Can Remember, including 103 Good Things, 5 Bad Kings and 2 Genuine Dates* (Harmondsworth: Penguin, 1960), 13.

9. Steven Rose, Leon J. Kamin, and Richard C. Lewontin, *Not in Our Genes: Biology, Ideology and Human Nature* (Harmondsworth: Penguin, 1984), 126.

10. Eric R. Wolf, *Europe and the Peoples without History* (Berkeley: University of California Press, 1982), 71.

11. For a brief discussion of how increasing social differences between Lowland and Highland Scotland led the inhabitants of the former region to regard those of the latter as a distinct "race" or "ethnicity," see Neil Davidson, "Scotland's Bourgeois Revolution," in *Scotland, Class and Nation*, edited by Chris Bambery (London: Bookmarks, 1999), 58–61, 120–21.

12. Wolf, *Europe and the Peoples without History*, 380–81.

13. The Twa are pygmies and consequently physically distinct from the other two, but in any event they composed only 1 percent of the population at the time of colonization.

14. Charlie Kimber, "Coming to Terms with Barbarism in Rwanda and Burundi," *International Socialism* 2:73 (Winter 1996), 128–29.

15. Thomas H. Eriksen, *Ethnicity and Nationalism: Anthropological Perspectives* (London: Pluto Press, 1993), 87–88.

16. Ibid., 82.

17. See chapter 3 in this volume; 51–52.

18. Anthony D. Smith, *National Identity* (Harmondsworth: Penguin, 1991), 21.

19. Ibid., 14.

20. Eriksen, *Ethnicity and Nationalism*, 3.

21. Max Weber [1910–14], *Economy and Society: An Outline of Interpretive Sociology*, edited by Guenther Roth and Claus Wittich, vol. 2 (Berkeley: University of California Press, 1978), 923, 926–40.

22. Banks, *Ethnicity*, 72. Banks suggests that the rise of Nazi Germany was a reason why Germans made less of their origins than, for example, Poles, but the "assimilationist" nature of German immigrants was well established long before 1933.

23. Lewis Carroll [1871], "Through the Looking Glass and What Alice Found There," in *The Complete Lewis Carroll* (Harmondsworth: Penguin, 1982), 196.

24. Stuart Hall, "Brave New World," *Marxism Today* 32, no. 10 (October 1988), 29.

25. Abner Cohen, *Two-Dimensional Man: An Essay on the Anthropology of Power and Symbolism in Complex Society* (Berkeley: University of California Press, 1974), 15.

26. No Sizwe [i.e., Neville Alexander], *One Azania, One Nation: The National Question in South Africa* (London: Zed Press, 1978), 137.

27. Weber, *Economy and Society*, vol. 1, 395.

28. Stuart Hall, "Our Mongrel Selves," *New Statesman and Society* (June 19, 1992), 6.

29. Stuart Hall [1988], "The New Ethnicities," in *Ethnicity*, edited by John Hutchinson and Anthony D. Smith (Oxford: Oxford University Press, 1996), 163.

30. John Hutchinson and Anthony D. Smith, preface to *Ethnicity*, v.

31. Eriksen, *Ethnicity and Nationalism*, 13–14.

32. Malcolm Cross, "Colonialism and Ethnicity: A Theory and Comparative Case Study," *Ethnic and Racial Studies* 1, no. 1 (January 1978), 40.

33. David Brown, "Why Is the Nation-State So Vulnerable to Ethnic Nationalism?," *Nations and Nationalism* 4, no. 1 (January 1998), 13.

34. Adam Kuper, *Culture: The Anthropologist's Account* (Cambridge, MA: Harvard University Press, 1999), 238–39. Kuper is South African and correctly describes himself as a liberal. See ibid., xi. Like that other exiled son of the British Dominions, the Australian Robert Hughes in *The Culture of Complaint*, he treads a fine line between acute commentary on the follies of much "radical" thought and dismissal of the problems it seeks to address.

35. Brown, "Why Is the Nation-State So Vulnerable to Ethnic Nationalism?," 13.

36. Misha Glenny, *The Fall of Yugoslavia* (Harmondsworth: Penguin, 1992), 141–42.

37. Andrew Bell-Fialkoff, "A Brief History of Ethnic Cleansing," *Foreign Affairs* 72, no. 3 (July 1993), 121.

38. Eric J. Hobsbawm [1992], "Ethnicity and Nationalism in Europe Today," in *Mapping the Nation*, edited by Gopal Balakrishnan (London: Verso, 1996), 260.

39. Ambalavaner Sivanandan [1985], "R[ace] A[wareness] T[raining] and the Degradation of Black Struggle," *Communities of Resistance* (London: Verso, 1990), 94.

40. Steven Fenton, *Ethnicity: Racism, Class and Culture* (Houndmills: Macmillan, 1999), 69.

41. Peter Alexander, *Racism, Resistance and Revolution* (London: Bookmarks, 1987), chapter 1.

42. Martin Barker, *The New Racism: Conservatives and the Ideology of the Tribe* (London: Junction Books, 1981), 4–5.

43. Theodore W. Allen, *The Invention of the White Race*, vol. 1, *Racial Oppression and Social Control* (London: Verso, 1994) 14–21, 32, 48, 65–66, 77–79, 92.

44. Kuper, *Culture*, xii–xiii.

45. *The Race Relations Act 1976*, S.3 (1), (2).

46. Herman Ouseley, preface to Commission for Racial Equality, *Racial Equality Means Quality: A Standard for Racial Equality for Local Government in England and Wales* (London: Commission for Racial Equality, 1995), 5.

47. No Sizwe (Neville Alexander), *One Azania, One Nation*, 137.

48. Alex Callinicos, *Race and Class* (London: Bookmarks, 1993), 32–33.

49. Richard J. Herrnstein and Charles Murray, *The Bell Curve: Intelligence and Class Structure in American Life* (New York: The Free Press, 1994), especially chapter 13.

50. Barker, *The New Racism*, 5.

51. In fact, many members of the Communications Workers Union refused to deliver Nazi election material, but not, alas, those delivering to Edinburgh postal district EH6.

52. Tom Nairn, "Does Tomorrow Belong to the Bullets or the Bouquets?," *New Statesman and Society* (June 19, 1992), 31. For similar arguments, couched within an explicit appeal to sociobiology, see van den Berghe, "Race and Ethnicity."

53. Bill Rolston, "Culture as a Battlefield: Political Identity and the State in the North of Ireland," *Race and Class* 39, no. 4 (April/June 1998), 28–30.

54. Kuper, *Culture*, 238–39.

55. James G. Kellas, *The Politics of Nationalism and Ethnicity* (Second edition, Houndmills: Macmillan, 1998), 65.

56. George Kerevan, "Milošević's 'Nationalism' Is Not Ours," *Scotsman* (April 5, 1999).

57. Michael Ignatieff, *Blood and Belonging: Journeys into the New Nationalism* (New York: Farrar, Straus and Giroux, 1993), 6.

58. Neil Davidson [1999], "Tom Nairn and the Inevitability of Nationalism," in *Holding Fast to an Image of the Past: Explorations in the Marxist Tradition* (Chicago: Haymarket Books, 2014), 35–37; Alex Callinicos, "Marxism and the National Question," in *Scotland, Class and Nation*.

59. Lord Acton [1862], "Nationality," in *Mapping the Nation*, 31.

60. Michael Billig, *Banal Nationalism* (London: Sage Publications, 1995), 55, 57.

61. Ibid., 47–48.

62. Davidson, "Tom Nairn and the Inevitability of Nationalism," 22–23; Donny Gluckstein, *The Nazis, Capitalism and the Working Class* (London: Bookmarks, 1999), chapter 1.

63. "Extract of a Letter from a Gentleman at Derby," *Gentleman's Magazine and Historical Chronicle* 16 (January 1746), 16.

64. Alan I. MacInnes, *Clanship, Commerce and the House of Stuart, 1603–1788* (East Linton: Tuckwell Press, 1996), 211; see also 32. Later the Hanoverian high command is no longer described as having a policy "verging" on "ethnic cleansing," but of "opting" for it without qualification. See ibid., 215.

65. James Hunter, *A Dance Called America* (Edinburgh: Mainstream, 1994), 237. Hunter recounts one of the more positive encounters between the Highland Scots and the Native Americans, in this case the MacDonalds of Glencoe and the Nez Perce, in his *Glencoe and the Indians* (Edinburgh: Mainstream, 1996).

66. James T. Callender, *The Political Progress of Great Britain; or an Impartial Account of the Principal Abuses in the Government of This Country from the Revolution in 1688: The Whole Tending to Prove the Ruinous Consequences of the Popular System of War and Conquest* (Edinburgh: Printed for Robertson and Berry, 1792), part 1, 1–2.

67. "Report of Committee to Consider Overtures from the Presbytery of Glasgow and from the Synod of Glasgow and Ayr on Irish Immigrants and the Education (Scotland) Act 1918, 29 May 1923," in *Report on the Schemes of the Church of Scotland with Legislative Acts Passed by the General Assembly* (Edinburgh: Church of Scotland, 1923), 750, 760–61. My emphasis. Steven Bruce has argued that this was an unrepresentative committee "whose views and enthusiasm were not shared by the majority"; the central point, he argues, is that the church lacked the willingness to act. See Bruce, "Sectarianism in Scotland: A Contemporary Assessment and Explanation," in *The Scottish Government Yearbook 1988*, edited by David McCrone and Alice Brown (Edinburgh: Unit for the Study of Government in Scotland, 1988), 165, note 25. In fact the membership of the committee included both the Moderator and the Procurator, that is, the leading officials of the Church of Scotland.

68. Valentin N. Voloshinov [1929], *Marxism and the Philosophy of Language* (Cambridge, MA: Harvard University Press, 1986), 19, 23.

69. Kuper, *Culture*, 247.
70. Banks, *Ethnicity*, 189.
71. Alasdair MacIntyre, "'Ought,'" in *Against the Self-Images of the Age: Essays on Ideology and Philosophy* (London: Duckworth, 1971), 156.

CHAPTER 2: WHAT IS NATIONAL CONSCIOUSNESS?

1. Michael Löwy, "Marxists and the National Question," *New Left Review* I/96 (March/April 1976), 81.
2. Joseph V. Stalin [1913], "Marxism and the National Question," in *Works*, vol. 2, *1907–1913* (Moscow: Foreign Languages Publishing House, 1953), 307.
3. Bob Mulholland, "What Is the National Question?," *Socialist Scotland* 1 (Autumn 1989), 18.
4. Eric J. Hobsbawm, *Nations and Nationalism since 1780: Program, Myth, Reality* (Cambridge: Cambridge University Press, 1990), 6.
5. Benedict Anderson [1983], *Imagined Communities: Reflections on the Rise and Spread of Nationalism* (Second, revised edition, London: Verso, 1991), 135–39.
6. Leon D. Trotsky [1933], "The Negro Question in America," in *Leon Trotsky on Black Nationalism and Self-Determination*, edited by George Breitman (New York: Pathfinder Press, 1978), 28.
7. Elie Kedourie [1960], *Nationalism* (London: Hutchinson University Library, 1966), 82.
8. Hugh Seton-Watson, *Nations and States: An Enquiry into the Origins of Nations and the Politics of Nationalism* (London: Taylor and Francis, 1977), 5.
9. See chapter 1 in this volume, 4–12.
10. For recent defenses of this "key dichotomy," see Michael Löwy, *Fatherland or Mother Earth? Essays on the National Question* (London: Pluto Press, 1998), 1, 27–29, and Alex Callinicos, "Marxism and the National Question," in *Scotland, Class and Nation*, edited by Chris Bambery (London: Bookmarks, 1999), 39, 40–42.
11. Hobsbawm, *Nations and Nationalism since 1780*, 7–8. Hobsbawm does some dexterous fence sitting with regard to his own position: "Neither objective nor subjective definitions are thus satisfactory, and both are misleading. In any case, agnosticism is the best initial posture of a student in the field, and so this book assumes no a priori definition of what constitutes a nation." On the same page, however, he comes down on what is essentially a subjectivist position: "As an initial working assumption, any sufficiently large body of people whose members regard themselves as members of a 'nation' will be treated as such." Ibid., 8.
12. Anderson, *Imagined Communities*, 6.
13. Valentin N. Voloshinov [1929], *Marxism and the Philosophy of Language* (Cambridge, MA: Harvard University Press, 1986), 11, 13.
14. Geoffrey de Ste Croix, *The Class Struggle in the Ancient Greek World* (London: Duckworth, 1981), 43. See also page 32.
15. Karl Marx [1847], *The Poverty of Philosophy: Answer to the Philosophy of Poverty by M. Proudhon*, in *Collected Works*, vol. 6 (London: Lawrence and Wishart, 1976), 211.
16. Georg Lukács [1923], "Class Consciousness," in *History and Class Consciousness: Studies in Marxist Dialectics* (London: Merlin Press, 1971), 51.
17. Edward P. Thompson [1963], *The Making of the English Working Class* (Second edition, Harmondsworth: Penguin, 1980), 8–9.

18. See, for example, Ronald Suny, "The Revenge of the Past: Socialism and Ethnic Conflict in Transcaucasia," *New Left Review* I/184 (November/December 1990), 9. For an explicit appeal to Thompson's authority, see ibid., note 7. In at least one case, that of so-called "proletarian Zionism," there has been an attempt to argue that national and class consciousness can become fused. See the discussion in Nathan Weinstock, *Zionism: False Messiah*, edited by Alan Adler (London: Pluto Press, 1979), appendix 3, "Borchov and the National Question," 274–79.

19. Hobsbawm has confused the issue further by arguing that two definitions of class can be found in Marx. One is based on objective class position (like that of de Ste Croix) and the other on subjective awareness of that position (like Thompson's). The latter is not, however, a definition of class but of class consciousness: "Class consciousness in the full sense only comes into existence at the historical moment when classes begin to acquire consciousness of themselves as such." How conscious would a proletarian have to be before she or he could be said to "exist" as a member of their class? And would they cease to be a member if their level of consciousness changed? See Eric J. Hobsbawm, "Class Consciousness in History," in *Aspects of History and Class Consciousness*, edited by István Mészáros (London: Routledge and Kegan Paul, 1971), 6, and "Notes on Class Consciousness," in *Worlds of Labour: Further Studies in the History of Labour* (London: Weidenfeld and Nicolson, 1984), 16.

20. I owe this formulation to Alex Callinicos, who offered it in his reply to the discussion during a meeting on "Base and Superstructure" at Marxism 1990 in London, July 13, 1990.

21. George Kerevan, "The Origins of Scottish Nationhood: Arguments within Scottish Marxism," *Bulletin of Scottish Politics* 1, no. 2 (Spring 1981), 119.

22. Anderson, *Imagined Communities*, 7.

23. Max Weber [1910–14], "Structures of Power," in *From Max Weber*, edited by C. Wright Mills and Hans H. Gerth (London: Routledge and Kegan Paul, 1948), 176.

24. Alfred Cobban [1945], *The Nation State and National Self-Determination* (Glasgow: Fontana, 1969), 108.

25. John Breuilly [1982], *Nationalism and the State* (Second edition, Manchester: Manchester University Press, 1993), 6.

26. Anthony D. Smith, *National Identity* (Harmondsworth: Penguin, 1991), 14.

27. Montserrat Guibernau, *Nationalisms: The Nation-State and Nationalism in the Twentieth Century* (Cambridge: Polity Press, 1996), 3.

28. Tom Nairn [1995], "Union and Empire," in *Faces of Nationalism: Janus Revisited* (London: Verso, 1997), 209.

29. Anthony D. Smith, *Nationalism and Modernism: A Critical Survey of Recent Theories of Nations and Nationalism* (London: Routledge, 1998), 73, 75.

30. Michael Biddiss, "Nationalism and the Molding of Modern Europe," *History* 79, no. 257 (October 1994), 414.

31. Alice Brown, David McCrone, and Lindsay Patterson, *Politics and Society in Scotland* (Houndmills: Macmillan, 1996), 191–92.

32. Michael Billig, *Banal Nationalism* (London: Sage Publications, 1995), 60.

33. Karl Marx and Friedrich Engels [1848], "Manifesto of the Communist Party,"

in *Political Writings*, vol. 1, *The Revolutions of 1848*, edited by David Fernbach (Harmondsworth: Penguin/New Left Review, 1974), 70.

34. Stuart Hall, "Brave New World," *Marxism Today* 32, no. 10 (October 1988), 28.

35. Ambalavaner Sivanandan, "All That Melts into Air Is Solid: The Hokum of New Times," in *Communities of Resistance* (London: Verso, 1990), 47.

36. Billig, *Banal Nationalism*, 138–39. These comments are clearly aimed at Lyotard's fatuous claim that "eclecticism is the degree zero of contemporary general culture: one listens to reggae, watches a western, eats McDonald's food for lunch and local cuisine at dinner, wears Paris perfume in Tokyo and 'retro' clothes in Hong Kong; knowledge is a matter for TV games." See Jean-François Lyotard [1979], *The Postmodern Condition: A Report on Knowledge* (Manchester: Manchester University Press, 1984), 76. The attempt by Smith to characterize Billig as a theorist "exploring novel postmodern dimensions" of nationalism is therefore quite incomprehensible, particularly since Smith himself quotes from this passage by Billig! See Smith, *Nationalism and Modernism*, 205, 224.

37. Guibernau, *Nationalisms*, 43.

38. Michael Billig, "From Codes to Utterances: Cultural Studies, Discourse and Psychology," in *Cultural Studies in Question*, edited by Marjorie Ferguson and Peter Golding (London: Sage Publications, 1997), 208.

39. Ross Poole, "On National Identity: A Response to Jonathan Ree," *Radical Philosophy* 62 (Autumn 1992), 14–15.

40. Billig, *Banal Nationalism*, 24, 60.

41. Edward P. Thompson, "Introduction: Custom and Culture," in *Customs in Common* (London: Merlin Press, 1991), 1.

42. Billig, *Banal Nationalism*, 8. The metonym is developed further on pages 39–43 and 49–51.

43. Voloshinov, *Marxism and the Philosophy of Language*, 91. Billig does not refer to Voloshinov directly in *Banal Nationalism* but acknowledges his debt to him in "From Codes to Utterances."

44. Hugh Cunningham [1981], "The Language of Patriotism," in *Patriotism: The Making and Unmaking of British National Identity*, vol. 1, *History and Politics*, edited by Raphael Samuel (London: Routledge, 1989), 58–59.

45. Bernard Crick, "Essays on Britishness," *Scottish Affairs* 2 (Winter 1993), 73–74.

46. Ernest Gellner, *Nations and Nationalism* (Oxford: Blackwell, 1983), 138.

47. Robert R. Palmer, "The National Idea in France before the Revolution," *Journal of the History of Ideas* 1, no. 1 (January 1940), 96, 98–99.

48. "Address from the Society of United Irishmen in Dublin, 1792," reproduced in Elaine W. McFarland, *Ireland and Scotland in the Age of Revolution: Planting the Green Bough* (Edinburgh: Edinburgh University Press, 1994), appendix 2, 250.

49. Peter J. Taylor, "The English and Their Englishness: 'A Curiously Mysterious, Elusive and Little Understood People,'" *Scottish Geographical Magazine* 107, no. 3 (1991), 148.

50. For the United Netherlands see Jonathan I. Israel, *The Dutch Republic: Its Rise, Greatness, and Fall, 1477–1806* (Oxford: Clarendon Press, 1998), 1085–87 and chapter 42; for Britain, see Linda Colley, "The Apotheosis of George III: Loyalty, Royalty and the British Nation, 1760–1830," *Past and Present* 102 (February 1983), 115–117.

51. Bernard Crick, *George Orwell: A Life* (London: Secker and Warburg, 1980), 22.

52. George Orwell [1945], "Notes on Nationalism," in *The Collected Essays, Journalism and Letters of George Orwell*, vol. 3, *As I Please, 1943–1945*, edited by Ian Angus and Sonia Orwell (Harmondsworth: Penguin, 1970), 411.

53. Johan H. Huizinga, "Patriotism and Nationalism in European History," in *Men and Ideas: History, the Middle Ages, the Renaissance* (London: Eyre & Spottiswoode, 1960), 97–99.

54. Any doubt that Orwell means "nationalism" where he writes "patriotism" can be dispelled by consulting John Newsinger, *Orwell's Politics* (Houndmills: Macmillan, 1999), chapter 4, a critical but sympathetic Marxist account that supersedes all previous discussion of the subject.

55. Billig, *Banal Nationalism*, 55–59.

56. Frederick M. Barnard, "National Culture and Political Legitimacy: Herder and Rousseau," *Journal of the History of Ideas* 44, no. 2 (April 1983), 231.

57. Quoted in Moses I. Finley [1954], "The Ancient Greeks and Their Nation," in *The Use and Abuse of History* (Harmondsworth: Penguin, 1987), 123.

58. John Plamenatz, "Two Types of Nationalism," in *Nationalism: The Nature and Evolution of an Idea*, edited by Eugene Kamenka (London: Edward Arnold, 1976), 23–24.

59. Smith, *Nationalism and Modernism*, 90.

60. Ibid., 74, 90.

61. Barnard, "National Culture and Political Legitimacy," 250–51.

62. Finley, "The Ancient Greeks and Their Nation," 131.

Chapter 3: National Consciousness to Nation-States

1. Quentin Skinner, *The Foundations of Modern Political Thought*, vol. 2, *The Age of Reformation* (Cambridge: Cambridge University Press, 1978), 351–52, 353, 354. Ian Birchall has argued, or, rather, asserted that Skinner is wrong, in an attempt to defend his thesis that Gracchus Babeuf, organizer of the Conspiracy of Equals against the Directory during the French Revolution, was engaged in the same struggle for freedom as the modern proletariat. See Ian H. Birchall, *The Spectre of Babeuf* (Houndmills: Macmillan, 1997), 3. Birchall makes a convincing case for Babeuf but would not, I trust, make the same case for Spartacus or Watt Tyler, other than in the most elementary sense that all three men were resisting exploitation and oppression. If this is not so then why do Marxists bother to distinguish between the slave, feudal, and capitalist modes of production? Karl Kautsky, although an elephantine pedant and ultimately a renegade, did nevertheless urge a sensible caution against "two dangers" that faced historical investigators who were also engaged in contemporary politics: "in the first place, they may attempt to mould the past entirely after the image of the present, and, in the second place, they may seek to behold the past in the light of the needs of present-day policy." Kautsky [1908], *Foundations of Christianity: A Study of Christian Origins* (London: Orbach and Chambers, no date of publication), 10.

2. Valentin N. Voloshinov [1929], *Marxism and the Philosophy of Language* (Cambridge, MA: Harvard University Press, 1986), 19.

3. Adrian Hastings, *The Construction of Nationhood: Ethnicity, Religion and Nationalism* (Cambridge: Cambridge University Press, 1997), 15–17.

4. Susan Reynolds [1984], *Kingdoms and Communities in Western Europe, 900–1300* (Second edition, Oxford: Clarendon Press, 1997), 250, 254, 255–56.

5. Susan Reynolds, "Medieval *Origines Gentium* and the Community of the Realm," *History* 68, no. 224 (October 1983), 377. Colin Kidd has argued that the Japhetan genealogy was dominant down to the seventeenth century at least in *British Identities before Nationalism: Ethnicity and Nationhood in the Atlantic World, 1600–1800* (Cambridge: Cambridge University Press, 1999), 9–10 and chapter 2 more generally.

6. Quoted in Robert Bartlett, *The Making of Europe: Conquest, Colonization and Cultural Change, 950–1350* (London: Allen Lane, 1993), 198.

7. Anthony D. Smith, *Theories of Nationalism* (London: Harper and Row, 1971), 167.

8. Bartlett, *The Making of Europe*, 202. As Reynolds writes: "There is no foundation at all for the belief, common among students of modern nationalism, that the word *natio* was seldom used in the Middle Ages except to describe the *nationes* into which university students were divided." *Kingdoms and Communities in Western Europe*, 256.

9. Bartlett, *The Making of Europe*, 201–02.

10. Josep R. Llobera, *The God of Modernity: The Development of Nationalism in Western Europe* (Providence: Berg, 1994), 153.

11. John R. Hale, *Renaissance Europe, 1480–1520* (Glasgow: Fontana, 1971), 55.

12. Reynolds, *Kingdoms and Communities in Western Europe*, 251–54.

13. Brendan O'Leary, "Ernest Gellner's Diagnoses of Nationalism: A Critical Overview, or, What Is Living and What Is Dead in Ernest Gellner's Philosophy of Nationalism?," in *The State of the Nation: Ernest Gellner and the Theory of Nationalism*, edited by John A. Hall (Cambridge: Cambridge University Press, 1998), 55.

14. Ernest Gellner, *Nations and Nationalism* (Oxford: Blackwell, 1983), 35, 141.

15. The most recent example, which specifically targets the writings of Eric Hobsbawm, can be found in Hastings, *The Construction of Nationhood*, a work that inspired William Ferguson to claim that Hastings had "exploded" the view that "nations, nationhood and nationalism cannot pre-date 1780." *The Identity of the Scottish Nation: An Historic Quest* (Edinburgh: Edinburgh University Press, 1998), 301. For similar remarks see also Fiona J. Watson, "The Enigmatic Lion: Scotland, Kingship and National Identity in the Wars of Independence," in *Image and Identity: The Making and Remaking of Scotland*, edited by Dauvit Broun, Richard. J. Finlay, and Michael Lynch (Edinburgh: John Donald, 1998), 31, note 58.

16. Ernest Gellner, "Reply to Critics," in *The Social Philosophy of Ernest Gellner*, edited by John A. Hall and Ian C. Jarvie (Amsterdam: Rodopi, 1996), 638.

17. John R. Hale, *The Civilization of Europe in the Renaissance* (London: Harper Collins, 1993), 68.

18. Hale, *Renaissance Europe*, 320.

19. J. Derrick McClure, "The Concept of Standard Scots," *Chapman* 23/24 (Spring 1979), 90–91.

20. Ibid., 91. Compare Eric J. Hobsbawm on this subject: "Dialects, as everyone knows, are just languages without an army and police force." *The Age of Empire, 1873–1914* (London: Weidenfeld and Nicolson, 1987), 156.

21. Michael Billig, *Banal Nationalism* (London: Sage Publications, 1995), 30, 31.

22. Lucien Febvre and Henri-Jean Martin, *The Coming of the Book: The Impact of Printing, 1450–1800* (London: New Left Books, 1976), 258–59.

23. Hale, *The Civilization of Europe in the Renaissance*, 68.

24. Ibid., 153–54.

25. Michael Mann, "The Emergence of Modern European Nationalism," in *Transitions to Modernity: Essays on Power, Wealth and Belief*, edited by John A. Hall and Ian C. Jarvie (Cambridge: Cambridge University Press, 1992), 162. See also Nigel Harris, *National Liberation* (Harmondsworth: Penguin, 1992), 28–29.

26. John W. Cairns, "Institutional Writings in Scotland Reconsidered," in *New Perspectives in Scottish Legal History*, edited by Albert K. R. Kirafy and Hector L. MacQueen (London: Frank Cass, 1984), 78.

27. Eric J. Hobsbawm, *Nations and Nationalism since 1780: Program, Myth, Reality* (Cambridge: Cambridge University Press, 1990), 46. It should be obvious from these observations that Hobsbawm does not believe that "nations, nationhood, and nationalism" simply appeared around 1780 without any preceding history of development, contrary to what is claimed in the references cited in note 15 above.

28. Peter Furtado, "National Pride in Seventeenth-Century England," in *Patriotism: The Making and Unmaking of British National Identity*, vol. 1, *History and Politics*, edited by Raphael Samuel (London: Routledge, 1989), 44.

29. Llobera, *The God of Modernity*, 141–42.

30. Quoted in Fernand Braudel, *Civilization and Capitalism*, vol. 2, *The Wheels of Commerce* (London: Fontana, 1982), 467.

31. It is therefore placing the existence of a full-blown English nationalism too early to argue, as Liah Greenfield does, that it arose during the reign of Henry VIII to legitimize the position of a "new" Henrican aristocracy based on merit rather than birth. See Greenfield, *Nationalism: Five Roads to Modernity* (Cambridge, MA: Harvard University Press, 1992), chapter 1. Nevertheless, Mann is surely right to argue that the transition from "nation" in "the medieval sense of a group united by common blood descent" to "the general population of the territorial state" had been accomplished in England before the outbreak of the War of the Three Kingdoms in 1638. See Michael Mann, *The Sources of Social Power*, vol. 1, *A History of Power from the Beginning to A.D. 1760* (Cambridge: Cambridge University Press, 1986), 463, 435. For an earlier version of this argument see Hans Kohn, "The Genesis and Character of English Nationalism," *Journal of the History of Ideas* 1, no. 1 (January 1940).

32. Ellen Meiksins Wood, *The Origin of Capitalism* (New York: Monthly Review Press, 1999), 13–14.

33. Such as the work of the "famous historian" to whom Wood presumably refers, the anti-Marxist zealot J. H. Hexter. See Hexter [1948–50], "The Myth of the Middle Class in Tudor England," in *Reappraisals in History* (London: Longmans, Green and Company, 1961), 71–75.

34. In one interview with Lee Humber and John Rees, conducted during 1992, Hill explained this decision on the grounds that "using the word 'bourgeoisie' is like a red rag to most academics. Even the most intelligent of them, Lawrence Stone for example, believe that the bourgeoisie must have something to do with the towns and that if you can prove that the gentry were the main capi-

talists in England in the seventeenth century you've disproved the idea of a bourgeois revolution. But to have to explain this every time you use the word bourgeois is a bore. It's much easier to just leave out the word bourgeois. . . . Initially I thought that I had to drop the jargon in order to get people to treat me seriously." "The Good Old Cause—An Interview with Christopher Hill," *International Socialism* 2:56 (Autumn 1992), 130–31.

35. Hal Draper, *Karl Marx's Theory of Revolution*, vol. 2, *The Politics of Social Classes* (New York: Monthly Review Press, 1978), 169.

36. See chapter 2 in this volume, 38–40.

37. John Breuilly, *Nationalism and the State* (Second edition, Manchester: Manchester University Press, 1993), 3–4.

38. Antonio Gramsci, "The Renaissance," in *Selections from the Cultural Writings*, edited by David Forgacs and Geoffrey Nowell-Smith (London: Lawrence and Wishart, 1985), 226, Q5§123, and "The Question of the Language and the Italian Intellectual Classes," ibid., 169, Q3§76. See also John Larner, *Italy in the Age of Dante and Petrarch, 1216–1380* (London: Longman, 1980), 1–9.

39. Billig, *Banal Nationalism*, 25.

40. Greenfield, *Nationalism*, 47.

41. For a useful synoptic account of the Swiss and Dutch states from their formation to their respective transformation into the Helvetic and Batavian Republics during the French Revolution, see Murray G. Forsyth, *Unions of States: The Theory and Practice of Confederation* (New York: Continuum International Publishing, 1981), chapter 2. The comments of Fredy Perlman on the United States that emerged from the War of Independence in 1784 can also be applied to its Swiss and Dutch predecessors: "The North American colonizers broke the traditional bonds of fealty and feudal obligation, but, unlike the French, they only gradually replaced the traditional bonds with bonds of patriotism and nationhood. They were not quite a nation; their reluctant mobilization of the colonial countryside had not fused them into one; and the multi-lingual, multi-cultural and socially divided underlying population resisted such a fusion." *The Continuing Appeal of Nationalism* (Detroit: Red and Black, 1985), 15. For a discussion of the American Civil War as the decisive moment in the formation of both national consciousness and nationalism in America, see Susan-Mary Grant, "'The Charter of Its Birthright': The Civil War and American Nationalism," *Nations and Nationalism* 4, no. 2 (July 1998).

42. L. L. Farrar, Kiernan McGuire, and John E. Thompson, "Dog in the Night: The Limits of European Nationalism, 1789–1895," *Nations and Nationalism* 4, no. 4 (October 1998), 550, 565.

43. Quoted in ibid., 555.

44. Quoted in Bruce Haddock, "State and Nation in Mazzini's Political Thought," *History of Political Thought* 20, no. 2 (Summer 1999), 321, 323.

45. Eugen Weber, *Peasants into Frenchmen: The Modernization of Rural France, 1870–1914* (Stanford: Stanford University Press, 1977), 67.

46. Ralph Miliband, "Barnave: A Case of Bourgeois Class Consciousness," in *Aspects of History and Class Consciousness*, edited by István Mészáros (London: Routledge and Kegan Paul, 1971), 22–23. Most discussions involve a similarly hierarchical conception of class consciousness, although with fewer levels. R. J. Morris, for

example, lists, in ascending order, "consensus," "labor consciousness," and "revolutionary class consciousness." See *Class and Class Consciousness in the Industrial Revolution, 1750–1850* (London: Macmillan, 1979), 37. Mann sees class consciousness involving four elements: an "identity" of common interests, an "opposition" to the interests of the capitalist class, a sense of "totality" that combines identity and opposition into a coherent worldview of the worker's situation within society, and finally the vision of an "alternative" type of society. See Michael Mann, *Consciousness and Action among the Western Working Class* (London: Macmillan, 1973), 13.

47. Miliband, "Barnave," 23.

48. Vladimir I. Lenin, "What Is to Be Done?," in *Collected Works*, vol. 5, *May 1901–February 1902* (Moscow: Foreign Languages Publishing House, 1961), 375 and 374–85 more generally. For an illuminating attempt to analyze class consciousness during the Industrial Revolution using strict Leninist categories, "trade-union consciousness" among them, see John Foster, *Class Struggle and the Industrial Revolution: Early Industrial Capitalism in Three English Towns* (London: Weidenfeld and Nicolson, 1974), especially 42–43.

49. Karl Marx, *Capital: A Critique of Political Economy*, vol. 1 (Harmondsworth: Penguin/New Left Review, 1976), 680. For an attempt to draw out the gap between the potential explanation of reformism as being found in the theory of commodity fetishism and the actual ad-hoc explanations advanced by Marx and Engels at various stages in their careers, see Carol Johnston, "The Problem of Reformism and Marx's Theory of Fetishism," *New Left Review* I/119 (January/February 1980). The significance of commodity fetishism and the related concept of alienation as the basis of the contradictory consciousness we call reformism has been demonstrated in detail by John Rees, *The Algebra of Revolution: The Dialectic and the Classical Marxist Tradition* (London: Routledge, 1998), 87–97, 220–25, 240–44.

50. Antonio Gramsci [1929–34], "The Study of Philosophy," in *Selections from the Prison Notebooks of Antonio Gramsci*, edited by Quintin Hoare and Geoffrey Nowell-Smith (London: Lawrence and Wishart, 1971), 327, 333, Q11§12.

51. Wilhelm Reich [1934], "What Is Class Consciousness?," in *Sex/Pol: Essays, 1929–1934*, edited by Lee Baxandall (New York: Vintage Books, 1972), 313. By "class consciousness" Reich means revolutionary class consciousness.

52. George Kerevan, "The Origins of Scottish Nationhood: Arguments within Scottish Marxism," *The Bulletin of Scottish Politics* 1, no. 2 (Spring 1981), 118–19.

53. Alex Callinicos, *Making History: Agency, Structure and Change in Social Theory* (Cambridge: Polity Press, 1987), 156–57.

54. Benedict Anderson [1983], *Imagined Communities: Reflections on the Rise and Spread of Nationalism* (Second, revised edition, London: Verso, 1991), 36.

55. Chris Harman, "The Return of the National Question," *International Socialism* 2:56 (Autumn 1992), 42–43.

56. R. W. Davies, *The Industrialization of Soviet Russia*, vol. 4, *Crisis and Progress in the Soviet Economy, 1931–1933* (Houndmills: Palgrave Macmillan, 1996), 485–88.

57. Alexander R. Luria, *Cognitive Development: Its Cultural and Social Foundations*, edited by Michael Cole (Cambridge, MA: Harvard University Press, 1976), 12–14, 163–64.

58. Georg Simmel [1903], "The Metropolis and Mental Life," in *On Individuality and Social Forms*, edited by Donald N. Levine (Chicago: University of Chicago Press, 1971), 325.

59. Tom Nairn [1975], "The Modern Janus," in *The Break-up of Britain: Crisis and Neo-nationalism* (London: Verso, 1981), 354.

60. Kerevan, "The Origins of Scottish Nationhood," 118–19.

61. Karl Marx [1843–44], "Critique of Hegel's Philosophy of Right. Introduction," in *Early Writings* (Harmondsworth: Penguin/New Left Review, 1975), 244.

62. Ernest Gellner, "Nationalism and Politics in Eastern Europe," *New Left Review* I/189 (September/October 1991), 121.

63. Breuilly, *Nationalism and the State*, 414.

64. Peter Linebaugh and Marcus Rediker, "The Many-Headed Hydra: Sailors, Slaves, and the Atlantic Working Class in the Eighteenth Century," *Journal of Historical Sociology* 3, no. 3 (September 1990), 245.

65. Valentin N. Voloshinov [1929], "Literary Stylistics 3: The Word and Its Social Function," in *Bahktin School Papers: Russian Poetics in Translation*, edited by Ann Shukman (Somerton: Old School House, 1988), 147.

66. Voloshinov, *Marxism and the Philosophy of Language*, 23.

67. Colley, "The Apotheosis of George III," 126.

Chapter 4: Marxism and Nationhood:
Two Replies to John Foster

1. Contrary to what Foster says, I am not so immodest as to claim "to be the first [Marxist] to write comprehensively on Scottish history," since I am obviously aware of the work of Angus Calder, Ian Carter, James Hunter, Victor Kiernan, and James D. Young, in addition to his own. My only claim is that I am the first to make a comprehensive case for Scottish nationhood being formed after the Union.

2. John Foster, "Nationality, Social Change and Class: Transformations of National Identity in Scotland," in *The Making of Scotland: Nation, Culture and Social Change*, edited by David McCrone, Stephen Kendrick, and Pat Straw (Edinburgh: Polygon Books, 1989), 35–36.

3. As I note in the first very first paragraph of the preface, *The Origins of Scottish Nationhood* began as the last chapter of a larger work on the bourgeois revolution in Scotland. That work provides a more appropriate setting for discussion of the economic aspects of Scottish development. There is a summary of the argument in Neil Davidson, "Scotland's Bourgeois Revolution," in *Scotland, Class and Nation* (London: Bookmarks, 1999).

4. See chapters 2 and 3 in this volume.

5. My misunderstanding is shared by, among others, a historian from an earlier generation than Foster, but one similarly associated with the Communist Party of Great Britain, Eric J. Hobsbawm: "The basic characteristic of the modern nation and everything connected with it is its modernity. This is now well understood . . ." Eric J. Hobsbawm, *Nations and Nationalism since 1780: Program, Myth, Reality* (Cambridge: Cambridge University Press, 1990), 14 and chapter 1, "The Nation as Novelty: From Revolution to Liberalism," more generally.

As this suggests, my view of the nation is not simply derived from sociologists like Ernest Gellner, as Foster insinuates, but from an entire modernist tradition, of which Marxism was part. It is worth noting that in every other respect Hobsbawm shares the same Popular Front–inspired view of contemporary nationalism as Foster himself: rejecting the "separatism" of the national movements within Britain on the one hand, while accepting the need to identify with working-class "patriotism" on the other. See, respectively, "Some Reflections on *The Break-up of Britain*," *New Left Review* I/105 (September/October 1977), and "Falklands Fallout," in *The Politics of Thatcherism*, edited by Stuart Hall and Martin Jacques (London: Lawrence and Wishart, 1983).

6. John Foster: "Capitalism and the Scottish Nation," *Scottish Marxist* 4 (June 1973), 9; "Capitalism and the Scottish Nation," in *The Red Paper on Scotland*, edited by Gordon Brown (Edinburgh: Edinburgh University Student Publications Board, 1975), 142; "Scottish Nationality and the Origins of Capitalism," *Scottish Capitalism: Class, State and Nation from before the Union to the Present*, edited by Tony Dickson (London: Lawrence and Wishart, 1980), 56; "Nationality, Social Change and Class," 35. See also John Foster and Charles Woolfson, *The Politics of the UCS Work-In* (London: Lawrence and Wishart, 1986), 57–58.

7. I do not, however, believe that "prior to the Union there was no Scottish capitalism," simply that, unlike in England during the same period, capitalism was not the dominant mode of production. Foster's carelessness with what I have actually written does not stop here. It is not true that I dismiss "the legal system and the ministry [of the Church of Scotland] as quasi-feudal corporations." I certainly describe the former in these terms (and offer evidence as to why this was the case), but I make a point of stating that because of this "it was left to *religion* to incubate a protonational consciousness" and that the Kirk was "the only institution over which the plebeians exercised any democratic control." *The Origins of Scottish Nationhood* (London: Pluto Press, 2000), 61, 62.

8. Foster, "Review of *The Origins of Scottish Nationhood*," *Historical Materialism* 10, no. 1 (2002), 268.

9. Davidson, *The Origins of Scottish Nationhood*, 55–56.

10. Edward Dunbar Dunbar, "Power of the Laird of a Barony," in *Social Life in Early Days: Illustrated by Letters and Family Papers* (Second series, Edinburgh: Edmonston and Douglas, 1866), 141–43.

11. Foster, "Review of *The Origins of Scottish Nationhood*," 269.

12. Isabel Guy, "The Scottish Export Trade, 1460–1599," in *Scotland and Europe, 1200–1850*, edited by T. C. Smout (Edinburgh: John Donald, 1986), 63–64, 69–72.

13. Margaret Sanderson, *Scottish Rural Society in the Sixteenth Century* (Edinburgh: John Donald, 1982), 65.

14. Gordon Donaldson, *Scotland: James V–James VII* (Edinburgh: Oliver and Boyd, 1965), 133.

15. Walter Makey, *The Church of the Covenant* (Edinburgh: John Donald, 1979), 2.

16. Foster, "Review of *The Origins of Scottish Nationhood*," 269.

17. Davidson, *The Origins of Scottish Nationhood*, 92–94, 170–71.

18. See ibid., chapter 10, and Christopher A. Whatley, *Scottish Society 1707–1830: Beyond Jacobitism, Towards Industrialization* (Manchester: Manchester University Press,

2000), 307–27. My own argument about the specificity of Scottish working-class development in the early nineteenth century, and its comparability with that of Russia a hundred years later, is in fact similar to the argument Foster makes about the Clydeside working class in the early twentieth century. I think my dates fit better, if only because the Clyde experience was not restricted to Scotland but comparable to that of Belfast and Sheffield. Compare Davidson, *The Origins of Scottish Nationhood*, 167–86, with John Foster, "Working-Class Mobilization on the Clyde 1917–1920," in *Challenges of Labour: Central and Western Europe 1917–1920*, edited by Chris Wrigley (London: Routledge, 1993), 156–59.

19. Foster, "Review of *The Origins of Scottish Nationhood*," 262.
20. Ibid., 270.
21. Ibid., 265.
22. Valentin N. Voloshinov [1929], *Marxism and the Philosophy of Language* (Cambridge, MA: Harvard University Press, 1986), 13. Presumably our contradictory interpretations of the term "sociological" are examples of the "multi-accentuality of the sign."
23. Davidson, *The Origins of Scottish Nationhood*, 3, 6.
24. Vladimir I. Lenin [1916], "Imperialism: The Highest Stage of Capitalism, a Popular Outline," in *Collected Works*, vol. 22, *December 1915–September 1916* (Moscow: Foreign Languages Publishing House, 1964), 266.
25. Vladimir. I. Lenin [1915], "Under a False Flag," in *Collected Works*, vol. 21, *August 1914–December 1915* (Moscow: Foreign Languages Publishing House, 1964), 146.
26. See, for example, references to "the achievements of ancient capitalism" during a discussion of the Roman Empire in Max Weber [1908], *The Agrarian Sociology of Ancient Civilizations* (London: Verso, 1998), 355.
27. Karl Marx [1857–58], *Grundrisse: Foundations of the Critique of Political Economy (Rough Draft)* (Harmondsworth: Penguin/New Left Review, 1973), 105.
28. Foster, "Review of *The Origins of Scottish Nationhood*," 265–66.
29. Norman Geras, *Marx and Human Nature: Refutation of a Legend* (London: Verso, 1983), 61–116.
30. Foster, "Review of *The Origins of Scottish Nationhood*," 266.
31. Paul James, "The Janus Face of History: Cleaving Marxist Theories of Nation and Nationalism," *Canadian Review of Studies of Nationalism* 18, no. 1–2 (1991), 16.
32. I discuss this briefly in relation to Engels in Neil Davidson [2001], "Marx and Engels on the Scottish Highlands," in *Holding Fast to an Image of the Past: Explorations in the Marxist Tradition* (Chicago: Haymarket Books, 2014), 59. In the same essay I also criticize Ephraim Nimni, "Marx, Engels and the National Question," *Science and Society* 53, no. 3 (Autumn 1989), an article with which Foster wrongly implies I am in agreement. See Davidson, "Marx and Engels on the Scottish Highlands," 57–58.
33. Foster, "Review of *The Origins of Scottish Nationhood*," 266.
34. Marx, *Grundrisse*, 495, 472, 486, 494. My italics.
35. In his monumental study of their politics, Hal Draper lists types of writing by Marx and Engels, starting with the first and most important, "books and major essays that were published under the control of the writer, with the usual opportunity for correction, revision, etc.," and finishing, sixth and least significant, with "private notes, notebooks and workbooks." Draper includes even as im-

portant a work as the *Grundrisse* in the latter category: the *Ethnographic Notebooks* fall somewhere below this in terms of how seriously they must be taken as part of the oeuvre. Hal Draper, *Karl Marx's Theory of Revolution*, vol. 2, *The Politics of Social Classes* (New York: Monthly Review Press, 1978), 3–4.

36. Foster, "Review of *The Origins of Scottish Nationhood*," 263.

37. Karl Marx and Friedrich Engels, "Manifesto of the Communist Party," in *Political Writings*, vol. 1, *The Revolutions of 1848*, edited by David Fernbach (Harmondsworth: Penguin/New Left Review, 1973), 86–87.

38. Karl Marx [1871], "The Civil War in France," in *Political Writings*, vol. 3, *The First International and After*, edited by David Fernbach (Harmondsworth: Penguin/New Left Review, 1973), 212.

39. Karl Marx [1875], "Critique of the Gotha Program," in *The First International and After*, 350.

40. Lenin, in line with most of the Second International, stressed both the centrality of national movements in the transition from feudalism to capitalism and the functionality of the nation-state form for capital. See Vladimir I. Lenin [1914], "The Right of Nations to Self-Determination," in *Collected Works*, vol. 20, *December 1913–August 1914* (Moscow: Foreign Languages Publishing House, 1964), 396–97. For the general background, see Chris Harman, "The Return of the National Question," *International Socialism* 2:56 (Autumn 1992), 19–33.

41. As Sanjay Seth notes, "The historical, cultural, linguistic and other dimensions of nationhood were relegated to a secondary position by Lenin's theory, as against the all-important question of determining which nations were oppressed and which were oppressors (it will be noted that to speak of nations as oppressed and oppressing is already to treat them as a 'given')." The difficulty is that Lenin did not allow "that a choice between one or the other might be necessary, because both socialist and nationalist consciousness were 'determinate'—they did not, even where nationalism was anti-imperialist, necessarily form a continuum in which progress from the former to the latter was a smooth transition." "Lenin's Reformulation of Marxism: The Colonial Question as a National Question," *History of Political Thought* 13, no. 1 (Spring 1992), 124, 126.

42. Lenin, "The Right of Nations to Self-Determination," 453–54.

43. Yulian V. Bromley, *Soviet Ethnography: Main Trends* (Moscow: Social Sciences Today Editorial Board, 1977), 65. But note also this other quote from Lenin: "Proletarian culture must be the logical development of the store of knowledge mankind has developed under the yoke of capitalist, landowner and bureaucratic society." "The Tasks of the Youth Leagues," in *Collected Works*, vol. 31, *April–December 1920* (Moscow: Foreign Languages Publishing House, 1966), 287.

44. Vladimir I. Lenin [1913], "Critical Remarks on the National Question," in *Collected Works*, vol. 20, 24.

45. Vladimir I. Lenin [1916], "The Discussion on Self-Determination Summed Up," in *Collected Works*, vol. 22, 325. Lenin's italics.

46. Ibid., 346. Lenin's italics.

47. Bromley, quoted in Tamara Dragadze, "The Place of 'Ethnos' Theory in Soviet Anthropology," in *Soviet and Western Anthropology*, edited by Ernest Gellner (London: Duckworth, 1980), 162. The first thing to note is that there is nothing remotely Marxist about this definition. And given Foster's hostility to—one feels

that this prefix is unavoidable—"bourgeois" sociology, it is interesting that the work of Bromley and his colleagues was welcomed by Ernest Gellner, the doyen of Western sociologists, for demonstrating the supposedly continuing vitality of Soviet intellectual life. Gellner was quite right to see an affinity between Western sociologists and their Soviet counterparts. Compare, for example, Bromley's definition of "ethnos" above with the definition of "an ethnic community" by the British political scientist Anthony D. Smith as "a collective proper name, a myth of common ancestry, shared historical memories, one or more differentiating elements of common culture, an association with a specific 'homeland,' and a sense of solidarity for significant sectors of the population." *National Identity* (Harmondsworth: Penguin, 1991), 21. Foster's discussion of Smith is deeply confused. He writes: "Smith sought to link ethnicity to national consciousness in terms of a myth of common ancestry or kinship and a common position within an international division of labour. Such characteristics are, however, 'virtually impossible to find today and have been since before the rise of capitalism.' Davidson finds only one of Smith's criteria relevant: that of 'shared identity,' which mirrors the subjective definition of Seton-Watson." Foster is confusing Smith's argument (ethnicity as a myth of common ancestry) with mine (ethnicity can be either be biological kinship, occupational location, or social identity). See chapter 1 in this volume.

48. Yulian V. Bromley, "The Object and the Subject of Ethnography," in *Soviet and Western Anthropology*, 153.
49. Bromley, *Soviet Ethnography*, 15. See also "The Object and the Subject of Ethnography," 155.
50. Bromley, *Soviet Ethnography*, 64.
51. In 1982 *Pravda* reported an announcement by then Soviet premier Yuri Andropov to the effect that national distinctions would outlast class distinctions. See *Pravda* (December 22, 1982).
52. Marcus Banks, *Ethnicity: Anthropological Constructions* (London: Routledge, 1996), 22–23.
53. Ibid., 23.
54. Ronald Suny, "Incomplete Revolution: National Movements and the Collapse of the Soviet Empire," *New Left Review* I/189 (September/October 1991), 113.
55. Suny describes the confusion that reigned at the annual conference of Soviet ethnographers following the attempted coup of August 1991 and the subsequent collapse of the USSR. See ibid., 111–12.
56. Foster, "Review of *The Origins of Scottish Nationhood*," 270.
57. Charles Woolfson, "Culture, Language, and the Human Personality," *Marxism Today* 21, no. 7 (Autumn 1977), 234.
58. Alex Callinicos, "The Politics of *Marxism Today*," *International Socialism* 2:29 (Summer 1985), 162.
59. Slavoj Žižek, "Postface: Georg Lukács as the Philosopher of Leninism," in *A Defense of History and Class Consciousness* (London: Verso, 2000), 173.
60. Foster, "Review of *The Origins of Scottish Nationhood*," 266.
61. Voloshinov died in a Stalinist labor camp around the same time that Dimitrov was making this apologia for Russian foreign policy. His work was written at a ferociously high level of abstraction—perhaps in a vain attempt to throw the heresy hunters off his track—but even so, to claim that it has anything in com-

mon with the politics of the bureaucratic ruling class that sent him to his death is quite grotesque.

62. Georgi Dimitrov, *The Working Class against Fascism* (London: Martin Lawrence, 1935), 69–72. Dimitrov attempts to enlist Lenin in his support with a decontextualized quotation from "On the National Pride of the Great Russians" (in much the same way as Bromley does with the same article and "The Tasks of the Youth Leagues," and Foster does with "Critical Remarks on the National Question").For the context, see Vladimir I. Lenin [1914], "On the National Pride of the Great Russians," in *Collected Works*, vol. 21, 103–04.

63. Neil Davidson, "Tom Nairn and the Inevitability of Nationalism," in *Holding Fast to an Image of the Past*, 31–34.

64. Foster, "Review of *The Origins of Scottish Nationhood*," 270.

65. David Harvey, "Working Men of All Countries, Unite!," in *Spaces of Hope* (Edinburgh: Edinburgh University Press, 2000), 50–51.

66. Foster, "Review of *The Origins of Scottish Nationhood*," 270.

67. See the report in the *Scots Independent*, new series, vol. 3, no. 10 (June 1938). Calgacus was the quasi-mythical leader whom Tacitus claims led the Picts to glorious defeat against the Romans at Mons Gropius in 87 AD.

68. Foster and Woolfson, *The Politics of the UCS Work-In*, 59. For an attempt "to use pre-existing national identities to split the new proletariat" by Sir Walter Scott, see Davidson, *The Origins of Scottish Nationhood*, 199.

69. Peter Linebaugh and Marcus Rediker, *The Many-Headed Hydra: The Hidden History of the Revolutionary Atlantic* (London: Verso, 2000), 352. For a reference to an earlier version of this argument by the same authors, see chapter 3 in this volume.

70. Foster, "Review of *The Origins of Scottish Nationhood*," 270.

71. Davidson, *The Origins of Scottish Nationhood*, 204–10.

72. Foster, "Scottish Nationality and the Origins of Capitalism."

73. Richard J. Finlay, "Keeping the Covenant: Scottish National Identity," in *Eighteenth-Century Scotland: New Perspectives*, edited by Thomas M. Devine and John R. Young (East Linton: Tuckwell Press, 1999), 120–21.

74. But see George Kerevan, "The Origins of Scottish Nationhood: Arguments within Scottish Marxism," *Bulletin of Scottish Politics* 1, no. 2 (1981), for one of the rare exceptions.

75. Davidson, *The Origins of Scottish Nationhood*, 5–6, 47, 213, note 14.

76. Richard. J. Finlay, "Understanding Scotland: The State of the Nation, 1707–1830," *Scottish Affairs* 37 (Autumn 2001), 132.

77. Ibid., 130–31.

78. Foster, "Nationality, Social Change and Class," 35.

79. Neal Ascherson, *Stone Voices: The Search for Scotland* (London: Granta Books, 2002), 269, 273–74.

80. Antonio Gramsci [1929–34], "Problems of Marxism," in *Selections from the Prison Notebooks*, edited by Quintin Hoare and Geoffrey Nowell-Smith (London: Lawrence and Wishart, 1971), 423, Q11§13.

81. Phillip Spencer and Howard Wollman, *Nationalism: A Critical Introduction* (London: Sage, 2002), 33.

82. Ernest Gellner, *Nations and Nationalism* (Oxford: Blackwell, 1983), 138.

83. Anthony D. Smith, *The Ethnic Origins of Nations* (Oxford: Blackwell, 1986); Liah

Greenfield, *Nationalism: Five Roads to Modernity* (Cambridge, MA: Harvard University Press, 1992); John Hutchinson, *Modern Nationalism* (London: Fontana Books, 1994); Adrian Hastings, *The Construction of Nationhood: Ethnicity, Religion and Nationalism* (Cambridge: Cambridge University Press, 1997); Emmanuel Todd, *La Diversité du monde: Famille et modernité* (Paris: Éditions du Seuil, 1999).

84. Tom Nairn, "Out of the Cage," *London Review of Books* 26, no. 12 (June 24, 2004), 13.

85. Hastings, *The Construction of Nationhood*, 205.

86. Attention! This is sarcasm, not a confession.

87. Davidson, *The Origins of Scottish Nationhood*, 55–56, 62–63.

88. Neil Davidson, *Discovering the Scottish Revolution, 1692–1746* (London: Pluto Press, 2003), chapter 3, "From Hanoverian Succession to Incorporating Union (1700–1707)."

89. Foster, "Marxists, Weberians and Nationality: A Response to Neil Davidson," *Historical Materialism* 12, no. 1 (2002), 171.

90. Karl Miller, *Electric Shepherd: A Likeness of James Hogg* (London: Faber and Faber, 2003), 145–49.

91. James Hogg [1824], *The Private Memoirs and Confessions of a Justified Sinner*, edited by John Wain (Harmondsworth: Penguin, 1987), 30, 38.

92. Ibid., 30, 37.

93. See the classic discussion in Georg Lukács [1937], *The Historical Novel* (Harmondsworth: Penguin, 1969), 32–33. For an application of this approach in relation to the figure of Henry Morton in *Old Mortality*, see Angus and Jenni Calder, *Scott* (London: Evans Brothers, 1969), 100–103.

94. Foster, "Marxists, Weberians and Nationality," 164–67.

95. Ibid., 155.

96. It may be, of course, that Foster considers anyone who does not share his interpretation of Marxism to be a Weberian by default—on the basis of his most recent response that seems quite likely—but I think that the range of theoretical options open to scholars is rather broader than either Marx or Weber, with the exception of the issue of social class, where all serious approaches ultimately derive from one or the other.

97. Max Weber [1904], *On the Methodology of the Social Sciences*, edited by Edward A. Shils and Henry A. Finch (Glencoe: The Free Press, 1949), 90.

98. See chapter 2 in this volume, 39.

99. See chapter 3 in this volume, 65.

100. See chapter 3 in this volume, 56–62.

101. Foster, "Marxists, Weberians and Nationality," 159.

102. Lenin, "Imperialism," 266.

103. Weber, *On the Methodology of the Social Sciences*, 44.

104. Max Weber [1895], "The Nation State and Economic Policy (Inaugural Lecture)," in *Political Writings*, edited by Peter Lassman and Ronald Spiers (Cambridge: Cambridge University Press, 1994), 5, 16–17.

105. Max Weber [1916], "Between Two Laws," in *Political Writings*, 75.

106. Max Weber [1922], "Structures of Power," in *From Max Weber: Essays in Sociology*, edited by Hans H. Gerth and C. Wright Mills (London: Routledge and Kegan Paul, 1948), 176, 179.

107. Foster, "Marxists, Weberians and Nationality," 166.

108. See chapter 3 in this volume, 55.

109. Foster, "Marxists, Weberians and Nationality," 160.

110. Karl Marx and Friedrich Engels [1845–46], *The German Ideology: Critique of Modern German Philosophy according to Its Representatives Feuerbach, B. Bauer and Stirner, and of German Socialism according to Its Various Prophets*, in *Collected Works*, vol. 5 (London: Lawrence and Wishart, 1976), 32.

111. Foster, "Marxists, Weberians and Nationality," 160.

112. Hobsbawm, *Nations and Nationalism since 1780*, 24.

113. Michael Mann, *The Sources of Social Power*, vol. 2, *The Rise of Classes and Nation-States, 1760–1914* (Cambridge: Cambridge University Press, 1993), 299–300.

114. Marx and Engels, *The German Ideology*, 73–74.

115. Hal Draper, *Karl Marx's Theory of Revolution*, vol. 1, *State and Bureaucracy* (New York: Monthly Review Press, 1978), 23–26; John Rees, "Engels' Marxism," *International Socialism* 2:65 (1994), special issue, *The Revolutionary Ideas of Frederick Engels* (1994), 47–56.

116. Friedrich Engels [1884], "[On the Early History of the Germans]," in *Collected Works*, vol. 26 (London: Lawrence and Wishart, 1990), 29, 30.

117. Friedrich Engels [1884], "[The Decline of Feudalism and the Rise of Nation States]," in *Collected Works*, vol. 26, 559, 560, 565.

118. Friedrich Engels [1884], "Marx and the *Neue Rheinische Zeitung* (1848–49)," in *Collected Works*, vol. 26, 124.

119. Foster, "Marxists, Weberians and Nationality," 157.

120. Geoffrey de Ste Croix, *The Class Struggle in the Ancient Greek World: From the Archaic Age to the Arab Conquests* (London: Duckworth, 1981), 43–44, 49–52.

121. See chapter 2 in this volume, 36–38.

122. Otto Bauer [1907], *The Question of Nationalities and Self-Determination*, edited by Ephraim J. Nimni (Minneapolis: University of Minnesota Press, 2000), 3.

123. See chapter 2 in this volume.

124. Karl Marx [1859], "Preface to *A Contribution to the Critique of Political Economy*," in *Early Writings* (Harmondsworth: Penguin/New Left Review, 1975), 425.

125. Georg Lukács [1923], "What Is Orthodox Marxism?," in *History and Class Consciousness: Studies in Marxist Dialectics* (London: Merlin Press, 1971), 9.

126. Georg Lukács [1923], "The Changing Function of Historical Materialism," in *History and Class Consciousness*, 238–39.

127. Hastings, *The Construction of Nationhood*, 19.

128. Alasdair MacIntyre, *A Short History of Ethics: A History of Moral Philosophy from the Homeric Age to the Twentieth Century* (London: Routledge and Kegan Paul, 1966), 2, 8.

129. See chapter 3 in this volume, 51–53 and, for example, Elie Kedourie [1960], *Nationalism* (London: Hutchinson University Library, 1966), 13–15.

130. Lucien Febvre [1942], *The Problem of Unbelief in the Sixteenth Century* (Cambridge, MA: Harvard University Press, 1982), 455, 460, 462.

131. For a summary of these problems, see Peter Burke, *The French Historical Revolution: The Annales School, 1929–89* (Cambridge: Polity Press, 1990), 30.

132. Foster et al., "Scottish Nationality and the Origins of Capitalism," 38.

133. Foster, "Marxists, Weberians and Nationality," 162, 163.

134. Vladimir I. Lenin [1916], "Letter to Inessa Armand, November 30, 1916," in *Collected Works*, vol. 35, *Letters: February 1912–December 1922* (Moscow: Foreign Languages Publishing House, 1972), 251.

135. Vladimir I. Lenin [1916], "The Socialist Revolution and the Right of Nations to Self-Determination," in *Collected Works*, vol. 22, 146–47. Extracts from the debate within the left of the Second International can be found in *Lenin's Struggle for a Revolutionary International: Documents: 1907–1916, The Preparatory Years*, edited by John Riddell (New York: Monad Press, 1984), 348–79.

136. Foster, "Marxists, Weberians and Nationality," 173.

CHAPTER 5: ENLIGHTENMENT AND ANTI-CAPITALISM

1. Michel Foucault [1984], "What Is Enlightenment?," in *The Foucault Reader: An Introduction to Foucault's Thought*, edited by Paul Rabinow (Harmondsworth: Penguin, 1986), 43. As these remarks suggest, Foucault cannot be uncomplicatedly recuperated in support of claims that Enlightenment is inherently oppressive. See Peter Dews [1979], "The *Nouvelle Philosophie* and Foucault," in *Towards a Critique of Foucault: Foucault, Lacan and the Question of Ethics*, edited by Mike Gane (London: Routledge, 1986), 75–77.

2. Alex Callinicos, *Is There a Future for Marxism?* (London: Macmillan, 1981), 50.

3. The Bible: "Again, a new commandment I write unto you, which thing is true in him and in you: because the darkness is past, and the true light now shineth" (1 John 1:8); the Qur'an: "Thou knewest not what the Scripture was, nor what the Faith. But We have made it a light whereby We guide whom We will of Our bondsmen. And lo! Thou verily dost guide unto a right path" (XLII, 52). The Torah is a different kind of document, which can be interpreted to include the whole of the Judaic tradition, written and oral. In the more traditional and restricted sense, however, the Torah is the five Mosaic books of the biblical Old Testament (i.e., from Genesis to Deuteronomy). "For the commandment is a lamp; and the teaching is a light; and the way to life is the rebuke that disciplines" (Proverbs 6:23). "Torah" can be translated as "teaching" rather than "law," making the holy text itself "the light."

4. Alexander Pope [1730], "Epitaph. Intended for Sir Isaac Newton, in Westminster-Abbey," in *The Poems of Alexander Pope*, edited by John Butt (London: Routledge, 1968), 808.

5. Anthony Arblaster, *Viva Liberta! Politics in Opera* (London: Verso, 1992), 60.

6. Wolfgang Amadeus Mozart and Emanuel Schikaneder [1791], *The Magic Flute* (London: Faber Music, 1980), 68.

7. Quoted in Timothy C. W. Blanning, "The Enlightenment in Catholic Germany," in *The Enlightenment in National Context*, edited by Roy Porter and Mikulas Teich (Cambridge: Cambridge University Press, 1981), 126.

8. Quoted in Roy Porter, *Enlightenment: Britain and the Creation of the Modern World* (London: Allen Lane, 2000), 465.

9. Jonathan I. Israel, *Radical Enlightenment: Philosophy and the Making of Modernity, 1650–1750* (Oxford: Oxford University Press, 2002), 159–60. Israel rightly devotes more space to Spinoza in his great work than to any other individual. See ibid., 159–327.

10. Baruch Spinoza [1670], *Tractatus Theologicus-Politicus* (Leiden: E. J. Brill, 1989), 53.

11. Quoted in Rosalie L. Colie, "Spinoza and the Early English Deists," *Journal of the History of Ideas* 20, no. 1 (January 1959), 28.

12. Michael C. W. Hunter, "'Aikenhead the Atheist': The Context and Consequences of Articulate Irreligion in the Late Seventeenth Century," in *Atheism from the Reformation to the Enlightenment*, edited by Michael C. W. Hunter and David Wooton (Oxford: Clarendon Press, 1992).

13. Robert Darnton [1980/1983], "A Police Inspector Sorts His Files: The Anatomy of the Republic of Letters," in *The Great Cat Massacre and Other Episodes in French Cultural History* (New York: Basic Books, 1984), 186–87.

14. Immanuel Kant [1783], "Answering the Question: What Is Enlightenment?," in *Political Writings*, edited by H. S. Reiss (Second, enlarged edition, Cambridge: Cambridge University Press, 1991), 54.

15. Edmund Gibbon [1776–88], *The Decline and Fall of the Roman Empire*, vol. 3 (London: Chandos Edition, no date identified), 582.

16. Adam Smith, *Lectures on Jurisprudence*, edited by Ronald L. Meek, David D. Raphael, and Peter G. Stein (Oxford: Oxford University Press, 1978), 14, 16.

17. Lord Kames, *Historical Law Tracts*, vol. 1 (Edinburgh: A. Millar, A. Kincaid and J. Bell, 1758), 56.

18. Walter Bagehot [1876], "Adam Smith as a Person," in *Works*, vol. 3, edited by Forrest Morgan (Hartford: Travelers' Insurance Company, 1889), 277.

19. Daniel Defoe [1701], "An Explanatory Preface to *The True-Born Englishman*," in *The Novels and Selected Writings of Daniel Defoe*, vol. 13, *The Shortest Way with Dissenters and Other Pamphlets* (Oxford: Shakespeare Head Press, 1927), 24.

20. Anne-Robert-Jacques Turgot [1750], "A Philosophical Review of the Successive Advances of the Human Mind," in *Turgot on Progress, Sociology and Economics* (Cambridge: Cambridge University Press, 1973), 42, 41.

21. Quoted in Darrell Moellendorf, "Racism and Rationality in Hegel's Philosophy of Subjective Spirit," *History of Political Thought* 13, no. 2 (April 1992), 255.

22. Thomas Jefferson [1818], "The Rockfish Gap Report to the Legislature of Virginia Relative to the University of Virginia, 1–14 August 1818," in *Revolutions, 1775–1830*, edited by Mervyn Williams (Harmondsworth: Penguin, 1971), 195–96. Jefferson served as president of the United States between 1801 and 1809. There could be no starker illustration of the decline of bourgeois civilization than a comparison between the magnificently resonant yet theoretically informed prose of the Declaration and the utterances of George W. Bush during his occupancy of the post once filled by Jefferson.

23. Blaise Pascal [1657–62], *Pensées* (Harmondsworth: Penguin, 1966), 154, note 423.

24. Baruch Spinoza [1675], "Tractatus Politicus," in *The Political Works*, edited by A. G. Wernham (Oxford: Clarendon Press, 1958), 265.

25. David Hume [1739], *A Treatise of Human Nature: Being an Attempt to Introduce the Experimental Method of Reasoning into Moral Subjects*, edited by Pall S. Ardal (London: Fontana, 1972), 156. See also 193.

26. Johann G. von Herder [1797], "Letters for the Advancement of Humanity (1793–1797)—Tenth Collection: Letter 115," in *Philosophical Writings*, edited by Michael N. Forster (Cambridge: Cambridge University Press, 2002), 386.

27. Robin Blackburn, *The Overthrow of Colonial Slavery, 1776–1848* (London: Verso, 1988), 145, 169–76; C. L. R. James, *The Black Jacobins: Toussaint L'Ouverture and*

the San Domingo Revolution (Revised edition, London: Alison and Busby, 1980), 69–75.

28. Sankar Muthu, *Enlightenment against Empire* (Princeton: Princeton University Press, 2003), 282.

29. Charles-Louis de Secondat Montesquieu [1748], *The Spirit of Laws*, edited by D.W. Carrithers (Berkeley: University of California Press, 1977), 262.

30. Georg W. F. Hegel [1830–31], *Lectures on the Philosophy of History* (London: H. G. Bohn, 1857), 95.

31. Michael Hardt and Antonio Negri, *Multitude: War and Democracy in the Age of Empire* (New York: Penguin, 2004), 307, 311, and 306–12 more generally.

32. Spinoza, *Tractatus Theologicus-Politicus*, 297.

33. Ibid., 56.

34. Voltaire to D'Alembert, September 2, 1768, in *Oeuvres complètes*, vol. 46 (Paris: Bernier Frères, 1880), 112.

35. Paul M. Siegel, *The Meek and the Militant: Religion and Power across the World* (London: Zed Books, 1986), 22.

36. Dorinda Outram, *The Enlightenment* (Cambridge: Cambridge University Press, 1995), 122–23; Derek E. D.Beales [1987], "Social Forces and Enlightened Policies," in *Enlightenment and Reform in Eighteenth-Century Europe* (London: I. B. Tauris, 2005), 9–10.

37. Thomas Jefferson [1776], "The Unanimous Declaration of the Thirteen United States of America, 4 July 1776," in *Revolutions*, 45.

38. Howard Zinn, *A People's History of the United States* (London: Harper and Row, 1980), 73.

39. Michael Bérubé, "It's Renaissance Time: New Historicism, American Studies, and American Identity," in *Public Access: Literary Theory and American Cultural Politics* (London: Verso, 1994), 205.

40. Terry Eagleton, *The Illusions of Postmodernism* (Oxford: Blackwell, 1994), 113.

41. Michel Foucault [1977], "Truth and Power," in *Power/Knowledge: Selected Interviews and Other Writings, 1972–1977*, edited by Colin Gordon (Brighton: Harvester Press, 1980), 133.

42. Partha Chatterjee, *Nationalist Thought and the Colonial World: A Derivative Discourse?* (London: Zed Books, 1999), 168.

43. Ellen Meiksins Wood, *The Origin of Capitalism: A Longer View* (London: Verso, 2002), 190.

44. Ibid., 183–89.

45. Robert Darnton, "The Case for the Enlightenment: George Washington's False Teeth," in *George Washington's False Teeth: An Unconventional Guide to the Eighteenth Century* (New York: W.W. Norton, 2003), 4.

46. Israel, *Radical Enlightenment*, 515–27; Porter, *Enlightenment*, 6–12; David Spadafora, *The Idea of Progress in Eighteenth-Century Britain* (New Haven: Yale University Press, 1990), 384.

47. Franco Venturi, *Utopia and Reform in the Enlightenment* (Cambridge: Cambridge University Press, 1971), 133.

48. Alasdair MacIntyre, *After Virtue: A Study in Moral Theory* (Second edition, London: Duckworth, 1985), 37.

49. Neil Davidson, *Discovering the Scottish Revolution, 1692–1746* (London: Pluto

Press, 2003), 275–78; "The Scottish Path to Capitalist Agriculture 3: The Enlightenment as Theory of Improvement (1747–1815)," *Journal of Agrarian Change* 5, no. 1 (January 2005).

50. Mikulas Teich, afterword to *The Enlightenment in National Context*, 216–17. See also Venturi, *Utopia and Reform in the Enlightenment*, 11.

51. David Hume [1752], "Of Interest," in *Political Essays*, edited by Knud Haakonssen (Cambridge: Cambridge University Press, 1994), 131.

52. Albert O. Hirschman, *The Passions and the Interests: Political Arguments for Capitalism before Its Triumph*, 20th anniversary ed. (Princeton: Princeton University Press, 1997), 66, 128–35.

53. Jürgen Habermas [1980], "Modernity—An Incomplete Project," in *Postmodern Culture*, edited by Hal Foster (London: Pluto Press, 1985), 18–19.

54. Louis Dupré, *The Enlightenment and the Intellectual Foundations of Modern Culture* (New Haven: Yale University Press, 2004), 4.

55. Alex Callinicos, *Social Theory: A Historical Introduction* (Cambridge: Polity Press, 1999), 56.

56. Christopher Hill, *Some Intellectual Consequences of the English Revolution* (London: Weidenfeld and Nicolson, 1997), 83, 77.

57. Margaret C. Jacob, *The Radical Enlightenment: Pantheists, Freemasons and Republicans* (London: George Allen and Unwin, 1981), 93–94.

58. Daniel Gordon [1999], "On the Supposed Obsolescence of the French Enlightenment," in *Postmodernism and the Enlightenment: New Perspectives on Eighteenth-Century French History* (London: Routledge, 2001), 204.

59. David McNally, *Against the Market: Political Economy, Market Socialism and the Marxist Critique* (London: Verso, 1993), 75–78.

60. Porter, *Enlightenment*, 470–73.

61. Karl Marx and Friedrich Engels [1848], "Manifesto of the Communist Party," in *Political Writings*, vol. 1, *The Revolutions of 1848*, edited by David Fernbach (Harmondsworth: Penguin/New Left Review, 1974), 85, 73.

62. Karl Marx [1873], "Postface to the Second Edition," in *Capital: A Critique of Political Economy*, vol. 1 (Harmondsworth: Penguin/New Left Review, 1976), 97.

63. Eagleton, *The Illusions of Postmodernism*, 5. See also 125.

64. Edward P. Thompson, *The Making of the English Working Class* (Revised edition, Harmondsworth: Penguin, 1980), 782.

65. Ibid., 81–82.

66. John Keane, *Tom Paine: A Political Life* (London: Bloomsbury Press, 1995), 307–08.

67. Thompson, *The Making of the English Working Class*, 106–07.

68. Robert Burns [1795], "A Man's a Man for a' That," in *The Canongate Burns: The Complete Poems and Songs of Robert Burns*, edited by Andrew Noble and Patrick Stewart Hogg (Edinburgh: Canongate Books, 2001), 512.

69. William Wordsworth [1803], "To Toussaint L'Ouverture," in *The Faber Book of Political Verse*, edited by Tom Paulin (London: Faber and Faber, 1986), 229.

70. Antonio Gramsci to Tatania Gramsci, August 17, 1931, in *Prison Letters* (London: Pluto Press, 1988), 156.

71. Friedrich Engels, "Refugee Literature—II. Program of the Blanquist Commune Refugees," in *Collected Works*, vol. 24 (London: Lawrence and Wishart,

1989), 16.

72. Vladimir I. Lenin, "Socialism and Religion," in *Collected Works*, vol. 10, *November 1905–June 1906* (Moscow: Foreign Languages Publishing House, 1965), 86.

73. Friedrich Engels [1886], "Ludwig Feuerbach and the End of Classical German Philosophy," in *Collected Works*, vol. 26 (London: Lawrence and Wishart, 1990), 398.

74. Vladimir I. Lenin [1913], "The Three Sources and Three Component Parts of Marxism," in *Collected Works*, vol. 15, *March–December 1913* (Moscow: Foreign Languages Publishing House, 1963), 29.

75. Leon D. Trotsky [1924], *Literature and Revolution* (London: Redwords, 1991), 225.

76. Stuart Macintyre, *A Proletarian Science: Marxism in Britain, 1917–1933* (London: Lawrence and Wishart, 1986), 71.

77. T. A. Jackson, *Solo Trumpet: Some Memories of Socialist Agitation and Propaganda* (London: Lawrence and Wishart, 1953), 24–25.

78. Duncan Hallas, "My Favorite Books," *Socialist Review* 163 (April 1993), 23.

79. Friedrich Engels, "Karl Marx's Funeral," in *Collected Works*, vol. 24, 467–68, 470.

80. See Macintyre, *A Proletarian Science*, 112–15; for Europe more generally, see Geoff Eley, *Forging Democracy: The History of the Left in Europe, 1850–2000* (Oxford: Oxford University Press, 2002), 403.

81. Ferdinand Mount, *Mind the Gap: The New Class Divide in Britain* (London: Short Books, 2004), 183 and 177–86 more generally.

82. Jonathan Rose, *The Intellectual Life of the British Working Classes* (New Haven: Yale University Press, 2001), 250.

83. Norman Stone, *Europe Transformed, 1878–1919* (London: Fontana Books, 1983), 114.

84. Barbara Ehrenreich, "For the Rationality Debate," originally published at www.zmag.org (last accessed February 2006; the page is no longer available).

85. Gareth Stedman Jones, *An End to Poverty? A Historical Debate* (London: Profile Books, 2004), 235.

86. Karl Marx [1843], "On the Jewish Question," in *Early Writings* (Harmondsworth: Penguin/New Left Review, 1975), 218, 221.

87. Friedrich Engels [1880], *Socialism: Utopian and Scientific*, in *Collected Works*, vol. 24, 286.

88. Robert M. May, *Threats to Tomorrow's World*, anniversary address delivered by the president of the Royal Society, November 30, 2005 (London: Royal Society, 2005), 4, 16–17, 23.

89. The Barna Update, "Americans Describe Their Views about Life after Death" (October 21, 2003), available at www.barna.org.

90. Paul Harris, "Would You Adam 'n' Eve It . . . Dinosaurs in Eden," *Observer* (May 22, 2005).

91. John Gray, *Al Qaeda and What It Means to Be Modern* (London: Faber and Faber, 2003), 23.

92. Mike Davis [1980], "Why the US Working Class Is Different," in *Prisoners of the American Dream: Politics and Economy in the History of the US Working Class* (London: Verso, 1986), 21–22.

93. Göran Therborn, *European Modernity and Beyond: The Trajectory of European Societies, 1945–2000* (London: Sage Publications, 1995), 275.

94. Barbara Ehrenreich, *Bait and Switch: The Futile Pursuit of the Corporate Dream* (London:

Granta Books, 2006), 221. See also chapter 5, "Networking with the Lord."

95. Theodor Adorno [1957], "The Stars Down to Earth: The *Los Angeles Times* Astrology Column: A Study in Secondary Superstition," in *The Stars Down to Earth and Other Essays in the Irrational in Culture*, edited by Stephen Crook (London: Routledge, 1994), 115.

96. Debora MacKenzie, "End of the Enlightenment," *New Scientist* (October 8, 2005), 41, 43.

97. Gilbert Achcar, *The Clash of Barbarisms: September 11 and the Making of the New World Disorder* (New York: Monthly Review Press, 2002), 89 and 85–89 more generally.

98. "'Intelligent Design' Teaching Ban," BBC News (December 20, 2005), available at news.bbc.co.uk.

99. May, *Threats to Tomorrow's World*, 22–23.

100. George Gilder, *The Spirit of Enterprise* (New York: Simon and Schuster, 1984), 19.

101. "Don't Despair," *Economist* (December 10, 2005), 13.

102. "The Root of All Evil?," broadcast on January 9 and 16, 2006, on Channel 4.

103. Francis Wheen, *How Mumbo-Jumbo Conquered the World: A Short History of Modern Delusions* (London: Fourth Estate, 2004), 193.

104. Karl Marx [1844], "A Contribution to the Critique of Hegel's *Philosophy of Right*. Introduction," in *Early Writings*, 244. Several non-Marxist radicals have been quicker to realize what Marx was actually saying than those who simply assimilate him to the Enlightenment. See, for example, George Orwell [1940], "Notes on the Way," in *The Collected Essays, Journalism and Letters of George Orwell*, vol. 2, *My Country Right or Left, 1940–1943*, edited by Sonia Orwell and Ian Angus (Harmondsworth: Penguin, 1970), 33; and Michel Foucault [1979], "Iran: The Spirit of a World without Spirit," in *Politics, Philosophy, Culture: Interviews and Other Writings, 1977–1984*, edited by Lawrence D. Kritzman (London: Routledge, 1988), 218.

105. Sigmund Freud [1927], "The Future of an Illusion," in *The Freud Reader*, edited by Peter Gay (New York: Vintage Books, 1995), 716. For a brief discussion of parallels between the views of Engels and Freud on religion, see Siegel, *The Meek and the Militant*, 37–38.

106. Richard Dawkins, preface to *Unweaving the Rainbow: Science, Delusion and the Appetite for Wonder* (Harmondsworth: Penguin, 1988), xi.

107. Rationalism in art can of course avoid the problem expressed here in science, as has been recently demonstrated by Philip Pullman's great trilogy, *His Dark Materials* (1994–2001).

108. Lenin, "Socialism and Religion," 86–87.

109. Ariel Dorfman, "Childhood as Underdevelopment," in *The Empire's Old Clothes: What the Lone Ranger, Babar and Other Innocent Heroes Do to Our Minds* (London: Pluto Press, 1983), 3–5.

110. Fisk encountered the phrase on the reverse of a campaign medal struck during the First World War and awarded to his grandfather. See Robert Fisk, *The Great War for Civilization: The Conquest of the Middle East* (London: Harper Perennial, 2005), ix.

111. Christopher Hitchens, "Against Rationalization," in *Love, Poverty and War: Journeys and Essays* (London: Atlantic Books, 2005), 413.

112. Christopher Hitchens, *Regime Change* (Harmondsworth: Penguin, 2003), 56. The conjunction of Islam and Fascism had first been made by Fred Halliday in his reports from revolutionary Iran in 1979, although far more tentatively than Halliday was later to claim. Compare the parallels Halliday actually draws in passing in "The Revolution Turns to Reaction," *New Statesman* (August 17, 1979), 264, and his subsequent claims to have identified "Islam with a Fascist Face" in "The Iranian Revolution and Its Implications," *New Left Review* I/166 (November/December 1987), 36–37.

113. Alan Massie, "The Trial of Christopher Hitchens," *Scotland on Sunday* (July 18, 2003).

114. Nick Cohen, "By the Left . . . about Turn," *Observer* (December 14, 2003).

115. Nick Cohen, "I Still Fight Oppression," *Observer* (August 7, 2005).

116. "Most of the orthodox Christians who fled into the Holy Roman Empire during the Turkish invasion of the Balkans after the fall of Constantinople in 1453 returned within 20 years, because they heard from those who had stayed behind that they were free to practice their religion and were not pressured to convert to Islam, whereas those who fled were constantly pressured to convert to Catholicism." See Amin Saikal, *Islam and the West: Conflict or Cooperation?* (Houndmills: Palgrave Macmillan, 2003), 33.

117. Edmund Burke [1790], *Reflections on the Revolution in France and on the Proceedings of Certain Societies in London Relative to That Event*, edited by Conor Cruise O'Brien (Harmondsworth: Penguin, 1968), 248–49. Elsewhere Cohen describes "the restoration of the Islamic Caliphate" as "a dream as impossible as communism." See "The Second Battle of Stalingrad," in *Pretty Straight Guys* (London: Faber and Faber, 2003), 124.

118. Joan Smith, "Muslim Anger Is Out of All Proportion: Being Angry Does Not Make You Right," *Independent on Sunday* (February 5, 2006).

119. Andrew Anthony, "The End of Freedom?," *Observer* (February 12, 2006).

120. Fred Halliday, "Fundamentalism and Political Power," in *Two Hours That Shook the World: September 11, 2001: Causes and Consequences* (London: Saqi Books, 2002), 66.

121. Wheen, *How Mumbo-Jumbo Conquered the World*, vii–xiv, chapter 1, 309–10.

122. Cohen, "The Second Battle of Stalingrad," 104.

123. Christopher Hitchens [1991], "Politically Correct," in *For the Sake of Argument: Essays and Minority Reports* (London: Verso, 1993), 227.

124. Robert Hughes [1994], *Culture of Complaint: The Fraying of America* (Revised and augmented edition, London: Harvill Press, 1995), 28.

125. Christopher Hitchens, "The Fraying of America: A Review of *Culture of Complaint*," in *The War of the Words: The Political Correctness Debate*, edited by Sarah Dunant (London: Virago Press, 1994), 139.

126. Onora O'Neill, "A Right to Offend?," *Guardian* (February 13, 2006).

127. Dick Taverne, *The March of Unreason: Science, Democracy, and the New Fundamentalism* (Oxford: Oxford University Press, 2005).

128. Dick Taverne, "Against Anti-science," *Prospect* (December 1999), available at www.prospectmagazine.co.uk.

129. Helene Guldberg, "How Can We Halt the 'March of Unreason,'" available at www.heleneguldberg.co.uk.

130. Martin Kettle, "When It Was No Longer Sweet and Noble to Kill for the Cause," *Guardian* (February 11, 2006).

131. Norman Geras, "Four Assumptions about Human Nature," in *The Enlightenment and Modernity*, edited by Norman Geras and Richard Wokler (Houndmills: Palgrave Macmillan, 2000), 157.

132. Halliday, "Fundamentalism and Political Power," 67.

133. 1 Corinthians 14:8.

134. See Perry Anderson, *Arguments within English Marxism* (London: Verso, 1980), 94–97, where Anderson makes clear the reactionary politics with which Swift was associated without ever indicating why he was able to write *Gulliver's Travels*. As Edward Thompson later said of this performance: "Perry . . . showed insufficient respect for Jonathan Swift . . . particularly because I regard *Gulliver's Travels* as the most savage indictment of the reasons of power that has ever been written. It still has a vitality of an extraordinary kind. And if, for political reasons, we try to devalue that, then somehow our categories are too limited." E. P. Thompson [1986], "Agenda for Radical History," in *Persons and Polemics: Historical Essays* (London: Merlin Press, 1994), 362.

135. Jonathan Swift [1726], *Gulliver's Travels*, edited by Peter Dixon and John Chalker (Harmondsworth: Penguin, 1967), 315–16. In his great essay on Swift, George Orwell claimed that Houyhnhnm society is the nearest to an ideal represented in *Gulliver's Travels*. This seems to be an unusual lapse of attention on Orwell's part, as Swift is far from endorsing the "Reason" of the Houyhnhnms. On the contrary, he is satirizing it. All the societies and their inhabitants described in the book embody different aspects of what Swift found abhorrent in his own milieu—which was virtually everything. See Orwell [1946], "Politics versus Literature: An Examination of *Gulliver's Travels*," in *The Collected Essays, Journalism and Letters of George Orwell*, vol. 4, *In Front of Your Nose, 1945–1950*, edited by Sonia Orwell and Ian Angus (Harmondsworth: Penguin, 1970), 246–47, 254–56.

136. Porter, *Enlightenment*, 463–64.

137. Mikhail Bakunin [1871], "God and the State," in *Bakunin on Anarchism*, edited by Sam Dolgoff (New York: Black Rose Press, 1980), 226–33; Marshall S. Shatz, *Jan Wacław Machajski: A Radical Critic of the Russian Intelligentsia and Socialism* (Pittsburgh: University of Pittsburgh Press, 1989), 32–42.

138. Irving L. Horowitz, *Radicalism and Revolt against Reason: The Social Theories of George Sorel with a Translation of his Essay on "The Decomposition of Marxism"* (London: Routledge, 1961), 100.

139. George Sorel [1908], *Reflections on Violence* (London: Collier Books, 1961), 54, 127.

140. Horowitz, *Radicalism and Revolt against Reason*, 100.

141. Quoted in Karl D. Bracher, *The German Dictatorship: The Origins, Structure, and Effects of National Socialism* (Harmondsworth: Penguin, 1970), 10.

142. Leon D. Trotsky [1934], "What Is National Socialism?," in *The Struggle against Fascism in Germany* (Harmondsworth: Penguin, 1975), 410, 413.

143. Leon D. Trotsky [1932], *The History of the Russian Revolution* (London: Pluto Press, 1977), 1191.

144. Henri Zuckier, "The Twisted Road to Genocide: On the Psychological Development of Evil during the Holocaust," *Social Research* 61, no. 2 (Summer 1994), 424. See also Enzo Traverso, *Understanding the Nazi Genocide: Marxism*

after Auschwitz (London: Pluto Press, 1999), 19–22.

145. Peter Novick, *The Holocaust and Collective Memory: The American Experience* (London: Bloomsbury, 2000), 63–169.

146. Theodor W. Adorno and Max Horkheimer [1944–47], *Dialectic of Enlightenment: Philosophical Fragments* (London: Verso, 1986), 6, 24, 32, 41, 42, 83, 208.

147. Charles Frankel, *The Faith of Reason: The Idea of Progress in the French Enlightenment* (New York: King's Crown Press, 1948), 157–58.

148. Traverso, *Understanding the Nazi Genocide*, 44.

149. Alex Callinicos, "Plumbing the Depths: Marxism and the Holocaust," *Yale Journal of Criticism* 14, no. 2 (Fall 2001), 387.

150. John Clellon Holmes, *Go* (New York: Scribner's, 1952), 37.

151. Leslie Fiedler, "The New Mutants," *Partisan Review* 32, no. 4 (Fall 1965), 515.

152. Norman Cohn [1957], *The Pursuit of the Millennium: Revolutionary Millenarians and Mystical Anarchists of the Middle Ages* (London: Paladin Books, 1970), 286.

153. Bob Dylan [1965], "Love Minus Zero/No Limit," in *Lyrics: 1962–1985* (London: Jonathan Cape, 1985), 260.

154. Bob Dylan [1965], "Tombstone Blues," in *Lyrics: 1962–1985*, 300.

155. Marvin Garson [1969], "History Is Now," in *Bamn (By Any Means Necessary): Outlaw Manifestos and Ephemera, 1965–70*, edited by Peter Stansell and David Zane Mairowitz (Harmondsworth: Penguin, 1971), 195.

156. Herbert Marcuse [1964], *One-Dimensional Man* (London: Sphere Books, 1968), 194, 200.

157. Luc Ferry and Alain Renaut [1991], preface to *Why We Are Not Nietzscheans*, edited by Luc Ferry and Alain Renaut (Chicago: Chicago University Press, 1997), viii.

158. Alex Callinicos, *Against Postmodernism: A Marxist Critique* (Houndmills: Polity Press, 1989), 168, 170.

159. Alan Sokal and Jean Bricmont, *Intellectual Impostures: Postmodern Philosophers' Abuse of Science* (London: Profile Books, 1998), 187–94.

160. Paul R. Gross and Norman Levitt, *Higher Superstition: The Academic Left and Its Quarrels with Science* (Baltimore: Johns Hopkins University Press, 1994), 32–34.

161. Michel Foucault [1975], *Discipline and Punish: The Birth of the Prison* (Harmondsworth: Penguin, 1979), 222. For parallels between Adorno and Foucault, see Alex Honneth, "Foucault's Theory of Society: A Systems-Theoretic Dissolution of the *Dialectic of Enlightenment*," in *Critique and Power: Recasting the Foucault/Habermas Debate*, edited by Michael Kelly (Cambridge, MA: MIT Press, 1994), 177–81.

162. Gilles Deleuze and Félix Guattari [1972], *Anti-Oedipus: Capitalism and Schizophrenia* (New York: Athlone Press, 1977), 112.

163. Jean-François Lyotard [1979], *The Postmodern Condition: A Report on Knowledge* (Manchester: Manchester University Press, 1984), xxiii–xxiv.

164. Quoted in Paul Berman, *A Tale of Two Utopias: The Political Journey of the Generation of 1968* (New York: W. W. Norton, 1996), 296.

165. Andrew Ross, introduction to *Universal Abandon: The Politics of Postmodernism*, edited by Andrew Ross (Minneapolis: University of Minneapolis Press, 1988), xii.

166. Sandra G. Harding, "A World of Sciences," in *Science and Other Cultures: Issues in Philosophies of Science and Technology*, edited by Robert Figueroa and Susan G.

Harding (London: Routledge, 2003), 52, 57, 61.

167. Paul Feyerabend, *Farewell to Reason* (London: Verso, 1987), 185–86. "*Anathema sit*" was—and perhaps still is—the papal denunciation of a person or doctrine, usually accompanied by excommunication.

168. Paul Feyerabend, *Science in a Free Society* (London: New Left Books, 1978), 9–10.

169. Alan Sokal, "Transgressing the Boundaries: Toward a Transformative Hermeneutics of Quantum Gravity," *Intellectual Impostures*, 199–200. For an earlier critique of postmodern appropriations of science, see Gross and Levitt, *Higher Superstition*, 78–82, 92–106, 126–48.

170. Quoted in Salvador Giner, *Mass Society* (London: Martin Robertson, 1976), 40.

171. Gross and Levitt, *Higher Superstition*, 21. Several writers, from varying political positions, have commented on the continuity between the original counter-Enlightenment and postmodernism. See, for example, Sokal and Bricmont, *Intellectual Impostures*, 186, and Wolin, *The Seduction of Unreason: The Intellectual Romance with Fascism from Nietzsche to Postmodernism* (Princeton: Princeton University Press, 2004), 3–7.

172. Chantal Mouffe, "Radical Democracy," in *Universal Abandon*, 38. "Oakeshott was a scoundrel," according to Edward Thompson as reported by Perry Anderson [1993], "In Memoriam: Edward Thompson," in *Spectrum: From Right to Left in the World of Ideas* (London: Verso, 2005), 187.

173. Jean-François Lyotard [1990], "The Wall, the Gulf and the Sun: A Fable," in *Political Writings* (London: University College London Press, 1993), 114.

174. Václav Havel, "The End of the Modern Era," *New York Times* (March 1, 1992).

175. John Sanbonmatsu, "Postmodernism and the Corruption of the Academic Intelligentsia," *The Socialist Register 2006: Telling the Truth*, edited by Leo Panitch and Colin Leys (London: Merlin Press, 2005), 198.

176. There is another argument, by Alasdair MacIntyre, that is far more rigorous in its construction, although it is so specific to its author, its recommendations so distant from contemporary preoccupations, that it is difficult to see how it could acquire any practical following: "What the Enlightenment made us for the most part blind to and what we need to recover is, so I shall argue, a conception of radical inquiry as embodied in a tradition, a conception according to which the standards of rational justification themselves emerge from and are part of the history in which they transcend the limitations of and provide remedies for the defects of their predecessors within the history of that tradition." See *Whose Justice? Which Rationality?* (London: Duckworth, 1988), 7.

177. Jonathan Glover, *Humanity: A Moral History of the Twentieth Century* (New Haven: Yale University Press, 1999), 310.

178. Roger Burbach, *Globalisation and Postmodern Politics: From Zapatistas to High-Tech Robber Barons* (London: Pluto Press, 2001), 10–11.

179. Roger Burbach, "For a Zapatista-Style Postmodernist Perspective," *Monthly Review* 47, no. 10 (March 1996), 37.

180. Notes from Nowhere, "Emergence," in *We Are Everywhere: The Irresistible Rise of Global Anticapitalism*, edited by Notes from Nowhere (London: Verso, 2003), 23.

181. Chalmers Johnson [2002], *Blowback: The Costs and Consequences of the American Empire* (Second edition, London: Henry Holt, 2004), xi–xvii, 8–19.

182. Larry Laudan, *Science and Relativism: Some Key Controversies in the Philosophy of*

Science (Chicago: University of Chicago Press, 1990), 163.

183. Elizabeth Wilson, "Rewinding the Video," in *Hallucinations: Life in the Post-Modern City* (London: Hutchinson Radius, 1988), 208–09.

184. James Holstun, *Ehud's Dagger: Class Struggle in the English Revolution* (London: Verso, 2000), 386.

185. Callinicos, *Social Theory*, 160.

186. Feyerabend, *Farewell to Reason*, 308–09.

187. Andrew Gamble, *Hayek: The Iron Cage of Liberty* (Boulder: Westview Press, 1996), 32–33.

188. Friedrich A. Hayek, *Collected Works*, vol. 1, *The Fatal Conceit: The Errors of Socialism*, edited by W. W. Bartley III (London: Routledge, 1988), 136.

189. Robert A. Nisbet, *History of the Idea of Progress* (New York: Basic Books, 1980), 352, 355.

190. The postmodern enthusiasm for Nietzsche tended to ignore his saner pronouncements, such as: "On the whole, scientific methods are at least as important as any other result of research: for it is upon the insight into method that the scientific spirit depends: and if these methods were lost, then all the results of science could not prevent a renewed triumph of superstition and nonsense." *Human, All-Too-Human*, excerpted in *The Portable Nietzsche*, edited by Walter Kaufman (Harmondsworth: Penguin, 1976), 63–64.

191. Allan Bloom, *The Closing of the American Mind: How Higher Education Has Failed Democracy and Impoverished the Souls of Today's Students* (Harmondsworth: Penguin, 1988), 219.

192. Friedrich W. Nietzsche [1888], *Twilight of the Idols*, in *Twilight of the Idols and The Anti-Christ* (Harmondsworth: Penguin, 1990), 35.

193. Friedrich W. Nietzsche [1888], *The Will to Power*, edited by Walter Kaufman (London: Vintage Books, 1968), 267, observation 481.

194. Alain Boyer, "Hierarchy and Truth," in *Why We Are Not Nietzscheans*, 2.

195. Friedrich W. Nietzsche [1886], *Beyond Good and Evil* (Harmondsworth: Penguin, 1990), 194.

196. Ishay Landa, "Nietzsche, the Chinese Worker's Friend," *New Left Review* I/236 (July/August 1999), 11, 15.

197. Laudan, *Science and Relativism*, 161.

198. Susan G. Harding, *Whose Science? Whose Knowledge? Thinking from Women's Lives* (Milton Keynes: Open University Press, 1991), 307.

199. Terry Eagleton, *After Theory* (London: Allen Lane, 2003), 135–36; "On Telling the Truth," in *The Socialist Register 2006: Telling the Truth*, 282.

200. Meera Nanda, "Restoring the Real: Rethinking Social Constructivist Theories of Science," *The Socialist Register 1997: Ruthless Criticism of All That Exists*, edited by Leo Panitch (London: Merlin Press, 1997), 305.

201. Hume, *A Treatise of Human Nature*, 159.

202. Paul Feyerabend, *Against Method: Outline of an Anarchist Theory of Knowledge* (London: New Left Books, 1975), 308–09. For a more recent attempt to defend the establishment of truth by popular acclaim, see Alan and Marten D. Shipman, *Knowledge Monopolies: The Academization of Society* (Exeter: Imprint Academic, 2006).

203. Andrew Collier, *Socialist Reasoning: An Inquiry into the Political Philosophy of Scientific Socialism* (London: Pluto Press, 1990), 148.

204. George Orwell [1949], *Nineteen Eighty-Four: A Novel* (Harmondsworth: Penguin, 1954), 212–15.
205. John Newsinger, *Orwell's Politics* (Houndmills: Macmillan, 1999), 124–30.
206. Richard Wolin, *The Seduction of Unreason*, 160.
207. Cindy Sheehan, "A New World Is Possible" (January 26, 2006), available at www.truth-out.org.
208. Julian L. Simon, "What Does the Future Hold? The Forecast in a Nutshell," in *The State of Humanity* (Oxford: Blackwell, 1995), 648, 659.
209. Thomas Pogge, *World Poverty and Human Rights* (Cambridge: Polity Press, 2002), 97–98.
210. Esther Leslie, *Walter Benjamin: Overpowering Conformism* (London: Pluto Press, 2000), 178, 231.
211. Max Horkheimer [1941], "The End of Reason," in *The Essential Frankfurt School Reader*, edited by Andrew Arato and Eike Gebhardt (Oxford: Blackwell, 1978), 30.

CHAPTER 6: ISLAM AND THE ENLIGHTENMENT

1. Louis Dupré, *The Enlightenment and the Intellectual Foundations of Modern Culture* (New Haven: Yale University Press, 2004), ix.
2. "Ziauddin Sardar Confronts the Commentators," *New Statesman* (February 6, 2006).
3. Abdulaziz Othman Altwaijri, *Enlightenment as an Islamic Concept* (Cairo: ISESCO, 2005), 18.
4. Thomas Paine [1795–96], *The Age of Reason* (London: Watts, 1938), 67.
5. Quoted in Bassam Tibi, "Culture and Knowledge: The Politics of Islamization of Knowledge as a Postmodern Project? The Fundamentalist Claim to De-Westernization," *Theory, Culture and Society* 12, no. 1 (February 1995), 16.
6. Antonio Gramsci [1929–34], "Problems of Marxism: Some Problems in the Study of the Philosophy of Praxis," in *Selections from the Prison Notebooks*, edited by Quintin Hoare and Geoffrey Nowell-Smith (London: Lawrence and Wishart, 1971), 394–95, Q16§9; Hugh R. Trevor-Roper [1961–63], "The Religious Origins of the Enlightenment," in *Religion, the Reformation and Social Change and Other Essays* (London: Macmillan, 1967), 233–35.
7. James Buchan, *Capital of the Mind: How Edinburgh Changed the World* (London: John Murray, 2003), 23.
8. Jonathan I. Israel, *Radical Enlightenment: Philosophy and the Making of Modernity, 1650–1750* (Oxford: Oxford University Press, 2002), 702–03. See also 572–73.
9. Edmund Gibbon [1776–88], *The Decline and Fall of the Roman Empire*, vol. 3 (London: Chandos Edition, no date identified), chapter 50; Hugh Goddard, *A History of Christian-Muslim Relations* (Edinburgh: Edinburgh University Press, 2000), 144–45; Roy Porter [1988], *Gibbon: Making History* (London: Phoenix Giants, 1995), 131.
10. Anthony Arblaster, *Viva Liberta! Politics in Opera* (London: Verso, 1992), 39.
11. Quoted in Paul M. Siegel, *The Meek and the Militant: Religion and Power across the World* (London: Zed Books, 1986), 179.
12. Amartya Sen, "East and West: The Reach of Reason," *The New York Review of Books* (July 20, 2000), 36.
13. Quoted in Iqbal Ghani Khan, "Scientific Concepts in Abu'l Fazl's *A'in-i Akbari*,"

in *Ikbar and His India*, edited by Irfan Habib (Delhi: Oxford University Press, 1997), 128.

14. See Neil Davidson, *We Cannot Escape History: States and Revolutions* (Chicago: Haymarket Books, 2015), xii–xv, and chapters 2 and 3.

15. Pervez A. Hoodbhoy, *Islam and Science: Religious Orthodoxy and the Battle for Rationality* (London: Zed Books, 1991), 126.

16. Ibn Khaldun [1377], *The Muqaddimah: An Introduction to History*, edited by N. J. Dawood (London: Routledge and Kegan Paul, 1967), 137, 142–52.

17. Joseph Needham [1956], *The Shorter Science and Civilization in China*, vol. 1 (Cambridge: Cambridge University Press, 1978), 253–54.

18. Jacques Gernet [1972], *A History of Chinese Civilization* (Second edition, Cambridge: Cambridge University Press, 1982), 476–77.

19. Christopher A. Bayly, *The Birth of the Modern World, 1780–1914* (Oxford: Blackwell, 2004), 15.

20. Bernard Lewis, *What Went Wrong? Western Impact and Middle Eastern Response* (London: Phoenix, 2002), 127.

21. Peter Gowan [1991], "The Gulf War, Iraq and Western Liberalism," in *The Global Gamble: Washington's Faustian Bid for World Dominance* (London: Verso, 1999), 167.

22. Quoted in Fernand Braudel [1963], *A History of Civilizations* (Harmondsworth: Penguin, 1993), 96.

23. Davidson, *We Cannot Escape History*, chapters 8–12.

24. Marx to Ruge, September 1843, in "Letters from the *Franco-German Yearbooks*," in *Early Writings* (Harmondsworth: Penguin/New Left Review, 1975), 208.

25. Ambalavaner Sivanandan, "Why Muslims Reject British Values," *Observer* (October 16, 2005).

CHAPTER 7: THE NECESSITY OF MULTIPLE NATION-STATES FOR CAPITAL

1. On these concepts see Hal Draper, *Karl Marx's Theory of Revolution*, vol. 1, *State and Bureaucracy* (New York: Monthly Review Press, 1978), 240.

2. Hannah Arendt [1951], *The Origins of Totalitarianism* (London: Andre Deutsch, 1986), 415–17; Cornelius Castoriadis [1949], "Socialism or Barbarism," in *Political and Social Writings*, vol. 1, *1946–1955: From the Critique of Bureaucracy to the Positive Content of Socialism*, edited by David Ames Curtis (Minneapolis: University of Minnesota Press, 1988), 86.

3. Karl Marx [1857–58], *Grundrisse: Foundations for the Critique of Political Economy (Rough Draft)* (Harmondsworth: Penguin/New Left Review, 1973), 414, 421, note 2. See also: Chris Arthur, "Capital, Competition and Many Capitals: A Reply to Finelli," in *The Culmination of Capital: Essays on Volume III of Marx's* Capital, edited by Martha Campbell and Geert Reuten (Houndmills: Palgrave, 2002), 128–48; Tony Cliff [1948], "The Nature of Stalinist Russia," in *Selected Works*, vol. 3, *Marxist Theory after Trotsky* (London: Bookmarks, 2003), 93–94; and Roman Rosdolsky [1967], *The Making of Marx's "Capital"* (London: Pluto Press, 1977), 41–53.

4. Karl Marx [1867], *Capital: A Critique of Political Economy*, vol. 1 (Harmondsworth: Penguin/New Left Review, 1976), 779.

5. Nikolai N. Bukharin [1915], *Imperialism and World Economy* (London: Merlin Press, 1972), 133–43; Rudolf Hilferding [1910], *Finance Capital: A Study of the Latest Phase of Capitalist Development*, edited by Tom Bottomore (London: Routledge and Kegan Paul, 1981), 234, 311; Vladimir I. Lenin [1915], introduction to Bukharin, *Imperialism and World Economy*, 12–14.

6. See, for example, Benno Teschke and Hannes Lacher, "The Changing 'Logics' of Capitalist Competition," *Cambridge Review of International Affairs* 20, no. 4 (December 2007), 576.

7. Ulrike Heider, *Anarchism: Left, Right and Green* (San Francisco: City Lights, 1994), 92–150.

8. Alan Greenspan, *The Age of Turbulence: Adventures in a New World* (London: Penguin, 2008), 52. In his account of Rand's influence Gary Weiss is so anxious to portray Greenspan as her acolyte that he makes no mention of these passages in which he has retreated from objectivism to a more conventional neoliberalism. See Weiss, *Ayn Rand Nation: The Hidden Struggle for America's Soul* (New York: St. Martin's Press, 2012), 208–35.

9. Evgeny Pashukanis [1924], *Law and Marxism: A General Theory*, edited by Chris Arthur (London: Ink Links, 1978), 139.

10. Fred Halliday, *Rethinking International Relations* (London: Macmillan, 1994), 91.

11. Ferdinand Tönnies [1887], *Community and Civil Society*, edited by Charles Loomis (East Lansing: University of Michigan Press, 1957), 221.

12. See, for example, Colin Leys, *Market-Driven Politics: Neoliberal Democracy and the Public Interest* (London: Verso, 2001), 26–27, and Robert Brenner, "Structure versus Conjuncture," *New Left Review* II/43 (January/February 2007), 84.

13. Michael Hardt and Antonio Negri, *Empire* (London: Harvard University Press, 2000), xi–xvi.

14. Leo Panitch and Samuel Gindin, "Global Capitalism and American Empire," in *The Socialist Register 2004: The New Imperial Challenge*, edited by Leo Panitch and Colin Leys (London: Merlin Press, 2003), 13–33.

15. Malcolm Bull, "States of Failure," *New Left Review* II/40 (July/August 2006), 22.

16. See, for example, Alexander Wendt, "Why a World State Is Inevitable," *European Journal of International Relations* 9, no. 4 (October 2003).

17. See William Robinson, *A Theory of Global Capitalism: Production, Class and State in a Transnational World* (Baltimore: Johns Hopkins University Press, 2004), 8; "The Pitfalls of Realist Analysis of Global Capitalism: A Critique of Ellen Meiksins Wood's *Empire of Capital*," *Historical Materialism* 15, no. 3 (2010). For critiques, see Paul Cammack, "Forget the Transnational State," Papers in the Politics of Global Competitiveness, No. 3, Institute for Global Studies, Manchester Metropolitan University (2007), accessible online at hdl.handle.net/2173/6759, and Adam David Morton, *Unravelling Gramsci: Hegemony and Passive Revolution in the Global Economy* (London: Pluto Press, 2007), 140–50.

18. Alex Callinicos, "Does Capitalism Need the State System?," *Cambridge Review of International Affairs* 20, no. 4 (December 2007), 544–45; Gonzalo Pozo-Martin, "Autonomous or Materialist Geopolitics?," *Cambridge Review of International Affairs* 20, no. 4 (December 2007), 556.

19. For the distinction, see Neil Davidson [2006], "From Uneven to Combined Development," in *We Cannot Escape History: States and Revolutions* (Chicago:

Haymarket Books, 2015). Callinicos has discussed the "combined" element of uneven and combined development elsewhere. See, for example, *Social Theory: A Historical Introduction* (Cambridge: Polity Press, 1999), 199.

20. Callinicos, "Does Capitalism Need the State System?," 544–45; Vladimir I. Lenin [1916], "Imperialism, the Highest Stage of Capitalism: A Popular Outline," in *Collected Works*, vol. 22 (Moscow: Foreign Languages Publishing House, 1964), 295.

21. Paul Ginsburg, *A History of Contemporary Italy: Society and Politics, 1943–1988* (Harmondsworth: Penguin, 1990), 17–38, 210–35; Morton, *Unravelling Gramsci*, 51–73.

22. Neil Davidson, *The Origins of Scottish Nationhood* (London: Pluto Press, 2000), 63–78, 102–06; *Discovering the Scottish Revolution, 1692–1746* (London: Pluto Press, 2003), 52–70, 220–27, 261–67; "The Scottish Path to Capitalist Agriculture 2: The Capitalist Offensive (1747–1815)," *Journal of Agrarian Change* 4, no. 4 (October 2004), 448–52.

23. Ellen Meiksins Wood, "Logics of Power: A Conversation with David Harvey," *Historical Materialism* 14, no. 4 (2006), 25; *Empire of Capital* (London: Verso, 2003), 141.

24. Neil Smith [1984], *Uneven Development: Nature, Capital, and the Production of Space* (Oxford: Blackwell, 1990), 142–43. It may be that as capitalist globalization proceeds, relatively small states may acquire new advantages, but clearly there is a lower limit beyond which this ceases to be the case. See, for example, Alberto Alesina and Enrico Spolaore, *The Size of Nations* (Cambridge, MA: MIT Press, 2003).

25. Vivek Chibber, "Capital Outbound," *New Left Review* II/36 (November/December 2005), 157.

26. Marx, *Grundrisse*, 85.

27. Alasdair MacIntyre [1958–59], "Notes from the Moral Wilderness," in *Alasdair MacIntyre's Engagement with Marxism: Selected Writings, 1953–1974*, edited by Paul Blackledge and Neil Davidson (Leiden: E. J. Brill/Historical Materialism, 2008), 55.

28. Göran Therborn, *What Does the Ruling Class Do When It Rules? State Apparatuses and State Power under Feudalism, Capitalism and Socialism* (London: New Left Books, 1978), 181.

29. Draper, *Karl Marx's Theory of Revolution*, vol. 1, *State and Bureaucracy*, 262.

30. Colin Barker, "The State as Capital," *International Socialism* 2:1 (July 1978), 20–23.

31. "Remarks by the President at a Campaign Event in Roanoke, Virginia," July 13, 2012. Available at www.whitehouse.gov.

32. Nigel Harris, *The Return of Cosmopolitan Capital: Globalization, the State and War* (London: I. B. Tauris, 2003), 4.

33. David Harvey, *A Brief History of Neoliberalism* (Oxford: Oxford University Press, 2005), 70–81; Neil Davidson, "What Is Neoliberalism?," in *Neoliberal Scotland: Class and Society in a Stateless Nation*, edited by Neil Davidson, Patricia McCafferty, and David Miller (Newcastle: Cambridge Scholars Press, 2010), 31–41.

34. Michael Mann, "The Autonomous Power of the State: Its Origins, Mechanisms, and Results," in *States in History*, edited by John A. Hall (Oxford: Blackwell, 1986), 133.

35. Brenner's unpublished Deutscher Prize Lecture of 1985, when he received the award for his contributions to *The Brenner Debate*, was called "The Autonomy of the State."

36. Benno Teschke, *The Myth of 1648: Class, Geopolitics and the Making of Modern International Relations* (London: Verso, 2003), 144–45.

37. Teschke and Lacher, "The Changing 'Logics' of Capitalist Competition," 574.

38. This alternative past is in any case highly implausible. Even Max Weber, who thought that capitalism had existed throughout human history, argued that prior to the late Middle Ages it took only "irrational" forms, by which he seems to have meant that it remained unsystematic, an "occasional economic activity" undertaken to raise money for particular purposes or supplement the income of officials: "The capitalism of the late middle ages began to be directed toward market opportunities, and the contrast between it and the capitalism of antiquity appears in the development after the cities have lost their freedom.... In antiquity the freedom of the cities was swept away by a bureaucratically organized world empire within which there was no longer a place for political capitalism." Accordingly, Weber did not think that capitalism in the modern "systematic" sense could have emerged under the Roman Empire or—by implication— any of the other great empires of antiquity. Weber [1919–20], *General Economic History* (London: George Allen and Unwin, 1923), 334–35.

39. Hannes Lacher, *Beyond Globalization: Capitalism, Territoriality and the Internal Relations of Modernity* (London: Routledge, 2006), 46.

40. Teschke and Lacher, "The Changing 'Logics' of Capitalist Competition," 574.

41. Justin Rosenberg, "Globalization Theory: A Post Mortem," *International Politics* 42, no. 1 (January 2005), 24–25.

42. Charles Tilly, *European Revolutions, 1492–1992* (Oxford: Blackwell, 1993), 30.

43. Louis Althusser [1976], *Machiavelli and Us* (London: Verso, 1999), 11.

44. Tom Nairn [1976], "The Twilight of the British State," in *The Break-up of Britain: Crisis and Neo-nationalism* (Second edition, London: Verso, 1981), 75.

45. Marx, *Capital*, vol. 1, 1019–1038.

46. Bukharin, *Imperialism and World Economy*, 128.

47. Christopher A. Bayly, *The Birth of the Modern World, 1780–1914: Global Connections and Comparisons* (Oxford: Blackwell, 2004), 426–30; David Cannadine, "The Context, Performance and Meaning of Ritual: The British Monarchy and the 'Invention of Tradition,' c. 1820–1977," in *The Invention of Tradition*, edited by Eric J. Hobsbawm and Terence Ranger (Cambridge: Cambridge University Press, 1983), 120–50.

48. Robert Brenner, "What Is, and What Is Not, Imperialism?," *Historical Materialism* 14, no. 4 (2006), 84.

49. Robert Brenner, *Merchants and Revolution: Commercial Change, Political Conflict, and London's Overseas Traders, 1550–1653* (Princeton: Princeton University Press, 1993), 618–25.

50. Charles Tilly, "Reflections on the History of European State-Making," in *The Formation of National States in Western Europe*, edited by Charles Tilly (Princeton: Princeton University Press, 1975), 76.

51. Benedict Anderson [1983], *Imagined Communities: Reflections on the Origin and Spread of Nationalism* (London: Verso, 2006), 50.

52. Chris Harman, "The State and Capitalism Today," *International Socialism* 2:51 (Summer 1991), 48.

53. Jean Comaroff and John Comaroff, "Millennial Capitalism: First Thoughts on

a Second Coming," in *Millennial Capitalism and the Culture of Neoliberalism*, edited by Jean Comaroff and John Comaroff (Durham: Duke University Press, 2001), 35. Poor Adam Smith! Is there any other thinker, except perhaps Marx himself, whose legacy has been so shamefully misappropriated and misused? See Neil Davidson, "The Posthumous Adventures of Adam Smith," in *Holding Fast to an Image of the Past: Explorations in the Marxist Tradition* (Chicago: Haymarket Books, 2014).

54. Callinicos, "Does Capitalism Need the State System?," 542.

55. See, for example, Pozo-Martin, "Autonomous or Materialist Geopolitics?," 556–59.

56. Lenin, "Imperialism," 187, 269, 276, 294.

57. Ernest Gellner, *Nations and Nationalism* (Oxford: Blackwell, 1983), 114–22; *Nationalism* (London: Weidenfeld and Nicolson, 1997), 47.

58. See, for example, Louis Althusser [1962], "Contradiction and Overdetermination," in *For Marx* (London: New Left Books, 1969), 236–41.

59. Anderson, *Imagined Communities*, xi, 1–2. For a critique, see Neil Davidson [2008], "Reimagined Communities," in *Holding Fast to an Image of the Past*, 195–202.

60. Bruce Russett, *Grasping the Democratic Peace: Principles for a Post–Cold War World*, with the collaboration of William Antholis, Carol Ember, Melvin Ember, and Zeev Maoz (Princeton: Princeton University Press, 1993), 30–40.

61. John Mearsheimer, *The Tragedy of Great Power Politics* (London: W. W. Norton, 2001), 3, 4.

62. Giovanni Arrighi, *The Long Twentieth Century: Money, Power and the Origins of Our Times* (London: Verso, 1994), 34–35.

63. David Harvey, *The New Imperialism* (Oxford: Oxford University Press, 2003), 27–30. Arrighi notes the differences between himself and Harvey, although in some places Harvey does employ the notion in ways similar to Arrighi. See, respectively, Giovanni Arrighi, *Adam Smith in Beijing: Lineages of the Twenty-First Century* (London: Verso, 2007), 212, note 2, and Harvey, *The New Imperialism*, 81.

64. David Harvey, "Reinventing Geography," in *Spaces of Capital: Toward a Critical Geography* (Edinburgh: Edinburgh University Press, 2001), 10.

65. Alex Callinicos, "David Harvey and Marxism," in *David Harvey: A Critical Reader*, edited by Noel Castree and Derek Gregory (Oxford: Blackwell, 2006), 52.

66. Harvey, *The New Imperialism*, 137–43.

67. Harvey, "Reinventing Geography," 9, 11.

68. Ibid., 34–35, 142–43; Arendt, *The Origins of Totalitarianism*, 121–302. The section of *The Origins of Totalitarianism* cited here (part 2) was published separately as *Imperialism* in 1968.

69. See, for example, David Harvey [1985], "The Geopolitics of Capital," in *Spaces of Capital*, or David Harvey [1982], *The Limits to Capital* (London: Verso, 2006).

70. Harvey, *The New Imperialism*, 140.

71. Ibid., 204–07; Michael Mann, *Incoherent Empire* (London: Verso, 2003), 51, 264.

72. Weber, *General Economic History*, 337.

73. Callinicos, "Does Capitalism Need the State System?," 540.

74. Samantha Ashman and Alex Callinicos, "Capital Accumulation and the State System: Assessing David Harvey's *The New Imperialism*," *Historical Materialism* 14, no. 4 (2006), 115.

75. Callinicos, "Does Capitalism Need the State System?," 542.
76. Hannes Lacher, "International Transformation and the Persistence of Territoriality: Toward a New Political Geography of Capitalism," *Review of International Political Economy* 12, no. 1 (February 2005), 35; Lacher, *Beyond Globalization*, 42, 60.
77. Althusser, "Contradiction and Overdetermination," 200–204.
78. Nicos Poulantzas [1968], *Political Power and Social Classes* (London: New Left Books, 1973), 14, 197–99.
79. John Rees, *The Algebra of Revolution: The Dialectic and the Classical Marxist Tradition* (London: Routledge, 1998), 247–49.
80. Georg Lukács [1923], "Reification and the Consciousness of the Proletariat," in *History and Class Consciousness: Studies in Marxist Dialectics* (London: Merlin Press, 1971), 162–63.
81. Alex Callinicos, "Periodizing Capitalism and Analyzing Imperialism: Classical Marxism and Capitalist Evolution," in *Phases of Capitalist Development: Booms, Crises and Globalizations*, edited by Robert Albritton, Makato Itoh, Richard Westra, and Alan Zuege (Houndmills: Palgrave, 2001), 38–40; Callinicos, "Does Capitalism Need the State System?," 542–43.
82. Alex Callinicos, *Is There a Future for Marxism?* (London: Macmillan, 1982), 138–39; Alex Callinicos, "Against the New Dialectics," *Historical Materialism* 13, no. 2 (2005), 57–58.
83. Marx to Engels, January 16, 1858, in *Collected Works*, vol. 40 (London: Lawrence and Wishart, 1983), 249.
84. Derek Sayer, *Marx's Method: Ideology, Science and Critique in* Capital (Brighton: Harvester, 1979), 101.
85. Georg Lukács, "What Is Orthodox Marxism?," in *History and Class Consciousness*, 9.
86. Marx, *Grundrisse*, 107–08; Marx, *Capital*, vol. 1, 102. See also Georg Lukács [1926], "Moses Hess and the Problem of Idealist Dialectics," in *Tactics and Ethics: Political Writings, 1919–1929*, edited by Rodney Livingstone (London: New Left Books, 1972), 221.
87. Bertell Ollman [1973], "Political Science: Prolegomenon to a Debate on Marx's Method," in *Dance of the Dialectic: Steps in Marx's Method* (Urbana: University of Illinois Press, 2003), 139.
88. I owe the notion of "entailment" to Colin Barker.
89. Karl Marx [1894], *Capital: A Critique of Political Economy*, vol. 3 (Harmondsworth: Penguin/New Left Review, 1981), 927.
90. Pozo-Martin, "Autonomous or Materialist Geopolitics?," 556–57.
91. Ellen Meiksins Wood, "The Separation of the Economic and Political under Capitalism," *New Left Review* I/127 (May/June 1981), 81–82.
92. Adam Smith [1776], *An Inquiry into the Nature and Causes of the Wealth of Nations*, edited by Edwin Cannan (Chicago: University of Chicago Press, 1976), book I, chapter 11, 278. See also Davidson, "The Posthumous Adventures of Adam Smith."
93. Ibid., book IV, chapters 7 and 8.
94. Marx, *Capital*, vol. 1, 606–07.
95. Ibid., 610.
96. Herbert Spencer [1884], *The Man versus the State, with Four Essays on Politics and*

Society, edited by Donald MacRae (Harmondsworth: Penguin, 1969).

97. Carl Schmitt [1932], "The Concept of the Political," in *The Concept of the Political* (Expanded edition, Chicago: University of Chicago Press, 2007), 63.

98. Joseph Schumpeter [1944], *Capitalism, Socialism and Democracy* (London: Routledge, 1994), 138–39.

99. Eric J. Hobsbawm, "Revolution," in *Revolution in History*, edited by Roy Porter and Mikulas Teich (Cambridge: Cambridge University Press, 1986), 27.

100. Draper, *Karl Marx's Theory of Revolution*, vol. 1, *State and Bureaucracy*, 321–24.

101. Bernard Porter, *Empire and Superempire: Britain, America and the World* (New Haven: Yale University Press, 2006), 49.

102. Fred Block [1977], "The Ruling Class Does Not Rule: Notes on the Marxist Theory of the State," in *Revising State Theory: Essays in Politics and Postindustrialization* (Philadelphia: Temple University Press, 1987), chapter 3.

103. Teschke, *The Myth of 1648*, 267.

104. The very development of "economics" as an academic discipline in the middle decades of the nineteenth century, out of elements of political economy and moral philosophy, was an expression of the formation of an ideology out of what had been—however inconsistently—a science. And like all central components of bourgeois ideology, it has permeated aspects of reformism, notably in the long-standing division between the so-called economic and political wings of the working-class movement, otherwise known as trade unions and Social-Democratic parties.

105. China Miéville, *Between Equal Rights: A Marxist Theory of International Law* (Leiden: E. J. Brill/Historical Materialism, 2005), 221.

106. Jairus Banaji, "The Fictions of Free Labour: Contract, Coercion, and So-Called Unfree Labour," *Historical Materialism* 11, no. 3 (2003), 79–80.

107. Chibber, "Capital Outbound," 155.

108. Max Weber's famous definition is: "A state is that human community which (successfully) lays claim to the *monopoly of legitimate physical violence* within a certain territory." Weber [1919], "The Profession and Vocation of Politics," in *Political Writings*, edited by Peter Lassman and Ronald Speirs (Cambridge: Cambridge University Press, 1994), 310–11. According to his own account, Michael Burawoy considered using the concept of an "internal state" within the factory but abandoned it precisely because he feared it would divert attention from the monopoly of violence supposedly enjoyed by actual states, and because it could also be extended to other institutions such as the family. He opted instead for the "politics of production" that gives his book its title. Burawoy, *The Politics of Production: Factory Regimes under Capitalism and Socialism* (London: Verso, 1985), 11. This is an example of a potentially fruitful line of inquiry being abandoned through Marxist adherence to a Weberian schema.

109. Timothy Mitchell, "Dreamland," in *Evil Paradises: Dreamworlds of Neoliberalism*, edited by Mike Davis and Daniel Bertrand Monk (New York: The New Press, 2007), 30.

110. Stephen Graham, *Cities under Siege: The New Military Urbanism* (London: Verso, 2010), xxiii.

111. Eric J. Hobsbawm, *Globalization, Democracy and Terrorism* (London: Little, Brown, 2007), 25.

112. Naomi Klein, *No Logo: Standing Up to the Brand Bullies* (London: Harper Collins, 2000), 204, 207.

113. Mike Davis, "The Political Economy of Late Imperial America," in *Prisoners of the American Dream: Politics and Economy in the History of the American Working Class* (London: Verso, 1986), 116.

114. Colin Barker, "A Note on the Theory of Capitalist States," *Capital and Class* 4 (Spring 1978); see also Barker, "The State as Capital." One of the problems here is that contributors tend to refer only to the first of these articles and not the more substantial second.

115. Barker, "The State as Capital," 25, 27–33.

116. Jeffrey Garten, "The Unsettling Zeitgeist of State Capitalism," *Financial Times* (January 14, 2008).

117. Andrew Graham, "If China Spends Its Trillions, Recession Could Be Averted," *Guardian* (October 15, 2008). Not everyone was so sanguine. The right-wing Scottish historian Niall Ferguson complained of the speech by Obama quoted earlier in this chapter: "It is bad enough to see state capitalism touted as an economic model by the Chinese Communist party. But to hear it deployed by the President of the United States as a rhetorical trope devoid of practical content makes this writer, for one, pine for the glad confident morning of 1989—when it really seemed the West had won, and a great regeneration had begun." See *The Great Degeneration: How Institutions Decay and Economies Die* (London: Allen Lane, 2012), 152. In the cases of Garten, Graham, and Ferguson, the model of state capitalism they have in mind is, in the words of Andrew Kliman, not that "of the former USSR, characterized by central 'planning' and the dominance of state property," but "a new global stage of capitalism, characterized by permanent state intervention, that arose in the 1930s with the New Deal and similar policy regimes." See "A Crisis for the Centre of the System," *International Socialism* 2:120 (Autumn 2008), 63.

118. Fred Block, "Beyond Relative Autonomy: State Managers as Historical Subjects," in *Revising State Theory*, 84.

119. Callinicos, "Does Capitalism Need the State System?," 543.

120. Ibid., 538; Chibber, "Capital Outbound," 157.

121. See chapter 3 in this volume, 62–63.

122. Harman, "The State and Capitalism Today," 16–17.

123. As Barker has pointed out, what counts as "national capital" is a complex matter. (See Barker, "The State as Capital," 33–37.) For our purposes, it can be taken to include all capitals, state and private, based in the nation-state of their origin, plus their overseas operations. More controversially, perhaps, I would argue that it should also include all those foreign capitals operating within the same nation-state to the extent that they are subject to its legal and fiscal regime. One consequence of this in the era of neoliberal globalization would of course be that some capitals will increasingly be claimed as "national" by two or more states: their state of origin and those other states upon whose territory they operate.

124. Joachim Hirsch [1974], "The State Apparatus and Social Reproduction: Elements of a Theory of the Bourgeois State," in *State and Capital: A Marxist Debate*, edited by John Holloway and Sol Picciotto (London: Edward Arnold, 1978), 100.

125. Mike Davis [2003], "Occupied America," in *In Praise of Barbarians: Essays against*

Empire (Chicago: Haymarket Books, 2007), 23, 26; Doug Henwood, "The 'Business Community,'" in *The Socialist Register 2006: Telling the Truth*, edited by Leo Panitch and Colin Leys (London: Merlin, 2005), 73; Kevin Phillips, *American Theocracy: The Peril and Politics of Radical Religion, Oil, and Borrowed Money in the 21st Century* (New York: Viking Penguin, 2006), 87.

126. See, for some preliminary remarks on this subject, Neil Davidson, "Neoliberal Regimes, the Far Right, and the Implications for Capital," in *Researching the Powerful: Public Sociology in Action*, edited by Lucy Brown, William Dinan, David Miller, and Ludek Stavinoha (London: Routledge, 2016).

127. Jonathan I. Israel, *The Dutch Republic: Its Rise, Greatness, and Fall, 1477–1806* (Oxford: Clarendon Press, 1998), 276–84.

128. Pepijn Brandon, "Marxism and the 'Dutch Miracle': The Dutch Republic and the Transition Debate," *Historical Materialism* 19, no. 3 (2011), 135–41.

129. Oliver James, *Affluenza: How to Be Successful and Stay Sane* (London: Vermillion, 2007), 321–22.

130. Ernest Mandel [1969], "The Inconsistencies of State Capitalism," in *Readings on "State Capitalism"* (London: International Marxist Group Publications, 1973), 17.

131. Cliff, "The Nature of Stalinist Russia," 90–92; Chris Harman [1982], "State Capitalism, the Arms Economy and the Crisis Today," in *Explaining the Crisis: A Marxist Reappraisal* (London: Bookmarks, 1984), 71–74, 84–86.

132. Michael Kidron [1969], "Maginot Marxism: Mandel's Economics," in *Capitalism and Theory* (London: Pluto Press, 1974), 80–81.

133. Liah Greenfield, *The Spirit of Capitalism: Nationalism and Economic Growth* (Cambridge, MA: Harvard University Press, 2001), 482.

134. Edward Luttwak, *Turbo-Capitalism: Winners and Losers in the Global Economy* (London: Weidenfeld and Nicolson, 1998), 128–29.

135. Ibid., 478.

136. Neil Davidson, *How Revolutionary Were the Bourgeois Revolutions?* (Chicago: Haymarket Books, 2012), 551-565.

137. Barker, "The State as Capital," 37.

138. Antonio Gramsci [1929–34], "State and Civil Society," in *Selections from the Prison Notebooks*, edited and translated by Quintin Hoare and Geoffrey Nowell-Smith (London: Lawrence and Wishart, 1971), 211, Q13§23.

139. Al Campbell, "The Birth of Neoliberalism in the United States: A Reorganization of Capitalism," in *Neoliberalism: A Critical Reader*, edited by Alfredo Saad-Filho and Deborah Johnston (London: Pluto Press, 2005), 188–89.

140. Andrew Gamble, *The Free Economy and the Strong State: The Politics of Thatcherism* (Houndmills: Macmillan, 1988), 194–97, 224–27.

141. Douglas Hurd, *An End to Promises: Sketch of a Government, 1970–74* (London: Collins, 1979), 29.

142. See chapter 8 in this volume.

143. Karl Marx, "Preface to *A Contribution to a Critique of Political Economy*," in *Early Writings* (Harmondsworth: Penguin/New Left Review, 1975), 424.

144. Marx, *Grundrisse*, 108.

145. Henryk Grossman [1943], "The Evolutionist Revolt against Classical Economics: II. In England—James Steuart, Richard Jones, Karl Marx," *Journal of Political Economy* 51, no. 6 (December 1943), 517.

146. Marx, *Grundrisse*, 414.

147. Marx, *Capital*, vol. 3, 205.

148. Marx, *Capital*, vol. 1, 874, 739.

149. Fernand Braudel, *Civilization and Capitalism, 15th–18th Century*, vol. 2, *The Wheels of Commerce* (London: Fontana Press, 1985), 554.

150. Benedict Anderson, "The New World Disorder," *New Left Review* I/193 (May/June 1992), 6; Harman, "The State and Capitalism Today," 32–38; Harvey, *A Brief History of Neoliberalism*, 35–36.

151. Harvey, "The Geopolitics of Capital," 328–29.

152. Pozo-Martin, "Autonomous or Materialist Geopolitics?," 560.

153. Smith, *An Inquiry into the Nature and Causes of the Wealth of Nations*, book V, chapter 1, 278.

154. Immanuel Kant [1795], "Perpetual Peace: A Philosophical Sketch," in *Political Writings*, edited by Hans Reiss (Cambridge: Cambridge University Press, 1991), 114.

155. Albert Hirschman [1976], *The Passions and the Interests: Political Arguments for Capitalism before Its Triumph*, 20th anniversary ed. (Princeton: Princeton University Press, 1996), 71, 132–35.

156. Robert Kagan, *The Return of History and the End of Dreams* (London: Atlantic Books, 2008), 8. For his invocation of Kant see ibid., 103.

157. Ibid., 24, 72.

158. Greenspan, *The Age of Turbulence*, 326–27.

159. Karl Kautsky [1914], "Imperialism," in *Lenin's Struggle for a Revolutionary International: Documents, 1907–1916*, edited by John Riddell (New York: Pathfinder Press, 1984), 180; Wood, *Empire of Capital*, 156–57.

160. Anderson, "The New World Disorder," 6.

161. Luttwak, *Turbo-Capitalism*, 149–50.

162. Wood, *Empire of Capital*, 143, 153.

163. Fareed Zakaria, "The Capitalist Manifesto: Greed Is Good (Up to a Point)," *Newsweek* (June 22, 2009), 39.

164. Wood, *Empire of Capital*, 168.

165. Ibid., 153–54.

166. Brenner, "What Is, and What Is Not, Imperialism?," 84–85.

167. Robert Brenner [1999], *The Economics of Global Turbulence: The Advanced Capitalist Economies from Long Boom to Long Downturn, 1945–2005* (London: Verso, 2006), 25.

168. Nikolai N. Bukharin [1920], "The Economics of the Transition Period," in *The Politics and Economics of the Transition Period*, edited by Kenneth J. Tarbuck (London: Routledge and Kegan Paul, 1979), 62.

169. Harman, "State Capitalism, the Arms Economy and the Crisis Today," 43–44.

170. Arrighi, *The Long Twentieth Century*, 227.

171. Arrighi, *Adam Smith in Beijing*, 130, 132.

172. Bukharin, *Imperialism and World Economy*, especially chapter 11.

173. Niall Ferguson, *The Pity of War* (Harmondsworth: Penguin, 1999), 32 and 31–33 more generally.

174. Bethmann-Hollweg to Baden, January 17, 1918, reproduced as an appendix in Egmont Zechlin [1964], "Cabinet versus Economic Warfare in Germany: Policy and Strategy during the Early Months of the First World War," in *The Origins*

of the First World War: Great Power Rivalry and German War Aims, edited by H.W. Koch (Second edition, London: Macmillan, 1984), 286.

175. Eric J. Hobsbawm, *The Age of Empire, 1875–1914* (London: Weidenfeld and Nicolson, 1987), 67–69.

176. Norman Stone, *World War One: A Short History* (London: Allen Lane, 2007), 23.

177. Alvin Offer, "Costs and Benefits, Prosperity and Security, 1870–1914," in *The Oxford History of the British Empire*, vol. 3, *The Nineteenth Century*, edited by Andrew Porter (Oxford: Oxford University Press, 1999), 706–07.

178. Wood, *Empire of Capital*, 45.

179. Bernadotte E. Schmitt and Harold C. Vedeler, *The World in the Crucible, 1914–1918* (New York: Harper and Row, 1984), 23. Compare Christopher Clark, *The Sleepwalkers: How Europe Went to War in 1914* (Harmondsworth: Penguin, 2013), 562.

180. Brenner, "What Is, and What Is Not, Imperialism?," 94; "Structure versus Conjuncture," 55.

181. Hobsbawm, *Globalization, Democracy and Terrorism*, 166.

182. Porter, *Empire and Superempire*, 112.

183. Mann, *Incoherent Empire*, 211.

184. Perry Anderson, "Jottings on the Conjuncture," *New Left Review* II/48 (November/December 2007), 13–17.

185. John Mearsheimer and Stephen Walt, *The Israel Lobby and U.S. Foreign Policy* (New York: Farrar, Straus and Giroux, 2007), 8, 316–19, 337–38.

186. Peter Novick, *The Holocaust and Collective Memory: The American Experience* (London: Bloomsbury, 1999), 166–67.

187. Jonathan Freedland, "Discard the Mythology of the 'Israeli Lobby,' the Reality Is Bad Enough," *Guardian* (March 18, 2009).

188. Patrick Cockburn, *The Occupation: War and Resistance in Iraq* (London: Verso, 2006), 2–3.

189. Emmanuel Todd, *After the Empire: The Breakdown of the American Order* (London: Constable, 2004), 123–44.

190. Boris Kagarlitsky, "From Global Crisis to Neo-imperialism: The Case for a Radical Alternative," in *The Politics of Empire: Globalization in Crisis* (London: Pluto Press in association with Transnational Institute, 2004), 266–67.

191. Retort, *Afflicted Powers: Capital and Spectacle in a New Age of War* (London: Verso, 2005), 74.

192. Richard Seymour, *The Liberal Defence of Murder* (London: Verso, 2008), 115.

193. Greenspan, *The Age of Turbulence*, 463.

194. Phillips, *American Theocracy*, 4.

195. Mearsheimer and Walt, *The Israel Lobby and U.S. Foreign Policy*, 255.

196. Alex Callinicos, *The New Mandarins of American Power* (Cambridge: Polity, 2003), 93–98; Harvey, *The New Imperialism*, 18–25, 74–86.

197. Zbigniew Brzezinski, *The Grand Chessboard: American Primacy and Its Geostrategic Imperatives* (New York: Basic Books, 1997), 158–73.

198. Tim Mason [1975], "Internal Crisis and Wars of Aggression, 1938–1939," in *Nazism, Fascism and the Working Class*, edited by Jane Caplan (Cambridge: Cambridge University Press, 1995), 126.

199. Francis Fox Piven, *The War at Home: The Domestic Costs of Bush's Militarism*

(New York: The New Press, 2004), 13–88; Wood, *Empire of Capital*, 166.

200. Piven, *The War at Home*, 27–29.

201. Arrighi, *Adam Smith in Beijing*, 178–203; Prem Shankar Jha, *The Twilight of the Nation State: Globalization, Chaos and War* (London: Pluto Press, 2006), 319–21; Immanuel Wallerstein, "The Curve of US Power," *New Left Review* II/40 (July/August 2006), 90–92.

202. Jha, *The Twilight of the Nation State*, 305.

203. Niall Ferguson, *Colossus: The Rise and Fall of the American Empire* (London: Allen Lane, 2004), 298.

204. Leo Panitch and Samuel Gindin, "Global Capitalism and American Empire," in *The Socialist Register 2004: The New Imperial Challenge*, edited by Leo Panitch and Colin Leys (London: Merlin Press, 2003), 24–25.

205. Callinicos, *The New Mandarins of American Power*, 122–27. On this point there is some agreement between Callinicos and Panitch and Gindin, to whose views he is otherwise consistently—and in my view correctly—opposed. See Panitch and Gindin, "Global Capitalism and American Empire," 24–25.

206. Chalmers Johnson, "No Longer the Lone Superpower," in *The World according to TomDispatch: America in the New Age of Empire*, edited by Tom Engelhardt (London: Verso, 2008), 52–58.

207. Miéville, *Between Equal Rights*, 139.

208. Owen Bowcott, "The New British Empire? UK Plans to Annex South Atlantic," *Guardian* (September 22, 2007); John Vidal and Owen Bowcott, "Scramble for the Seabed: Or How Rockall Could Be the Key to a British Oil Bonanza," *Guardian* (September 22, 2007).

209. Luke Harding, "Kremlin Sees Energy as New Battleground in Security Strategy," *Guardian* (May 14, 2009).

210. Kagarlitsky, "From Global Crisis to Neo-imperialism," 274, note 3.

211. Thomas G. Otte, "The Great Carnage," *New Statesman* (December 14–20, 2012), 21.

212. Harsh V. Pant, "Rising China in India's Vicinity: A Rivalry Takes Shape in Asia," *Cambridge Review of International Affairs* 26, no. 1 (March 2013), 12–14.

213. Halliday, *Rethinking International Relations*, 81.

214. Ellen Meiksins Wood, *The Pristine Culture of Capitalism: An Essay on Old Regimes and Modern States* (London: Verso, 1991), 28–31; Wood, "A Reply to Critics," *Historical Materialism* 15, no. 3 (2007), 153; and Etienne Balibar, "The Nation Form: History and Ideology," in Etienne Balibar and Immanuel Wallerstein, *Race, Class and Nation: Ambiguous Legacies* (London: Verso, 1991), 89–90.

215. Callinicos, "Does Capitalism Need the State System?," 545.

216. Claudia von Braunmühl, "On the Analysis of the Bourgeois Nation State within the World Market Context: An Attempt to Develop a Methodological and Theoretical Approach," in *State and Capital*, 173.

217. Smith, *An Inquiry into the Nature and Causes of the Wealth of Nations*, book V, chapter 2, 375–76.

218. Marquis de Condorcet [1776], "Réflexions sur le commerce des blés," in *Oeuvres de Condorcet*, vol. 11, edited by A. Condorcet O'Connor and M. F. Arago (Paris: Didot, 1849), 170–71.

219. Joris Luyendijk, *Swimming with Sharks: My Journey into the World of the Bankers*

(London: Guardian Books and Faber and Faber, 2015), 260–61.

220. André Malraux [1933], *Man's Estate* (London: Hamish Hamilton, 1948), 176.

221. Greenfield, *Spirit of Capitalism*, 473.

222. Randolph Bourne, "Unfinished Fragment on the State," in *Untimely Papers*, edited by James Oppenheim (New York: B.W. Huebsch, 1919), 145.

223. Nationalism affects all classes, of course, not only capitalists and workers; but for the purposes of this argument I am using a "two-class" model that does not exist anywhere in pure form, nor is ever likely to.

224. Georg Lukács [1924], *Lenin: A Study in the Unity of His Thought* (London: New Left Books, 1970), 66.

225. See chapter 3 in this volume, 67–71.

226. Tom Nairn, "Terrorism and the Opening of Black Pluto's Door," in Tom Nairn and Paul James, *Global Matrix: Nationalism, Globalism and State-Terrorism* (London: Pluto Press, 2005), 233.

227. Ludwig von Mises [1920], *Nation, State and Economy: Contributions to the Politics and History of Our Time* (Indianapolis: Liberty Fund, 2006).

228. Friedrich von Hayek, *The Road to Serfdom* (London: George Routledge, 1944), 103–07. Hayek seems to have been the first person to use the term "classism" to describe discriminatory behavior toward a group on the basis of their class. See ibid., 104.

229. See, for example, Martin J. Wolf, *Why Globalization Works: The Case for the Global Market Economy* (New Haven: Yale University Press, 2004), 36–38, 98–99, 122–26.

230. Quoted in Richard Vinen, *Thatcher's Britain: The Politics and Social Upheaval of the 1980s* (London: Simon and Schuster, 2009), 51–52.

231. Harvey, *A Brief History of Neoliberalism*, 84.

232. Terry Eagleton, *After Theory* (London: Allen Lane, 2003), 28.

233. George Steiner, "The State of Europe: Christmas Eve, 1989," *Granta* 30: *New Europe!* (December 1990), 131.

234. Christopher Hughes, *Chinese Nationalism in the Global Era* (London: Routledge, 2006).

235. Mark Beissinger, "Nationalisms That Bark and Nationalisms That Bite: Ernest Gellner and the Substantiation of Nations," in *The State of the Nation: Ernest Gellner and the Theory of Nationalism*, edited by John Hall (Cambridge: Cambridge University Press, 1998), 176.

236. Luttwak, *Turbo-Capitalism*, 128.

237. Ian Kershaw, *Fateful Choices: Ten Decisions That Changed The World, 1940–1941* (London: Allen Lane, 2007), 105–06, 380.

238. Norman Stone, *World War One*, 97.

239. Peter Gowan, "British Euro-Solipsism," in *The Question of Europe*, edited by Peter Gowan and Perry Anderson (London: Verso, 1996), 99–103.

240. Harvey, *A Brief History of Neoliberalism*, 86.

241. Raymond Williams, *Toward 2000* (Harmondsworth: Penguin, 1983), 192.

242. Montserrat Guibernau, *Nationalisms: The Nation-State and Nationalism in the Twentieth Century* (Cambridge: Polity Press, 1996), 114.

243. Anderson, *Imagined Communities*, 53.

244. Greenfield, *Spirit of Capitalism*, 483.

245. William Peter Blatty, *Exorcist* (London: Corgi Books, 1972), 282.

246. Panitch and Gindin, "Global Capitalism and American Empire," 4–9; Teschke and Lacher, "The Changing 'Logics' of Capitalist Competition," 578.

247. National Security Council [1950], "NCS-68: United States Objectives and Programs for National Security," *Naval College Review* 27 (May/June 1975), 9. My emphasis.

248. See, for example, John Maclean [1919], "The Coming War with America," in *In the Rapids of Revolution: Essays, Articles and Letters, 1902–1903*, edited by Nan Milton (London: Alison and Busby, 1977), 182–90, and Leon D. Trotsky [1924], "Perspectives of World Development," in *Europe and America: Two Speeches on Imperialism* (New York: Pathfinder Press, 1971), 28–37.

249. James Heartfield, *An Unpatriotic History of the Second World War* (Winchester: Zero Books, 2012), 142 and 139–46 more generally.

250. Arrighi, *Adam Smith in Beijing*, 312.

251. Barry Eichengreen, *Exorbitant Privilege: The Rise and Fall of the Dollar* (Oxford: Oxford University Press, 2012), 154–57.

252. Peter Hennessy, *Having It So Good: Britain in the Fifties* (London: Allen Lane, 2006), 426, 450.

CHAPTER 8: FAR-RIGHT SOCIAL MOVEMENTS AS A PROBLEM FOR CAPITAL

1. Gracchus Babeuf [1796], "Manifesto of the Equals," in *Revolution from 1789 to 1906*, edited by Raymond Postgate (London: Grant Richards, 1920), 54–55; James Bronterre O'Brien [1837], "A View of Social Development," in *From Cobbett to the Chartists: Nineteenth Century*, vol. 1, *1815–1848*, edited by Max Morris (London: Lawrence and Wishart, 1948), 161; Friedrich Engels [1845], "Speeches in Elberfeld: February 15, 1845," in *Collected Works*, vol. 4 (London: Lawrence and Wishart, 1975), 262; Alexander Herzen [1864], "To an Opponent: Letter 1," in *Selected Philosophical Works* (Moscow: Foreign Languages Publishing House, 1956), 549.

2. Karl Marx and Friedrich Engels [1845–46], *The German Ideology: Critique of Modern German Philosophy according to Its Representatives Feuerbach, B. Bauer and Stirner, and of German Socialism according to Its Various Prophets*, in *Collected Works*, vol. 5 (London: Lawrence and Wishart, 1976), 486.

3. Marx to Engels, December 10, 1869, in *Collected Works*, vol. 43 (London: Lawrence and Wishart, 1988), 396.

4. Paul Byrne, *Social Movements in Britain* (London: Routledge, 1997), 18–19, 64–74.

5. Hilary Wainwright, introduction to Sheila Rowbotham, Lynne Segal, and Hilary Wainwright, *Beyond the Fragments: Feminism and the Making of Socialism* (London: Merlin Press, 1979), 6–18.

6. Stanley Aronowitz, *How Class Works: Power and Social Movements* (New Haven: Yale University Press, 2003), 147–48.

7. Byrne, *Social Movements in Britain*, 74.

8. Jaume Torras, "Peasant Counter-revolution?," *Journal of Peasant Studies* 5, no. 1 (October 1977), 74, 75.

9. Ronald Fraser, *Napoleon's Cursed War: Popular Resistance in the Spanish Peninsular War, 1808–1814* (London: Verso, 2008), 480.

10. Christopher Duggan, *The Force of Destiny: A History of Italy since 1796* (London: Allen Lane, 2007), 121, 123.

11. Eric Foner, *A Short History of Reconstruction* (New York: Harper and Row, 1990), 186–87.

12. Elizabeth Fox-Genovese and Eugene Genovese, *Fruits of Merchant Capital: Slavery and Bourgeois Property in the Rise and Expansion of Capitalism* (Oxford: Oxford University Press, 1983), 263.

13. Theodore Allen, *The Invention of the White Race*, vol. 2, *The Origin of Racial Oppression in Anglo-America* (London: Verso, 1997), 249.

14. Stephen E. Tolnay and E. M. Beck, *A Festival of Violence: An Analysis of Southern Lynching, 1882–1930* (Chicago: University of Illinois Press, 1992), 28.

15. Albert Szymanski, "Racial Discrimination and White Gain," *American Sociological Review* 41, no. 3 (June 1976), 412–13.

16. W. E. B. Du Bois [1935], *Black Reconstruction in America, 1860–1880: An Essay toward a History of the Part Which Black Folk Played in That Attempt to Reconstruct Democracy in America, 1860–1880* (New York: Athenaeum, 1969), 700–701.

17. Eamonn McCann, "After 5 October 1968," *International Socialism* 1:51 (April/June 1972), 10–11.

18. See chapter 7 in this volume, 212–220.

19. John Stauber and Sheldon Rampton, *Toxic Sludge Is Good for You! Lies, Damn Lies and the Public Relations Industry* (Monroe: Common Courage Press, 1995).

20. Nir Rosen, "Thugs on the Payroll," *New Statesman* (March 21, 2011), 34.

21. Donatella della Porta and Mario Diani [1995], *Social Movements: An Introduction* (Oxford: Blackwell, 2006), 217.

22. Anthony Giddens, *A Contemporary Critique of Historical Materialism*, vol. 1, *Power, Property and the State* (London: Macmillan, 1981), 16–18, 21.

23. Gregor McLennan, "Post-Marxism and the 'Four Sins' of Modernist Theorizing," *New Left Review* I/218 (July/August 1996), 62–63.

24. See chapter 7 in this volume, 191–92, 224.

25. Rajani Palme Dutt, *Fascism and Social Revolution* (London: Martin Lawrence, 1934), 82.

26. Leon D. Trotsky [1932], "The Only Road," in *The Struggle against Fascism in Germany* (Harmondsworth: Penguin, 1975), 265.

27. Leon D. Trotsky [1932], "What Next? Vital Questions for the German Proletariat," in *The Struggle against Fascism in Germany*, 125.

28. Leon D. Trotsky [1933], "What Is National Socialism?," in *The Struggle against Fascism in Germany*, 413.

29. David Forgacs, "The Left and Fascism: Problems of Definition and Strategy," in *Rethinking Italian Fascism: Capitalism, Populism and Culture*, edited by David Forgacs (London: Lawrence and Wishart, 1986), 36; Nicos Poulantzas [1970], *Fascism and Dictatorship* (London: New Left Books, 1974), 61–62.

30. Friedrich von Hayek, *The Road to Serfdom* (London: Routledge, 1944), 20, 124–25.

31. Ibid., 52–53.

32. Friedrich von Hayek, Letter to the *Times* (August 3, 1978).

33. Friedrich Pollock [1941], "State Capitalism: Its Possibilities and Limitations," in *The Essential Frankfurt School Reader*, edited by Andrew Arato and Eike Geb-

hardt (Oxford: Blackwell, 1978), 72.

34. Robert A. Brady, *Business as a System of Power* (New York: Columbia University Press, 1943), 181.

35. G. D. H. Cole, *The Intelligent Man's Guide to the Post-war World*, (London: Victor Gollancz, 1947), 122.

36. Franz Neumann, *Behemoth: The Structure and Practice of National Socialism* (London: Victor Gollancz, 1942), 295–96.

37. See, for example, respectively: Donny Gluckstein, *The Nazis, Capitalism and the Working Class* (London: Bookmarks, 1999), 162; John Gray, *Liberalism* (Buckingham: Open University Press, 1986), 36; Roger Eatwell, "Conceptualizing the Right: Marxism's Central Errors," in *The Nature of the Right: American and European Politics and Political Thought since 1789*, edited by Roger Eatwell and Noel O'Sullivan (London: Pinter Publishers, 1989), 30.

38. Georg W. F. Hegel [1830–31], *The Philosophy of History* (New York: Dover Publications, 1956), 11.

39. Max Weber [1910–14], *Economy and Society: An Outline of Interpretive Sociology*, vol. 1, edited by Guenther Roth and Claus Wittich (Berkeley: University of California Press, 1978), 24–26.

40. Zygmunt Bauman [1989], *Modernity and the Holocaust* (Second edition, Oxford: Polity Press, 1991), 18.

41. Stephen Eric Bonner, *Reclaiming the Enlightenment: Toward a Politics of Radical Engagement* (New York: Columbia University Press, 2004), 112.

42. Ulrich Herbert, "Labor and Extermination: Economic Interest and the Primacy of *Weltanschauung* in National Socialism," *Past and Present* 138 (February 1993), 195.

43. Ernest Mandel, *The Meaning of the Second World War* (London: Verso, 1986), 90–93.

44. Benjamin Madley, "From Africa to Auschwitz: How German South West Africa Incubated Ideas and Methods Adopted and Developed by the Nazis in Eastern Europe," *European History Quarterly* 35, no. 3 (July 2005).

45. Norman Geras, *The Contract of Mutual Indifference: Political Philosophy after the Holocaust* (London: Verso, 1998), 158, 164.

46. Ernst Nolte, *Theorien über den Faschismus* (Cologne: Kiepenheuer und Witsch, 1967), 21.

47. Alex Callinicos, "Plumbing the Depths: Marxism and the Holocaust," *Yale Journal of Criticism* 14, no. 2 (June 2001), 403, 406.

48. Peter Sedgwick, "The Problem of Fascism," *International Socialism* 1:42 (February/March 1970), 34. Callinicos actually ascribes this thought to Joel Geier, who expressed it from the floor during a discussion at Marxism 1993. See Callinicos, "Plumbing the Depths," 413, note 95.

49. Richard Evans, *The Coming of the Third Reich* (London: Allen Lane, 2003), 22–76; Ian Kershaw, *Fateful Choices: Ten Decisions That Changed the World, 1940–1941* (London: Allen Lane, 2007), 438–44; Sabby Sagall, *Final Solutions: Human Nature, Capitalism, and Genocide* (London: Pluto Press, 2013), 196–210.

50. Detlev Peukert [1982], *Inside Nazi Germany: Conformity, Opposition and Racism in Everyday Life* (Harmondsworth: Penguin, 1989), 44.

51. Robert O. Paxton, *The Anatomy of Fascism* (Harmondsworth: Penguin, 2004), 147.

52. Götz Aly, *Hitler's Beneficiaries: Plunder, Racial War, and the Nazi Welfare State* (New

York: Metropolitan Books, 2006).

53. Gluckstein, *The Nazis, Capitalism, and the Working Class*, chapter 9; Peukert, *Inside Nazi Germany*, 118–25.

54. Tim Mason [1975], "The Primacy of Politics: Politics and Economics in National Socialist Germany," in *Nazism, Fascism and the Working Class*, edited by Jane Caplan (Cambridge: Cambridge University Press, 1995), 74.

55. Peukert, *Inside Nazi Germany*, 176–78; Adam Tooze, *The Wages of Destruction: The Making and Breaking of the Nazi Economy* (New York: Viking, 2006), 358–59, 513–15.

56. Ian Kershaw, *Hitler, 1889–1936: Hubris* (London: Allen Lane, 1998), 563, 567–68, 713.

57. Eatwell, "Conceptualizing the Right," 21.

58. Francisco de Oliveira, "The Duckbilled Platypus," *New Left Review* II/24 (November/December 2003), 45.

59. Karin Fischer, "The Influence of Neoliberals in Chile, before, during, and after Pinochet," in *The Road from Mont Pèlerin: The Making of the Neoliberal Thought Collective*, edited by Philip Mirowski and Dieter Plehwe (Cambridge, MA: Harvard University Press, 2009), 317.

60. Paxton, *The Anatomy of Fascism*, 149–50.

61. Roger Griffin, "Revolution from the Right: Fascism," in *Revolutions and the Revolutionary Tradition in the West, 1560–1991*, edited by David Parker (London: Routledge, 2000), 189.

62. Anton Pelinka, "Right-Wing Populism: Concept and Typology," in *Right-Wing Populism in Europe: Politics and Discourse*, edited by Ruth Wodak, Majid KhosraviNik, and Brigitte Mral (London: Bloomsbury, 2013), 15–17.

63. Alejandro Dabat and Luis Lorenzano [1982], *Argentina, the Malvinas and the End of Military Rule* (Revised and expanded translation, London: Verso, 1984), 21–25; Gino Germani, "Fascism and Class," in *The Nature of Fascism*, edited by S. J. Woolf (London: Weidenfeld and Nicolson, 1968), 65–95.

64. Michael Mann, *Fascists* (Cambridge: Cambridge University Press, 2004), 367–68.

65. Peter Mair, *Ruling the Void: The Hollowing of Western Democracy* (London: Verso, 2013), 45.

66. Trotsky, "What Next?," 125.

67. Neil Davidson, *How Revolutionary Were the Bourgeois Revolutions?* (Chicago: Haymarket Books, 2012), 490–97.

68. Reinhard Heinisch, "Austria: The Structure and Agency of Austrian Populism," in *Twenty-First Century Populism: The Spectre of Western European Democracy*, edited by Daniele Albertazzi and Duncan McDonnell (Houndmills: Palgrave Macmillan, 2008), 82.

69. Griffin, "Revolution from the Right," 198.

70. Daniele Albertazzi and Duncan McDonnell, "The Scepter and the Spectre," introduction to *Twenty-First Century Populism*, 5.

71. Daniel Trilling, *Bloody Nasty People: The Rise of Britain's Far Right* (London: Verso, 2012), 147.

72. Robert Ford and Matthew Goodwin, *Revolt on the Right: Explaining Support for the Radical Right in Britain* (Abingdon: Routledge, 2014), 146 and see chapter 4 more generally for evidence of working-class support for UKIP.

73. Chip Berlet and Matthew N. Lyons, *Right-Wing Populism in America: Too Close for Comfort* (New York: The Guilford Press, 2000), 347–48.

74. Ibid., 349.

75. Nigel Harris [1968], *Beliefs in Society: The Problem of Ideology* (Harmondsworth: Penguin, 1971), 115–16.

76. George Monbiot, "The Tea Party Movement: Deluded and Inspired by Billionaires," *Guardian* (October 25, 2010).

77. Della Porta and Diani, *Social Movements*, 20.

78. Thomas Frank, *What's the Matter with America? The Resistible Rise of the American Right* (London: Secker and Warburg, 2004), 175, 247.

79. Sara Diamond, *Roads to Dominion: Right-Wing Movements and Political Power in the United States* (New York: The Guilford Press, 1995), 6.

80. Mike Davis, "What's the Matter with America? A Debate with Thomas Frank," in *In Praise of Barbarians: Essays against Empire* (Chicago: Haymarket Books, 2007), 50.

81. Ibid.

82. Marx and Engels, *The German Ideology*, 59.

83. Ibid., 52–53; Karl Marx [1845], "[Theses on Feuerbach]," in *Collected Works*, vol. 5, 7, thesis 3.

84. Antonio Gramsci [1929–35], "The Study of Philosophy," in *Selections from the Prison Notebooks*, edited by Quintin Hoare and Geoffrey Nowell-Smith (London: Lawrence and Wishart, 1971), 333–34, Q11§12.

85. Georg Lukács [1923], "Class Consciousness," in *History and Class Consciousness: Essays on Marxist Dialectics* (London: Merlin Press, 1971), 51.

86. John Rees, *The Algebra of Revolution: The Dialectic and the Classical Marxist Tradition* (London: Routledge, 1998), 260, note 134.

87. Georg Lukács [1924], *Lenin: A Study in the Unity of His Thought* (London: New Left Books, 1970), 56.

88. Ibid.

89. Berlet and Lyons, *Right-Wing Populism in America*, 348.

90. Chip Berlet, "The Violence of Right-Wing Populism," *Peace Review* 7, no. 3/4 (1995), 285.

91. Joe Bageant, *Deer Hunting with Jesus: Dispatches from America's Class War* (New York: Three Rivers Press, 2007), 81–82; see also Davis, "What's the Matter with America?," 57.

92. Paul Taggart, *The New Populism and the New Politics: New Protest Parties in Sweden in a Comparative Perspective* (New York: St. Martin's Press, 1996), 17–18.

93. Alexandra Cole, "Old Right or New Right? The Ideological Positioning of Parties of the Far Right," *European Journal of Political Research* 44, no. 2 (March 2005), 222–23.

94. Magnus Marsdal, "Loud Values, Muffled Interests: Third Way Social Democracy and Right-Wing Populism," in *Right-Wing Populism in Europe*, 51.

95. Carolyn Gallaher, "Mainstreaming the Militia," in *Spaces of Hate: Geographies of Discrimination and Intolerance in the USA*, edited by Colin Flint (New York: Routledge, 2004), 186.

96. Michael Kimmel, *Angry White Men: American Masculinity at the End of an Era* (New York: Nation Books, 2013), 281.

97. Lisa McGirr, *Suburban Warriors: The Origins of the New American Right* (Princeton:

Princeton University Press, 2001), 163.

98. Kevin Phillips, *American Theocracy: The Peril and Politics of Radical Religion, Oil, and Borrowed Money in the 21st Century* (New York: Viking Penguin, 2006), 393–94.

99. Frank, *What's the Matter with America?*, 6.

100. Ibid., 8, 109.

101. Phillips, *American Theocracy*, 394, 370–71.

102. Mark Lilla, "The Tea Party Jacobins," *New York Review of Books* (May 27, 2010).

103. Jonathan Raban, "Say What?," *Guardian* (October 16, 2010).

104. Ed Pilkington, "Immigrants Go into Hiding as Alabama Rules That Looking Illegal Is Enough," *Guardian* (October 15, 2011).

105. Immigration Policy Center, "Bad for Business: How Alabama's Anti-immigrant Law Stifles State Economy" (November 3, 2011), available at www.immigrationpolicy.org.

106. Rory Carroll, "Growing Power of the Gay Dollar Sees Off Legal Threats in America's Deep South," *Observer* (March 2, 2014).

107. Eric Lipton, Nicholas Confessore, and Nelson Schwartz, "Business Groups See Loss of Sway over House G.O.P.," *New York Times* (October 9, 2013).

108. Jon Huntsman, "Republicans Must Stop Scrapping and Change Course," *Financial Times* (October 24, 2013).

109. Chris Gifford, "The Rise of Post-imperial Populism: The Case of Right-Wing Euroscepticism in Britain," *European Journal of Political Research* 45, no. 5 (August 2006), 858, 865.

110. See chapter 7 in this volume, 241–42.

111. Gonzalo Vina, "Almost One in Five UK Companies Favor Leaving the EU," *Bloomberg Businessweek* (April 14, 2013).

112. "Nearly Half of Small Business Owners Want to Leave the European Union," *Mail on Sunday* (January 20, 2013).

113. Andrew Rawnsley, "It's Not Just the Tories Who Should Beware UKIP in the Local Elections," *Observer* (April 21, 2013).

114. Ford and Goodwin, *Revolt on the Right*, 277.

115. Eric J. Hobsbawm [2002], "Politics and Culture in the New Century," in *Fractured Times: Culture and Society in the Twentieth Century* (London: Little, Brown, 2013), 45.

116. Timothy Garten Ash, "This Epochal Crisis Requires Us to Resolve the Paradox of Capitalism," *Guardian* (May 7, 2009); Anthony Giddens, *The Third Way: The Renewal of Social Democracy* (Cambridge: Polity, 1998), 15; John Gray, "Maggie's Gift to Gordon," *New Statesman* (September 24, 2007), 46.

117. Alan Sinfield [1997], "The Politics and Cultures of Discord (1997)," in *Literature, Politics and Culture in Postwar Britain* (Third edition, London: Continuum, 2004), 349.

118. Marco D'Eramo, "Populism without the People," *New Left Review* II/82 (July/August 2013).

119. Mike Davis, "Last White Election?," *New Left Review* II/79 (January/February 2013), 44.

120. Vladimir I. Lenin [1916], "The Discussion on Self-Determination Summed Up," in *Collected Works*, vol. 22, *December 1915–July 1916* (Moscow: Foreign Languages Publishing House, 1964), 356.

121. Ibid.

CHAPTER 9: A SCOTTISH WATERSHED

1. The Scottish Parliament consists of seventy-three constituency members, elected through first past the post, and fifty-six party-list members, elected on a D'Hondt-style "additional member" system, the most disproportionate of proportional-representation methods, which tops up the constituency results and so further rewards the largest parties, even though it also allows for some smaller-party representation. Thus the Scottish Socialist Party and the Greens won six and seven MSPs respectively in 2003, each getting around 5 percent of the vote.

2. Tom Nairn, "Scotland and Europe," *New Left Review* I/83 (January/February 1974), 71, citing T. C. Smout, *A History of the Scottish People, 1560–1830* (London: Fontana, 1969), 33; *The Break-up of Britain: Crisis and Neo-nationalism* (Second, revised edition, London: Verso, 1981), 92–125.

3. Nairn, "Scotland and Europe," 73; *The Break-up of Britain*, 113.

4. Tom Nairn, "Ukania under Blair," *New Left Review* II/1 (January/February 2000), 76.

5. Tom Nairn, "Old and New Scottish Nationalism," in *The Break-up of Britain*, 178–79.

6. Tom Nairn, "The Twilight of the British State," *New Left Review* I/101–02 (February/April 1977), 59–60; *The Break-up of Britain*, 89–90.

7. For the historical formation of Scottish national consciousness, see my *The Origins of Scottish Nationhood* (London: Pluto Press, 2000), 47–203; and for a critique of Nairn's work down to 1999, see [1999] "Tom Nairn and the Inevitability of Nationalism," in *Holding Fast to an Image of the Past: Explorations in the Marxist Tradition* (Chicago, 2014).

8. For examples of each, see: James Foley and Pete Ramand, *Yes: The Radical Case for Scottish Independence* (London: Pluto Press, 2014); Peter McColl, "The Green Activist," *Scottish Left Review* 73 (November/December 2012); and Cat Boyd and Jenny Morrison, *Scottish Independence: A Feminist Response* (Edinburgh: Word Power Books, 2014).

9. Daniel Bensaïd, "Leaps! Leaps! Leaps!," *International Socialism* 2:95 (Summer 2002), 77; *Lenin Reloaded: Towards a Politics of Truth*, edited by Sebastian Budgen, Stathis Kouvelakis, and Slavoj Žižek (Durham: Duke University Press, 2007), 153.

10. At a 2012 conference, the SNP leadership had reversed the party's long-standing policy of quitting NATO, telling the membership it was "necessary" to win the referendum. Salmond and Sturgeon insisted—despite the obvious contradiction—that they would however also retain the existing policy of evicting Britain's nuclear-armed Trident submarines from their deep-water base on the Clyde.

11. Suki Sangha and David Jamieson, "The Radical Independence Campaign," *RS21* 2 (Autumn 2014), 29.

12. Paul Hutcheon, "The Growth of the Yes Movement," *Sunday Herald* (September 21, 2014).

13. The Common Weal project was set up by Robin McAlpine, founding editor of the *Scottish Left Review* (SLR), with the aim of developing broadly Social-Democratic policies that it hoped might be adopted by either Labour or the SNP. Under McAlpine, the SLR took a similarly agnostic approach to independence.

The new SLR editor, Gregor Gall, an SSP member, is pro-independence, as his editorial in SLR 83 (October 2014) declares.

14. See for example Jonathan Freedland, "If Britain Loses Scotland It Will Feel Like an Amputation," *Guardian* (September 5, 2014).

15. George Kerevan, "Vote's Biggest Loser Is Scottish Labour," *Scotsman* (September 20, 2014).

16. See the Red Paper Collective, "The Question Isn't Yes or No," *Scottish Left Review* 73 (November/December 2012). The Red Paper Collective is a pro-Union think tank of Communist Party (CP) and Labour trade-union officials and academics; John Foster, the CP's international secretary, is a leading light. The No campaign also had the support of George Galloway, the ex-Glasgow Labour MP who broke with the party over Iraq to become the one-man vanguard of Respect. Galloway set out on a speaking tour to save the Union, repeating Darling's nostrums of economic doom at greater volume: "Do you honestly think that a UK company is going to situate in a more socialist Scotland when the Tory government had created the perfect low-tax, low-regulation, low-wage capitalist environment?" *"Just Say Naw . . .": An Evening with George Galloway*, Respect 2014, [3]. The logic of this argument is that the left should just crawl away and die, or (same difference) schmooze its way into the New Labour hierarchy, as Galloway would clearly like to do.

17. "UK RIP?," *Economist* (September 13, 2014); Fred Dews, "Lord George Robertson: 'Forces of Darkness Would Love Scottish Split from United Kingdom,'" *Brookings Now* (April 7, 2014).

18. Tom Gordon, "One Year On: Will Better Together Change Their Tactics?," *Sunday Herald* (June 23, 2013).

19. John Robertson, "Fairness in the First Year? BBC and ITV Coverage of the Scottish Independence Campaign from September 2012 to September 2013," Creative Futures Institute, University of the West of Scotland, available at issuu.com.

20. Will Hutton, "We Have 10 Days to Find a Settlement to Save the Union," *Observer* (September 7, 2014); Jason Cowley, "A Shattered Union," *New Statesman* (September 13, 2014); Martin Kettle, "Don't Let Alex Salmond Blind You to the Yes Campaign's Dark Side," *Guardian* (September 17, 2014); Philip Stephens, "The World Is Saying No to Scottish Separation," *Financial Times* (September 12, 2014). For a definitive refutation of the "ethnic campaign" myth, see Foley and Ramand, *Yes*, 38–40.

21. Polly Toynbee, "Scottish Referendum: Shared Values Matter More than Where the Border Lies," *Guardian* (August 19, 2014); Seumas Milne, "Salmond's Scotland Won't Be an Escape from Tory Britain," *Guardian* (September 11, 2014).

22. Nairn, "The Twilight of the British State," 59–60; *The Break-up of Britain*, 89–90.

23. The president of the European Commission was also wheeled out to say that an independent Scotland would have to reapply for EU membership, though there is no legal basis for this.

24. Sarah Neville and Clive Cookson, "Ruling Elite Aghast as Union Wobbles," *Financial Times* (September 12, 2014).

25. Kiran Stacey, George Parker, Mure Dickie, and Beth Rigby, "Scottish Referendum: How Complacency Nearly Lost a United Kingdom," *Financial Times* (September 19, 2014).

26. Judith Duffy, "An Explosive Breach of the Rules: Salmond Blasts Treasury as Its BBC Email Is Exposed," *Sunday Herald* (September 14, 2014). Shortly after this, BBC political editor Nick Robinson asked Salmond at an Edinburgh press conference about possible loss of tax revenues if RBS moved to London: "Why should a Scottish voter believe you, a politician, against men who are responsible for billions of pounds of profits?"—terms he would never have used addressing Cameron. That evening on BBC News, Robinson claimed that Salmond had not answered. Footage from the press conference, which soon went viral on the Internet, showed Salmond giving a six-minute answer to that and other points raised by Robinson in the subsequent exchange. This was the reason for the Yes campaign protest outside BBC headquarters, reported in the unionist media as an alarming attack on press freedom.

27. Among the major unions, ASLEF (railway workers), national CWU (postal workers), USDAW (shopworkers), and the sad remnants of the NUM (miners), all notoriously right-wing, came out for No. Only the Scottish RMT (transport workers), the Prison Officers' Association, and the habitually rebellious Edinburgh, Stirling, Fife, and Falkirk branch of the CWU supported a Yes vote.

28. George Monbiot noted the addition of "another weasel word" to Labour's lexicon, along with "reform," meaning privatization, and "partnership," meaning selling out to big business: "once solidarity meant making common cause with the exploited," now it meant "keeping faith with the banks, the corporate press, cuts, a tollbooth economy and market fundamentalism." "A Yes Vote in Scotland Would Unleash the Most Dangerous Thing of All—Hope," *Guardian* (September 9, 2014).

29. The parties made different if overlapping offers: Labour, the ability to set and control income tax by up to 15p in the pound; the Conservatives and Lib Dems, to set and control all Scottish income tax; Labour and the Conservatives, control of housing benefit; the Lib Dems, control of capital-gains tax and inheritance tax.

30. Lord Ashcroft Polls, Post Referendum Scotland Poll, September 18–19, 2014.

31. Ashcroft and YouGov polls, accessed through Curtice.

32. For an analysis, see Yiannis Mavris, "Greece's Austerity Election," *New Left Review* 76 (July/August 2012).

33. Personal communication with the author, October 9, 2014.

34. The process of selecting a new Labour parliamentary candidate for Falkirk began after sitting MP Eric Joyce launched a drunken assault (head buttings, etc.) on fellow members of the House of Commons. It rapidly descended into a turf war, with skullduggery on both sides, between the Mandelson faction and local union officials, culminating with Miliband's decision to call in the Scottish police to investigate his party comrades.

35. Allan Brogan, "Out with the Old: In with the New?," *Scottish Left Review* 83 (October 2014), 7.

36. Kate Devlin, "Darling Says No Campaign Needs to Win Well to Avoid 'Neverendum,'" *Herald* (May 14, 2013).

37. Scott to Southey, June 4, 1812, in *The Letters of Sir Walter Scott*, vol. 3, *1811–1814*, edited by H. J. C. Grierson (London: Constable, 1932), 125–26.

Index

140; revolution and, 248; Scotland,
78, 94, 295, 296–97, 298, 305; Sorel
view, 154; Soviet Union, 72; US,
255. *See also* lumpen-proletariat
World War I. *See* First World War
World War II. *See* Second World War
Wrigley, Terry, xviii

xenophobia, 18–19, 53, 273, 274

Yemen, 258
Yugoslavia, xiv, xix, 2, 3, 15, 23, 198,
235, 300

Zakaria, Fareed, 223
Zinn, Howard, 128–29
Zionism, 33–34
Žižek, Slavoj, 91